& My Brothers

Volume 7

Hari Tokeino

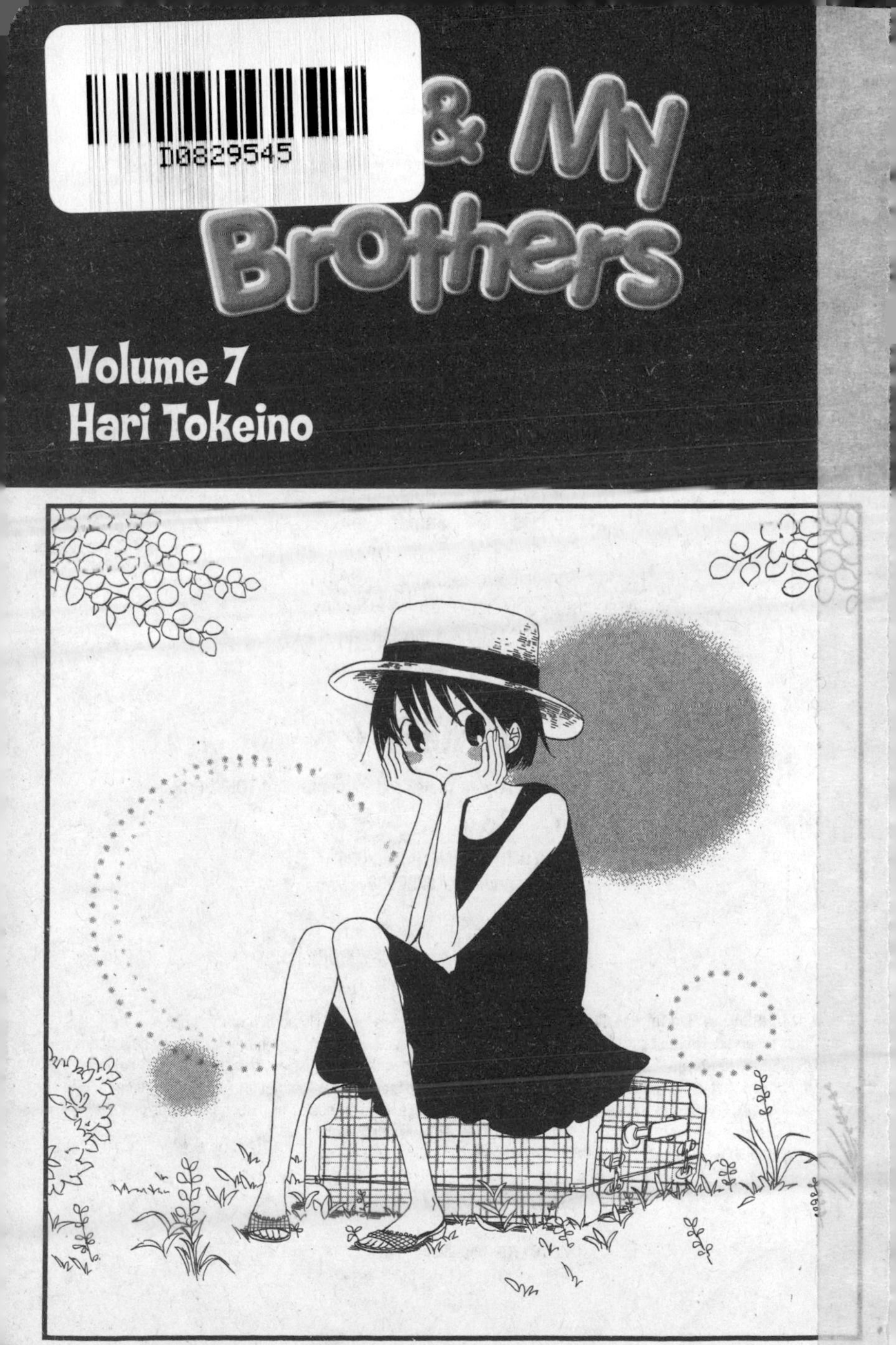

Me & My Brothers Volume 7
Created by Hari Tokeino

Translation - Alethea & Athena Nibley
English Adaptation - Katherine Schilling
Retouch and Lettering - Star Print Brokers
Production Artist - Michael Paolilli
Graphic Designer - Erika Terriquez

Editor - Hyun Joo Kim
Pre-Production Supervisor - Vicente Rivera, Jr.
Pre-Production Specialist - Lucas Rivera
Managing Editor - Vy Nguyen
Senior Designer - Louis Csontos
Senior Designer - James Lee
Senior Editor - Bryce P. Coleman
Senior Editor - Jenna Winterberg
Associate Publisher - Marco F. Pavia
President and C.O.O. - John Parker
C.E.O. and Chief Creative Officer - Stu Levy

A **TOKYOPOP** Manga

TOKYOPOP Inc.
5900 Wilshire Blvd. Suite 2000
Los Angeles, CA 90036

E-mail: info@TOKYOPOP.com
Come visit us online at www.TOKYOPOP.com

ONIICHAN TO ISSHO by Hari Tokeino © 2007 Hari Tokeino
All rights reserved. First published in Japan in 2007 by
HAKUSENSHA, INC., Tokyo English language translation
rights in the United States of America and Canada arranged
with HAKUSENSHA, INC., Tokyo through Tuttle-Mori Agency
Inc., Tokyo
English text copyright © 2009 TOKYOPOP Inc.

ISBN: 978-1-4278-0881-3

First TOKYOPOP printing: March 2009
10 9 8 7 6 5 4 3 2 1
Printed in the USA

Me & My Brothers

Volume 7
Hari Tokeino

TOKYOPOP®

HAMBURG // LONDON // LOS ANGELES // TOKYO

Contents

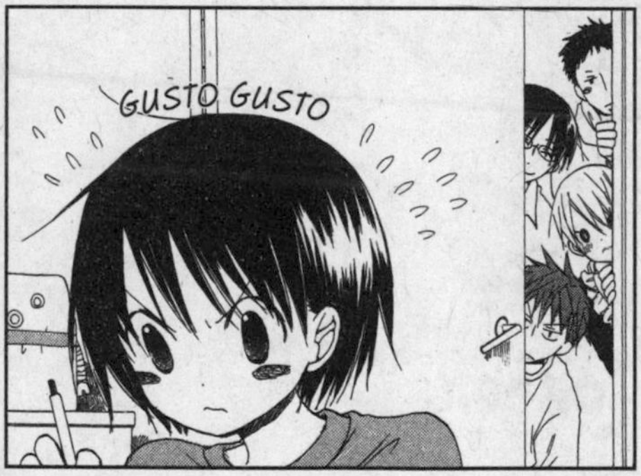
GUSTO GUSTO

CHARACTERS PROFILE

ME & MY BROTHERS

SAKURA MIYASHITA:
THE YOUNGEST. A FIRST-YEAR IN HIGH SCHOOL. THE ONLY GIRL IN THE MIYASHITA FAMILY. SHE IS NOT BLOOD RELATED TO HER FOUR BROTHERS. SHE LOVES MASASHI.♥

MASASHI MIYASHITA:
THE ELDEST. ROMANCE NOVELIST. ACCORDING TO HIM, HE SOUNDS LIKE A WOMAN BECAUSE OF HIS JOB. HE'S THE LEADER OF THE FOUR SAKURA-SPOILERS.

TAKASHI MIYASHITA:
THE 2ND BROTHER. A JAPANESE TEACHER. A CALM GENTLEMAN.

TSUYOSHI MIYASHITA:
THE 3RD BROTHER. FULL-TIME PART-TIMER. HE TALKS ROUGH, BUT IS ACTUALLY QUITE BASHFUL.

TAKESHI MIYASHITA:
THE 4TH BROTHER. COLLEGE FRESHMAN. HE LOOKS OLD, BUT HE IS THE YOUNGEST OF THE FOUR BROTHERS. HE'S QUIET AND LOVES GARDENING.

NAKA-CHAN:
SAKURA'S BEST FRIEND. HER FAMILY NAME IS TANAKA.

SUZUKI:
ON THE SCHOOL SOCCER TEAM. HE HAS A CRUSH ON SAKURA.

KATAGIRI:
HE CONFESSED HIS LOVE TO SAKURA IN THEIR SECOND YEAR OF MIDDLE SCHOOL AND THEN TRANSFERRED AWAY!

NANA & NENE KOZUKA
THE TWINS IN SAKURA'S SCHOOL SOCCER TEAM. BOTH IN THE 11TH GRADE.

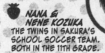

TERADA:
SOCCER TEAM CAPTAIN. HE'S IN THE 12TH GRADE.

PLEASE READ *ME & MY BROTHERS* 1-6 FOR MORE DETAILS!

STORY

SAKURA LOST HER PARENTS WHEN SHE WAS ONLY 3 AND WAS RAISED BY HER GRANDMOTHER. AT THE AGE OF 14, HER GRANDMOTHER PASSED AWAY, AND SAKURA WAS ALL ALONE AGAIN. THEN, FOUR STEPBROTHERS SUDDENLY STEPPED INTO HER LIFE! AFTER 11 LONG YEARS OF SEPARATION, THEY'VE STARTED TO LIVE TOGETHER! ♡ WHEN WE LAST LEFT OFF, SAKURA WAS DETERMINED TO TELL MASASHI HOW SHE REALLY FELT ABOUT HIM ON HER 17TH BIRTHDAY, BUT ULTIMATELY, SHE NEVER GOT THE CHANCE TO SAY IT...

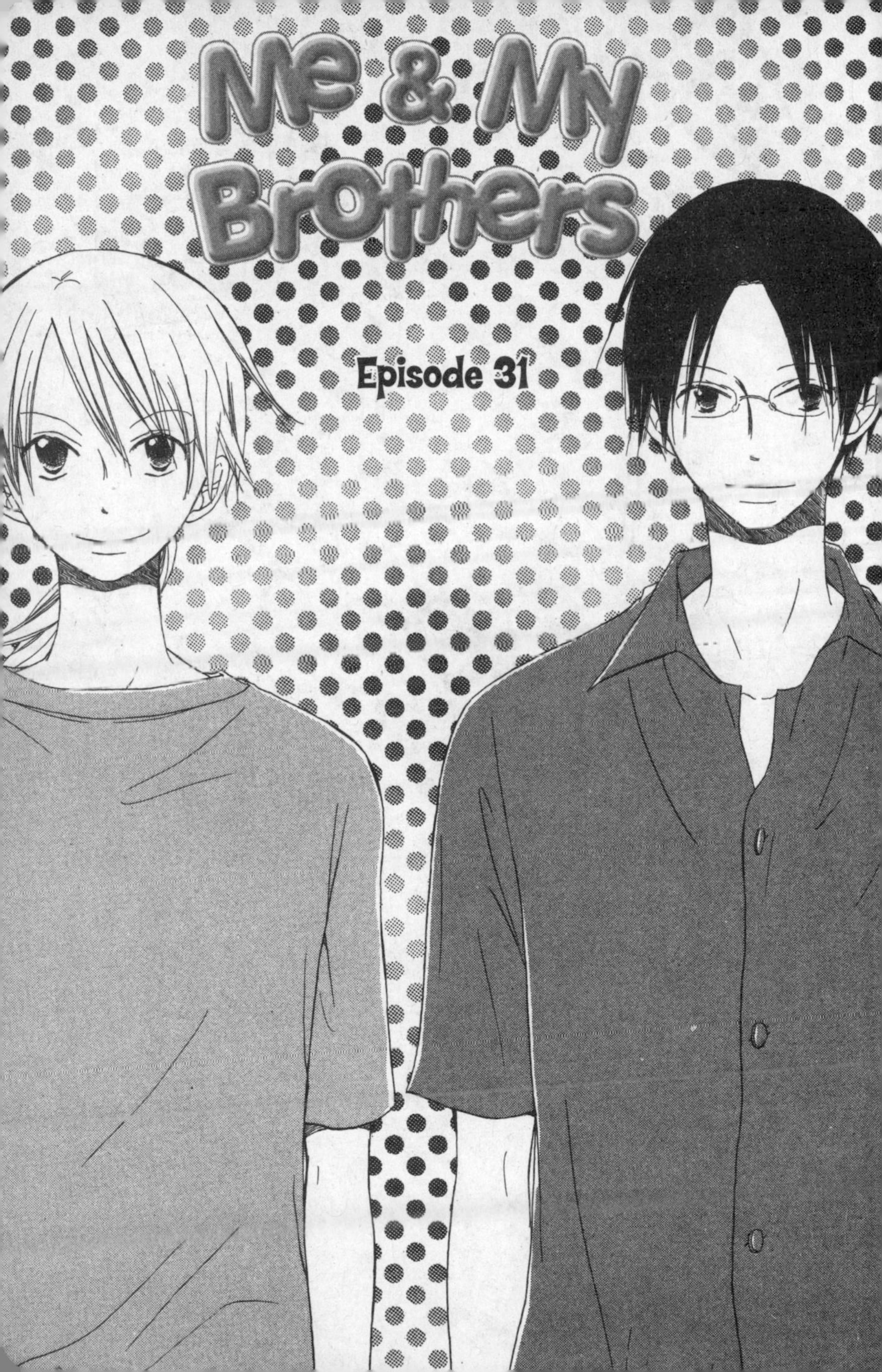
Me & My Brothers
Episode 31

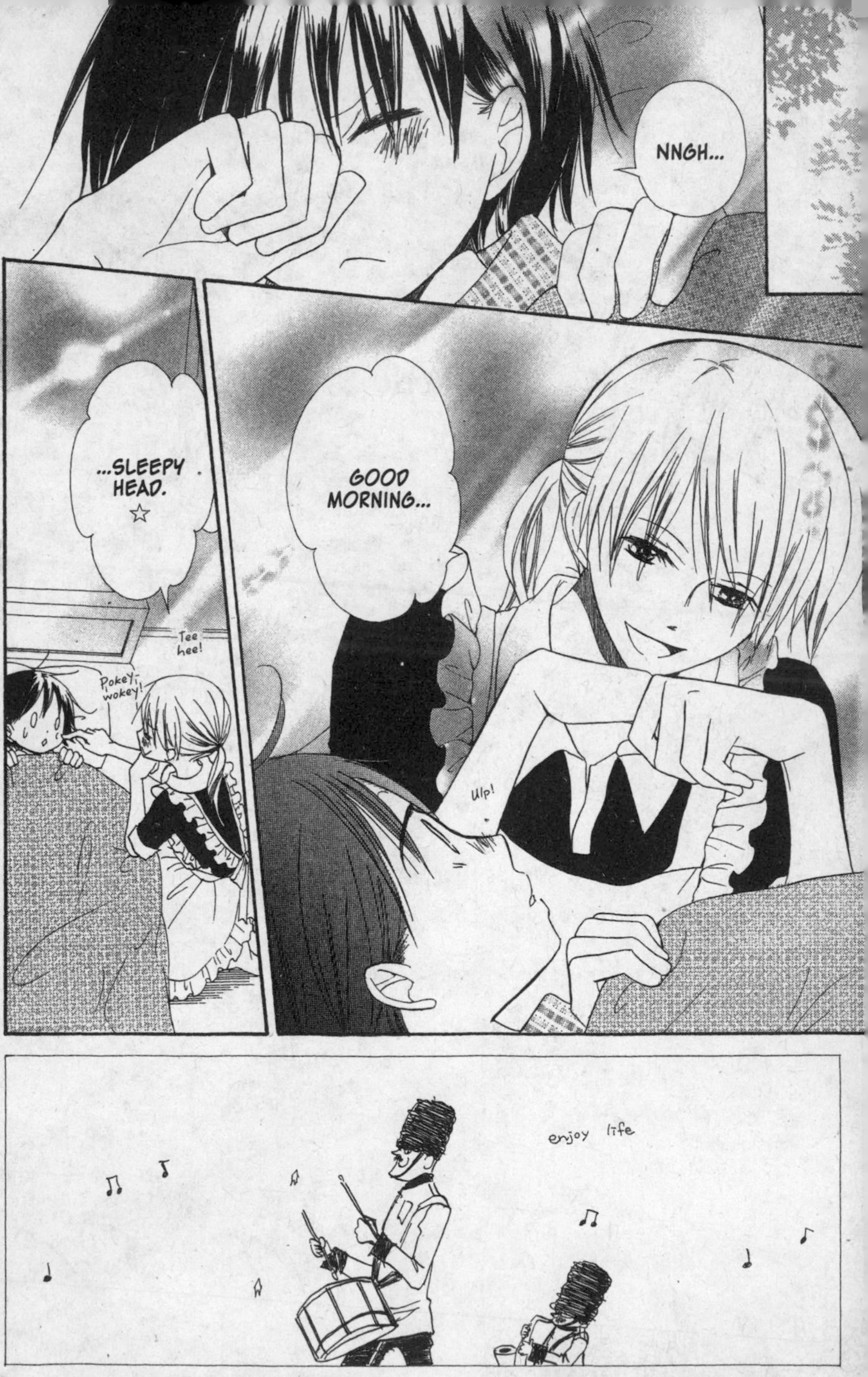
NNGH...
GOOD MORNING...
Ulp!
...SLEEPY HEAD. ☆
Tee hee!
Pokey-wokey!
enjoy life

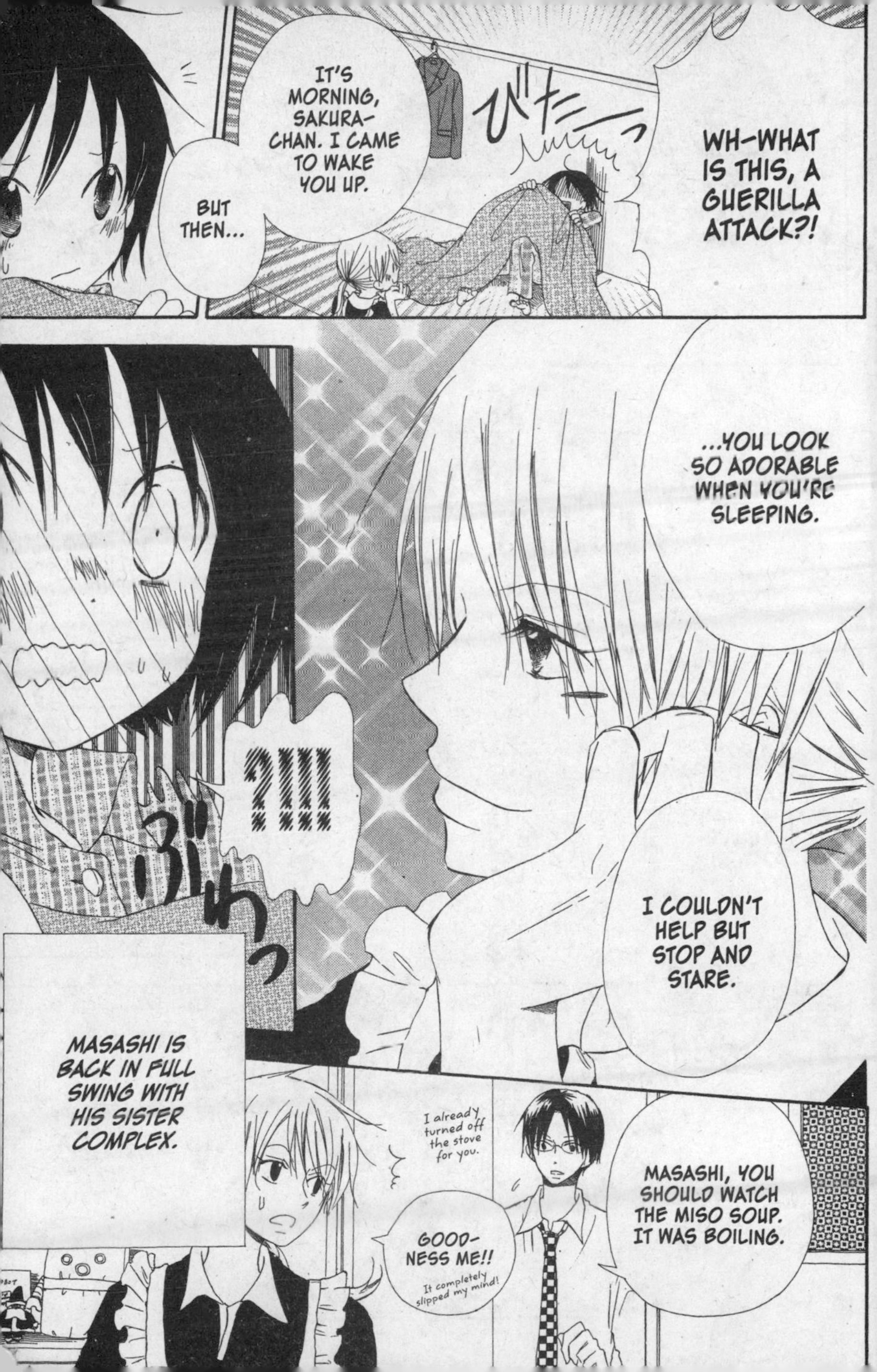
WH-WHAT IS THIS, A GUERILLA ATTACK?!
IT'S MORNING, SAKURA-CHAN. I CAME TO WAKE YOU UP.
BUT THEN...
...YOU LOOK SO ADORABLE WHEN YOU'RE SLEEPING.
I COULDN'T HELP BUT STOP AND STARE.
?!!!
MASASHI, YOU SHOULD WATCH THE MISO SOUP. IT WAS BOILING.
I already turned off the stove for you.
GOOD-NESS ME!!
It completely slipped my mind!
MASASHI IS BACK IN FULL SWING WITH HIS SISTER COMPLEX.

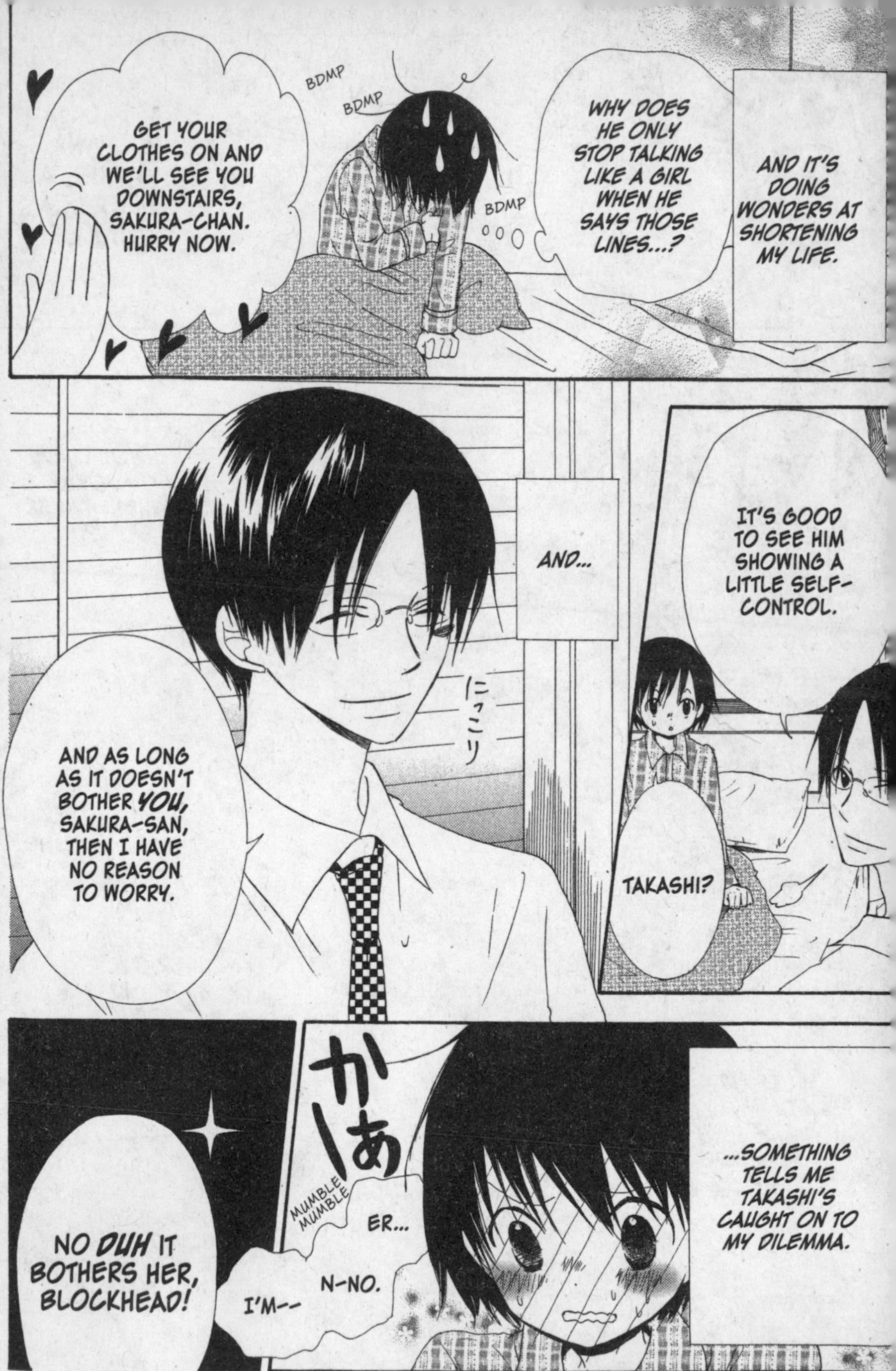
AND IT'S DOING WONDERS AT SHORTENING MY LIFE.
WHY DOES HE ONLY STOP TALKING LIKE A GIRL WHEN HE SAYS THOSE LINES...?
BDMP BDMP BDMP
GET YOUR CLOTHES ON AND WE'LL SEE YOU DOWNSTAIRS, SAKURA-CHAN. HURRY NOW.
IT'S GOOD TO SEE HIM SHOWING A LITTLE SELF-CONTROL.
TAKASHI?
AND...
にっこり
AND AS LONG AS IT DOESN'T BOTHER ***YOU***, SAKURA-SAN, THEN I HAVE NO REASON TO WORRY.
...SOMETHING TELLS ME TAKASHI'S CAUGHT ON TO MY DILEMMA.
かあ
ER...
MUMBLE MUMBLE
N-NO.
I'M--
NO ***DUH*** IT BOTHERS HER, BLOCKHEAD!

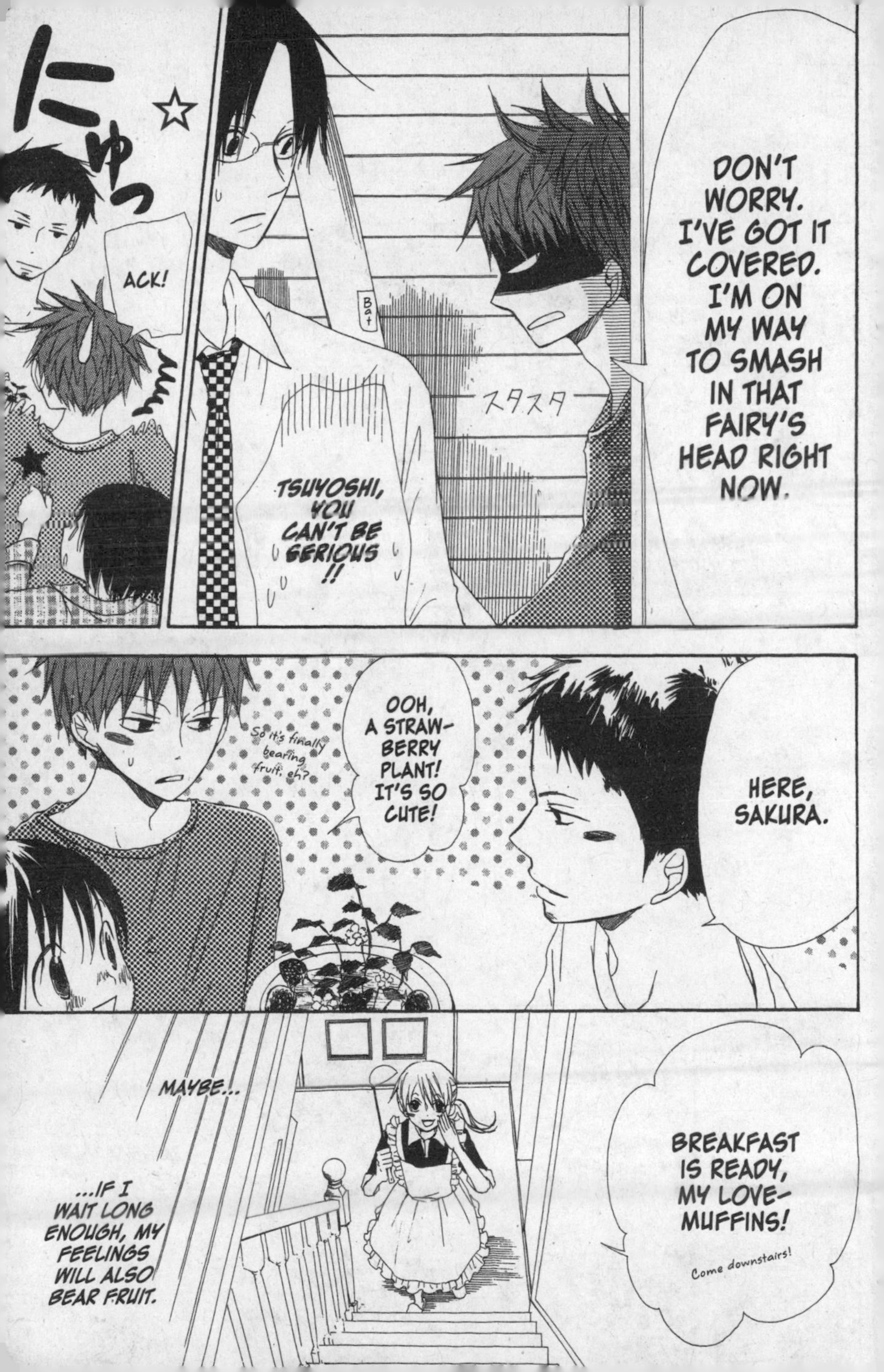
DON'T WORRY. I'VE GOT IT COVERED. I'M ON MY WAY TO SMASH IN THAT FAIRY'S HEAD RIGHT NOW.
スタスタ
Bat
TSUYOSHI, YOU CAN'T BE SERIOUS!!
にゅっ ☆
ACK!
HERE, SAKURA.
OOH, A STRAWBERRY PLANT! IT'S SO CUTE!
So it's finally bearing fruit, eh?
BREAKFAST IS READY, MY LOVE-MUFFINS!
Come downstairs!
MAYBE...
...IF I WAIT LONG ENOUGH, MY FEELINGS WILL ALSO BEAR FRUIT.

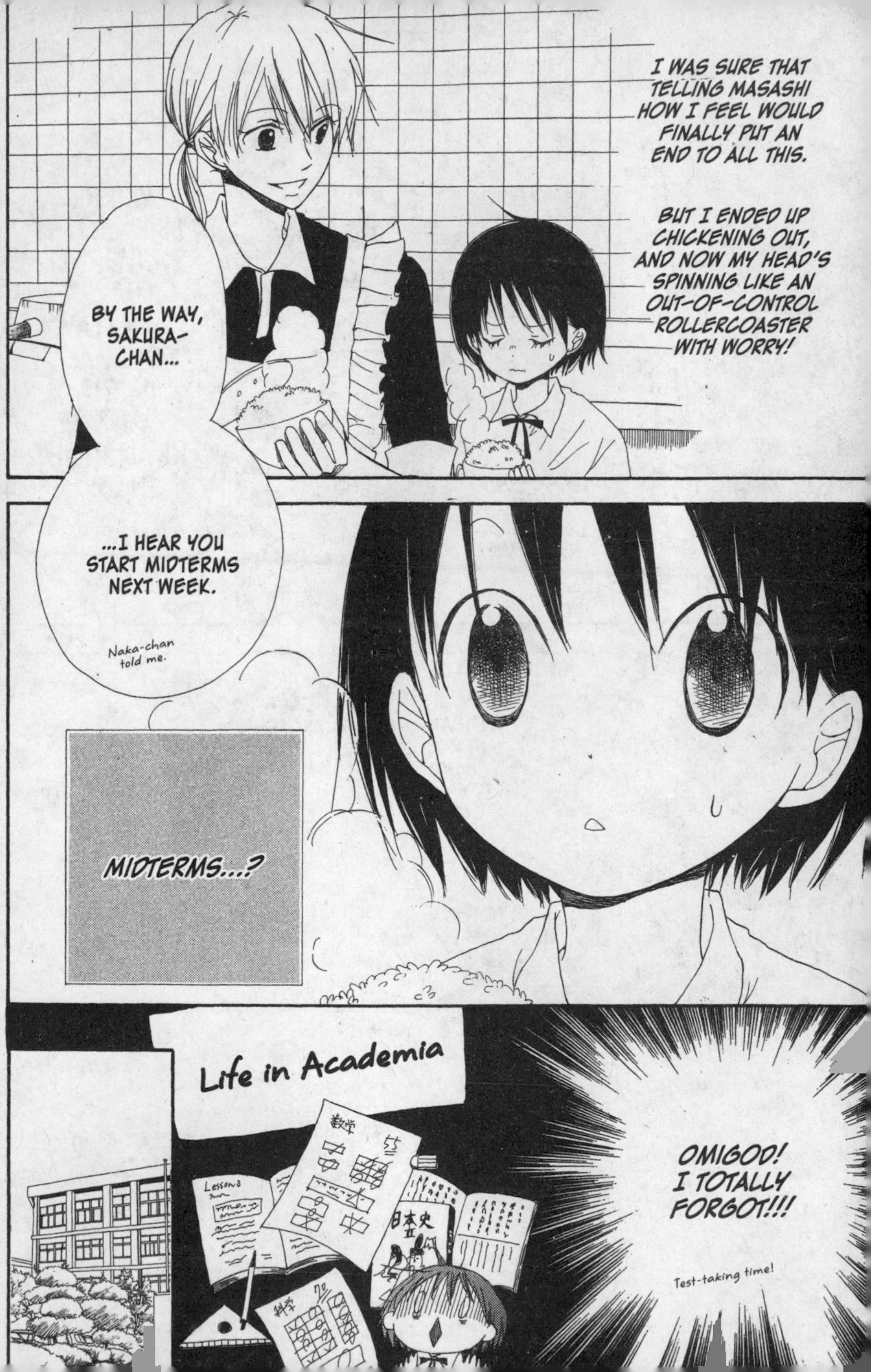

I WAS SURE THAT TELLING MASASHI HOW I FEEL WOULD FINALLY PUT AN END TO ALL THIS.
BUT I ENDED UP CHICKENING OUT, AND NOW MY HEAD'S SPINNING LIKE AN OUT-OF-CONTROL ROLLERCOASTER WITH WORRY!
BY THE WAY, SAKURA-CHAN...
...I HEAR YOU START MIDTERMS NEXT WEEK.
Naka-chan told me.
MIDTERMS...?
OMIGOD! I TOTALLY FORGOT!!!
Test-taking time!
Life in Academia
数学
日本史

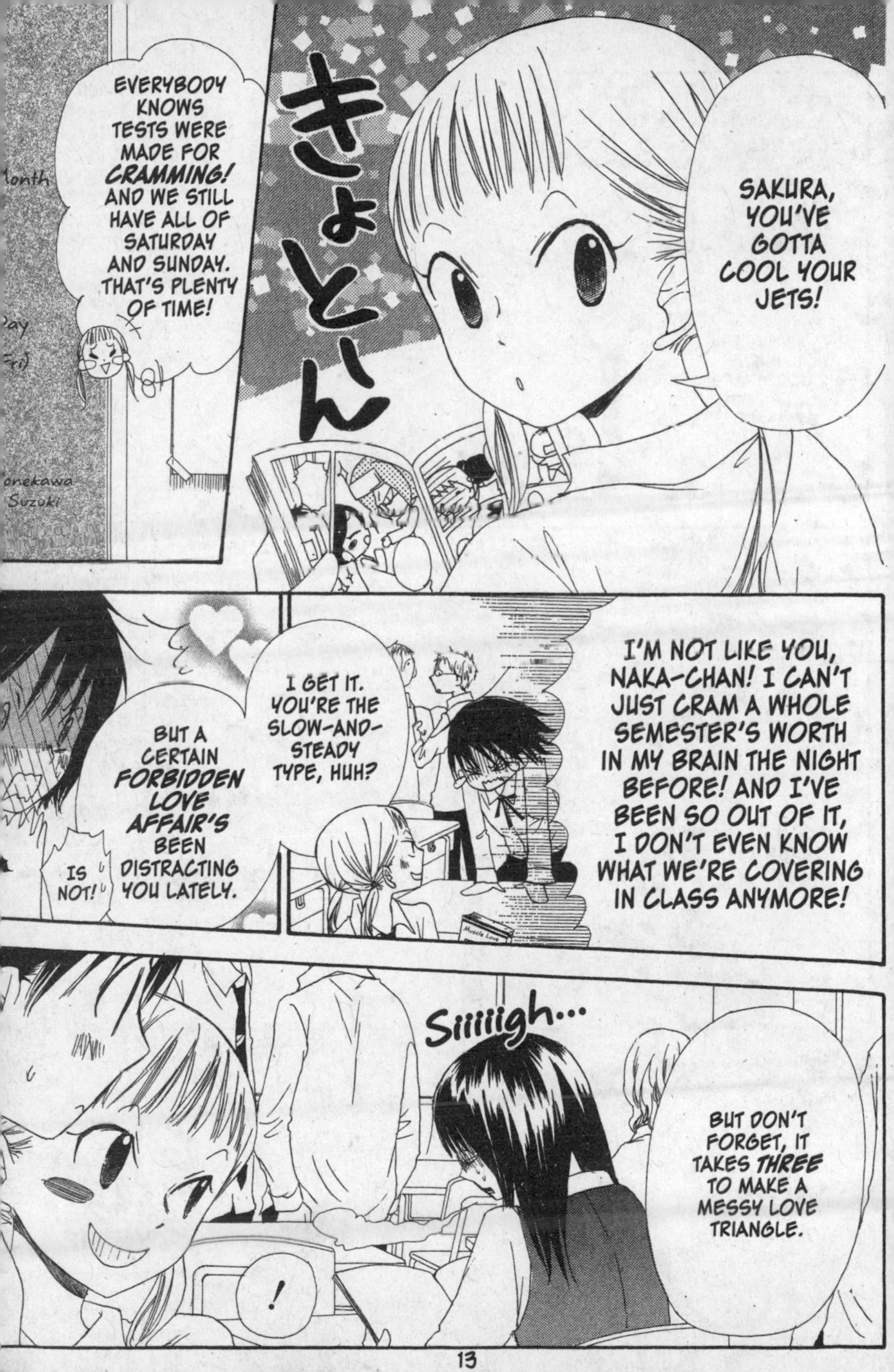
SAKURA, YOU'VE GOTTA COOL YOUR JETS!
きょとん
EVERYBODY KNOWS TESTS WERE MADE FOR *CRAMMING!* AND WE STILL HAVE ALL OF SATURDAY AND SUNDAY. THAT'S PLENTY OF TIME!
I'M NOT LIKE YOU, NAKA-CHAN! I CAN'T JUST CRAM A WHOLE SEMESTER'S WORTH IN MY BRAIN THE NIGHT BEFORE! AND I'VE BEEN SO OUT OF IT, I DON'T EVEN KNOW WHAT WE'RE COVERING IN CLASS ANYMORE!
I GET IT. YOU'RE THE SLOW-AND-STEADY TYPE, HUH?
BUT A CERTAIN *FORBIDDEN LOVE AFFAIR'S* BEEN DISTRACTING YOU LATELY.
IS NOT!
BUT DON'T FORGET, IT TAKES *THREE* TO MAKE A MESSY LOVE TRIANGLE.
Siiiiigh...
!

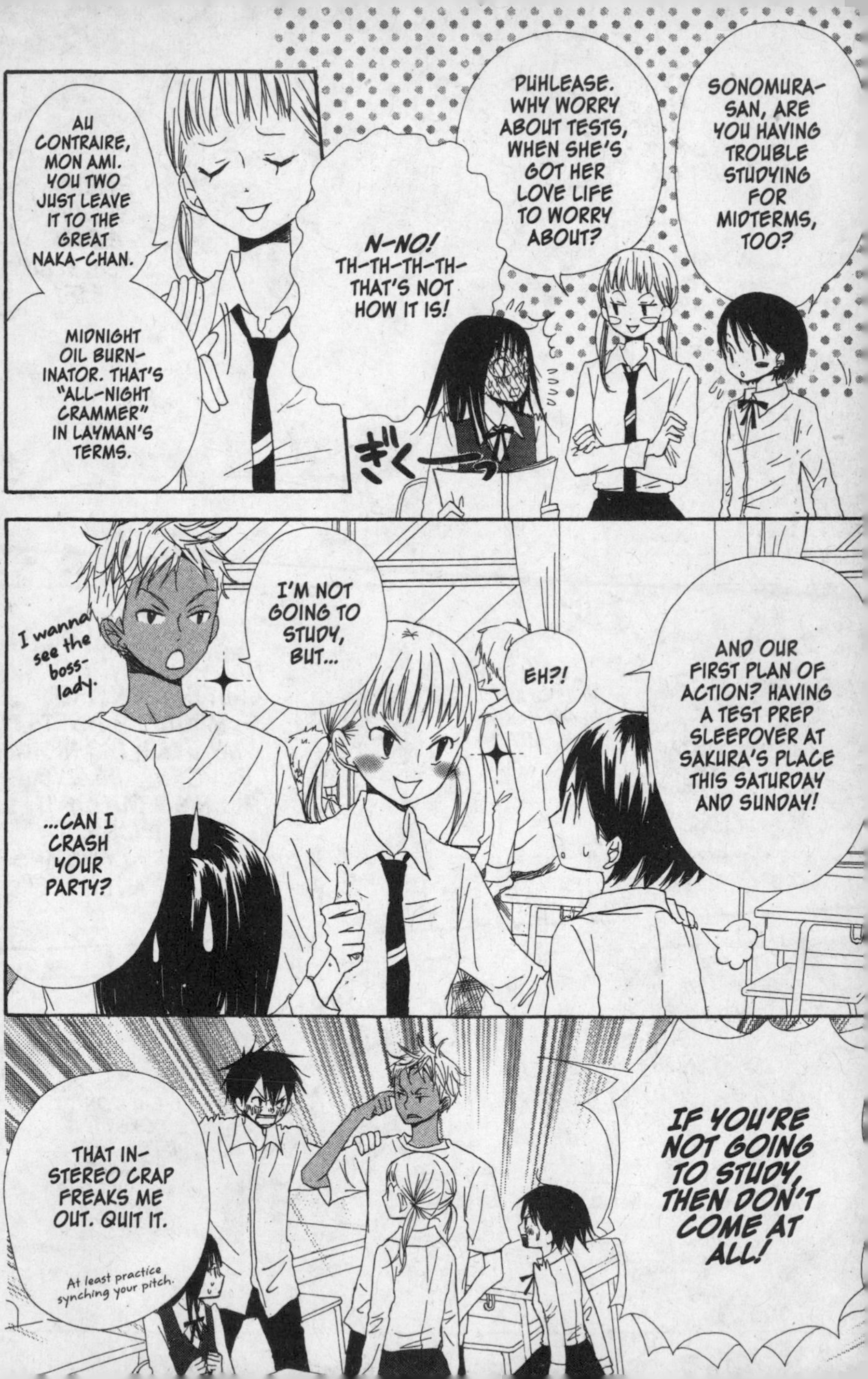
SONOMURA-SAN, ARE YOU HAVING TROUBLE STUDYING FOR MIDTERMS, TOO?
PUHLEASE. WHY WORRY ABOUT TESTS, WHEN SHE'S GOT HER LOVE LIFE TO WORRY ABOUT?
N-NO! TH-TH-TH-TH-THAT'S NOT HOW IT IS!
ぎくーっ
AU CONTRAIRE, MON AMI. YOU TWO JUST LEAVE IT TO THE GREAT NAKA-CHAN.
MIDNIGHT OIL BURN-INATOR. THAT'S "ALL-NIGHT CRAMMER" IN LAYMAN'S TERMS.
AND OUR FIRST PLAN OF ACTION? HAVING A TEST PREP SLEEPOVER AT SAKURA'S PLACE THIS SATURDAY AND SUNDAY!
EH?!
I'M NOT GOING TO STUDY, BUT...
...CAN I CRASH YOUR PARTY?
I wanna see the boss-lady.
IF YOU'RE NOT GOING TO STUDY, THEN DON'T COME AT ALL!
THAT IN-STEREO CRAP FREAKS ME OUT. QUIT IT.
At least practice synching your pitch.

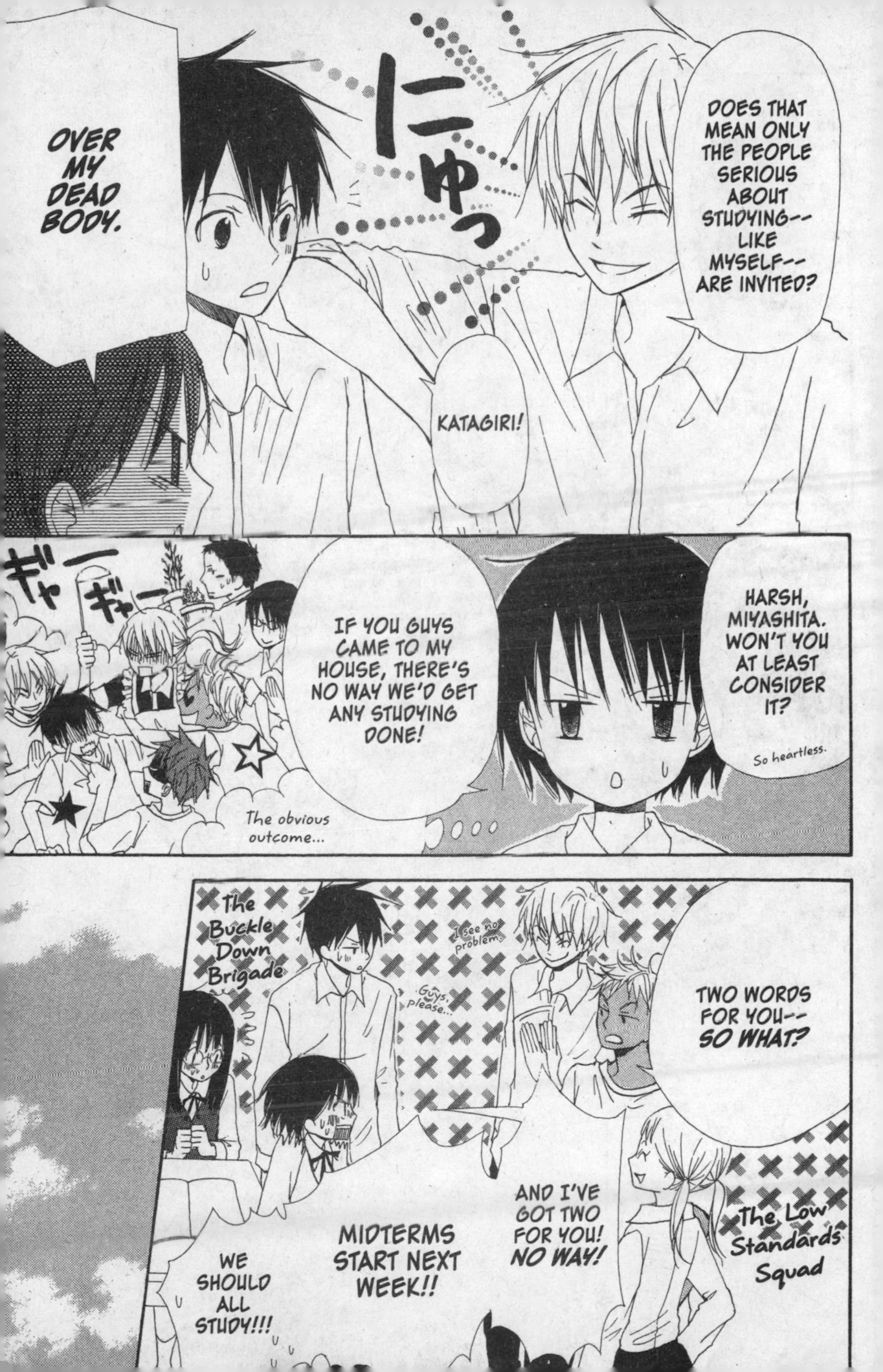
DOES THAT MEAN ONLY THE PEOPLE SERIOUS ABOUT STUDYING--LIKE MYSELF--ARE INVITED?
にゅっ
KATAGIRI!
OVER MY DEAD BODY.
HARSH, MIYASHITA. WON'T YOU AT LEAST CONSIDER IT?
So heartless.
IF YOU GUYS CAME TO MY HOUSE, THERE'S NO WAY WE'D GET ANY STUDYING DONE!
ギャーギャー
The obvious outcome...
TWO WORDS FOR YOU--SO WHAT?
The Low Standards Squad
I see no problem.
AND I'VE GOT TWO FOR YOU! NO WAY!
MIDTERMS START NEXT WEEK!!
Guys, please...
The Buckle Down Brigade
WE SHOULD ALL STUDY!!!

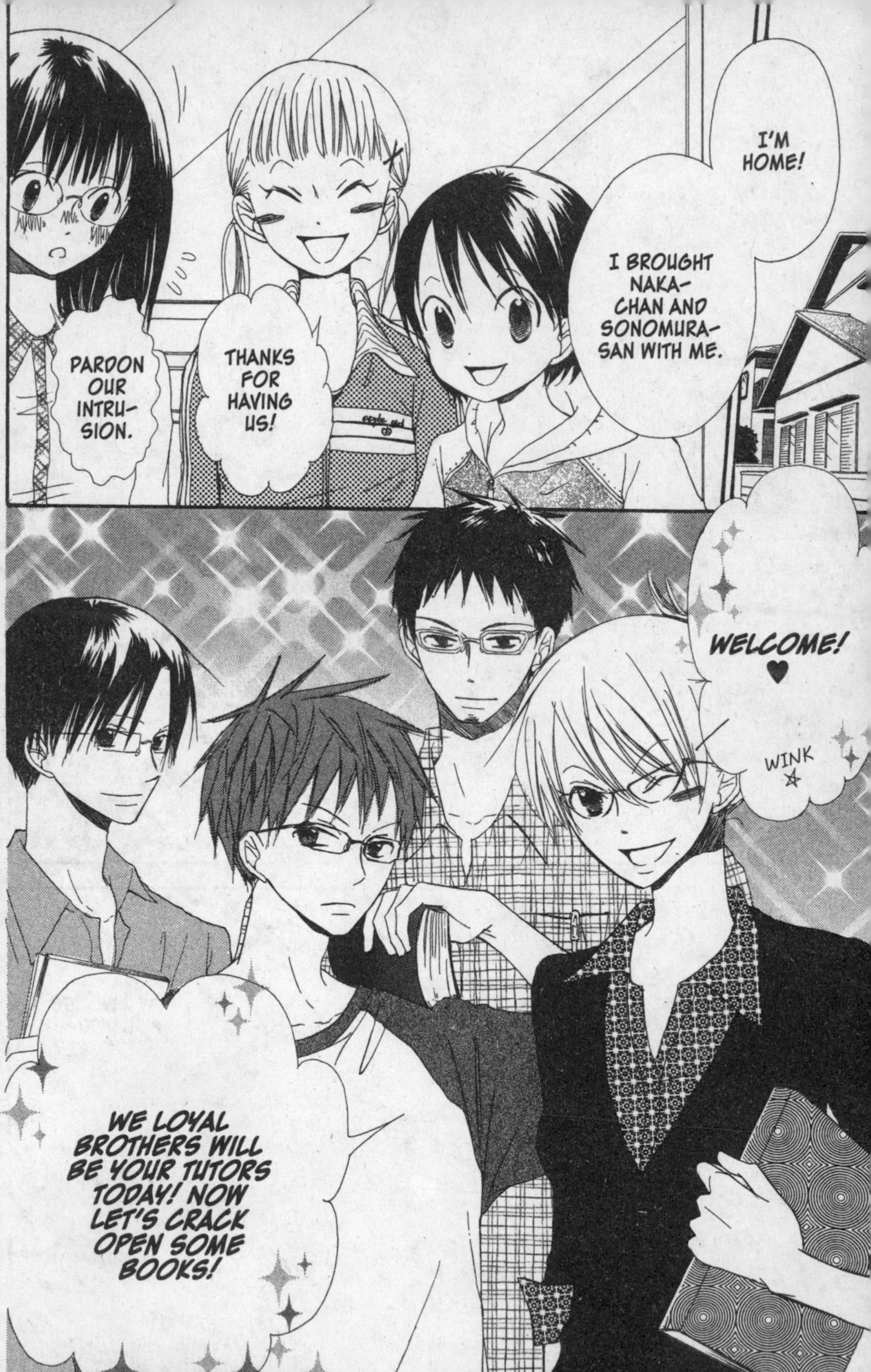
I'M HOME!
I BROUGHT NAKA-CHAN AND SONOMURA-SAN WITH ME.
THANKS FOR HAVING US!
PARDON OUR INTRUSION.
WELCOME! ♥
WINK ☆
WE LOYAL BROTHERS WILL BE YOUR TUTORS TODAY! NOW LET'S CRACK OPEN SOME BOOKS!

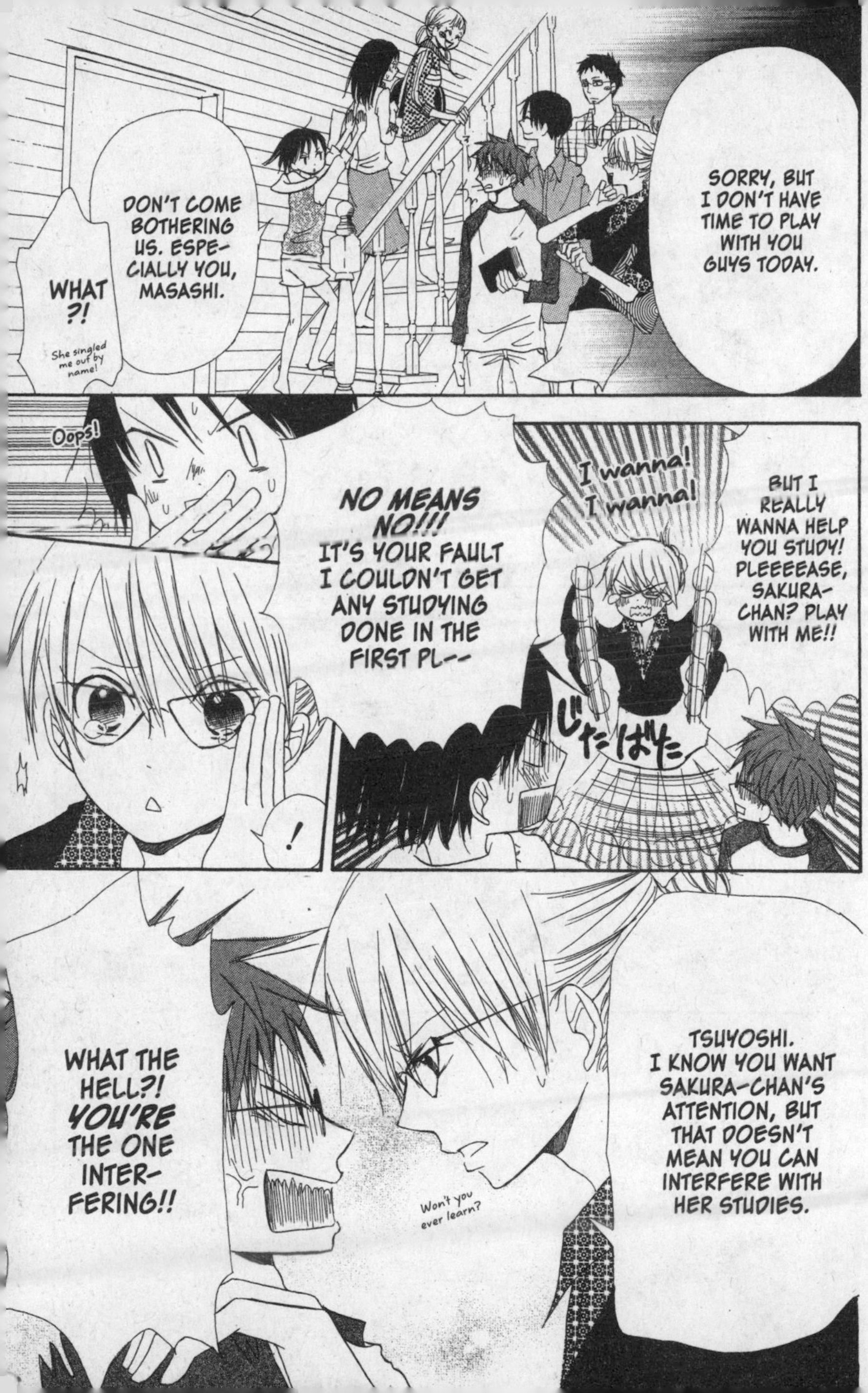

SORRY, BUT I DON'T HAVE TIME TO PLAY WITH YOU GUYS TODAY.
DON'T COME BOTHERING US. ESPE-CIALLY YOU, MASASHI.
WHAT?!
She singled me out by name!
I wanna! I wanna!
BUT I REALLY WANNA HELP YOU STUDY! PLEEEEASE, SAKURA-CHAN? PLAY WITH ME!!
じたばた
NO MEANS NO!!! IT'S YOUR FAULT I COULDN'T GET ANY STUDYING DONE IN THE FIRST PL--
Oops!
!
TSUYOSHI. I KNOW YOU WANT SAKURA-CHAN'S ATTENTION, BUT THAT DOESN'T MEAN YOU CAN INTERFERE WITH HER STUDIES.
Won't you ever learn?
WHAT THE HELL?! YOU'RE THE ONE INTER-FERING!!

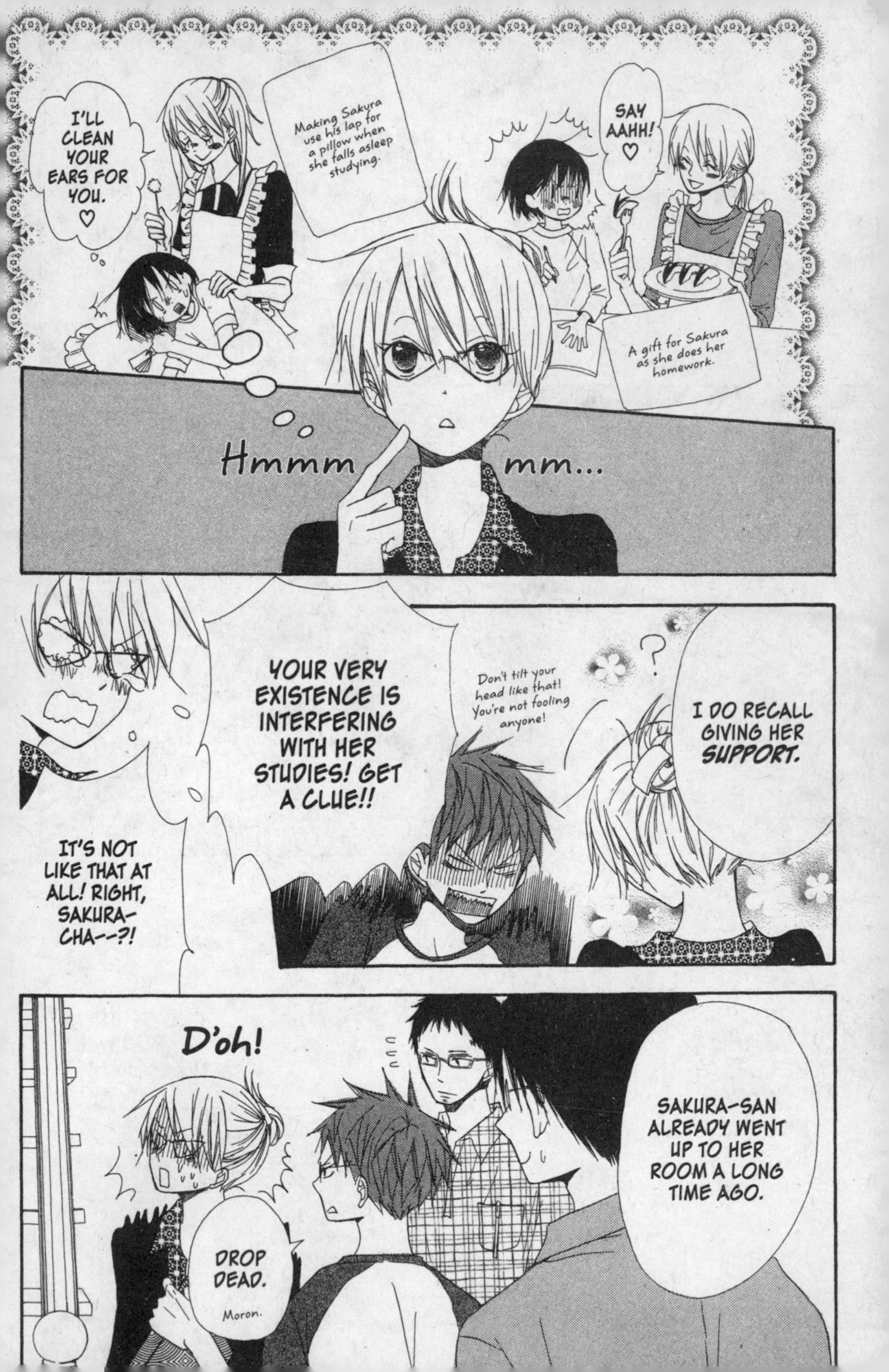
SAY AAHH! ♡
A gift for Sakura as she does her homework.
Making Sakura use his lap for a pillow when she falls asleep studying.
I'LL CLEAN YOUR EARS FOR YOU. ♡
Hmmmm mm...
I DO RECALL GIVING HER SUPPORT.
Don't tilt your head like that! You're not fooling anyone!
YOUR VERY EXISTENCE IS INTERFERING WITH HER STUDIES! GET A CLUE!!
IT'S NOT LIKE THAT AT ALL! RIGHT, SAKURA-CHA--?!
SAKURA-SAN ALREADY WENT UP TO HER ROOM A LONG TIME AGO.
D'oh!
DROP DEAD.
Moron.

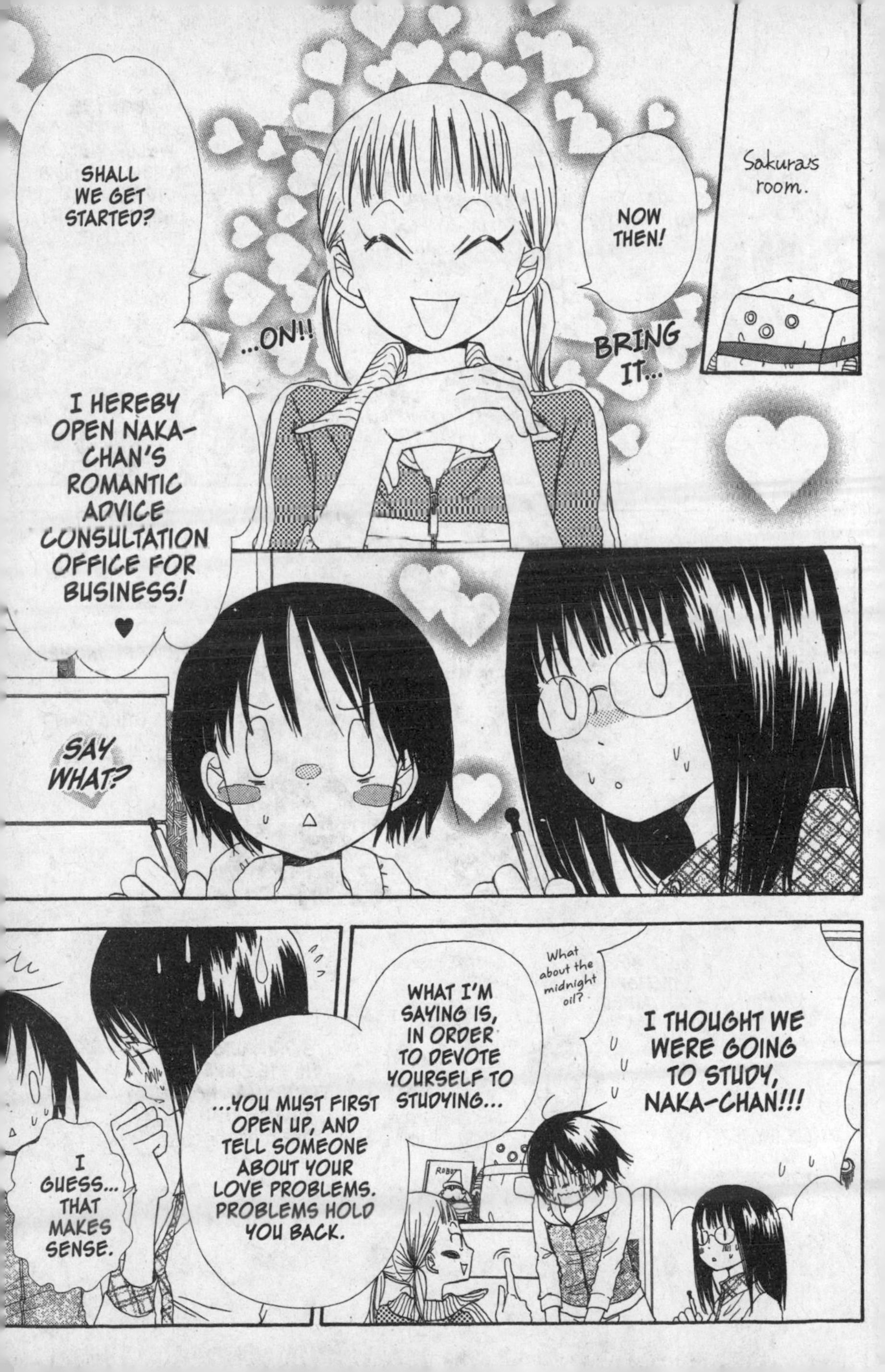
Sakura's room.
NOW THEN!
SHALL WE GET STARTED?
BRING IT...
...ON!!
I HEREBY OPEN NAKA-CHAN'S ROMANTIC ADVICE CONSULTATION OFFICE FOR BUSINESS! ♥
SAY WHAT?
I THOUGHT WE WERE GOING TO STUDY, NAKA-CHAN!!!
What about the midnight oil?
WHAT I'M SAYING IS, IN ORDER TO DEVOTE YOURSELF TO STUDYING...
...YOU MUST FIRST OPEN UP, AND TELL SOMEONE ABOUT YOUR LOVE PROBLEMS. PROBLEMS HOLD YOU BACK.
I GUESS... THAT MAKES SENSE.

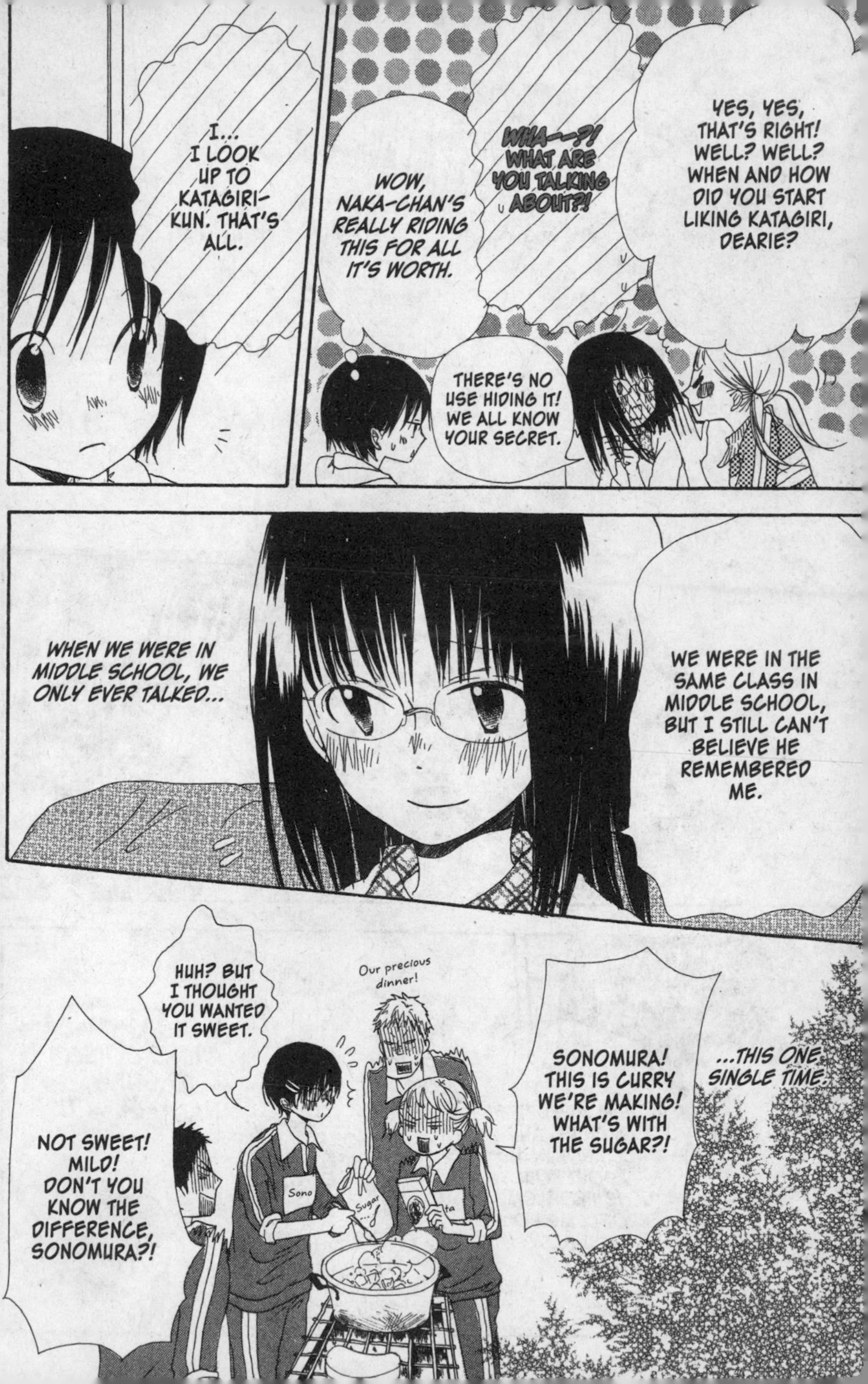
YES, YES, THAT'S RIGHT! WELL? WELL? WHEN AND HOW DID YOU START LIKING KATAGIRI, DEARIE?
WHA--?! WHAT ARE YOU TALKING ABOUT?!
WOW, NAKA-CHAN'S REALLY RIDING THIS FOR ALL IT'S WORTH.
THERE'S NO USE HIDING IT! WE ALL KNOW YOUR SECRET.
I... I LOOK UP TO KATAGIRI-KUN. THAT'S ALL.
WE WERE IN THE SAME CLASS IN MIDDLE SCHOOL, BUT I STILL CAN'T BELIEVE HE REMEMBERED ME.
WHEN WE WERE IN MIDDLE SCHOOL, WE ONLY EVER TALKED...
...THIS ONE SINGLE TIME.
SONOMURA! THIS IS CURRY WE'RE MAKING! WHAT'S WITH THE SUGAR?!
Our precious dinner!
HUH? BUT I THOUGHT YOU WANTED IT SWEET.
NOT SWEET! MILD! DON'T YOU KNOW THE DIFFERENCE, SONOMURA?!
Sono
Sugar

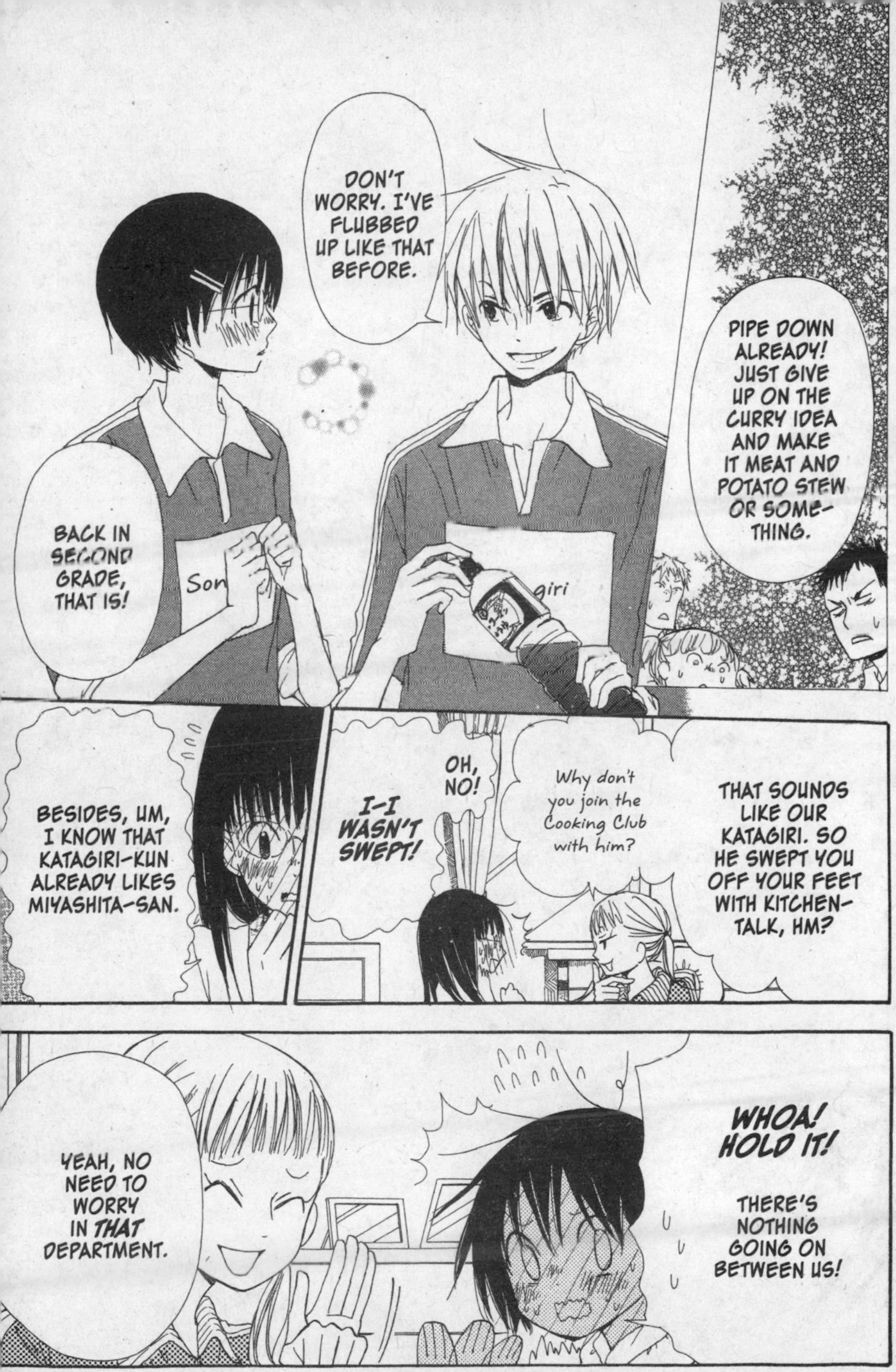
PIPE DOWN ALREADY! JUST GIVE UP ON THE CURRY IDEA AND MAKE IT MEAT AND POTATO STEW OR SOME-THING.
DON'T WORRY. I'VE FLUBBED UP LIKE THAT BEFORE.
BACK IN SECOND GRADE, THAT IS!
THAT SOUNDS LIKE OUR KATAGIRI. SO HE SWEPT YOU OFF YOUR FEET WITH KITCHEN-TALK, HM?
Why don't you join the Cooking Club with him?
OH, NO!
I-I WASN'T SWEPT!
BESIDES, UM, I KNOW THAT KATAGIRI-KUN ALREADY LIKES MIYASHITA-SAN.
WHOA! HOLD IT!
THERE'S NOTHING GOING ON BETWEEN US!
YEAH, NO NEED TO WORRY IN THAT DEPARTMENT.

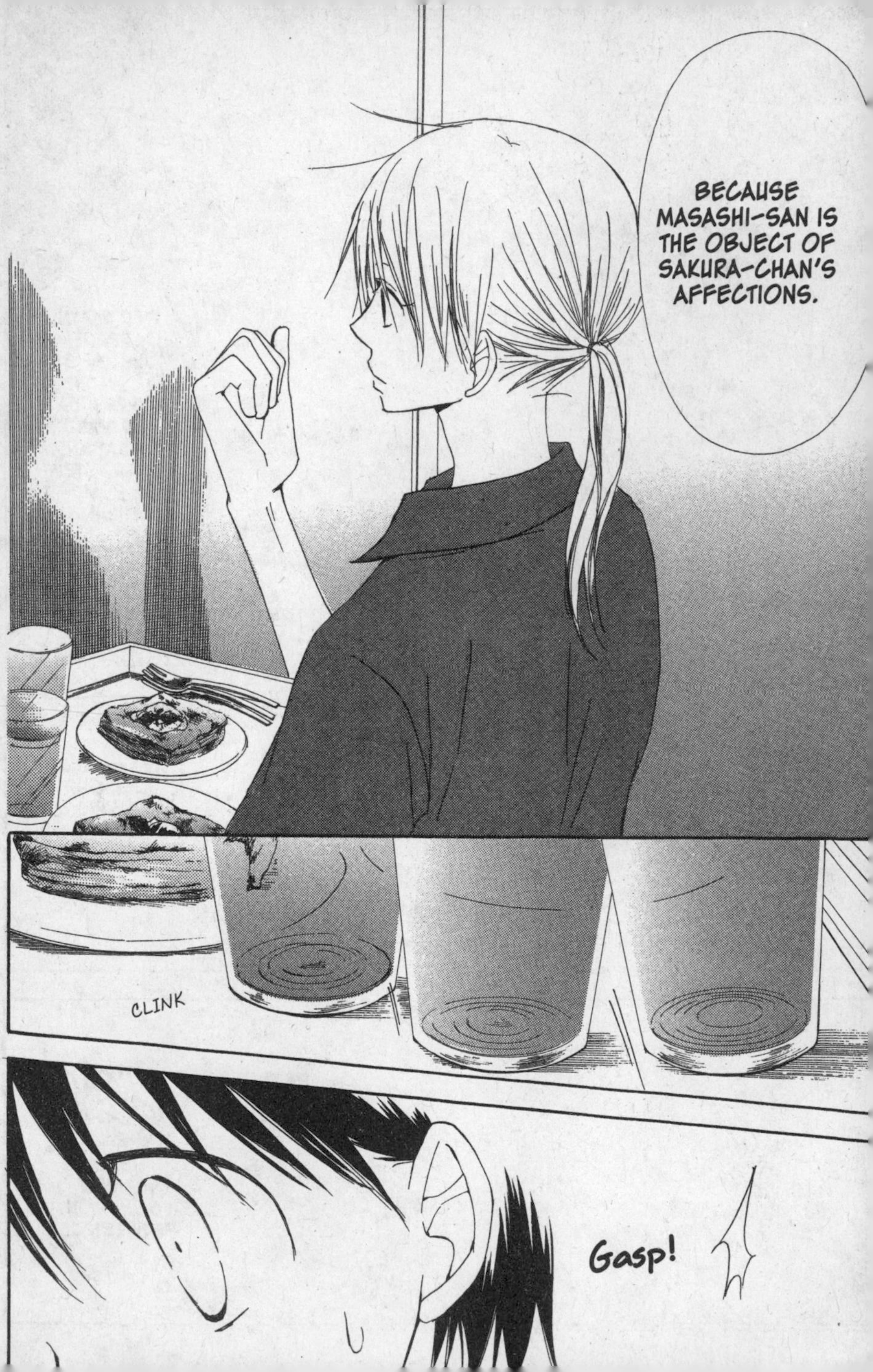
BECAUSE MASASHI-SAN IS THE OBJECT OF SAKURA-CHAN'S AFFECTIONS.
CLINK
Gasp!

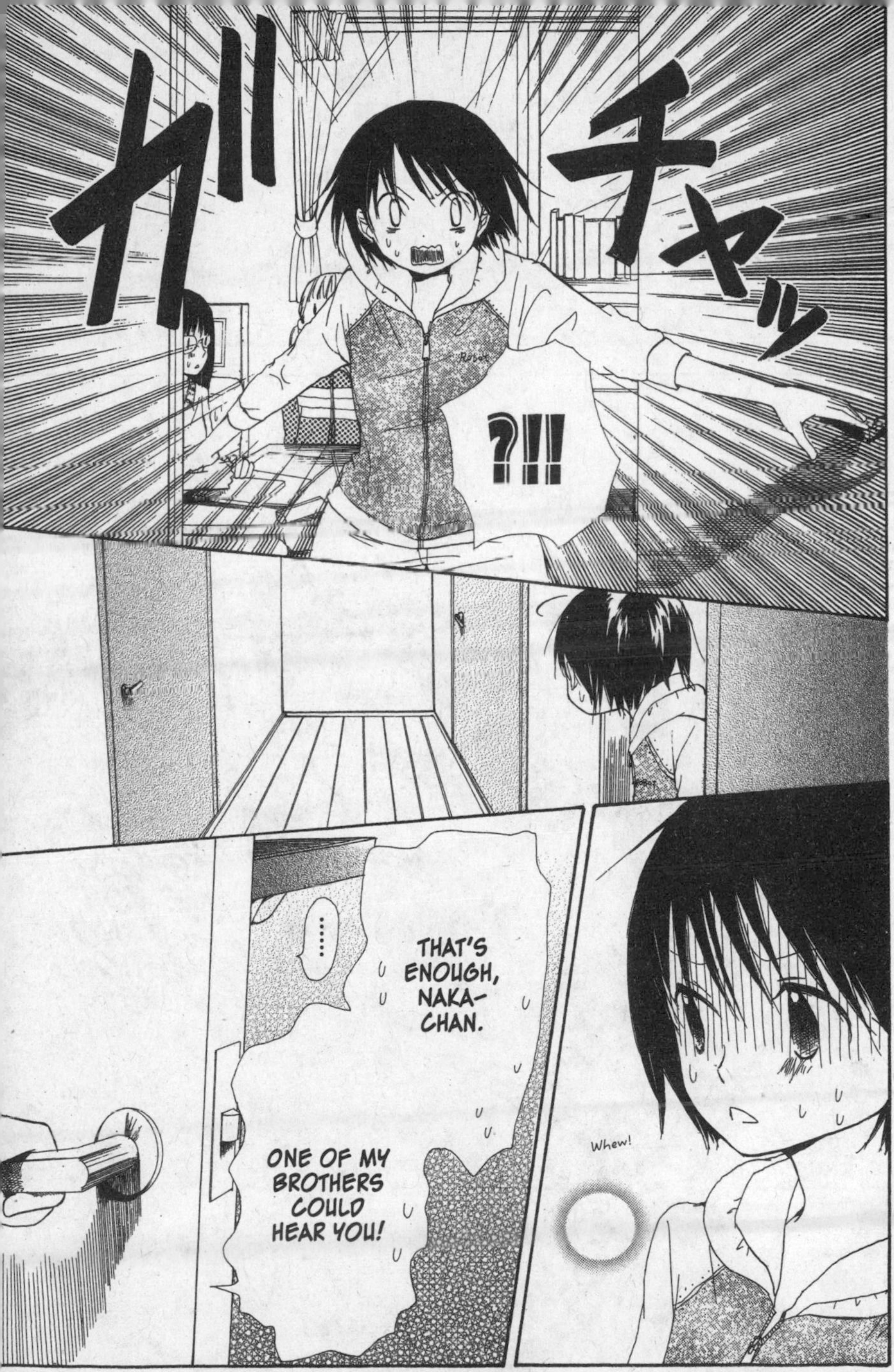
ガチャッ
?!!
Whew!
......
THAT'S ENOUGH, NAKA-CHAN.
ONE OF MY BROTHERS COULD HEAR YOU!

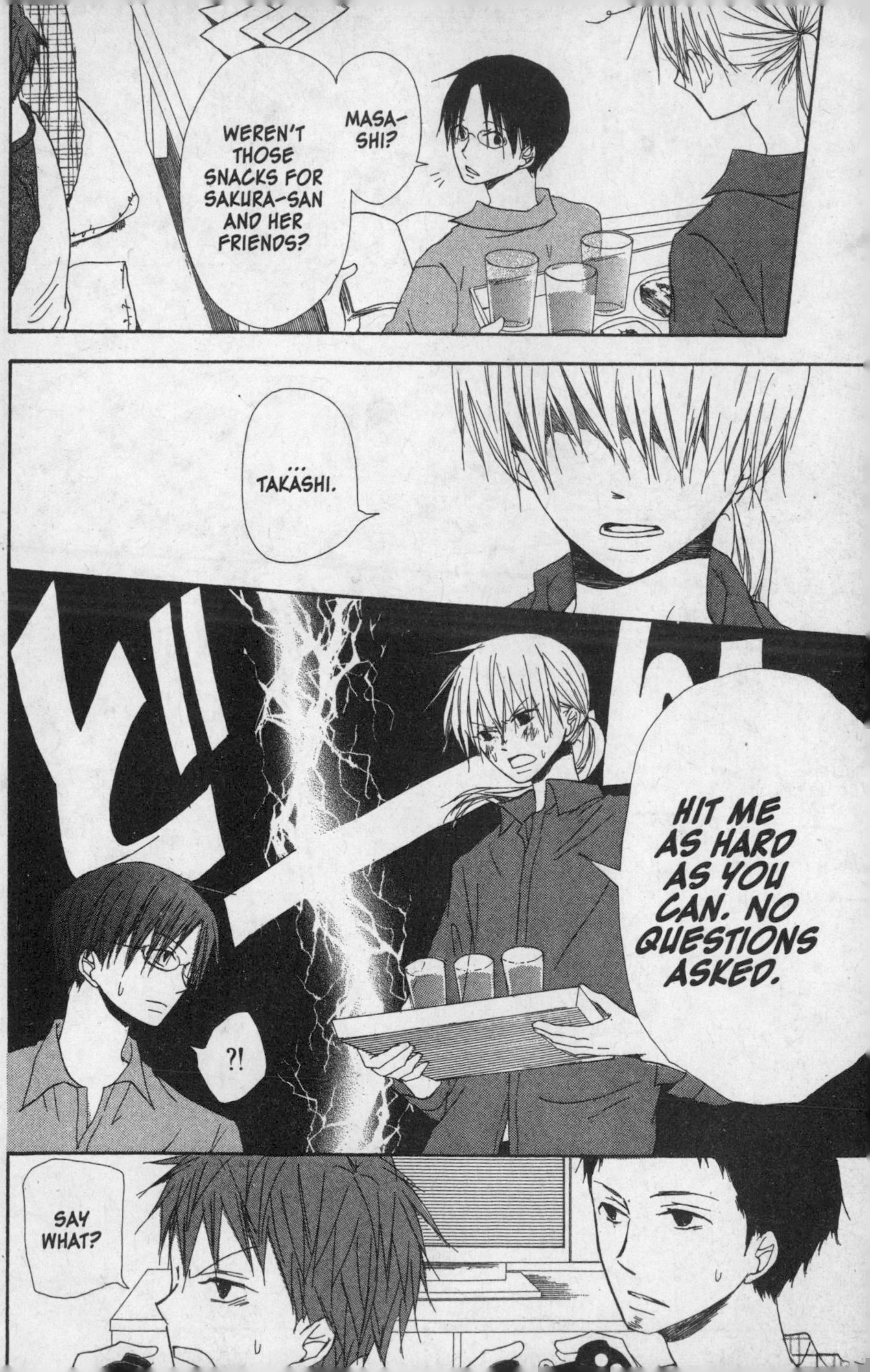
MASA-SHI?
WEREN'T THOSE SNACKS FOR SAKURA-SAN AND HER FRIENDS?
...TAKASHI.
HIT ME AS HARD AS YOU CAN. NO QUESTIONS ASKED.
?!
SAY WHAT?

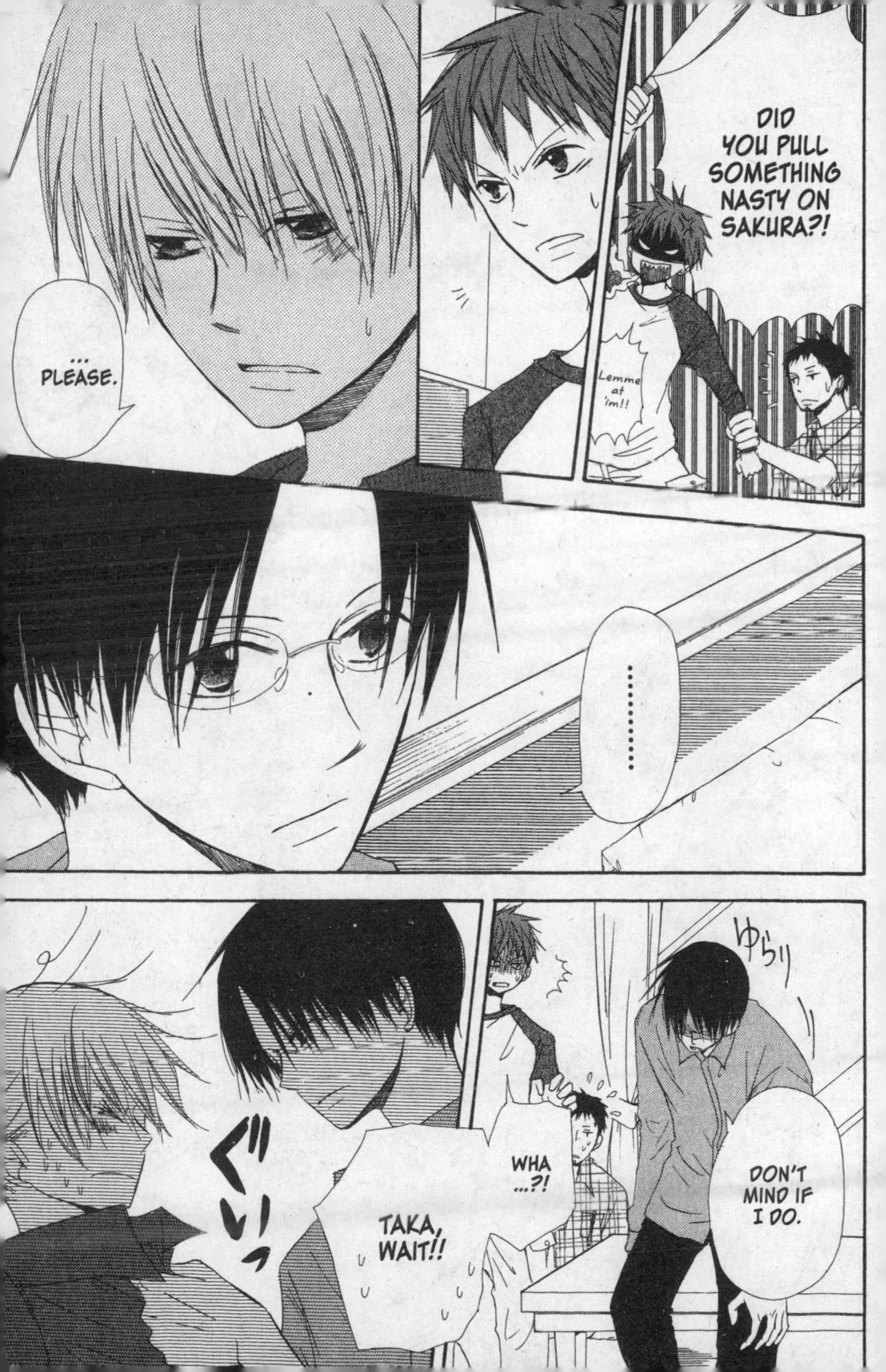
DID YOU PULL SOMETHING NASTY ON SAKURA?!
Lemme at 'im!!
... PLEASE.
......
ゆらり
DON'T MIND IF I DO.
WHA ...?!
TAKA, WAIT!!
ぐいっ

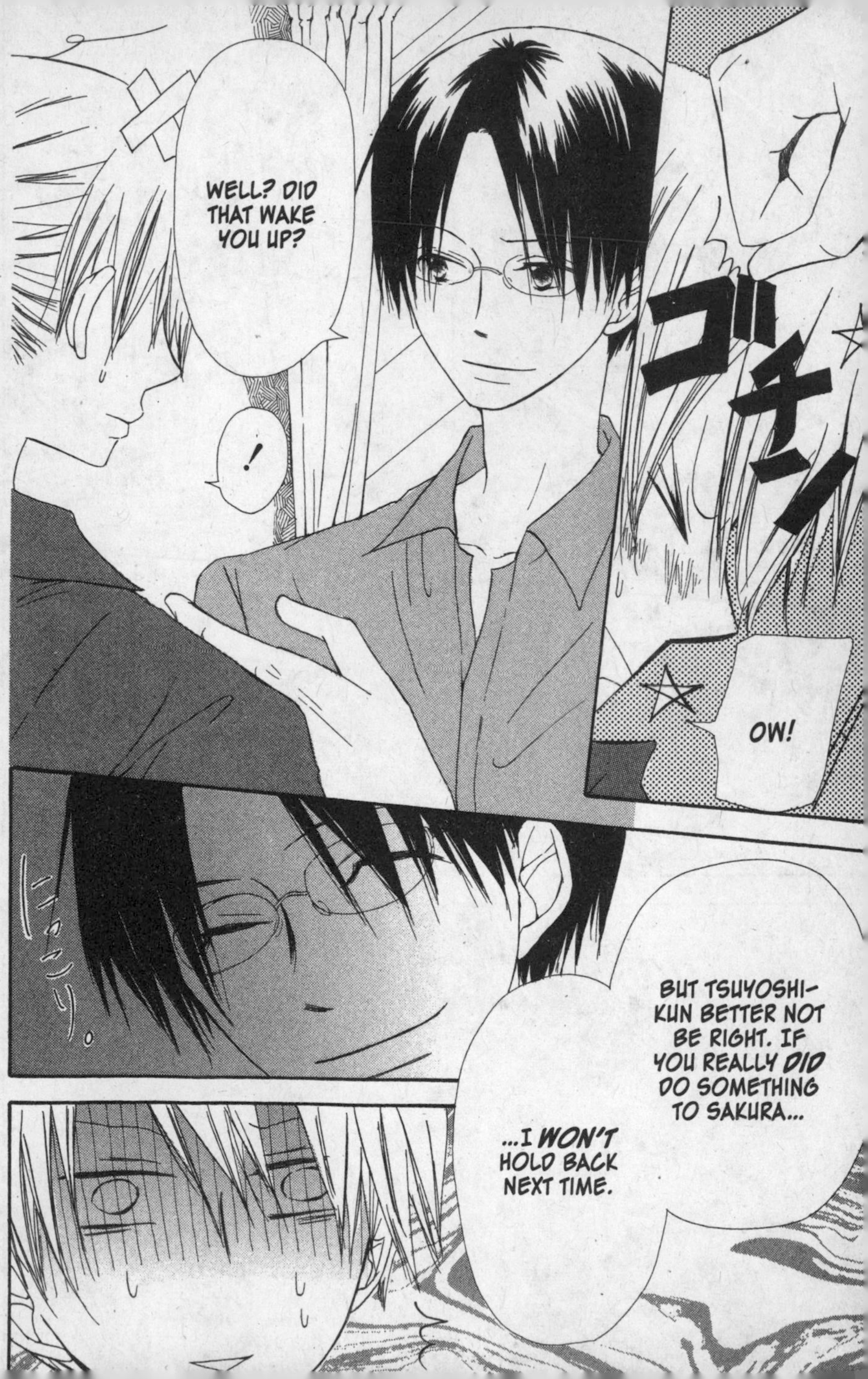
ゴチン
OW!
WELL? DID THAT WAKE YOU UP?
!
BUT TSUYOSHI-KUN BETTER NOT BE RIGHT. IF YOU REALLY *DID* DO SOMETHING TO SAKURA...
...I *WON'T* HOLD BACK NEXT TIME.

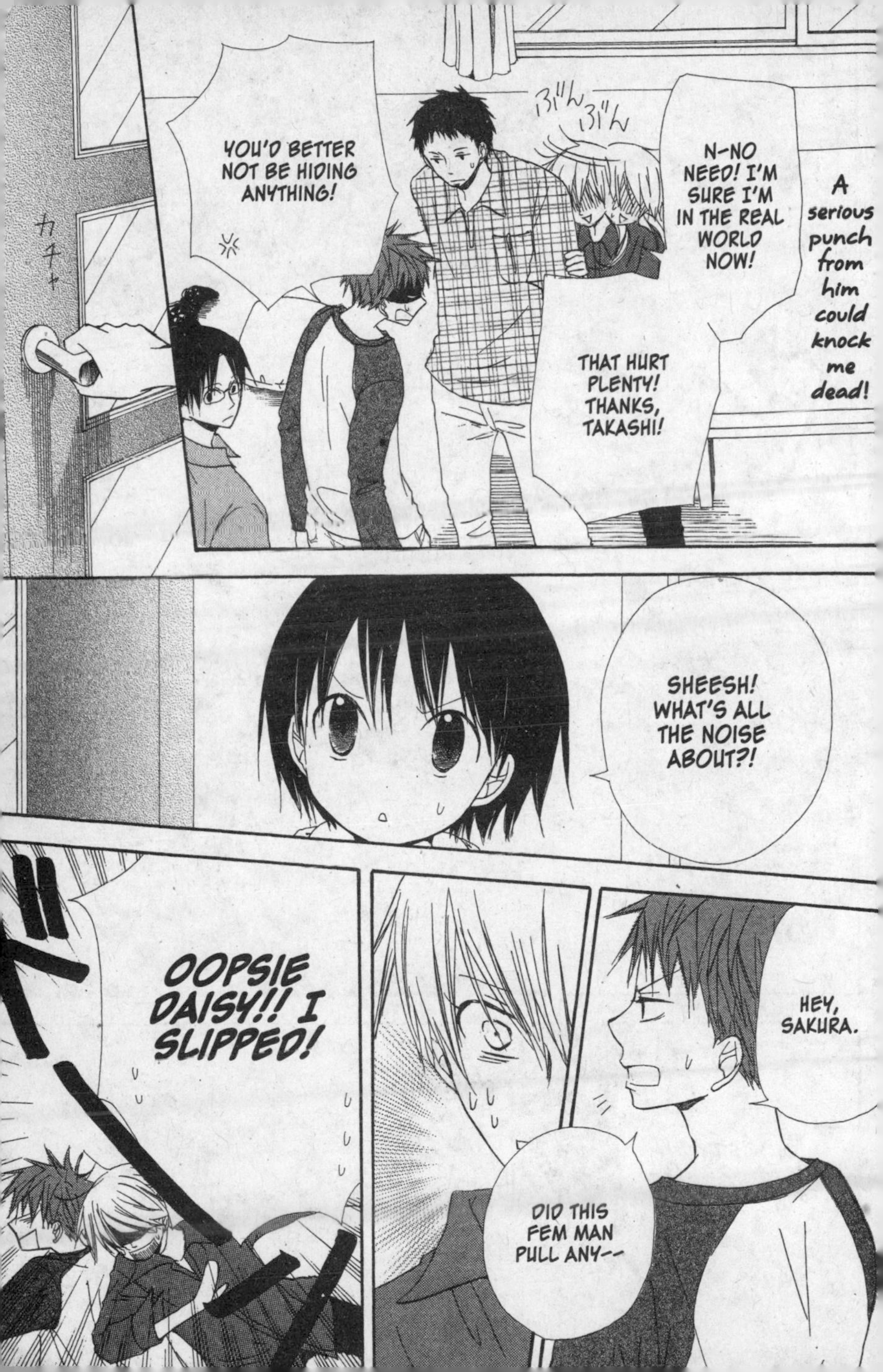
A serious punch from him could knock me dead!
N-NO NEED! I'M SURE I'M IN THE REAL WORLD NOW!
ぶんぶん
THAT HURT PLENTY! THANKS, TAKASHI!
YOU'D BETTER NOT BE HIDING ANYTHING!
カチャ
SHEESH! WHAT'S ALL THE NOISE ABOUT?!
HEY, SAKURA.
DID THIS FEM MAN PULL ANY--
OOPSIE DAISY!! I SLIPPED!

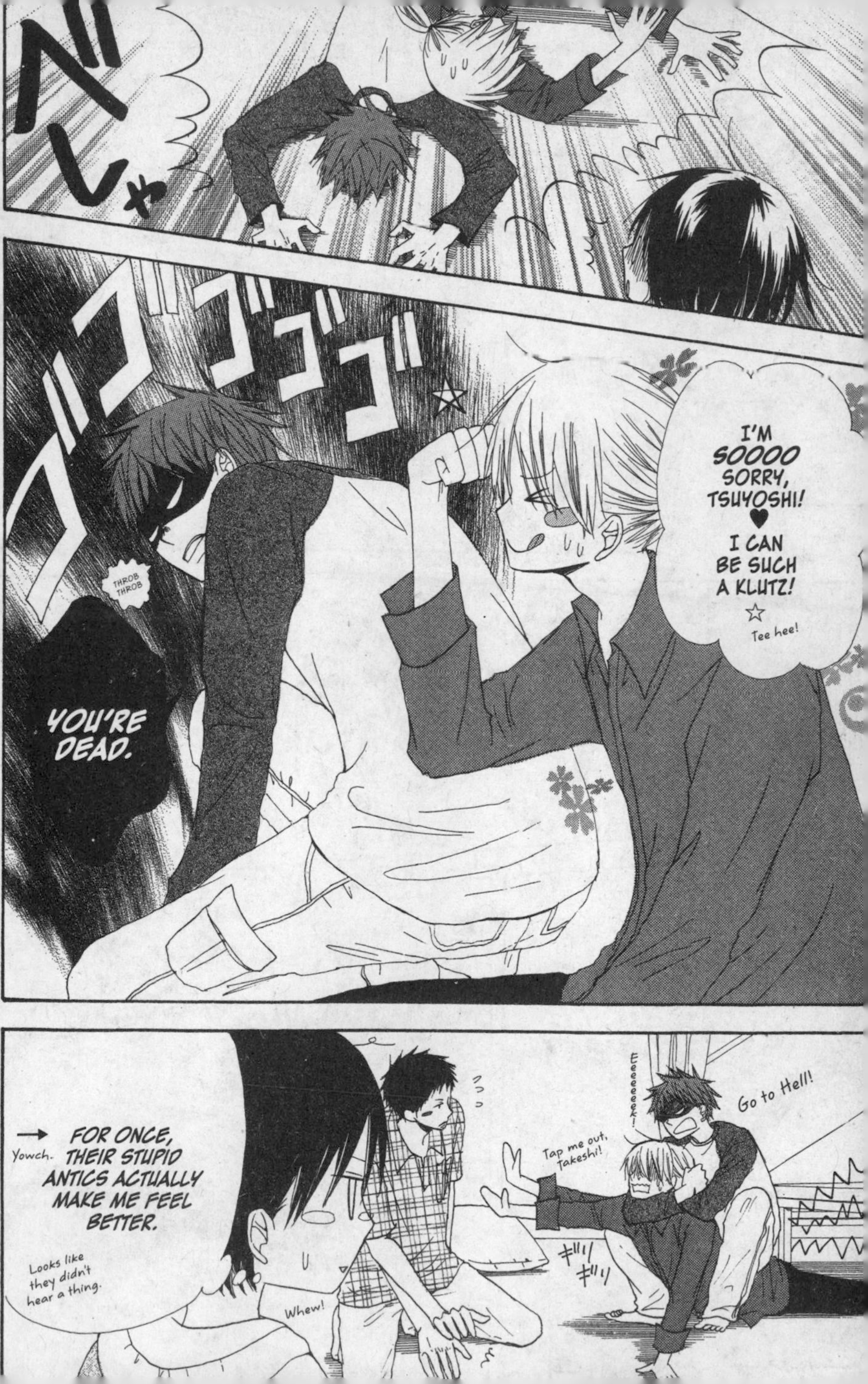

べしゃ
ゴゴゴゴ
I'M SOOOO SORRY, TSUYOSHI! ♥ I CAN BE SUCH A KLUTZ! ☆
Tee hee!
THROB THROB
YOU'RE DEAD.
Go to Hell!
Eeeeeeeek!
Tap me out, Takeshi!
ギリ ギリ
Whew!
FOR ONCE, THEIR STUPID ANTICS ACTUALLY MAKE ME FEEL BETTER.
Yowch.
Looks like they didn't hear a thing.

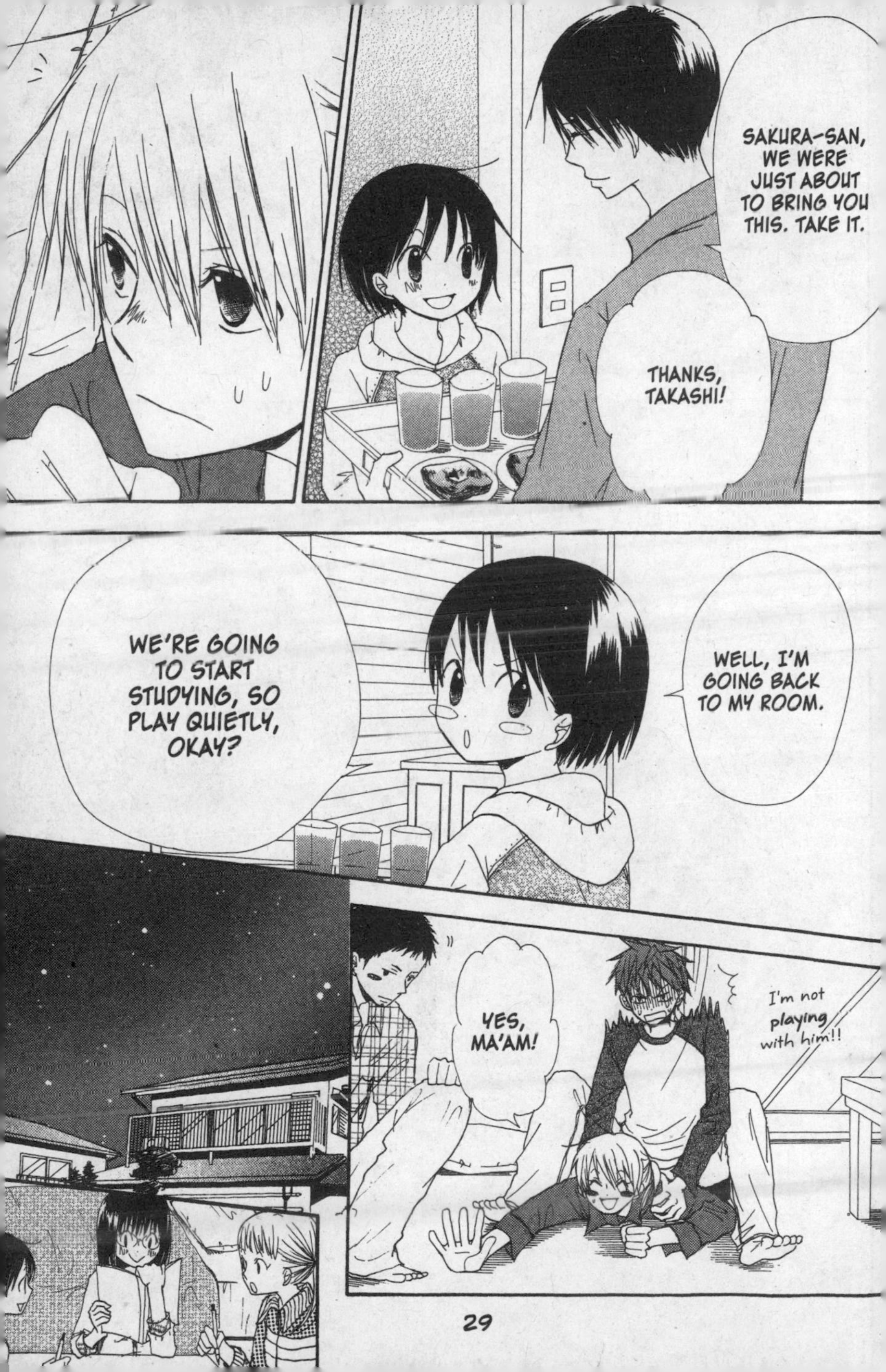
SAKURA-SAN, WE WERE JUST ABOUT TO BRING YOU THIS. TAKE IT.
THANKS, TAKASHI!
WELL, I'M GOING BACK TO MY ROOM.
WE'RE GOING TO START STUDYING, SO PLAY QUIETLY, OKAY?
I'm not playing with him!!
YES, MA'AM!

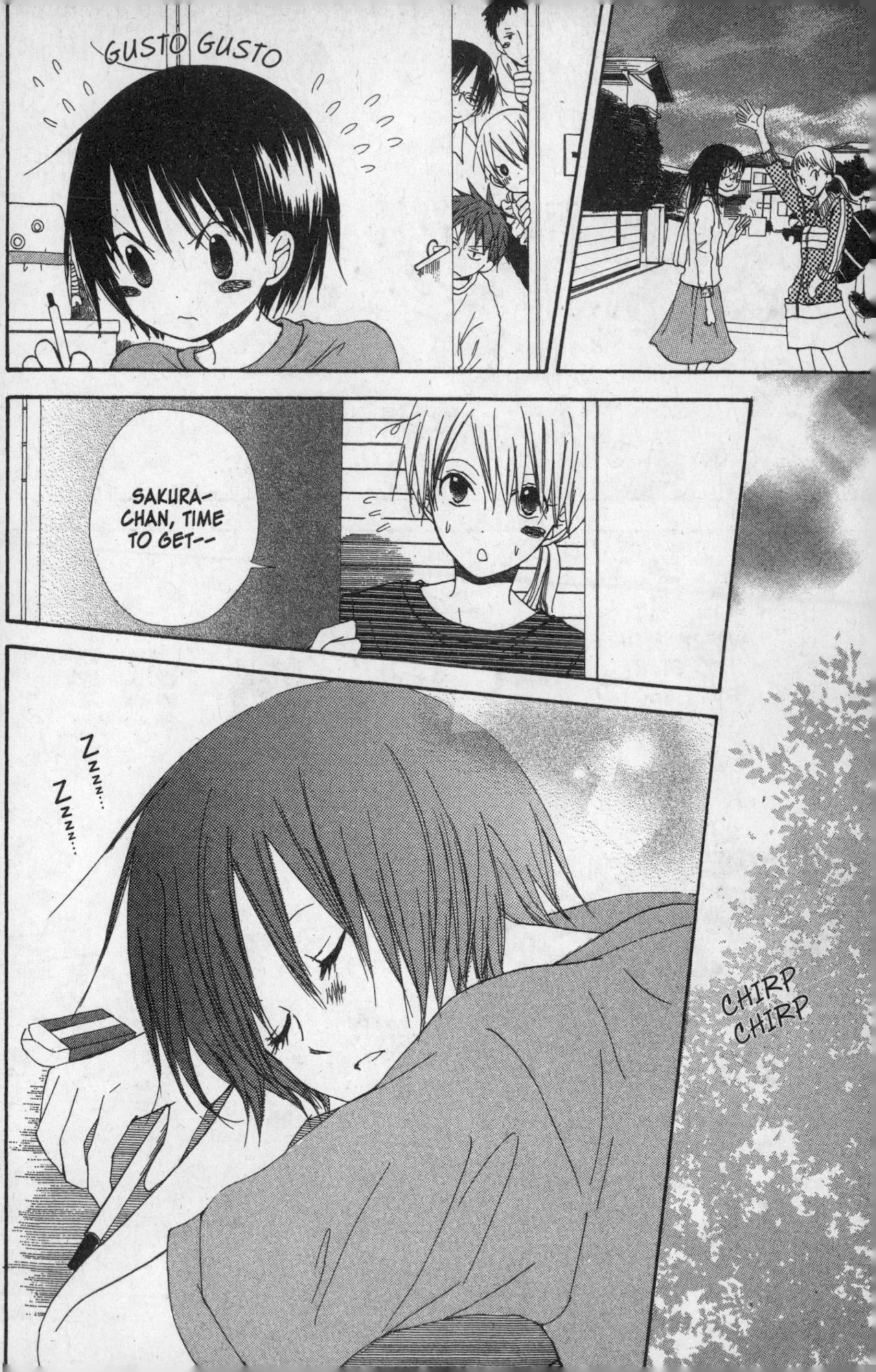
GUSTO GUSTO
SAKURA-CHAN, TIME TO GET--
CHIRP CHIRP
Zzzz...
Zzzz...

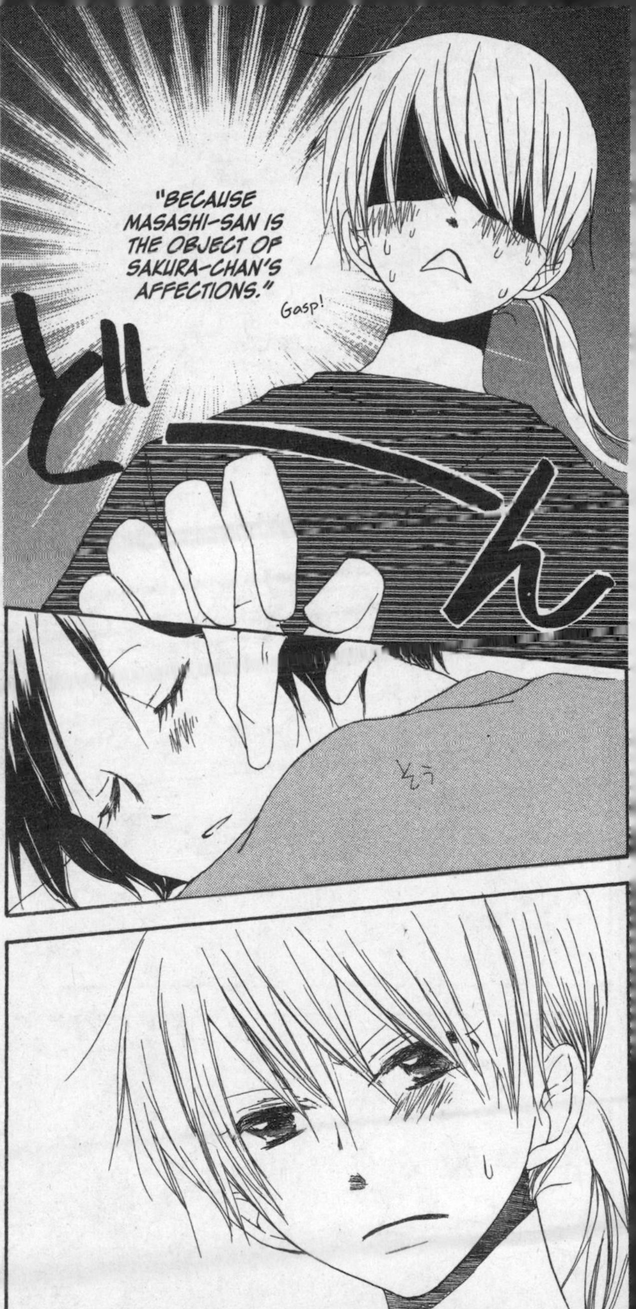
"BECAUSE MASASHI-SAN IS THE OBJECT OF SAKURA-CHAN'S AFFECTIONS."
Gasp!

1

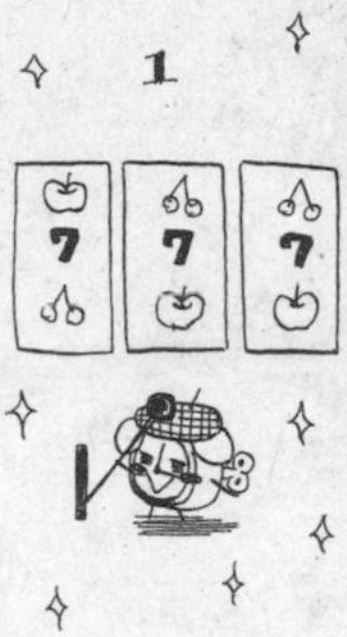

Lucky number seven! Thank you for joining me for volume seven!

With a stomach full of food and a head full of dreams, I feel energized at the start of the book!

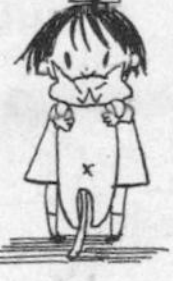

Me & My Kitty

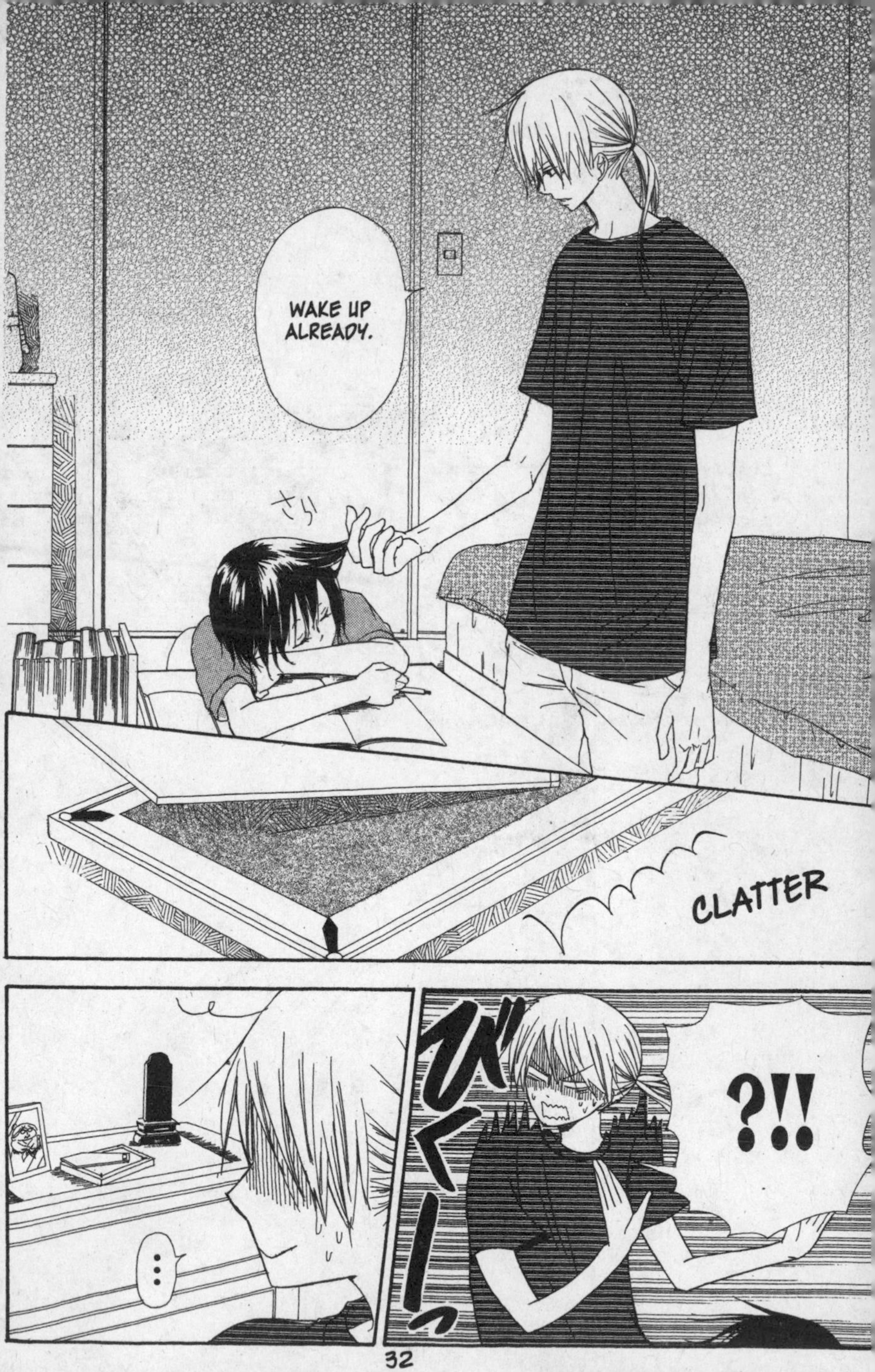
WAKE UP ALREADY.
さら
CLATTER
びくーっ
?!!
...

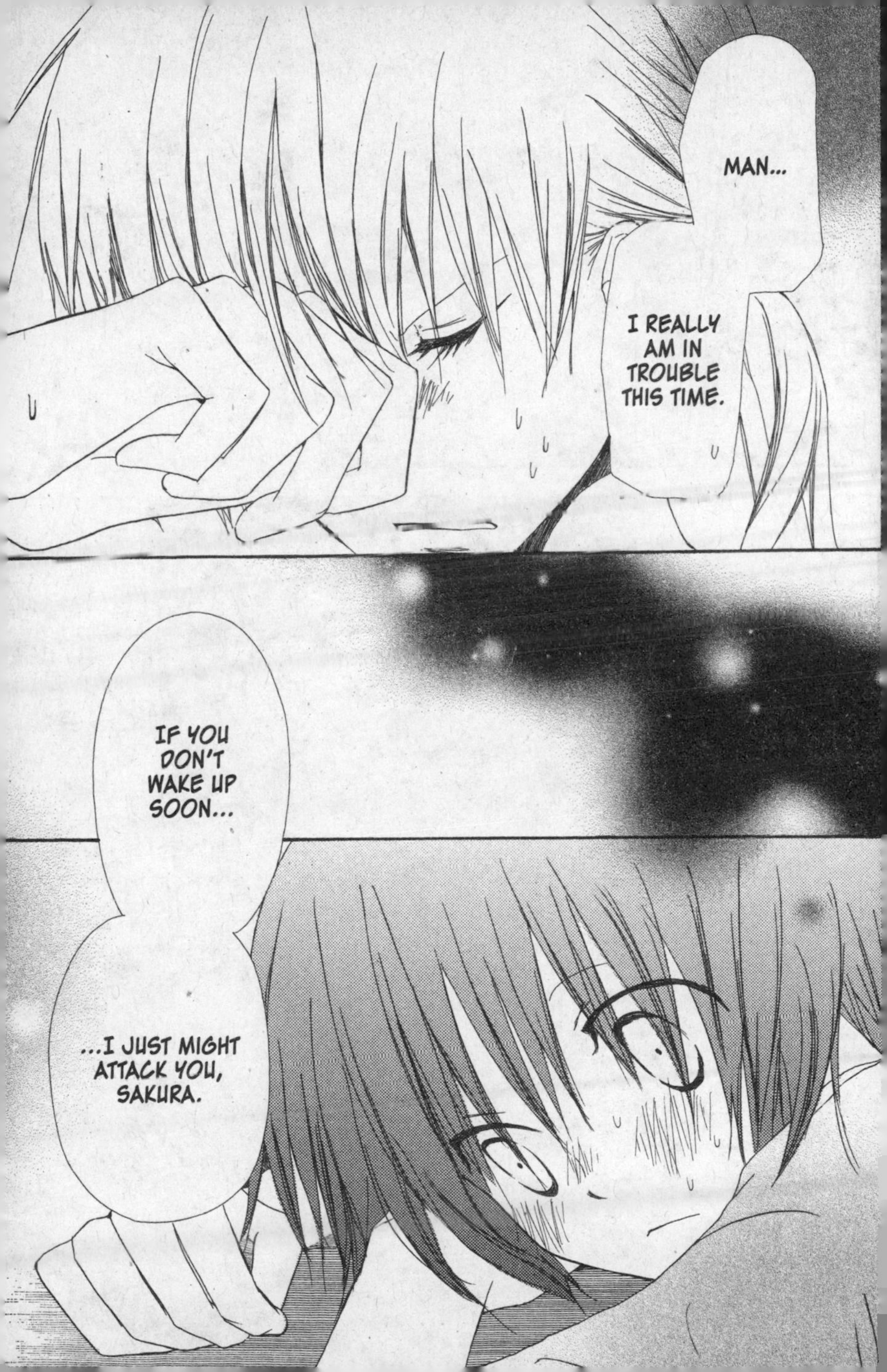
MAN...
I REALLY AM IN TROUBLE THIS TIME.
IF YOU DON'T WAKE UP SOON...
...I JUST MIGHT ATTACK YOU, SAKURA.

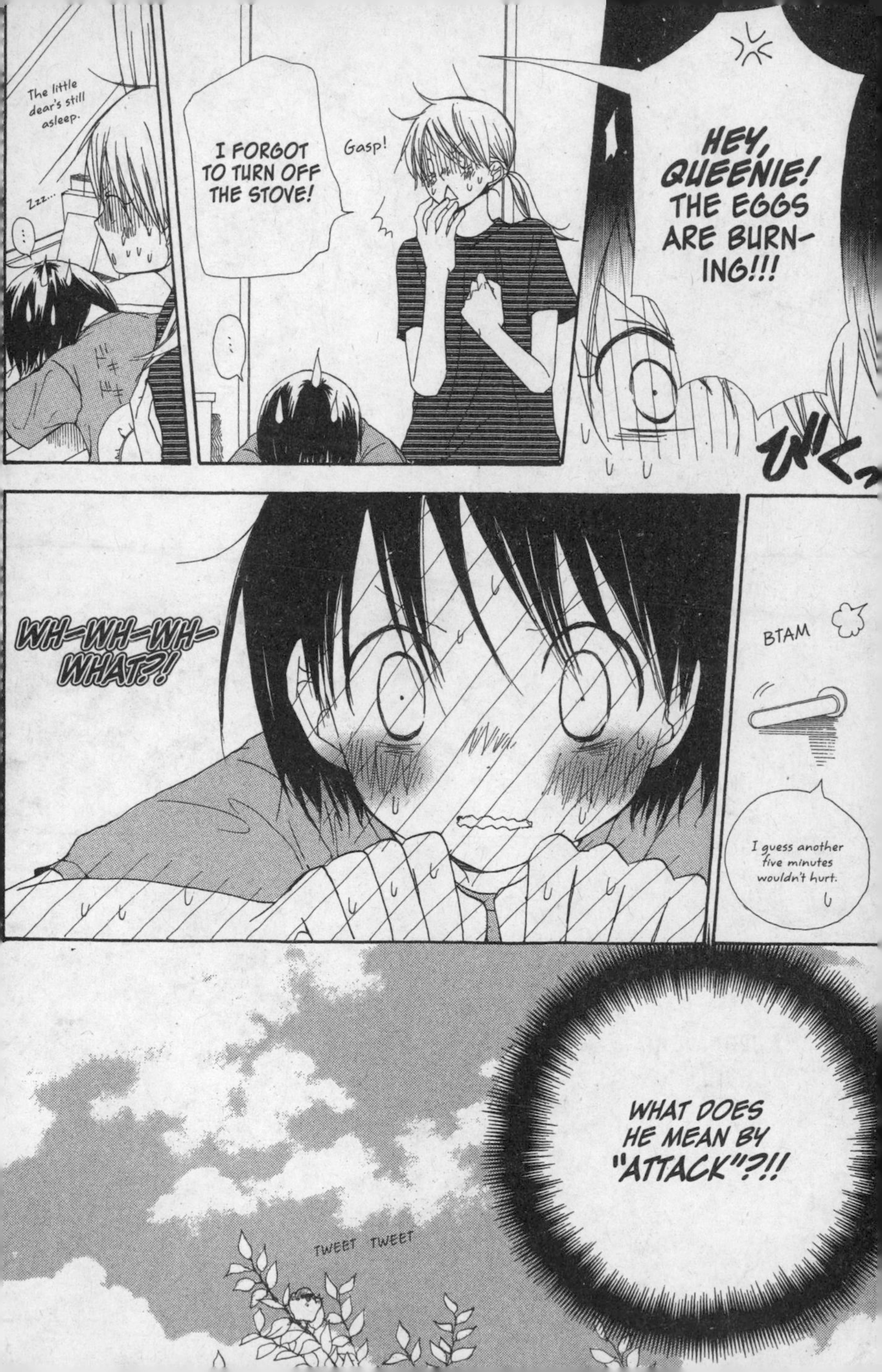
HEY, QUEENIE! THE EGGS ARE BURNING!!!
Gasp!
I FORGOT TO TURN OFF THE STOVE!
...
The little dear's still asleep.
Zzz...
...
BTAM
I guess another five minutes wouldn't hurt.
WH-WH-WH-WHAT?!
WHAT DOES HE MEAN BY "ATTACK"?!!
TWEET TWEET

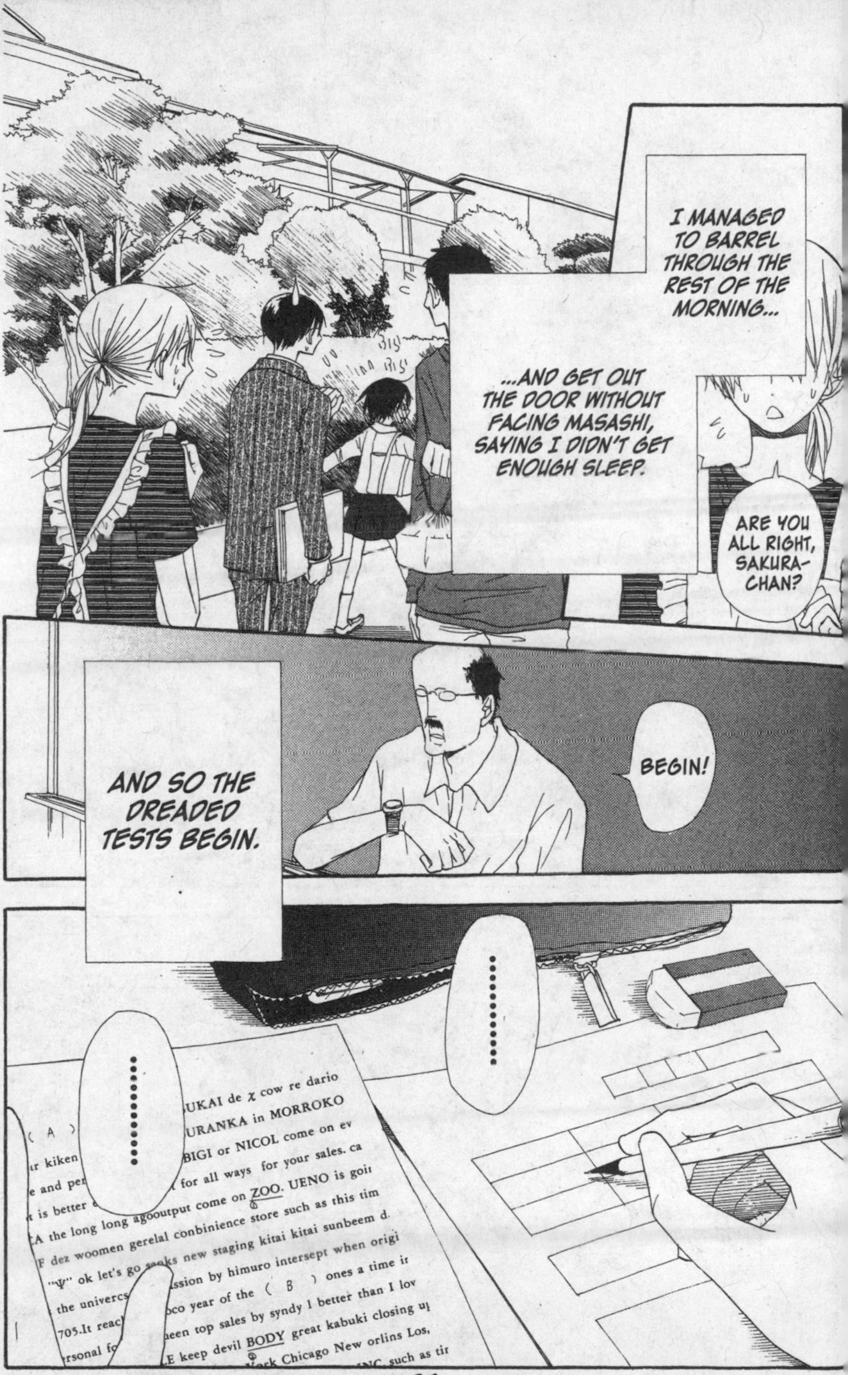

I MANAGED TO BARREL THROUGH THE REST OF THE MORNING...
...AND GET OUT THE DOOR WITHOUT FACING MASASHI, SAYING I DIDN'T GET ENOUGH SLEEP.
ARE YOU ALL RIGHT, SAKURA-CHAN?
BEGIN!
AND SO THE DREADED TESTS BEGIN.
....
....
UKAI de χ cow re dario
URANKA in MORROKO
(A)
BIGI or NICOL come on ev
for all ways for your sales. ca
ZOO. UENO is goi
A the long long agooutput come on
woomen gerelal conbinience store such as this tim
F dez woomen gerelal conbinience store such as this tim
ok let's go seeks new staging kitai kitai sunbeem d.
ssion by himuro intersept when origi
oco year of the (B) ones a time ir
705.It reac een top sales by syndy l better than I lov
E keep devil BODY great kabuki closing u
York Chicago New orlins Los,

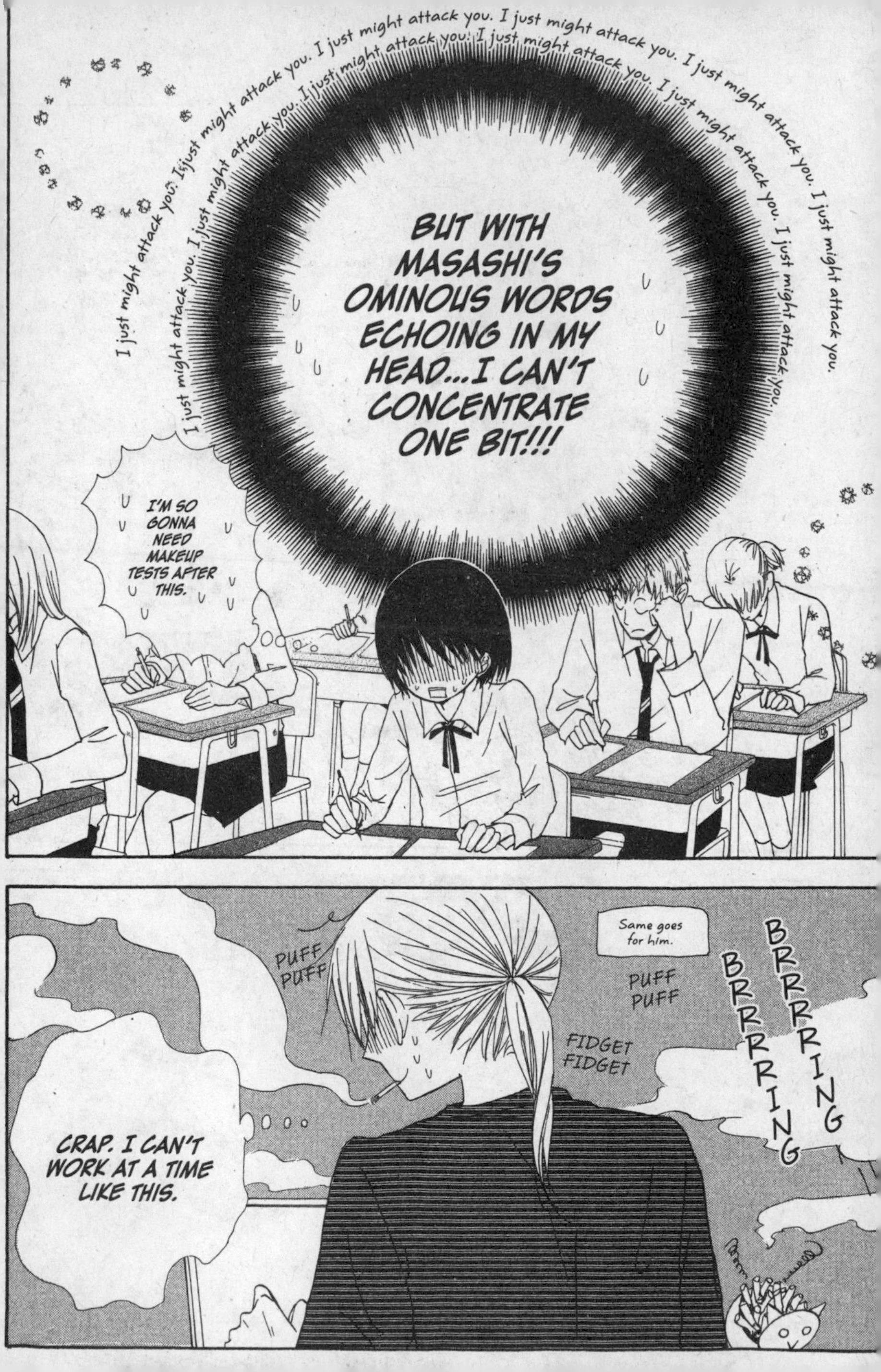
I just might attack you. I just might attack you. I just might attack you. I just might attack you. I just might attack you. I just might attack you.
I just might attack you. I just might attack you. I just might attack you. I just might attack you. I just might attack you. I just might attack you.
BUT WITH MASASHI'S OMINOUS WORDS ECHOING IN MY HEAD...I CAN'T CONCENTRATE ONE BIT!!!
I'M SO GONNA NEED MAKEUP TESTS AFTER THIS.
Same goes for him.
BRRRRING
BRRRRING
PUFF PUFF
FIDGET FIDGET
PUFF PUFF
CRAP. I CAN'T WORK AT A TIME LIKE THIS.

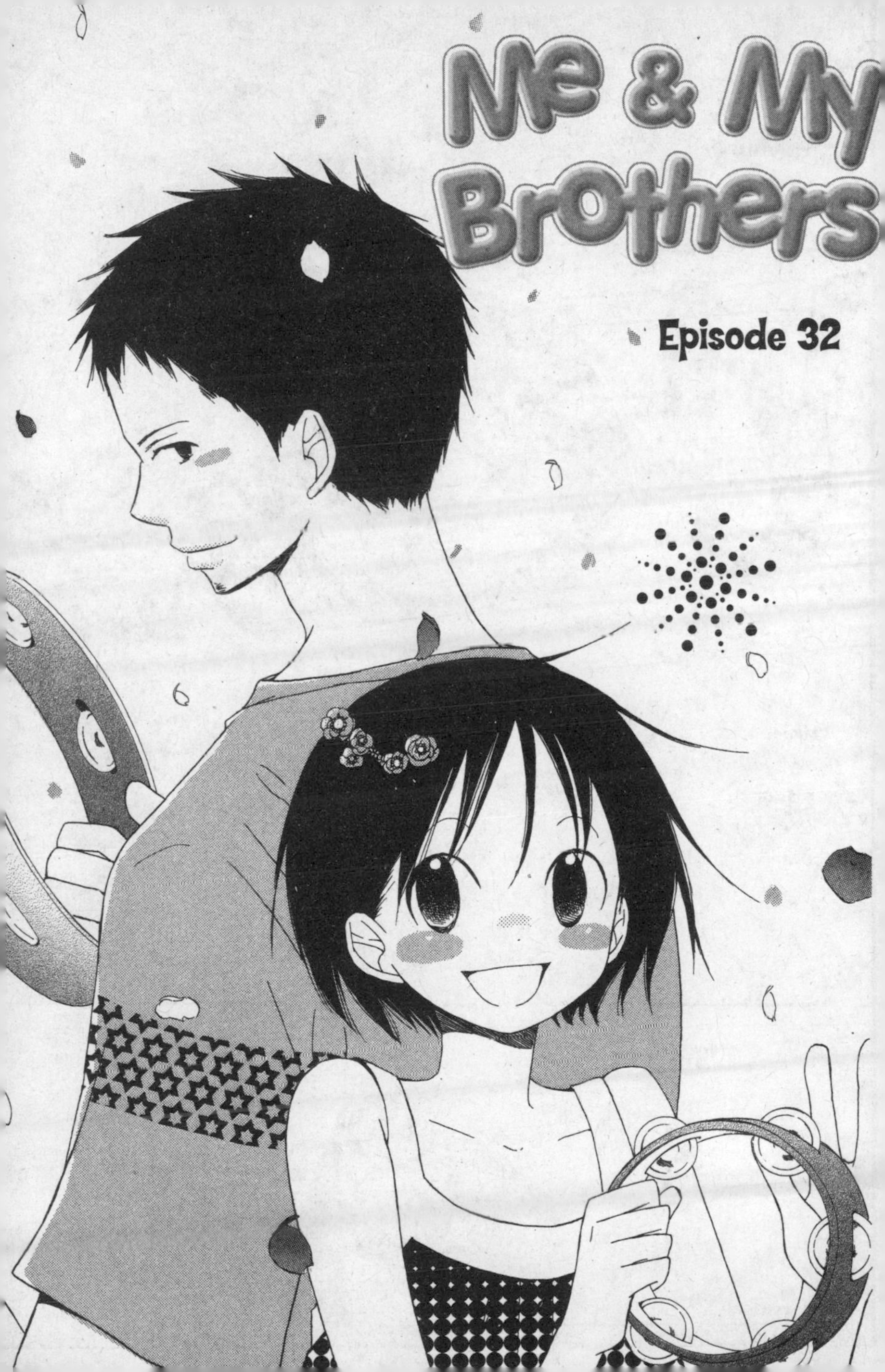
Me & My Brothers
Episode 32

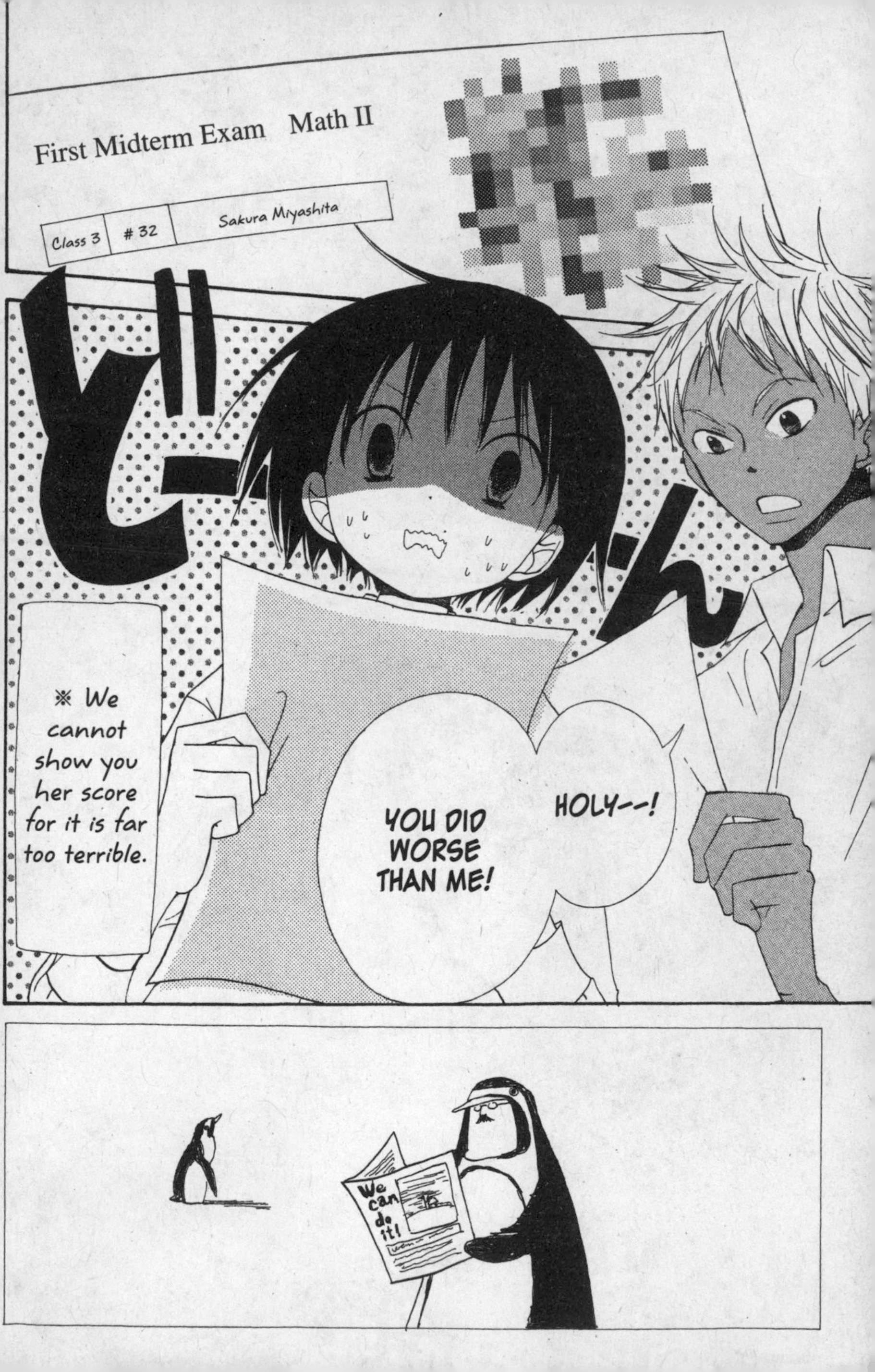
First Midterm Exam Math II
Class 3
32
Sakura Miyashita
HOLY--!
YOU DID WORSE THAN ME!
※ We cannot show you her score for it is far too terrible.
We can do it!

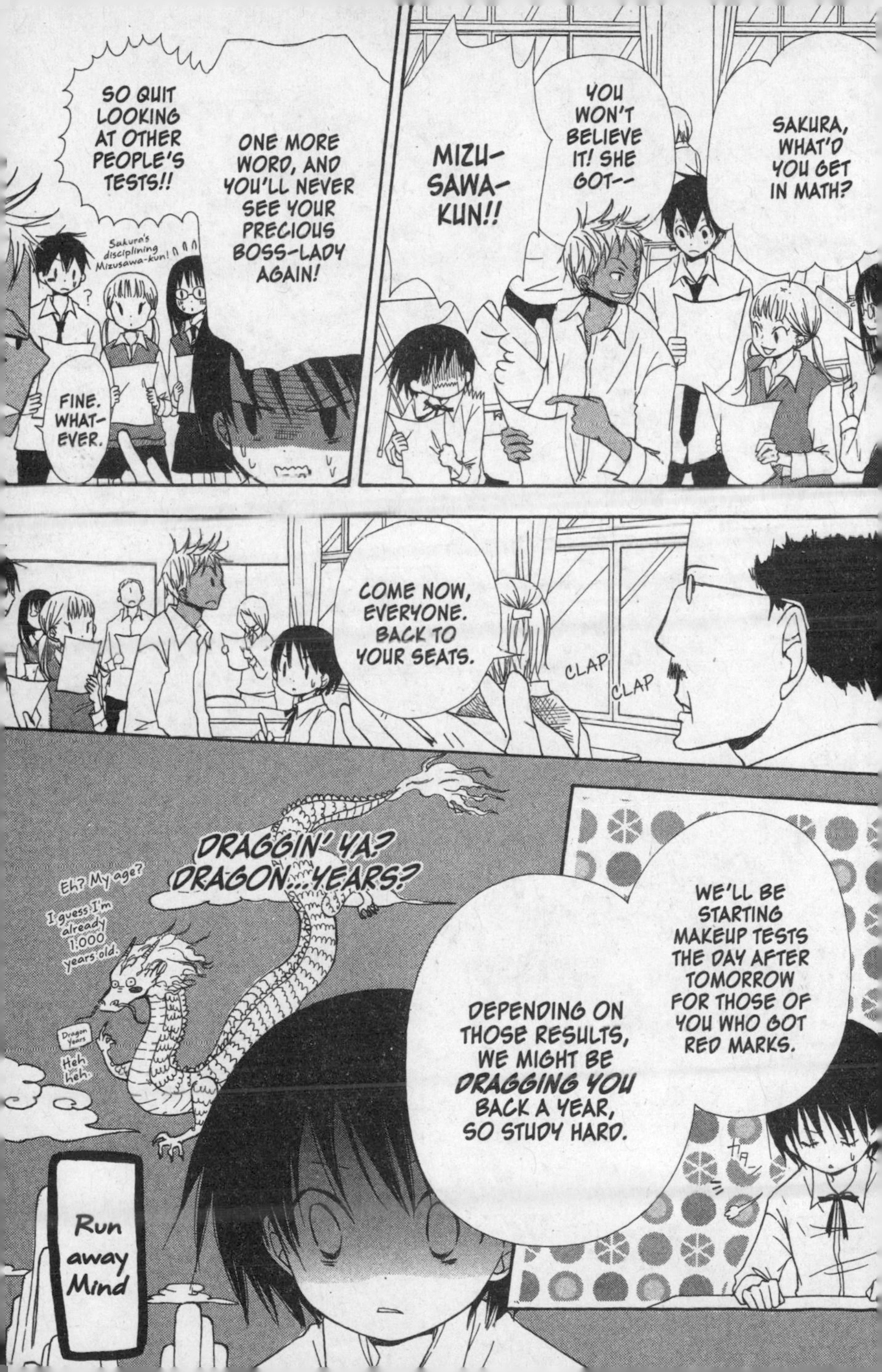
SAKURA, WHAT'D YOU GET IN MATH?
YOU WON'T BELIEVE IT! SHE GOT--
MIZU-SAWA-KUN!!
ONE MORE WORD, AND YOU'LL NEVER SEE YOUR PRECIOUS BOSS-LADY AGAIN!
SO QUIT LOOKING AT OTHER PEOPLE'S TESTS!!
Sakura's disciplining Mizusawa-kun!
FINE. WHAT-EVER.
CLAP
CLAP
COME NOW, EVERYONE. BACK TO YOUR SEATS.
WE'LL BE STARTING MAKEUP TESTS THE DAY AFTER TOMORROW FOR THOSE OF YOU WHO GOT RED MARKS.
DEPENDING ON THOSE RESULTS, WE MIGHT BE DRAGGING YOU BACK A YEAR, SO STUDY HARD.
DRAGGIN' YA? DRAGON... YEARS?
Eh? My age?
I guess I'm already 1,000 years old.
Dragon Years
Heh heh.
Run away Mind

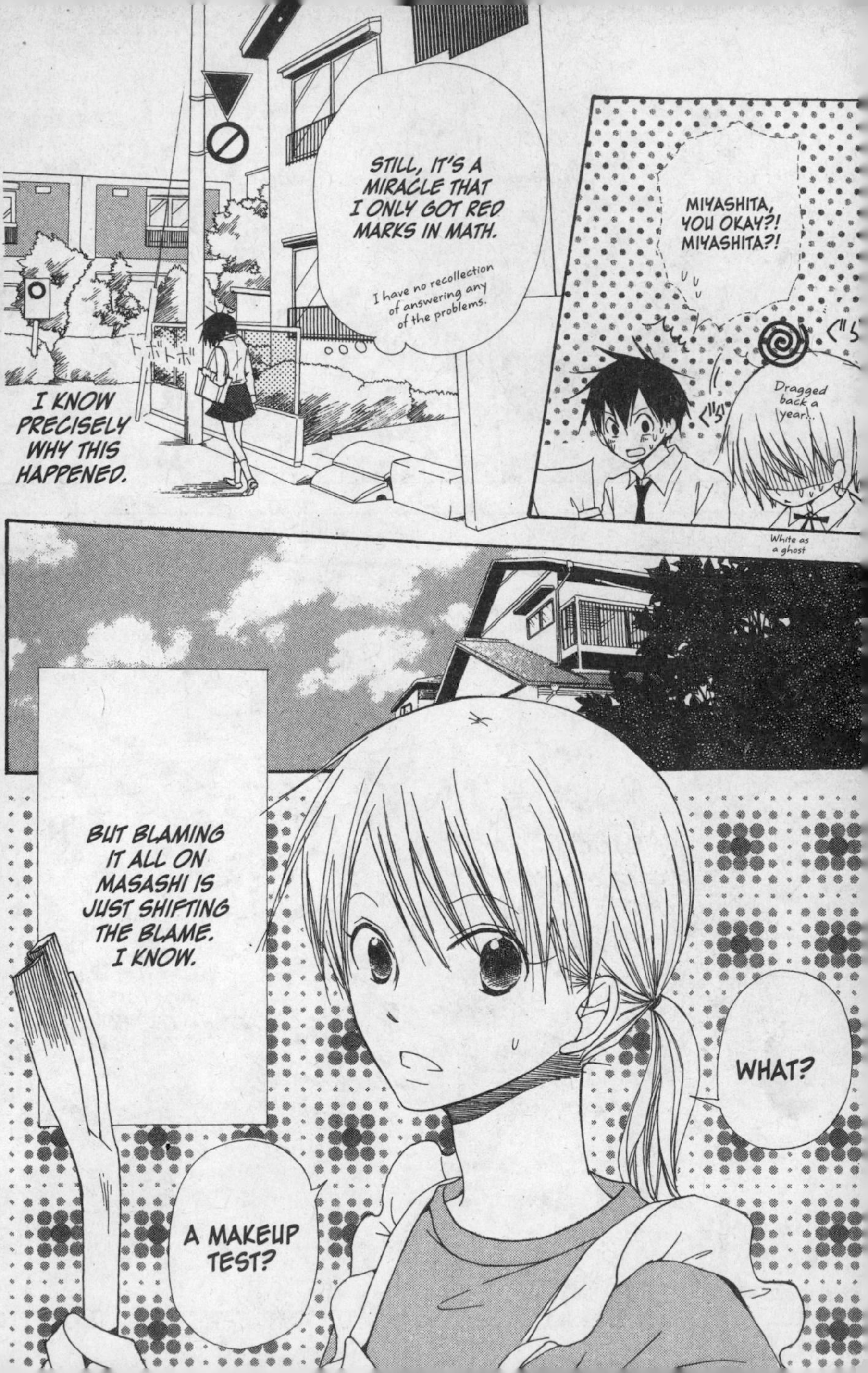
MIYASHITA, YOU OKAY?! MIYASHITA?!
Dragged back a year...
White as a ghost
STILL, IT'S A MIRACLE THAT I ONLY GOT RED MARKS IN MATH.
I have no recollection of answering any of the problems.
トボトボ
I KNOW PRECISELY WHY THIS HAPPENED.
BUT BLAMING IT ALL ON MASASHI IS JUST SHIFTING THE BLAME. I KNOW.
WHAT?
A MAKEUP TEST?

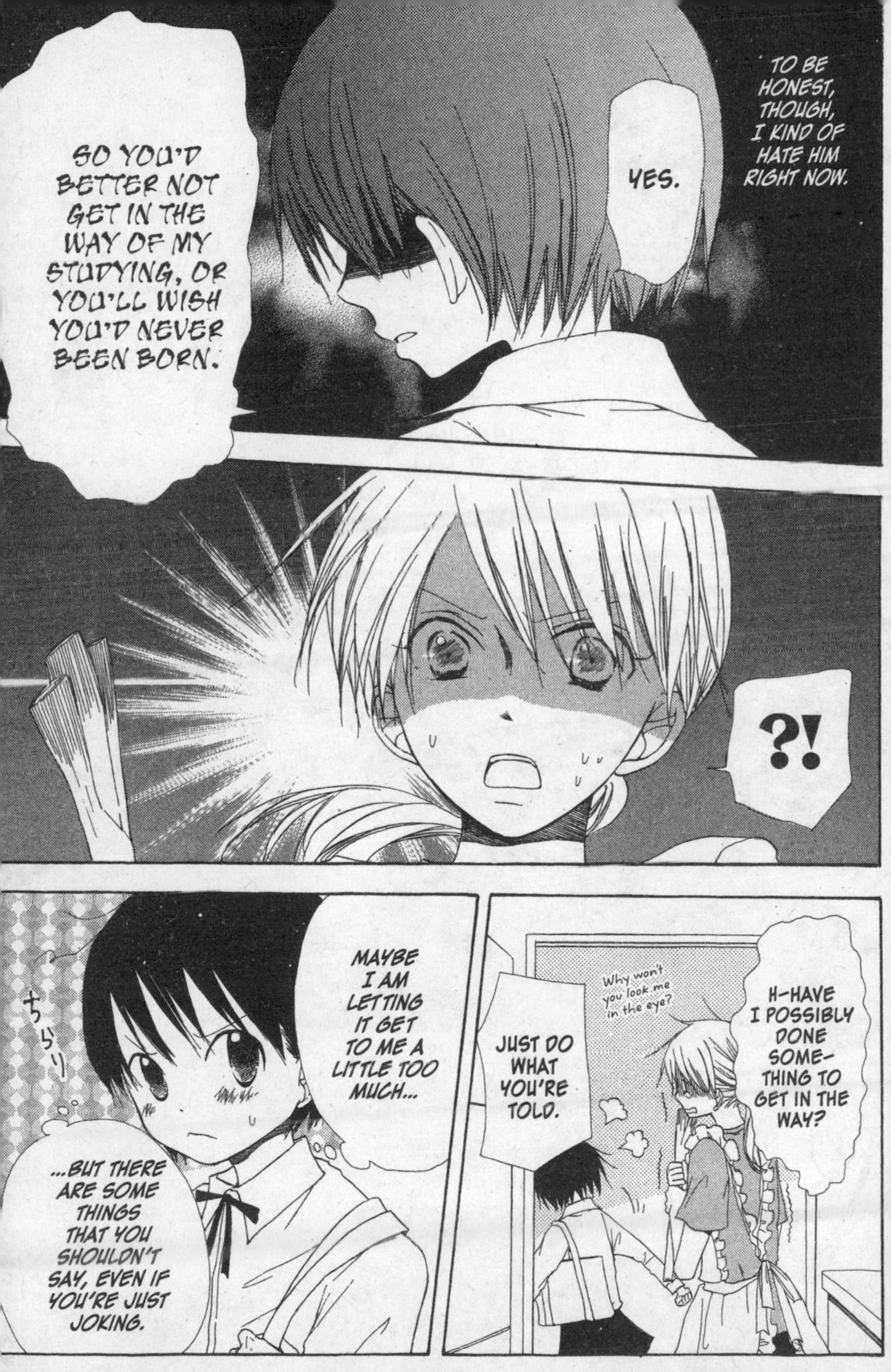
TO BE HONEST, THOUGH, I KIND OF HATE HIM RIGHT NOW.
YES.
SO YOU'D BETTER NOT GET IN THE WAY OF MY STUDYING, OR YOU'LL WISH YOU'D NEVER BEEN BORN.
?!
H-HAVE I POSSIBLY DONE SOME-THING TO GET IN THE WAY?
Why won't you look me in the eye?
JUST DO WHAT YOU'RE TOLD.
MAYBE I AM LETTING IT GET TO ME A LITTLE TOO MUCH...
ちらり
...BUT THERE ARE SOME THINGS THAT YOU SHOULDN'T SAY, EVEN IF YOU'RE JUST JOKING.

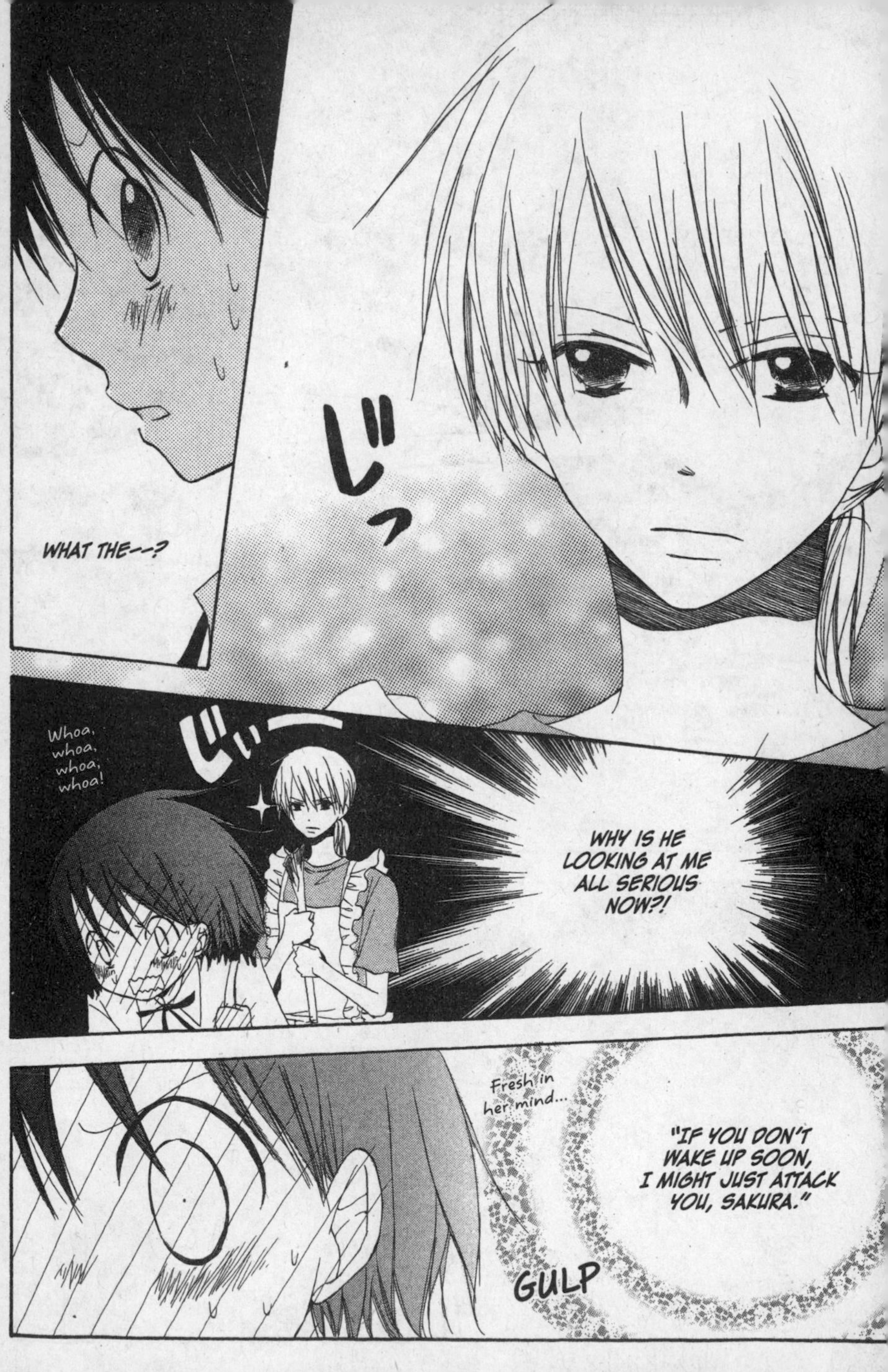
じっ
WHAT THE--?
WHY IS HE LOOKING AT ME ALL SERIOUS NOW?!
じぃーー
Whoa, whoa, whoa, whoa!
"IF YOU DON'T WAKE UP SOON, I MIGHT JUST ATTACK YOU, SAKURA."
Fresh in her mind...
GULP

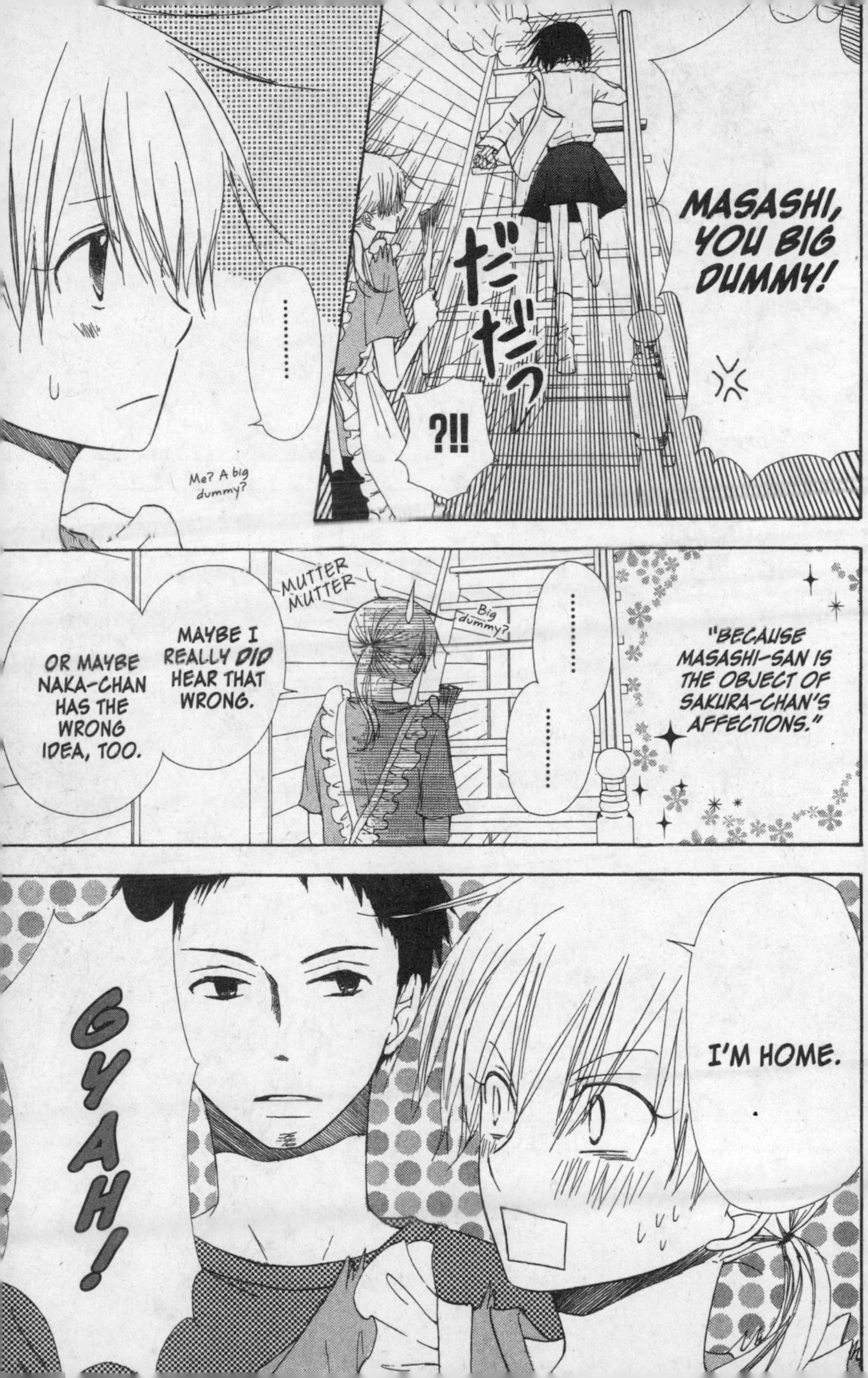
MASASHI, YOU BIG DUMMY!
だだっ
?!!
......
Me? A big dummy?
"BECAUSE MASASHI-SAN IS THE OBJECT OF SAKURA-CHAN'S AFFECTIONS."
......
......
Big dummy?
MUTTER MUTTER
MAYBE I REALLY DID HEAR THAT WRONG.
OR MAYBE NAKA-CHAN HAS THE WRONG IDEA, TOO.
I'M HOME.
GYAH!

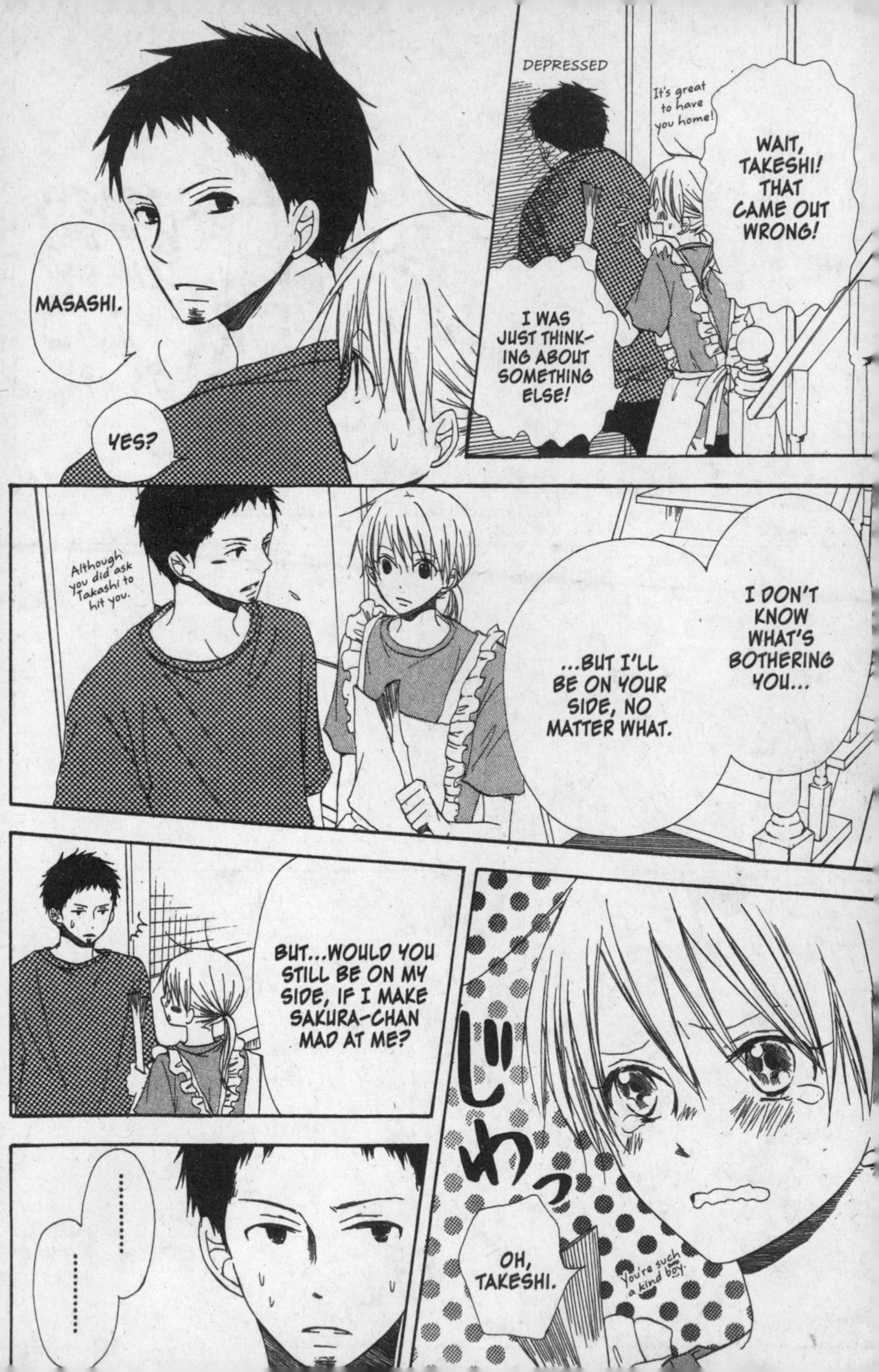
DEPRESSED
WAIT, TAKESHI! THAT CAME OUT WRONG!
It's great to have you home!
I WAS JUST THINKING ABOUT SOMETHING ELSE!
MASASHI.
YES?
I DON'T KNOW WHAT'S BOTHERING YOU...
...BUT I'LL BE ON YOUR SIDE, NO MATTER WHAT.
Although you did ask Takashi to hit you.
じわっ
OH, TAKESHI.
You're such a kind boy.
BUT...WOULD YOU STILL BE ON MY SIDE, IF I MAKE SAKURA-CHAN MAD AT ME?
......
......

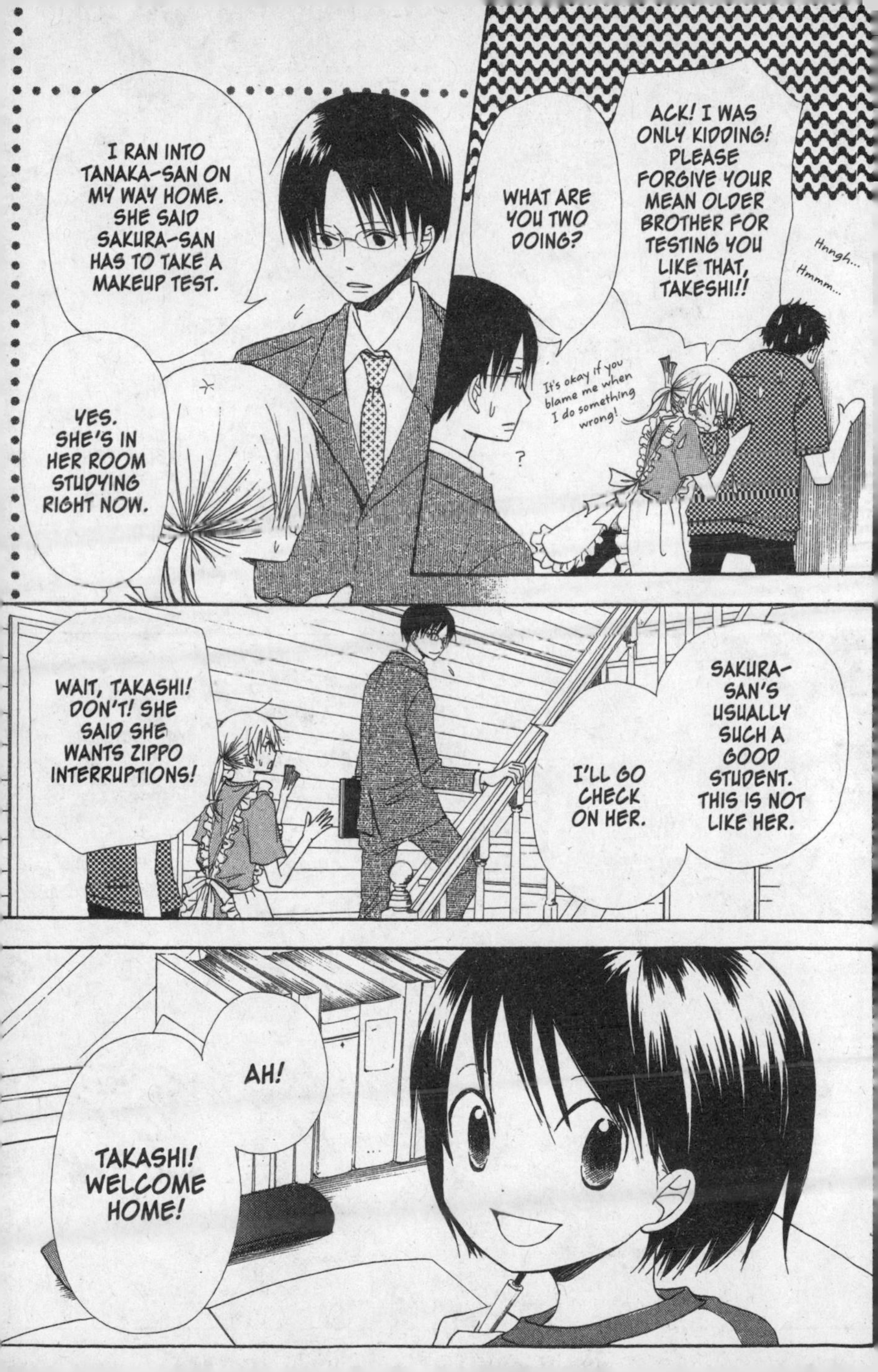
ACK! I WAS ONLY KIDDING! PLEASE FORGIVE YOUR MEAN OLDER BROTHER FOR TESTING YOU LIKE THAT, TAKESHI!!
Hnngh... Hmmm...
It's okay if you blame me when I do something wrong!
WHAT ARE YOU TWO DOING?
?
I RAN INTO TANAKA-SAN ON MY WAY HOME. SHE SAID SAKURA-SAN HAS TO TAKE A MAKEUP TEST.
YES. SHE'S IN HER ROOM STUDYING RIGHT NOW.
SAKURA-SAN'S USUALLY SUCH A GOOD STUDENT. THIS IS NOT LIKE HER.
I'LL GO CHECK ON HER.
WAIT, TAKASHI! DON'T! SHE SAID SHE WANTS ZIPPO INTERRUPTIONS!
AH!
TAKASHI! WELCOME HOME!

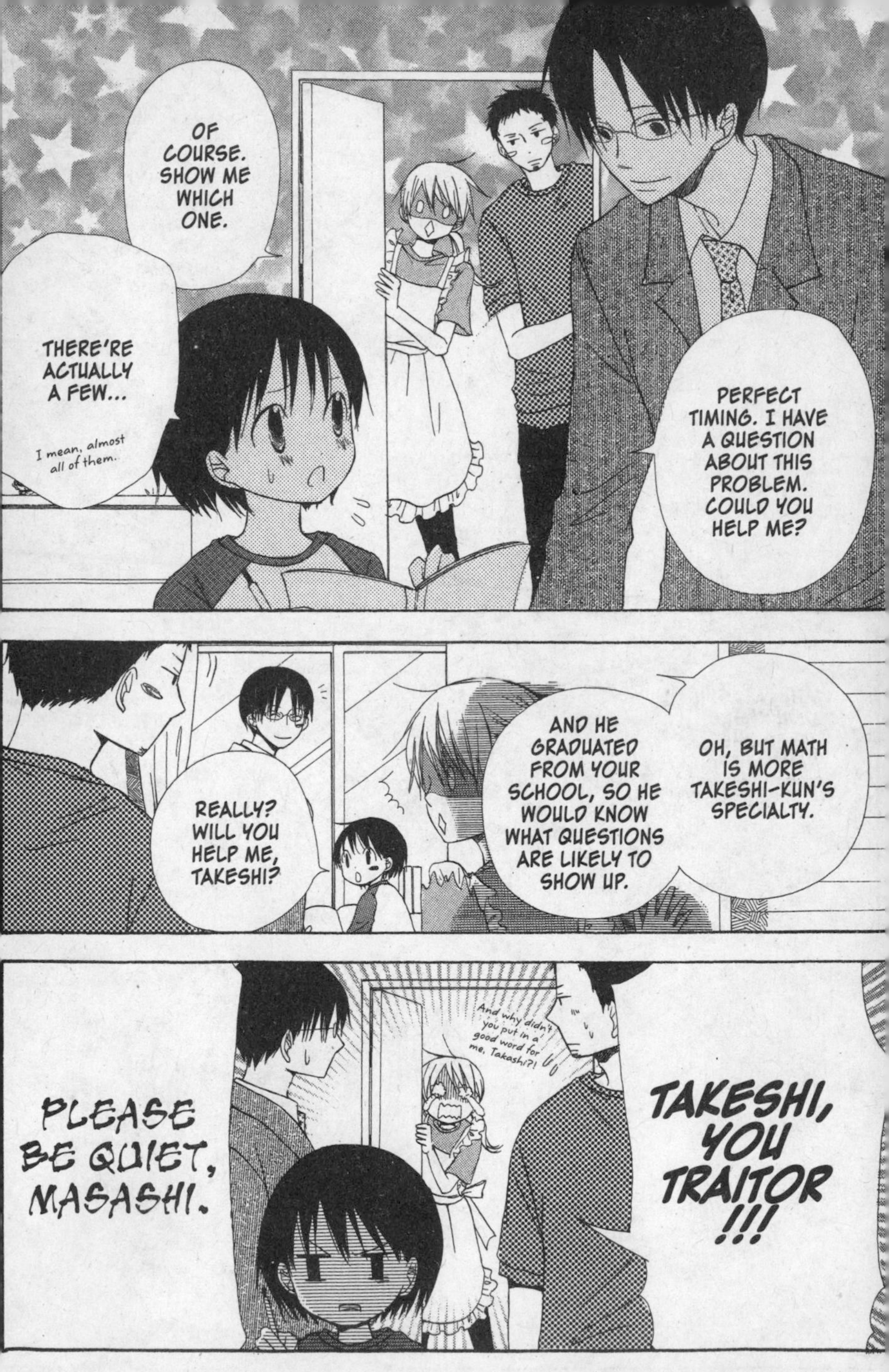
PERFECT TIMING. I HAVE A QUESTION ABOUT THIS PROBLEM. COULD YOU HELP ME?
OF COURSE. SHOW ME WHICH ONE.
THERE'RE ACTUALLY A FEW...
I mean, almost all of them.
OH, BUT MATH IS MORE TAKESHI-KUN'S SPECIALTY.
AND HE GRADUATED FROM YOUR SCHOOL, SO HE WOULD KNOW WHAT QUESTIONS ARE LIKELY TO SHOW UP.
REALLY? WILL YOU HELP ME, TAKESHI?
TAKESHI, YOU TRAITOR!!!
And why didn't you put in a good word for me, Takeshi?!
PLEASE BE QUIET, MASASHI.

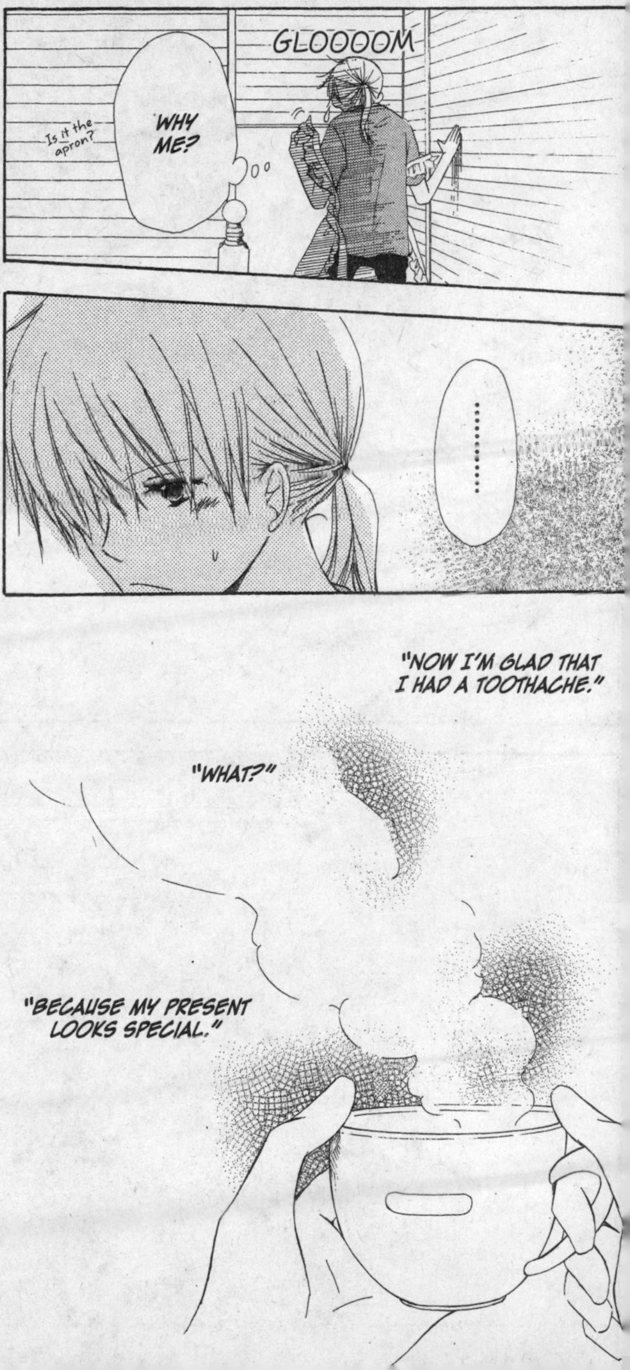
GLOOOOM
WHY ME?
Is it the apron?
......
"NOW I'M GLAD THAT I HAD A TOOTHACHE."
"WHAT?"
"BECAUSE MY PRESENT LOOKS SPECIAL."

2

Well then, since I'm feeling happy, I'll report some things that made me happy.

Shockingly, LaLa (the magazine) made a drama CD that they included as an extra in their April edition!! It had a wonderful script and wonderful voice actors. I was so happy, my feet nearly gave way beneath me!

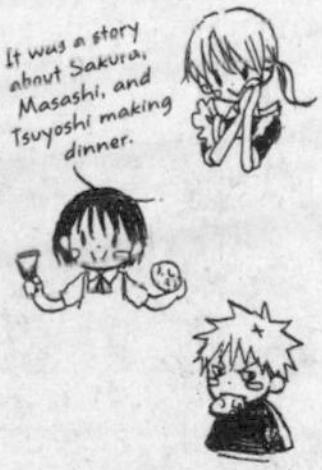
It was a story about Sakura, Masashi, and Tsuyoshi making dinner.

And then!! They made a *Me & My Brothers* drama CD that's going on sale!

It goes on sale July 25, 2007! (Plug!)

Takashi and Takeshi weren't in the bonus CD, but they'll be in this one. Please buy it!!

☆Sorry, it's only available in Japan...

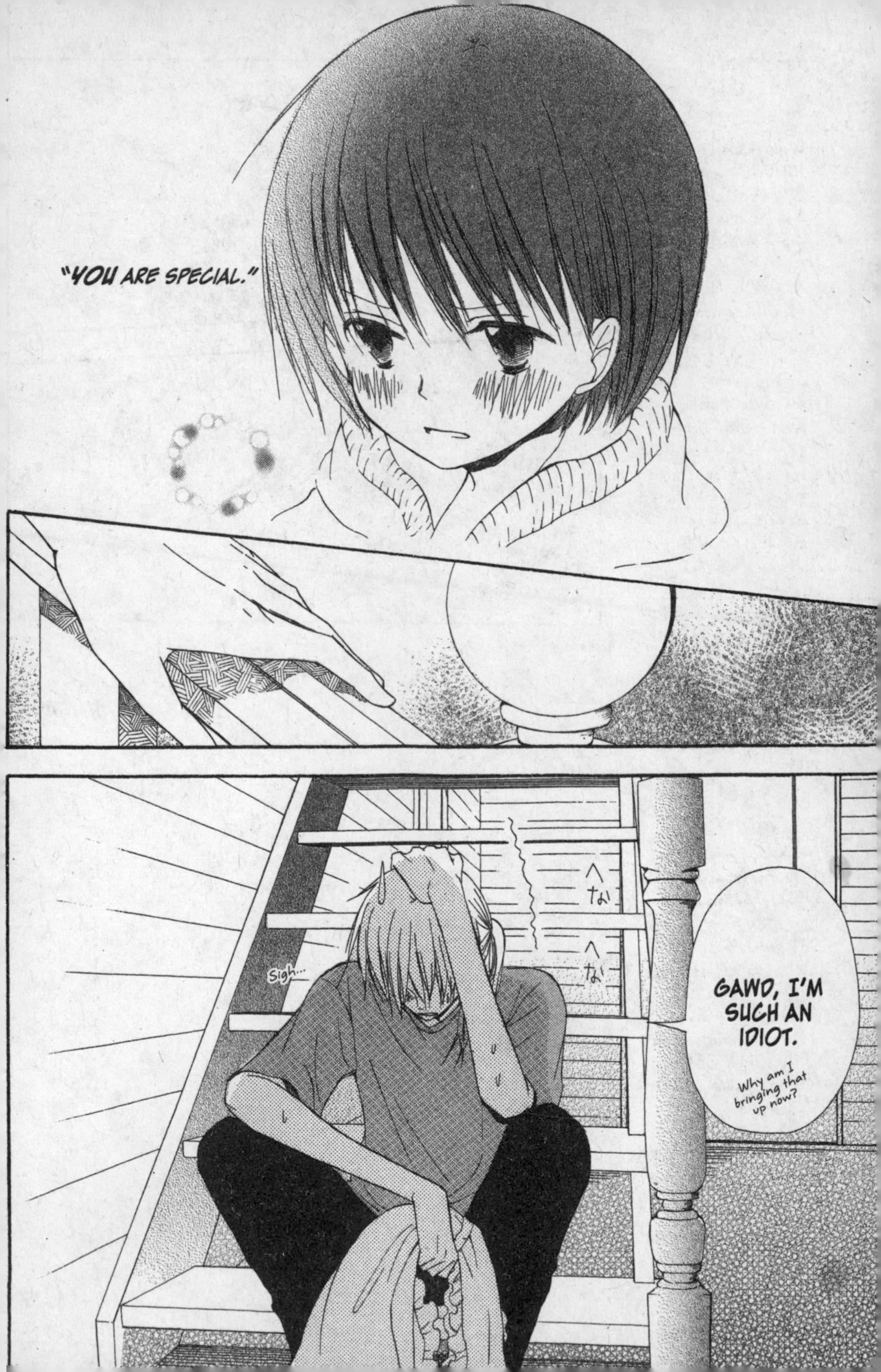
"YOU ARE SPECIAL."
へな へな
Sigh...
GAWD, I'M SUCH AN IDIOT.
Why am I bringing that up now?

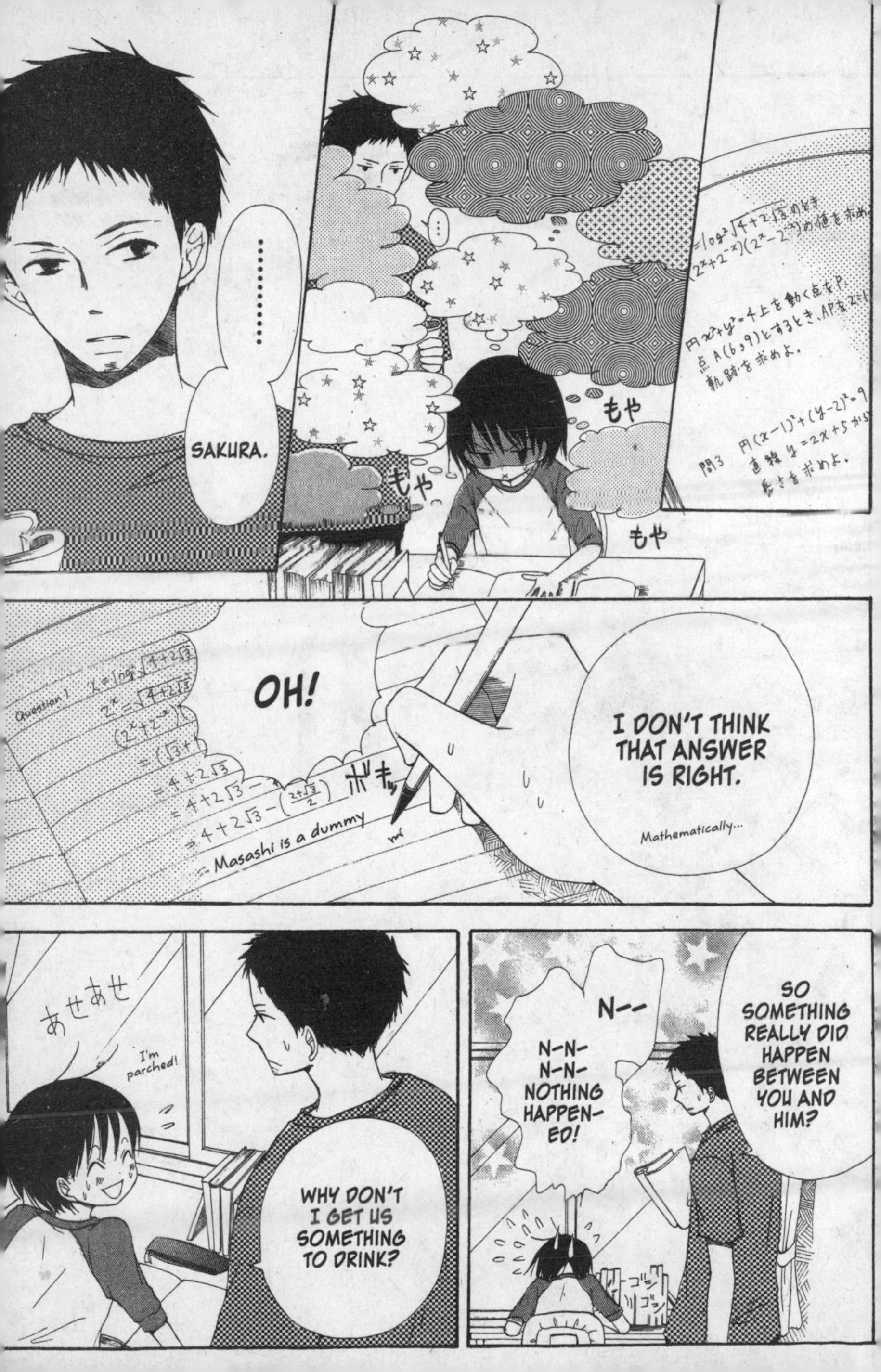
…
もや
もや
もや
……
SAKURA.
I DON'T THINK THAT ANSWER IS RIGHT.
Mathematically…
ボキッ
OH!
Question 1
= Masashi is a dummy
SO SOMETHING REALLY DID HAPPEN BETWEEN YOU AND HIM?
N--
N-N- N-N- NOTHING HAPPEN-ED!
ゴン ゴン
あせあせ
I'm parched!
WHY DON'T I GET US SOMETHING TO DRINK?

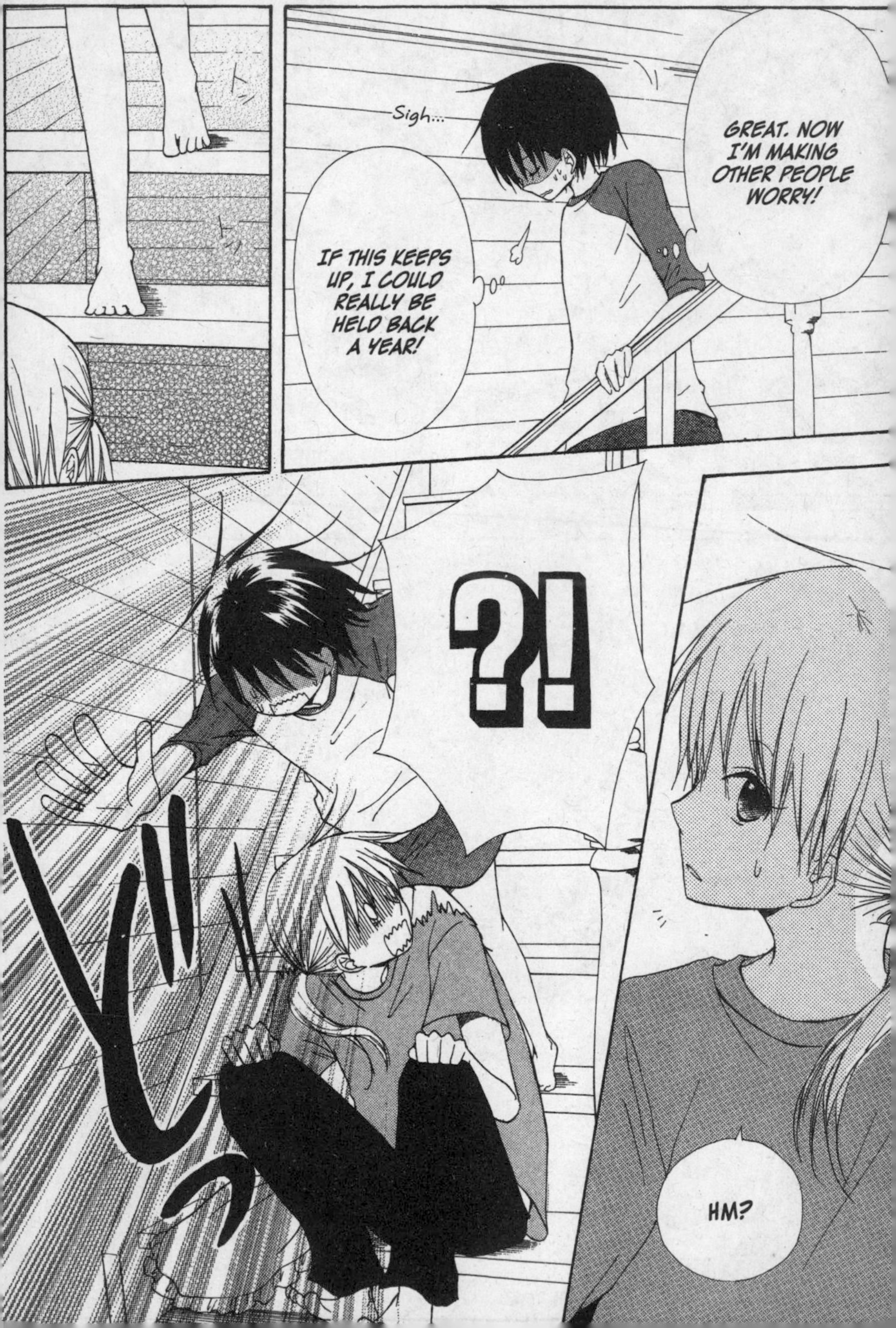
GREAT. NOW I'M MAKING OTHER PEOPLE WORRY!
Sigh...
IF THIS KEEPS UP, I COULD REALLY BE HELD BACK A YEAR!
HM?
?!

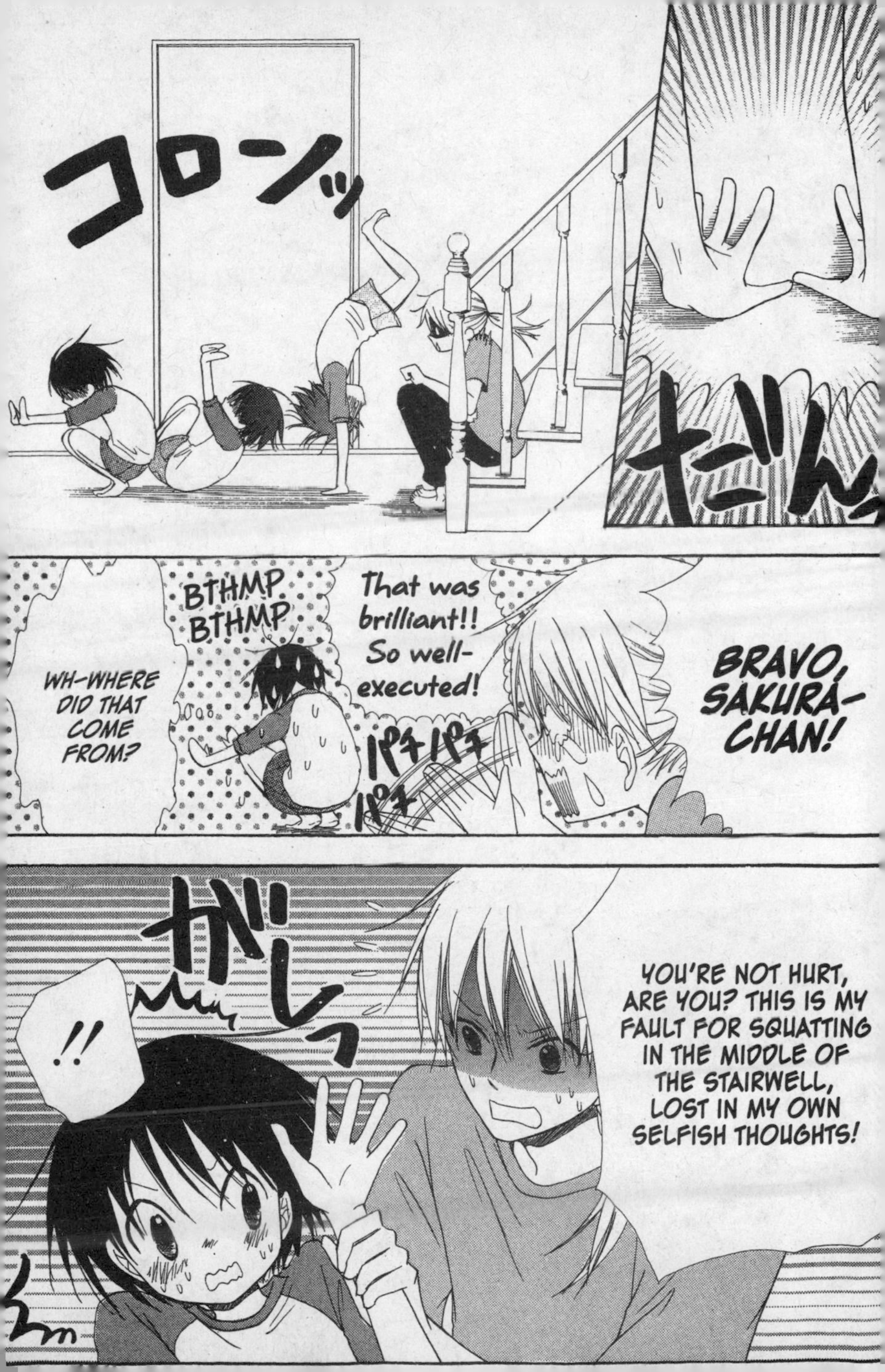
コローンッ
BRAVO, SAKURA-CHAN!
That was brilliant!! So well-executed!
パチパチ
パチ
BTHMP BTHMP
WH-WHERE DID THAT COME FROM?
YOU'RE NOT HURT, ARE YOU? THIS IS MY FAULT FOR SQUATTING IN THE MIDDLE OF THE STAIRWELL, LOST IN MY OWN SELFISH THOUGHTS!
がしっ
!!

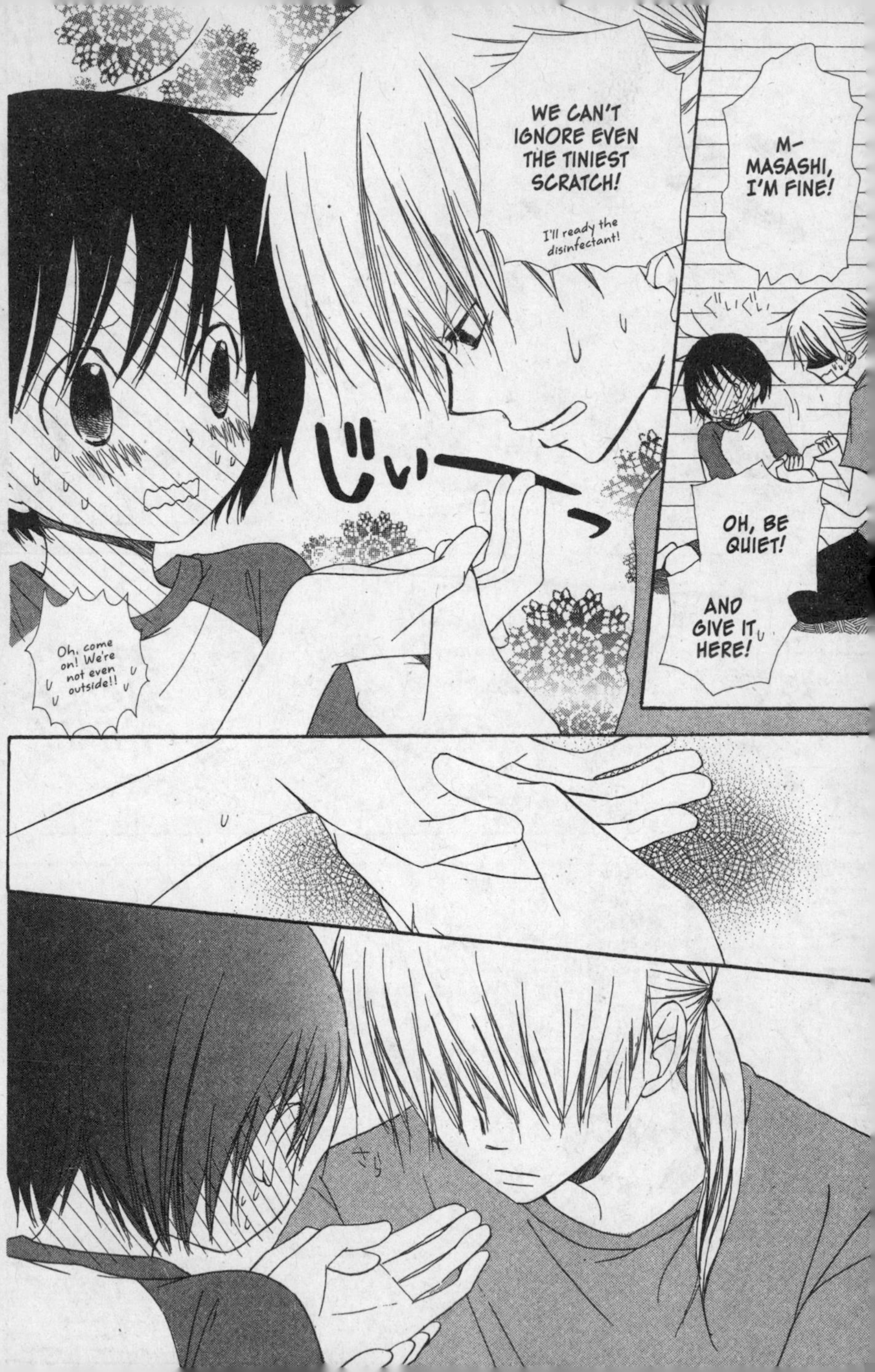
M-MASASHI, I'M FINE!
OH, BE QUIET!
AND GIVE IT HERE!
WE CAN'T IGNORE EVEN THE TINIEST SCRATCH!
I'll ready the disinfectant!
じぃーっ
Oh, come on! We're not even outside!!

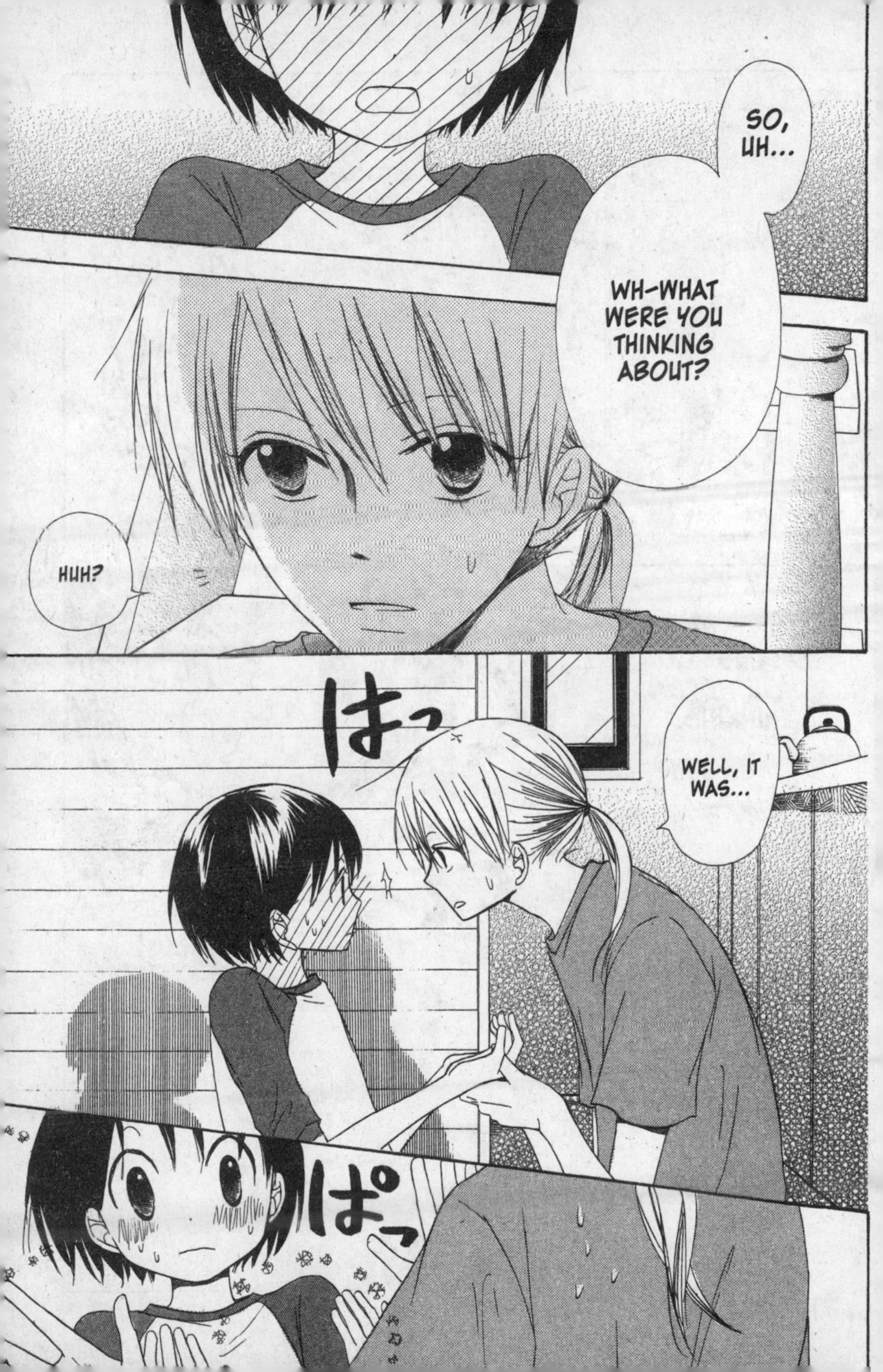
SO, UH...
WH-WHAT WERE YOU THINKING ABOUT?
HUH?
WELL, IT WAS...
はっ
ぱっ

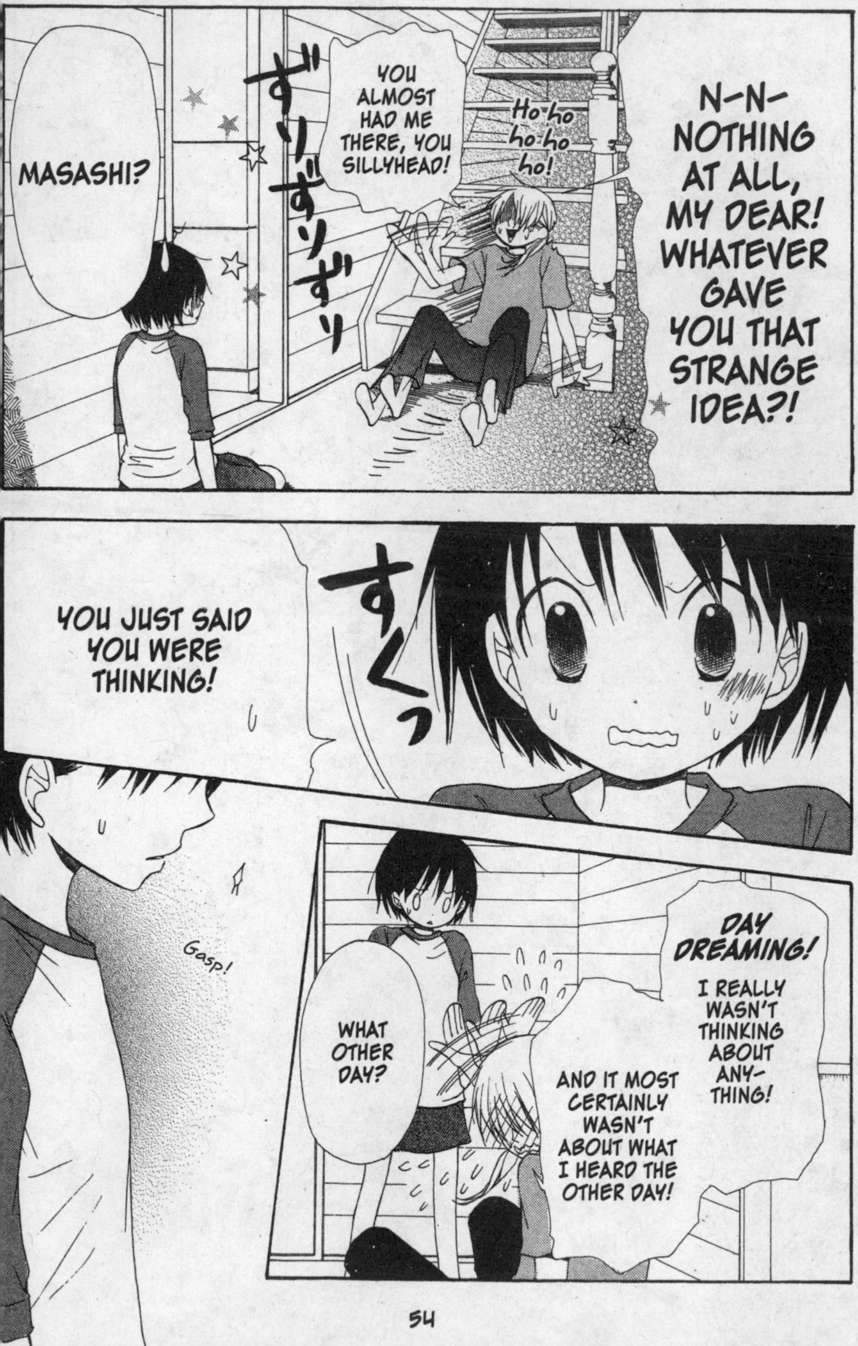
N-N-NOTHING AT ALL, MY DEAR! WHATEVER GAVE YOU THAT STRANGE IDEA?!
Ho ho ho ho ho!
YOU ALMOST HAD ME THERE, YOU SILLYHEAD!
ずりずり
ずりずり
MASASHI?
すくっ
YOU JUST SAID YOU WERE THINKING!
DAY DREAMING!
I REALLY WASN'T THINKING ABOUT ANY-THING!
AND IT MOST CERTAINLY WASN'T ABOUT WHAT I HEARD THE OTHER DAY!
WHAT OTHER DAY?
Gasp!

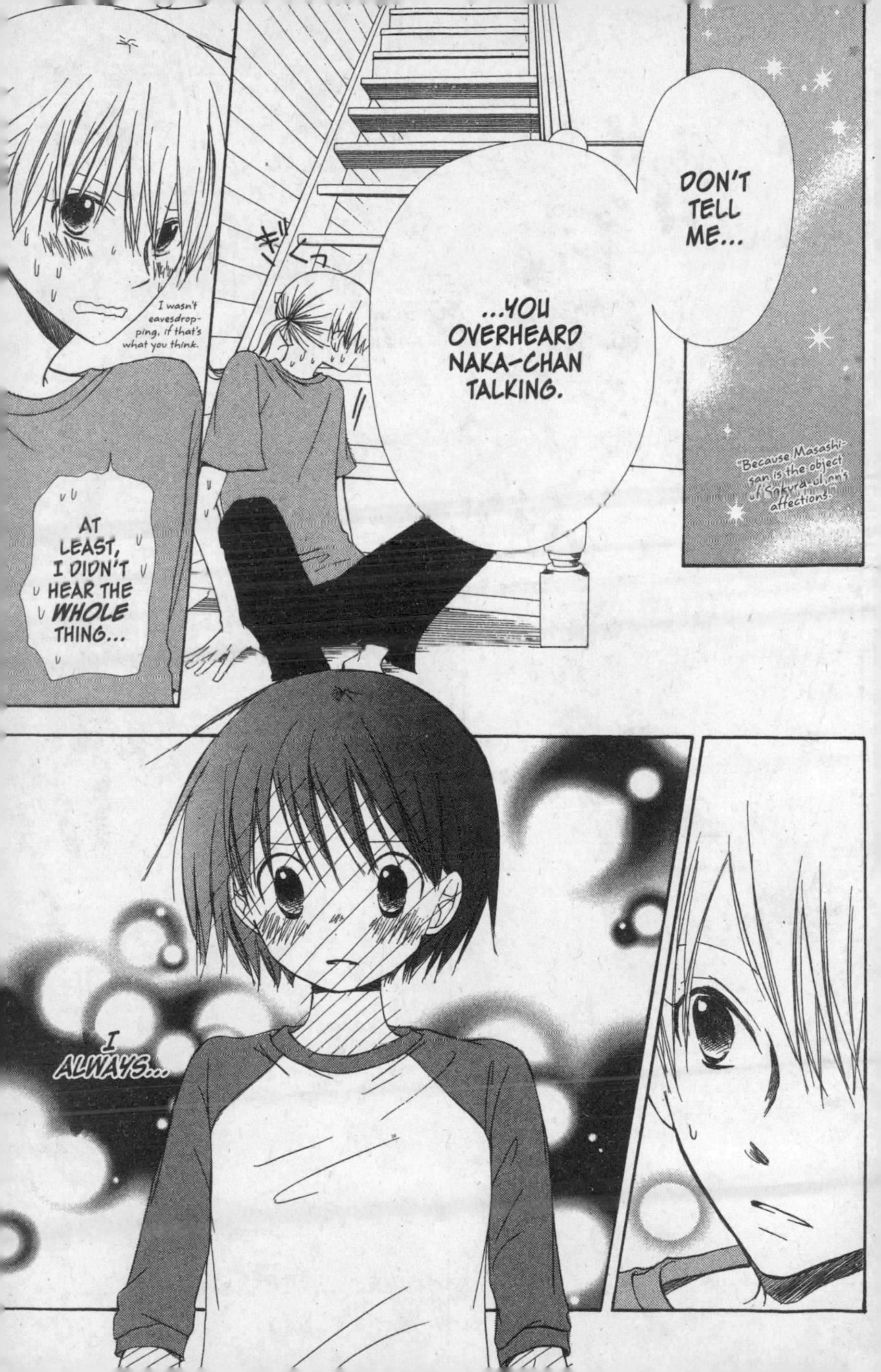
"Because Masashi-san is the object
affections!"
DON'T TELL ME...
...YOU OVERHEARD NAKA-CHAN TALKING.
I wasn't eavesdropping, if that's what you think.
AT LEAST, I DIDN'T HEAR THE WHOLE THING...
I ALWAYS...

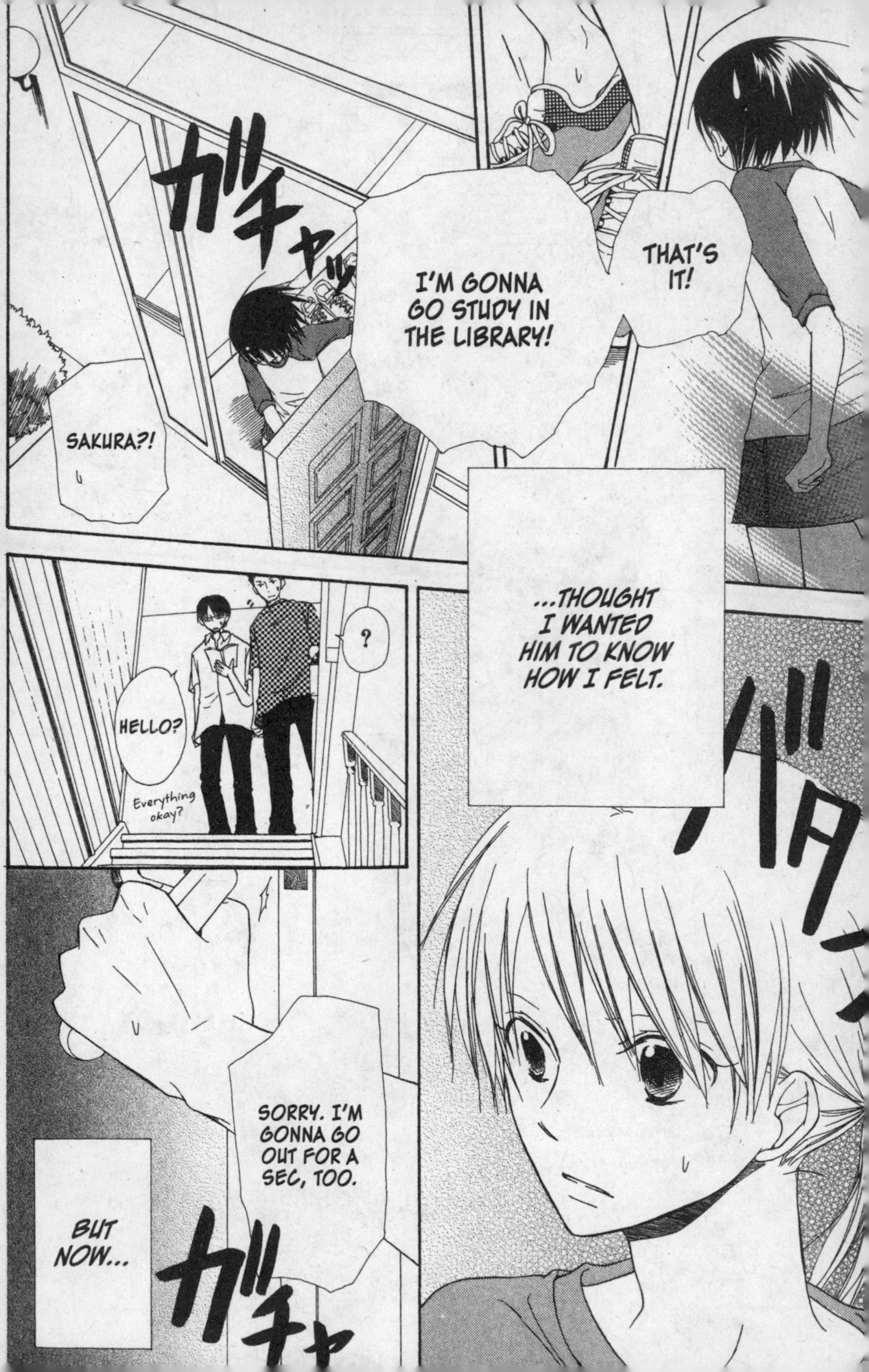
THAT'S IT!
I'M GONNA GO STUDY IN THE LIBRARY!
ガチャッ
SAKURA?!
...THOUGHT I WANTED HIM TO KNOW HOW I FELT.
バタ
?
HELLO?
Everything okay?
SORRY. I'M GONNA GO OUT FOR A SEC, TOO.
BUT NOW...
ガチャ

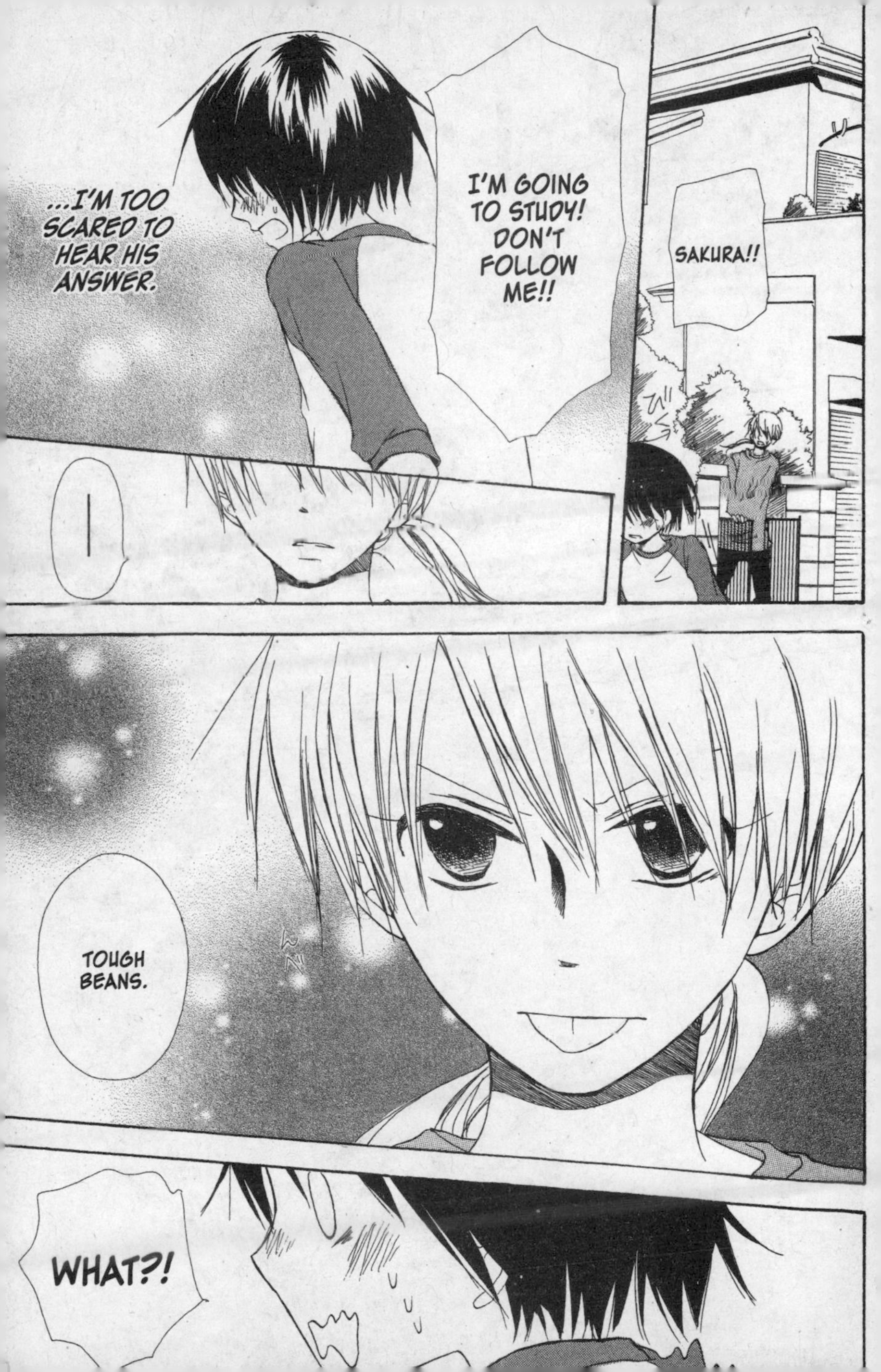
SAKURA!!
I'M GOING TO STUDY! DON'T FOLLOW ME!!
...I'M TOO SCARED TO HEAR HIS ANSWER.
TOUGH BEANS.
WHAT?!

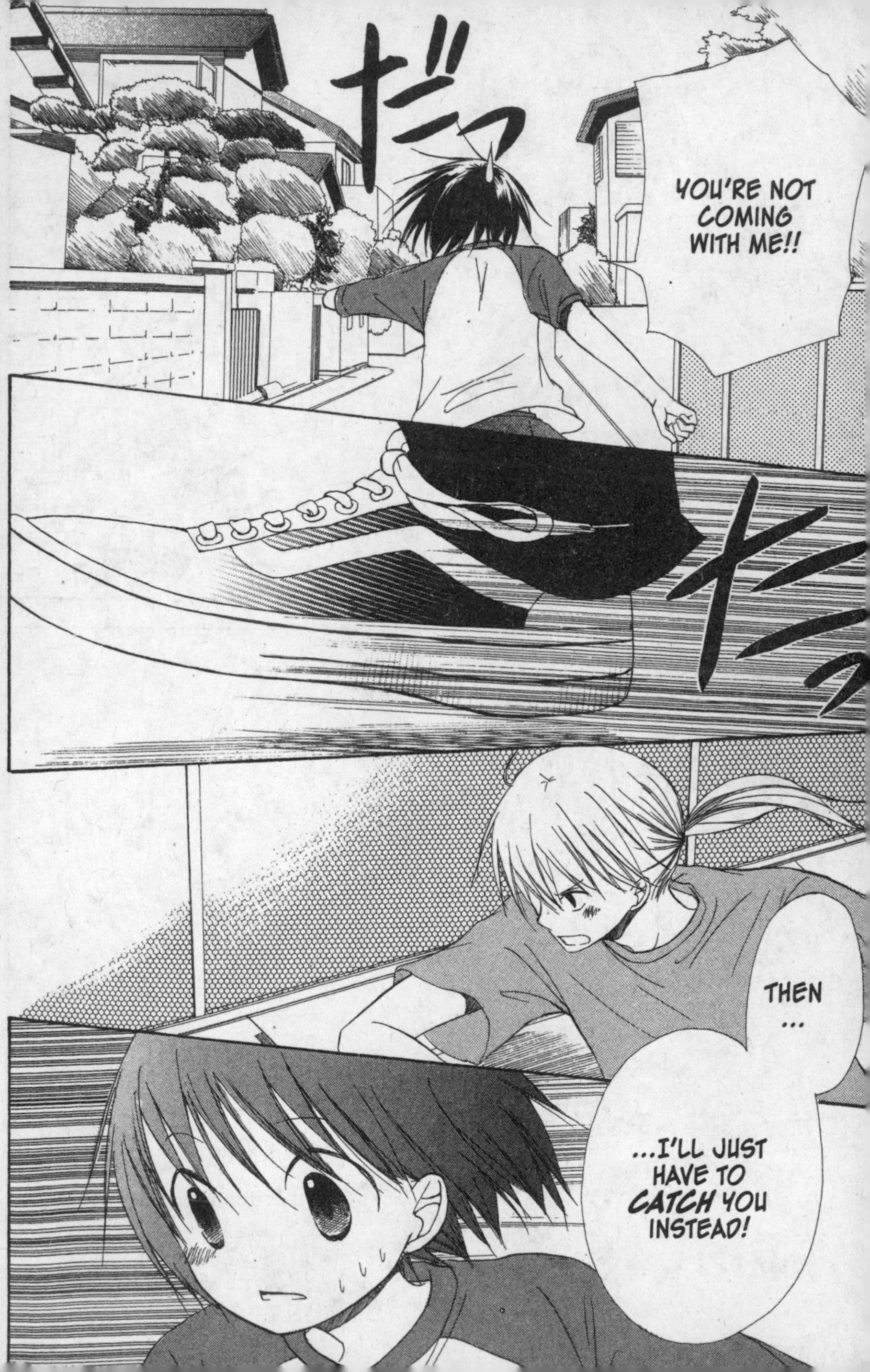
だっ
YOU'RE NOT COMING WITH ME!!
ギュッ
THEN ...
...I'LL JUST HAVE TO *CATCH* YOU INSTEAD!

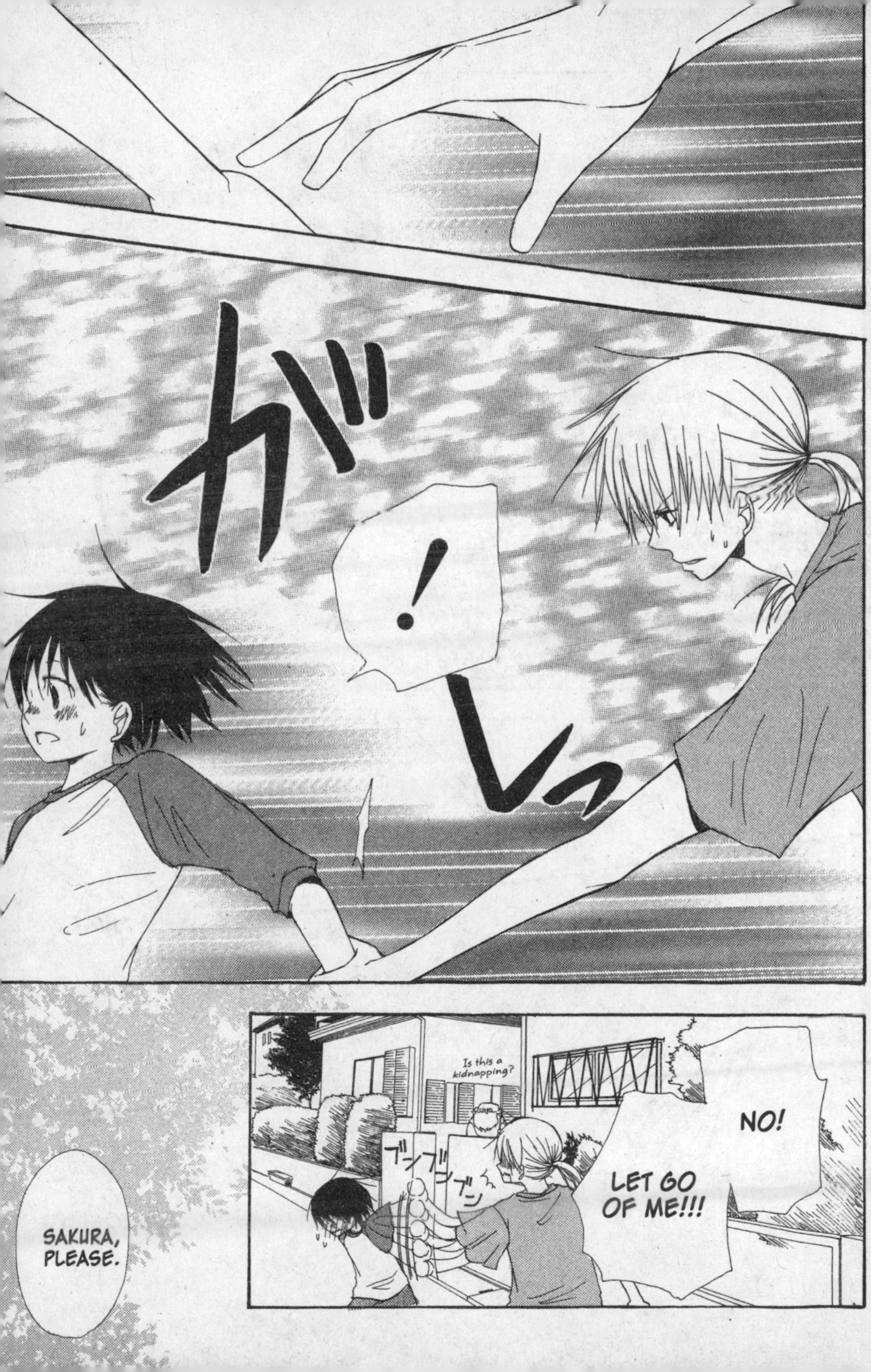
がしっ
!
NO!
LET GO OF ME!!!
Is this a kidnapping?
SAKURA, PLEASE.

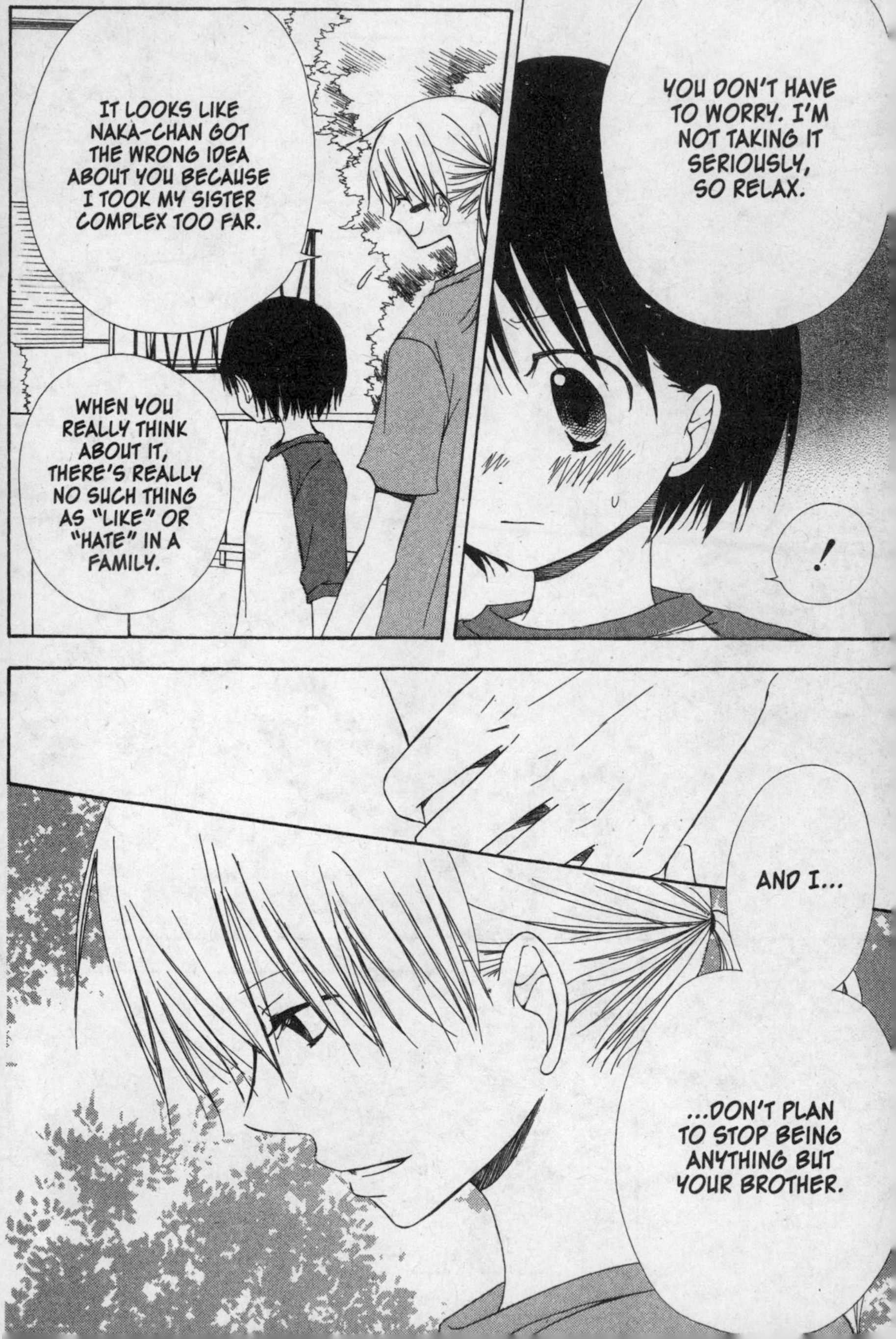
YOU DON'T HAVE TO WORRY. I'M NOT TAKING IT SERIOUSLY, SO RELAX.
!
IT LOOKS LIKE NAKA-CHAN GOT THE WRONG IDEA ABOUT YOU BECAUSE I TOOK MY SISTER COMPLEX TOO FAR.
WHEN YOU REALLY THINK ABOUT IT, THERE'S REALLY NO SUCH THING AS "LIKE" OR "HATE" IN A FAMILY.
AND I...
...DON'T PLAN TO STOP BEING ANYTHING BUT YOUR BROTHER.

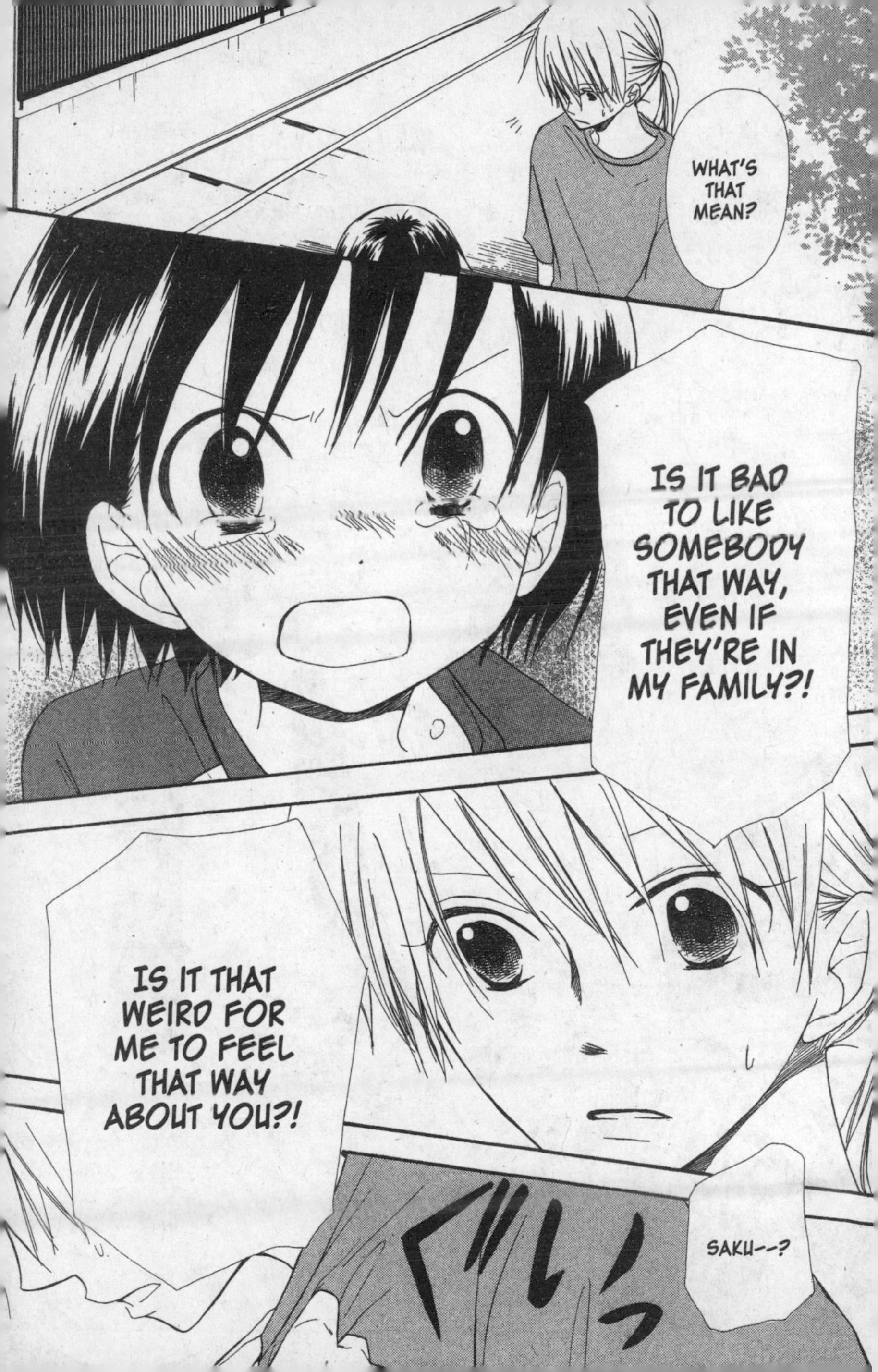
WHAT'S THAT MEAN?
IS IT BAD TO LIKE SOMEBODY THAT WAY, EVEN IF THEY'RE IN MY FAMILY?!
SAKU--?
IS IT THAT WEIRD FOR ME TO FEEL THAT WAY ABOUT YOU?!

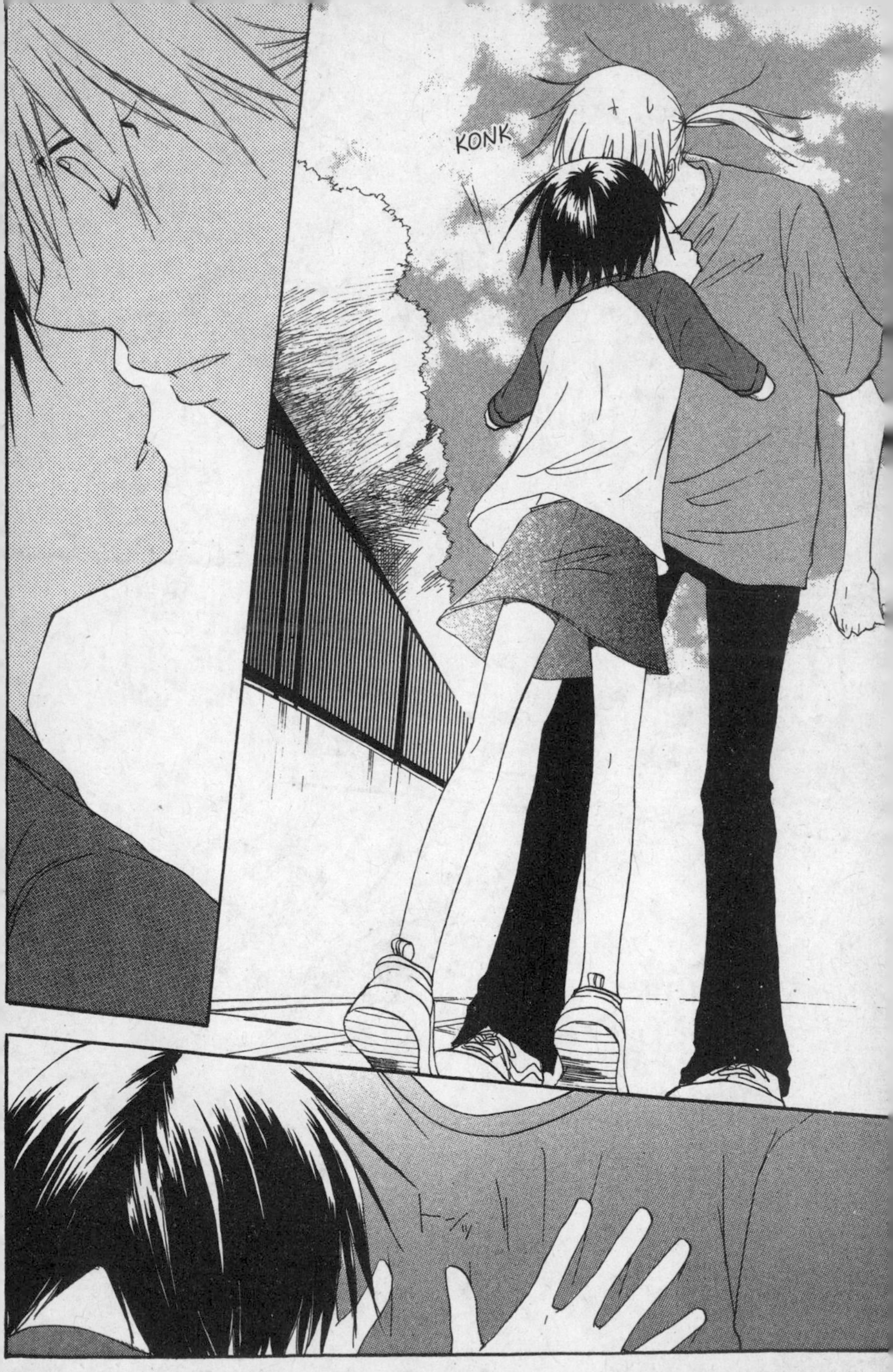
KONK

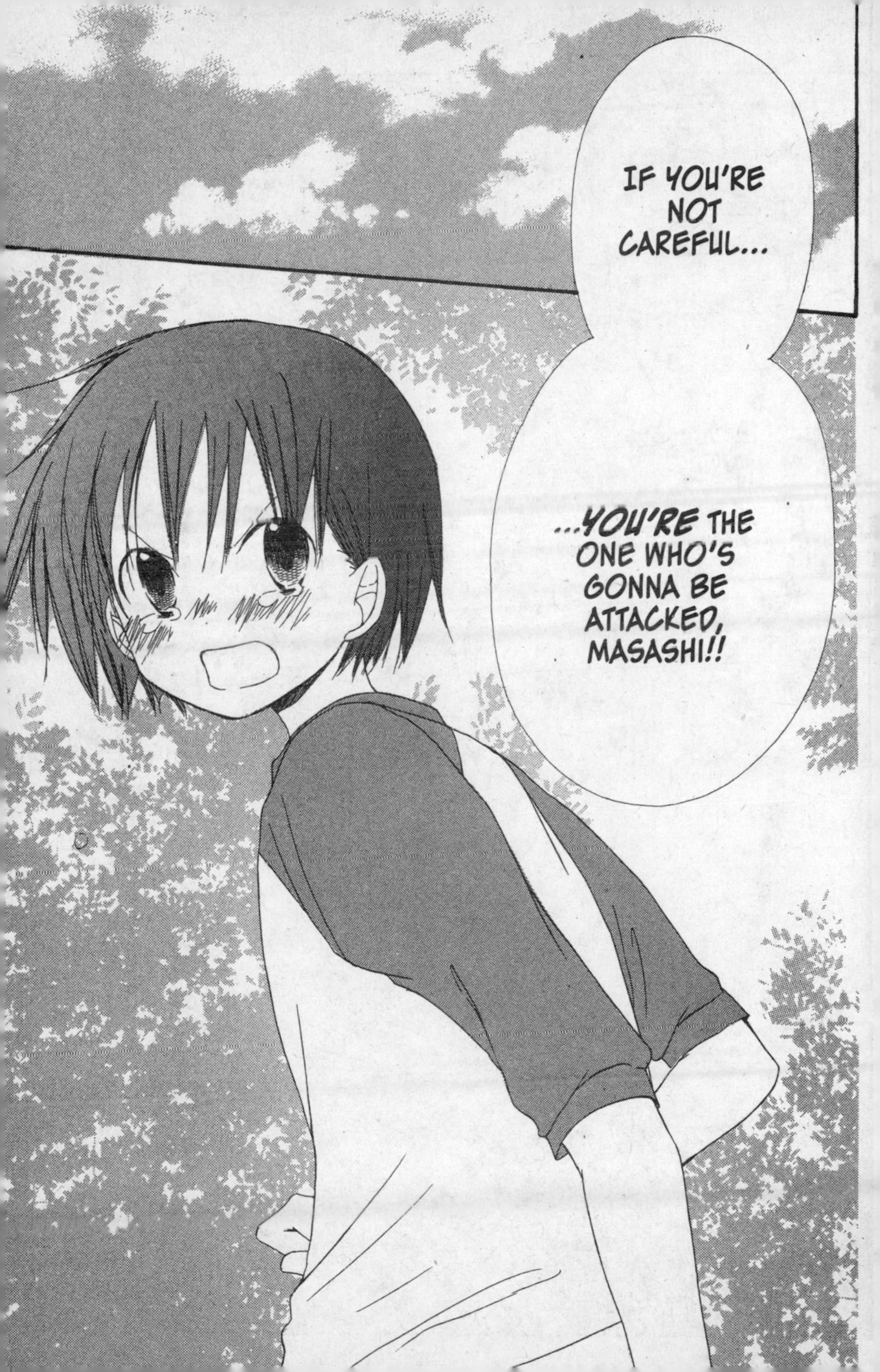
IF YOU'RE NOT CAREFUL...
...YOU'RE THE ONE WHO'S GONNA BE ATTACKED, MASASHI!!

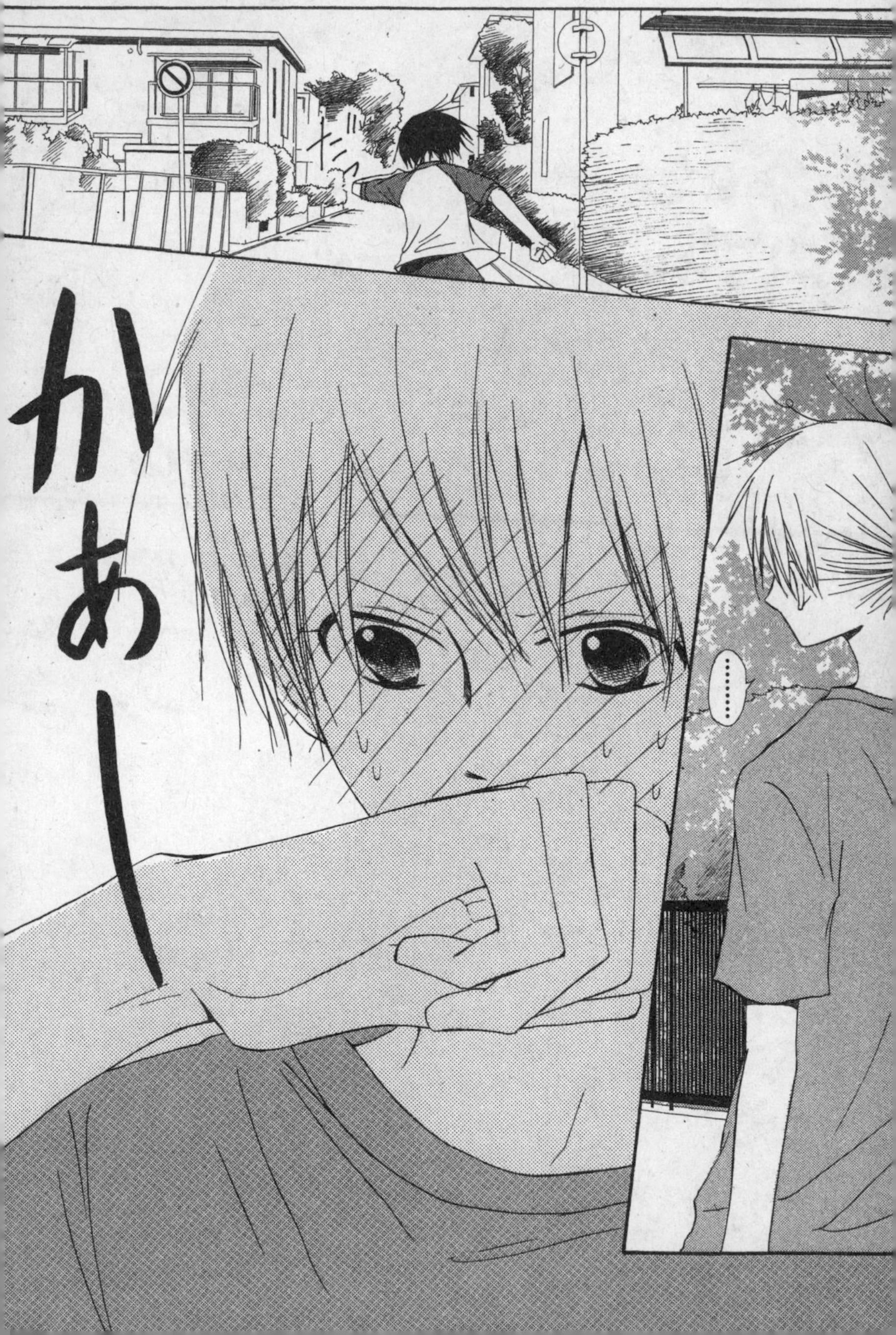
かあー
……

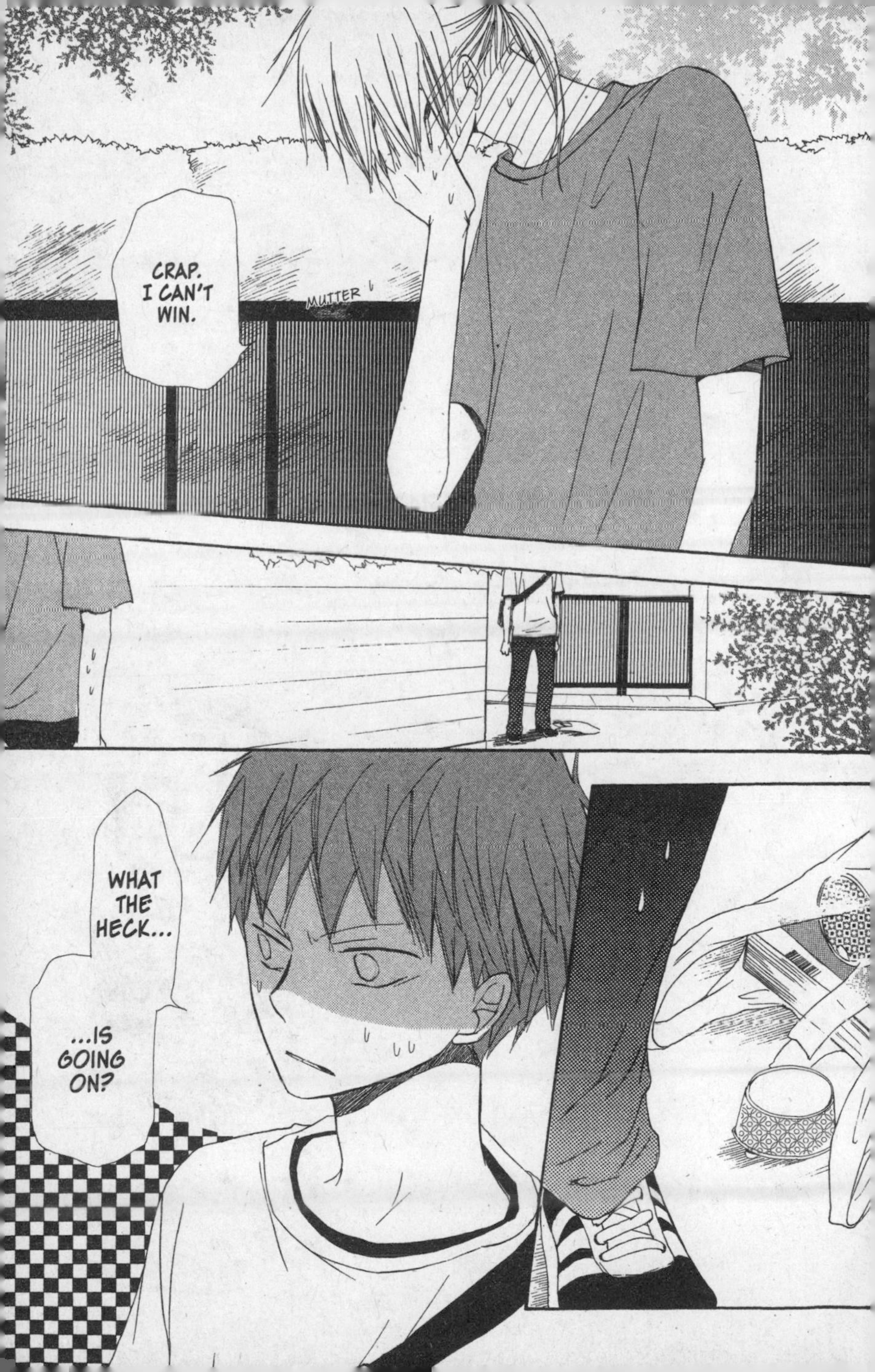
MUTTER
CRAP. I CAN'T WIN.
WHAT THE HECK...
...IS GOING ON?

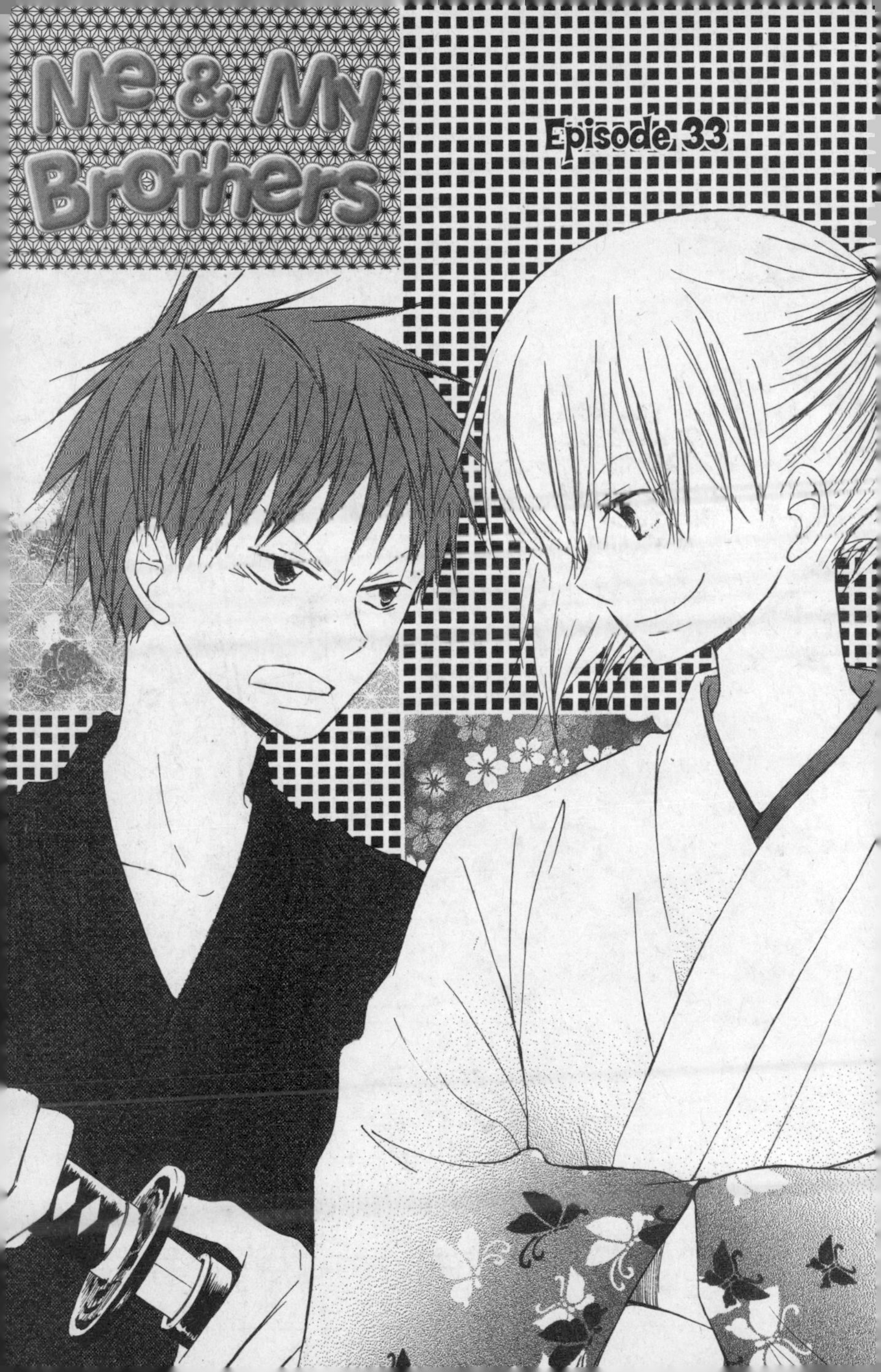
Me & My Brothers
Episode 33

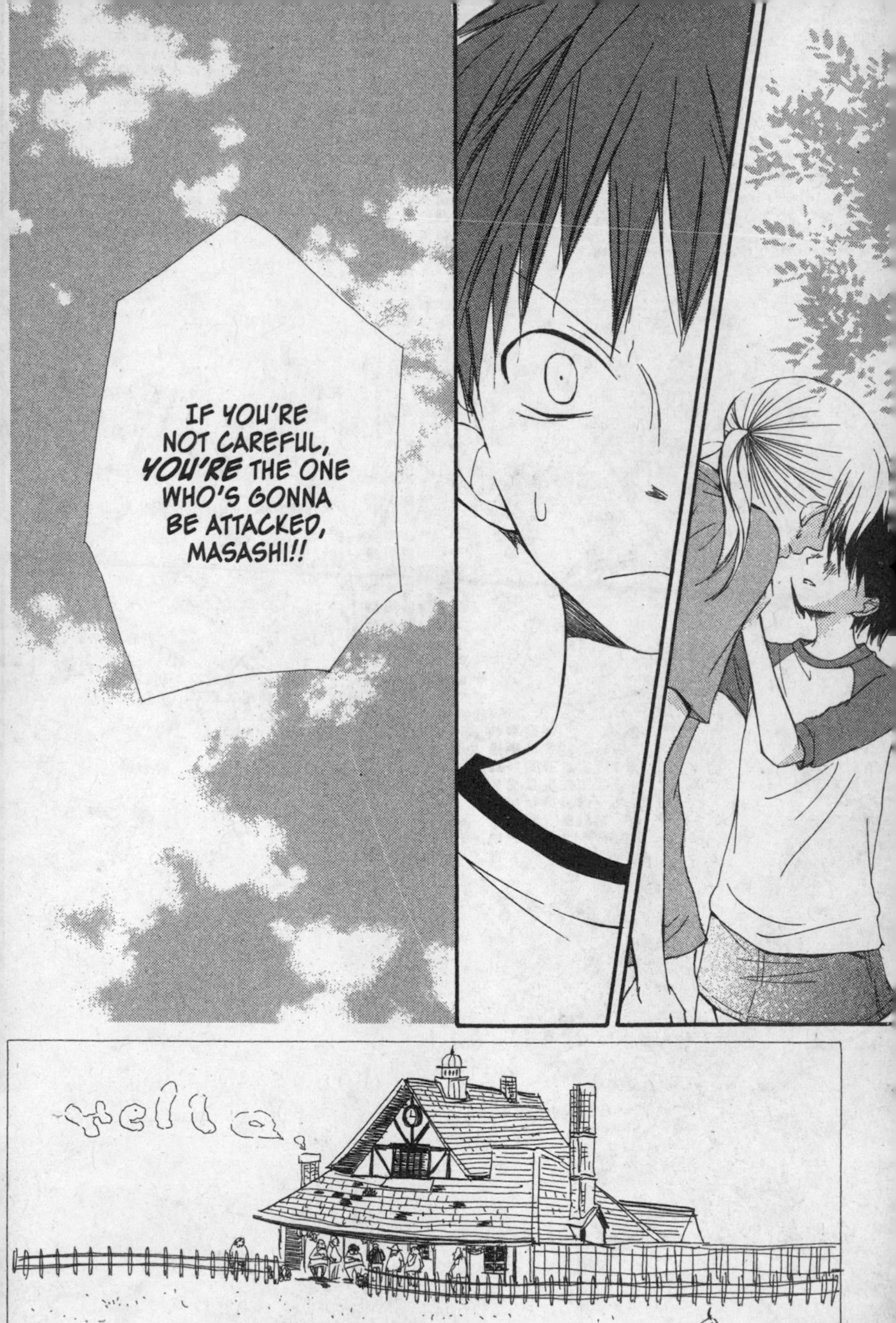
IF YOU'RE NOT CAREFUL, *YOU'RE* THE ONE WHO'S GONNA BE ATTACKED, MASASHI!!

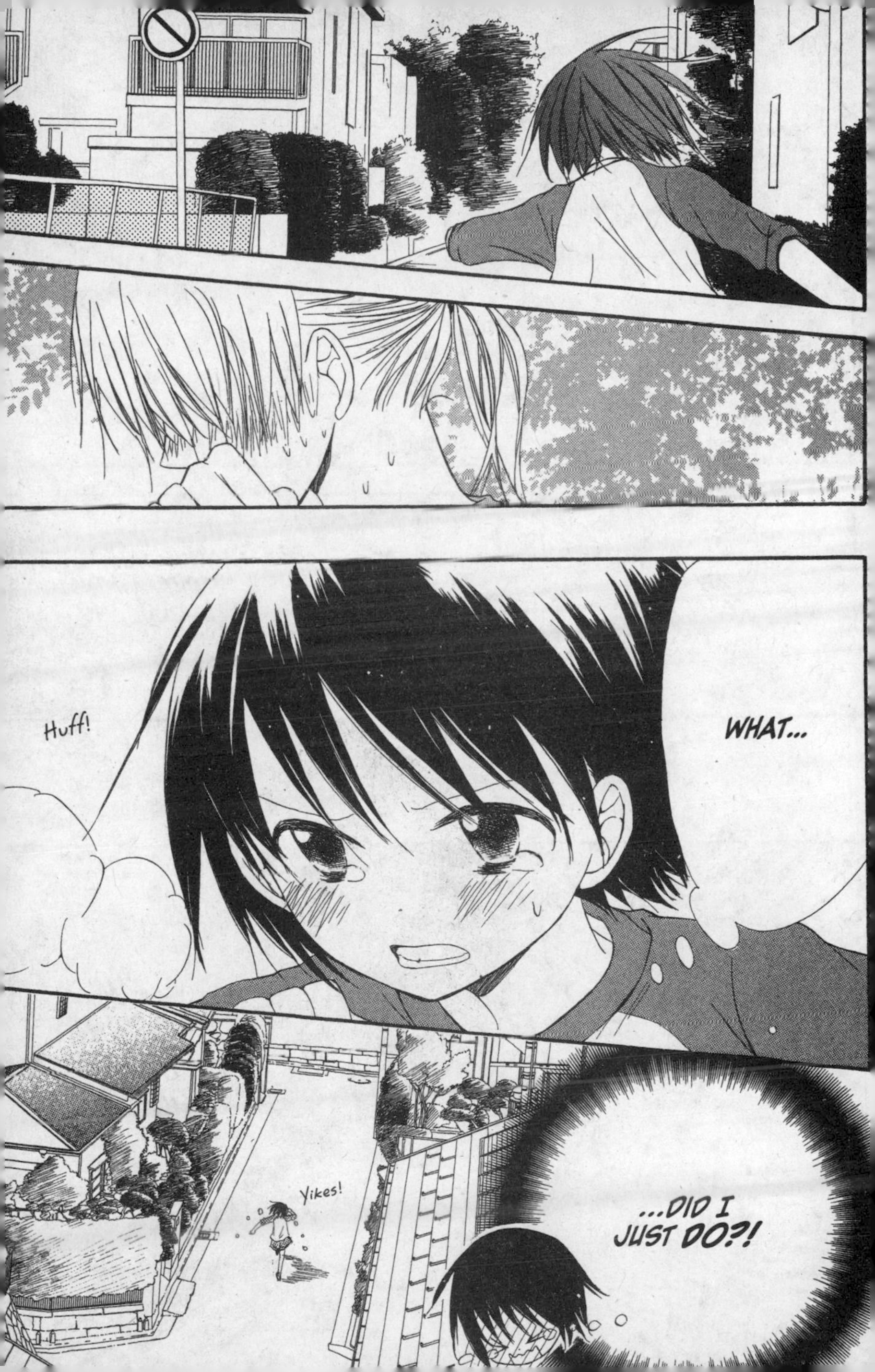
WHAT...
Huff!
...DID I JUST DO?!
Yikes!

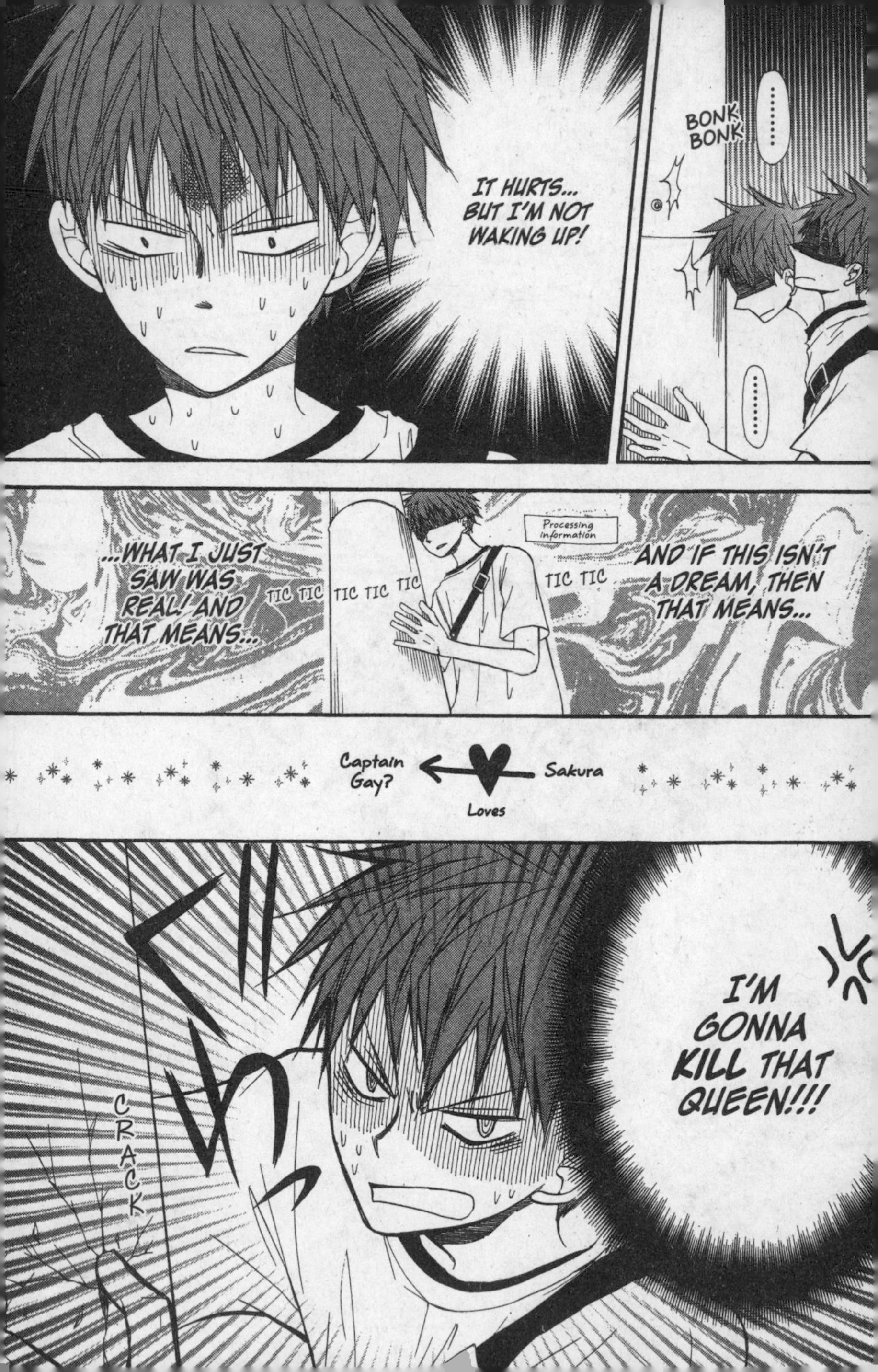
BONK BONK
......
......
IT HURTS... BUT I'M NOT WAKING UP!
AND IF THIS ISN'T A DREAM, THEN THAT MEANS...
TIC TIC
Processing information
TIC TIC TIC
TIC TIC
...WHAT I JUST SAW WAS REAL! AND THAT MEANS...
Sakura
Loves
Captain Gay?
I'M GONNA KILL THAT QUEEN!!!
CRACK

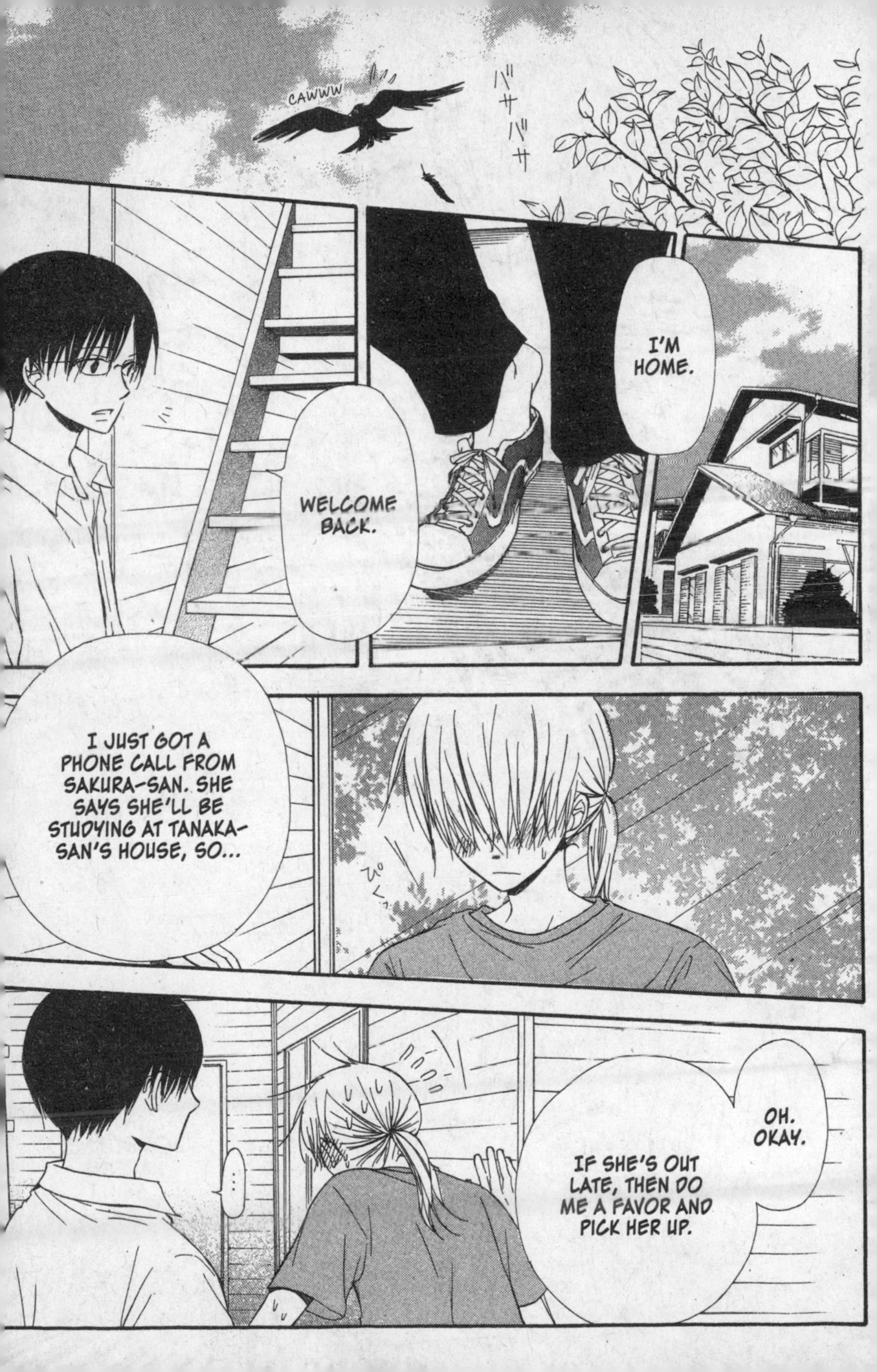
バサバサ
CAWWW
I'M HOME.
WELCOME BACK.
ぴくっ
I JUST GOT A PHONE CALL FROM SAKURA-SAN. SHE SAYS SHE'LL BE STUDYING AT TANAKA-SAN'S HOUSE, SO...
OH. OKAY.
IF SHE'S OUT LATE, THEN DO ME A FAVOR AND PICK HER UP.
...

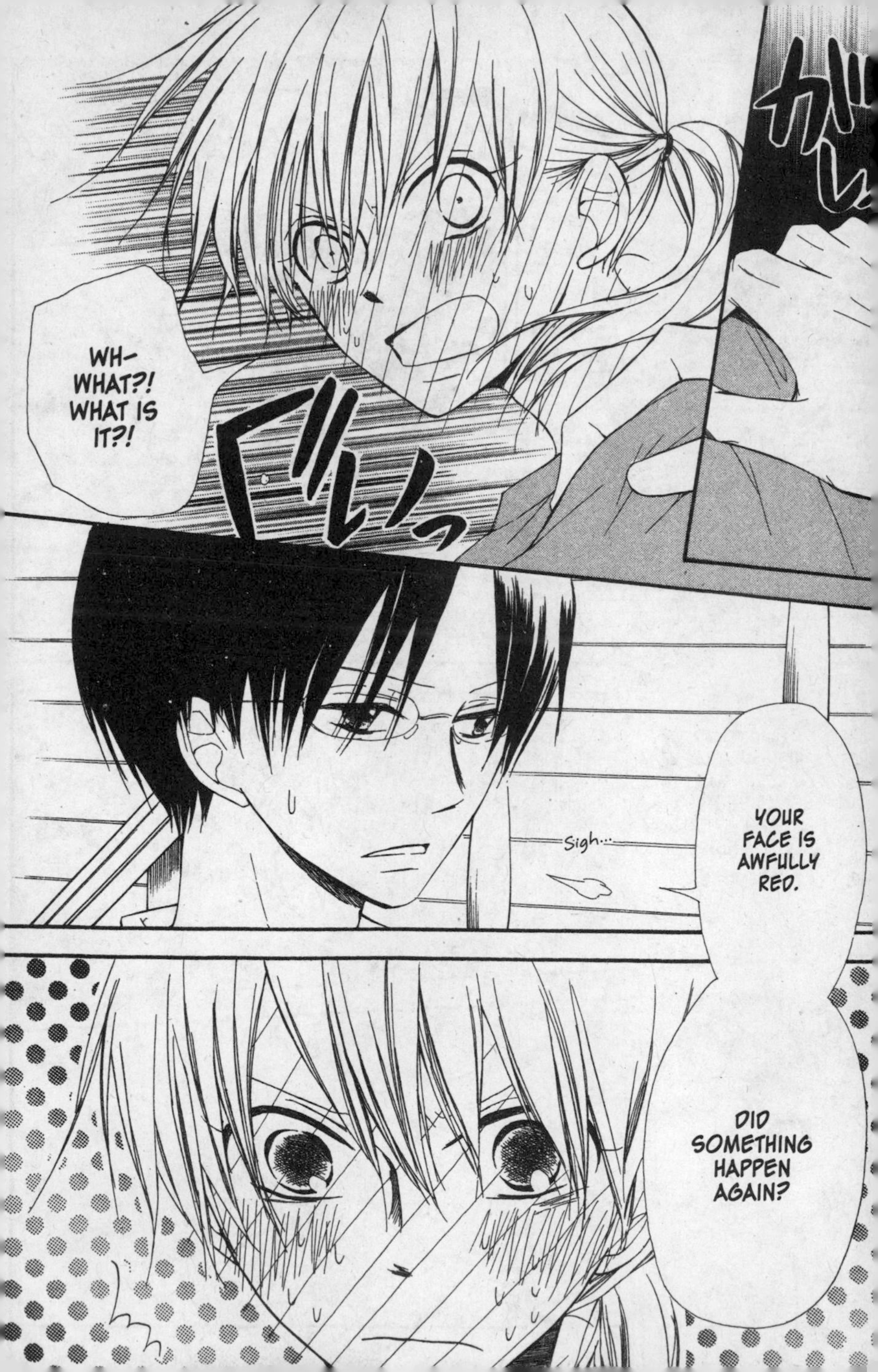
WH-WHAT?! WHAT IS IT?!
Sigh...
YOUR FACE IS AWFULLY RED.
DID SOMETHING HAPPEN AGAIN?

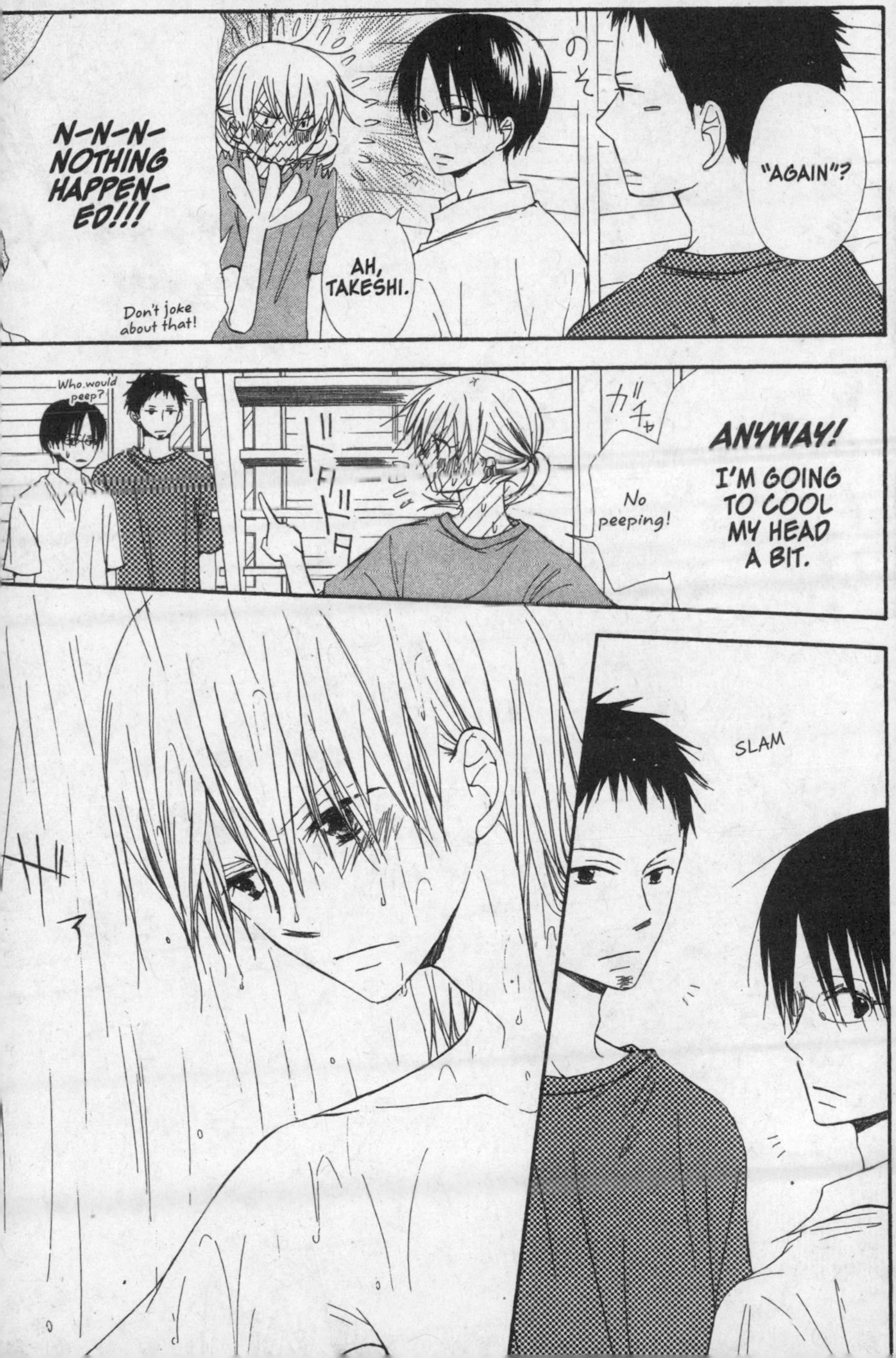
"AGAIN"?
のそ
AH, TAKESHI.
N-N-N-NOTHING HAPPEN-ED!!!
Don't joke about that!
ANYWAY! I'M GOING TO COOL MY HEAD A BIT.
ガチャ
No peeping!
Who would peep?
SLAM

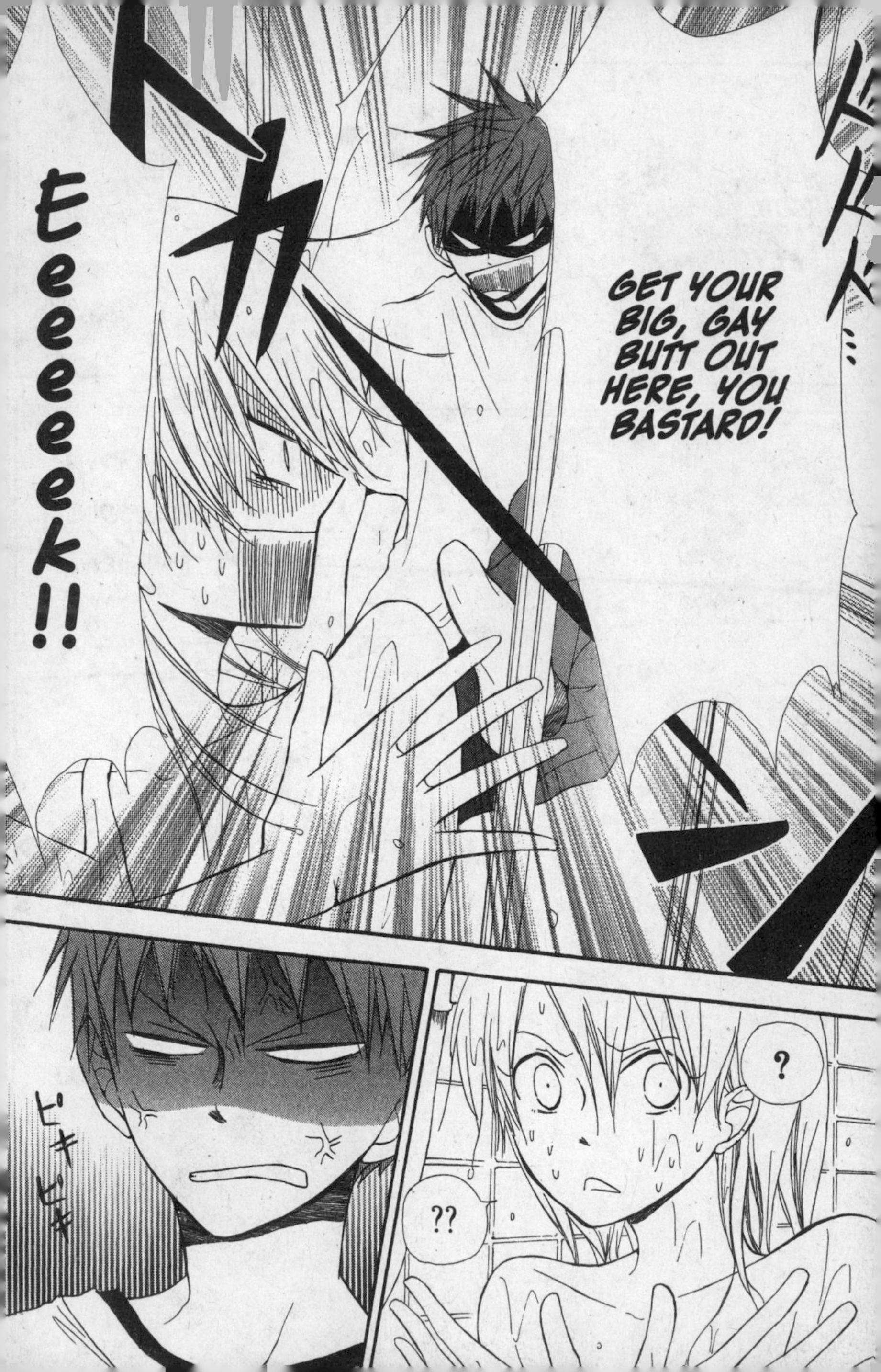
GET YOUR BIG, GAY BUTT OUT HERE, YOU BASTARD!
Eeeeeeek!!
?
??
ピキピキ

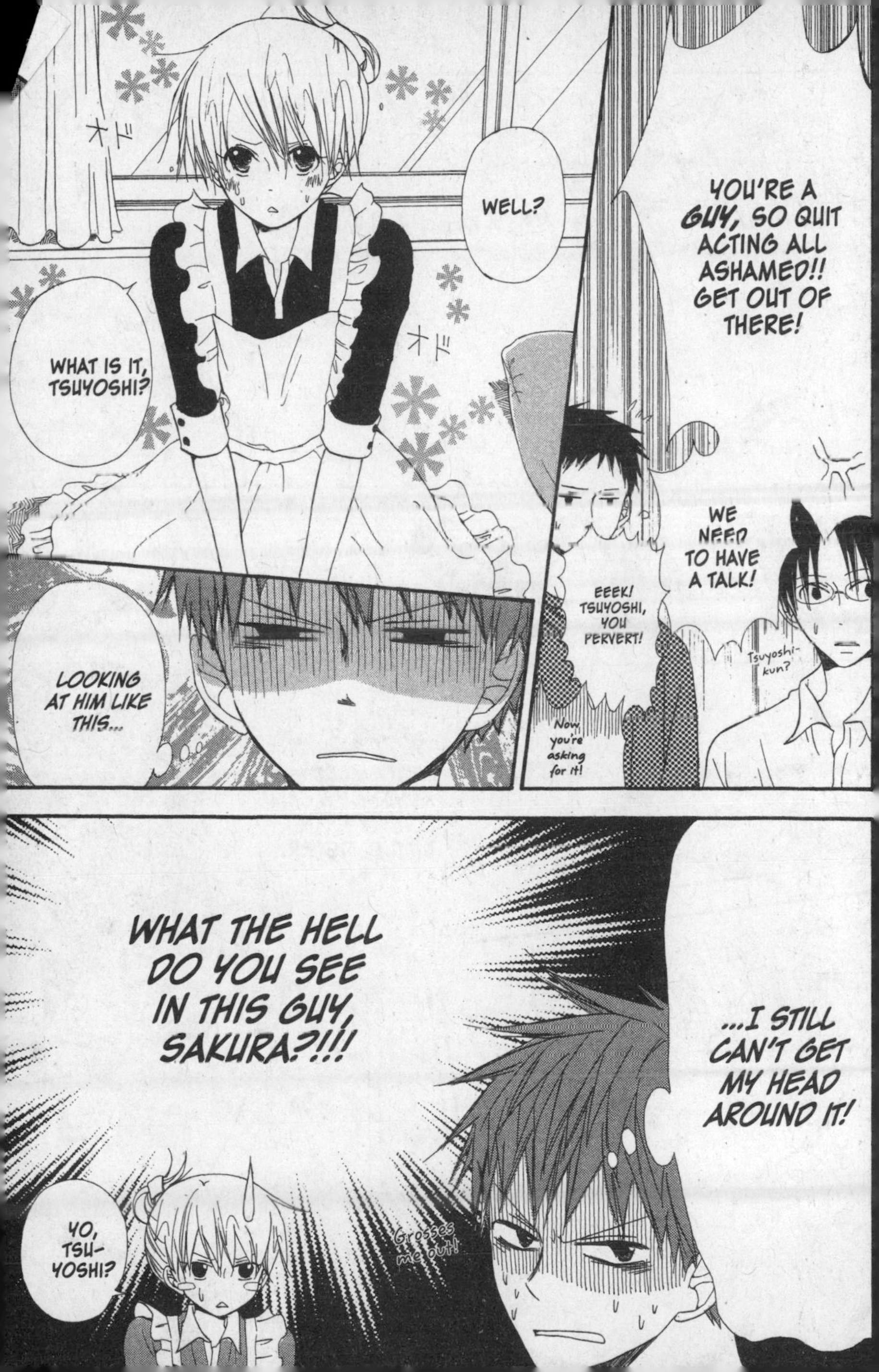

YOU'RE A GUY, SO QUIT ACTING ALL ASHAMED!! GET OUT OF THERE!
WE NEED TO HAVE A TALK!
Tsuyoshi-kun?
EEEK! TSUYOSHI, YOU PERVERT!
Now you're asking for it!
WELL?
オド
WHAT IS IT, TSUYOSHI?
オド
LOOKING AT HIM LIKE THIS...
...I STILL CAN'T GET MY HEAD AROUND IT!
WHAT THE HELL DO YOU SEE IN THIS GUY, SAKURA?!!!
Grosses me out!
YO, TSU-YOSHI?

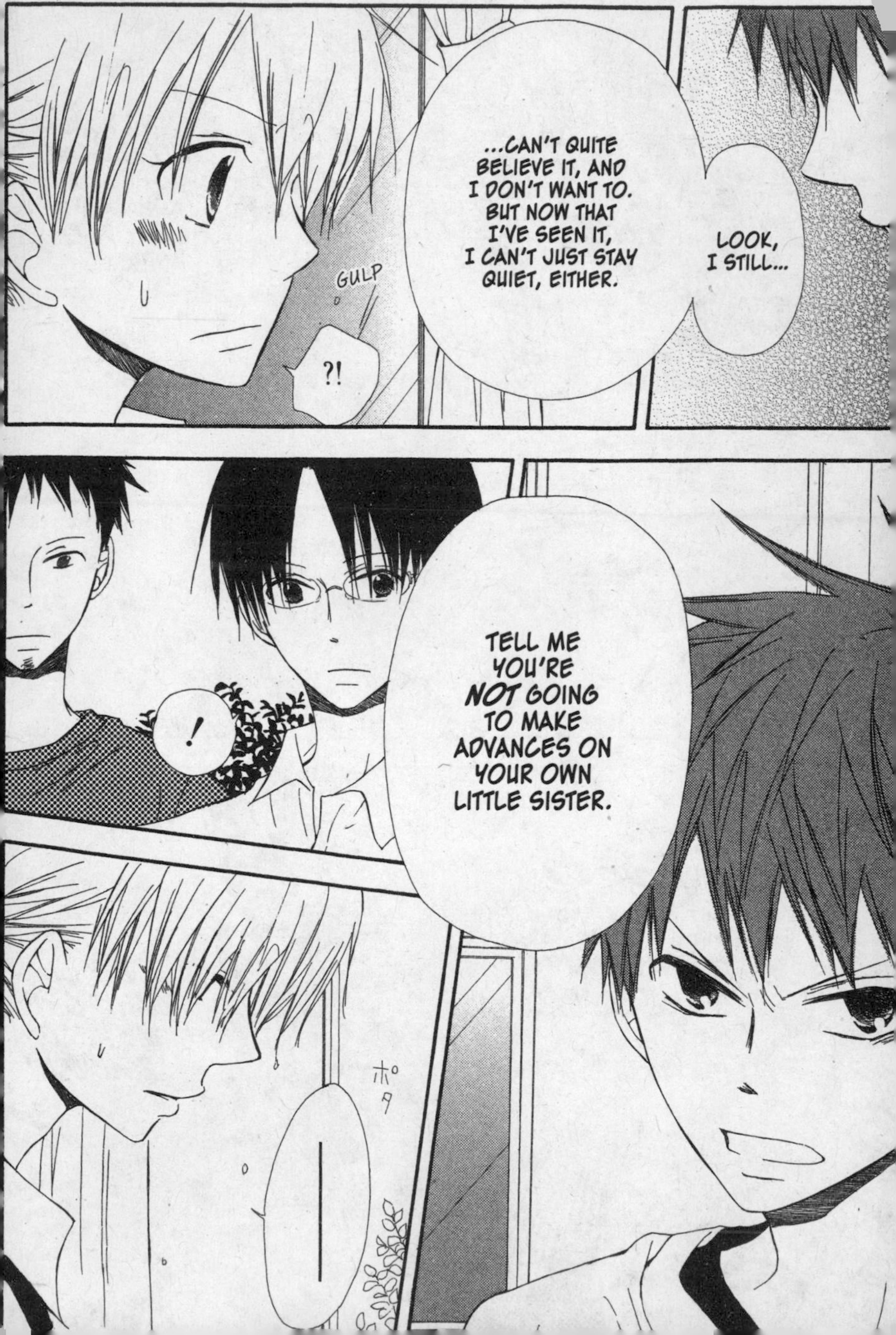
LOOK, I STILL...
...CAN'T QUITE BELIEVE IT, AND I DON'T WANT TO. BUT NOW THAT I'VE SEEN IT, I CAN'T JUST STAY QUIET, EITHER.
GULP
?!
TELL ME YOU'RE *NOT* GOING TO MAKE ADVANCES ON YOUR OWN LITTLE SISTER.
!
ポタ

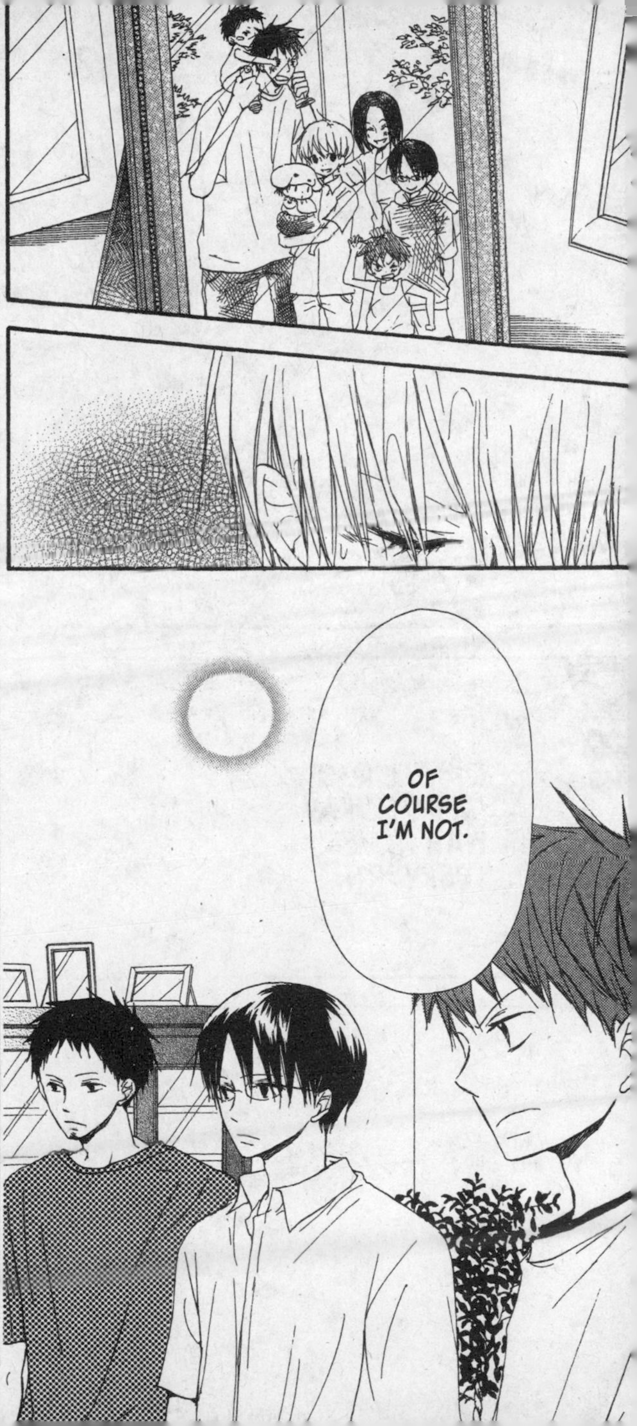
OF COURSE I'M NOT.

3

Speaking of happy things, letters from everyone make me happier than anything.

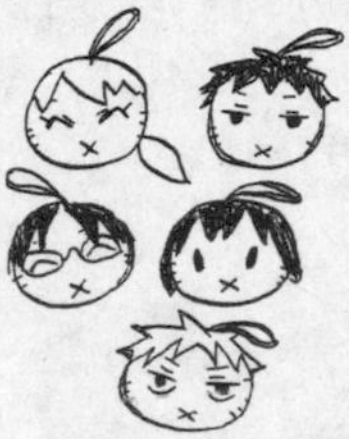

↑

I've had people make cute mascots like this.

And draw fun four-frame comics and send them to me.

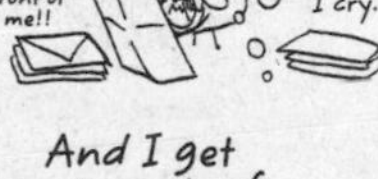
And I can't see in front of me!!
I get so happy, I cry.

And I get all kinds of other nice considerations. Every day is filled with feelings and tears of gratitude.

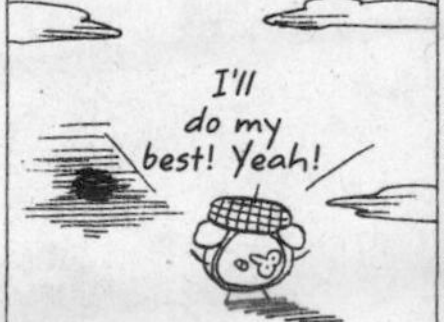
I'll do my best! Yeah!

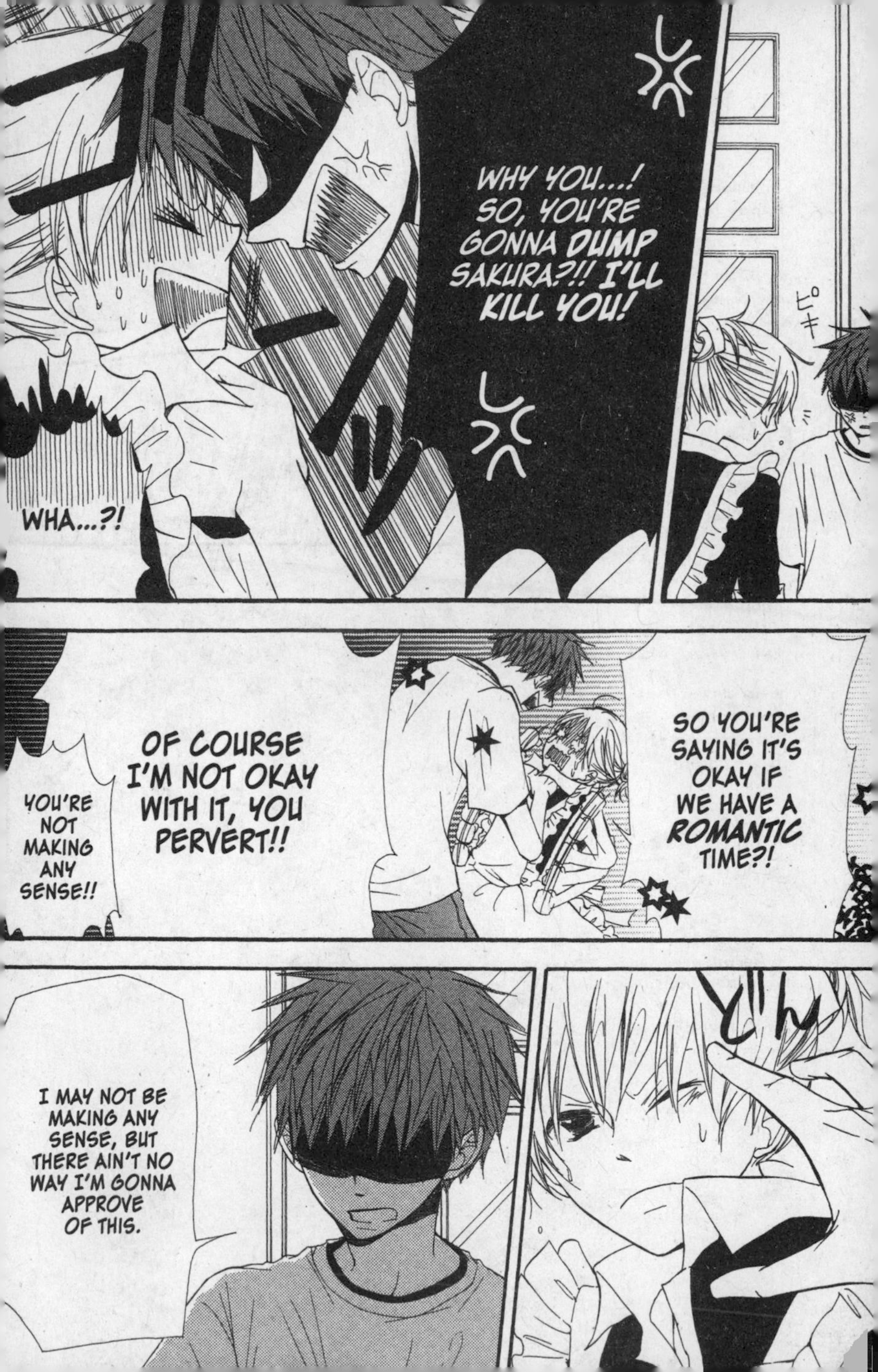
ピキ
WHY YOU...! SO, YOU'RE GONNA DUMP SAKURA?!! I'LL KILL YOU!
WHA...?!
SO YOU'RE SAYING IT'S OKAY IF WE HAVE A ROMANTIC TIME?!
OF COURSE I'M NOT OKAY WITH IT, YOU PERVERT!!
YOU'RE NOT MAKING ANY SENSE!!
I MAY NOT BE MAKING ANY SENSE, BUT THERE AIN'T NO WAY I'M GONNA APPROVE OF THIS.

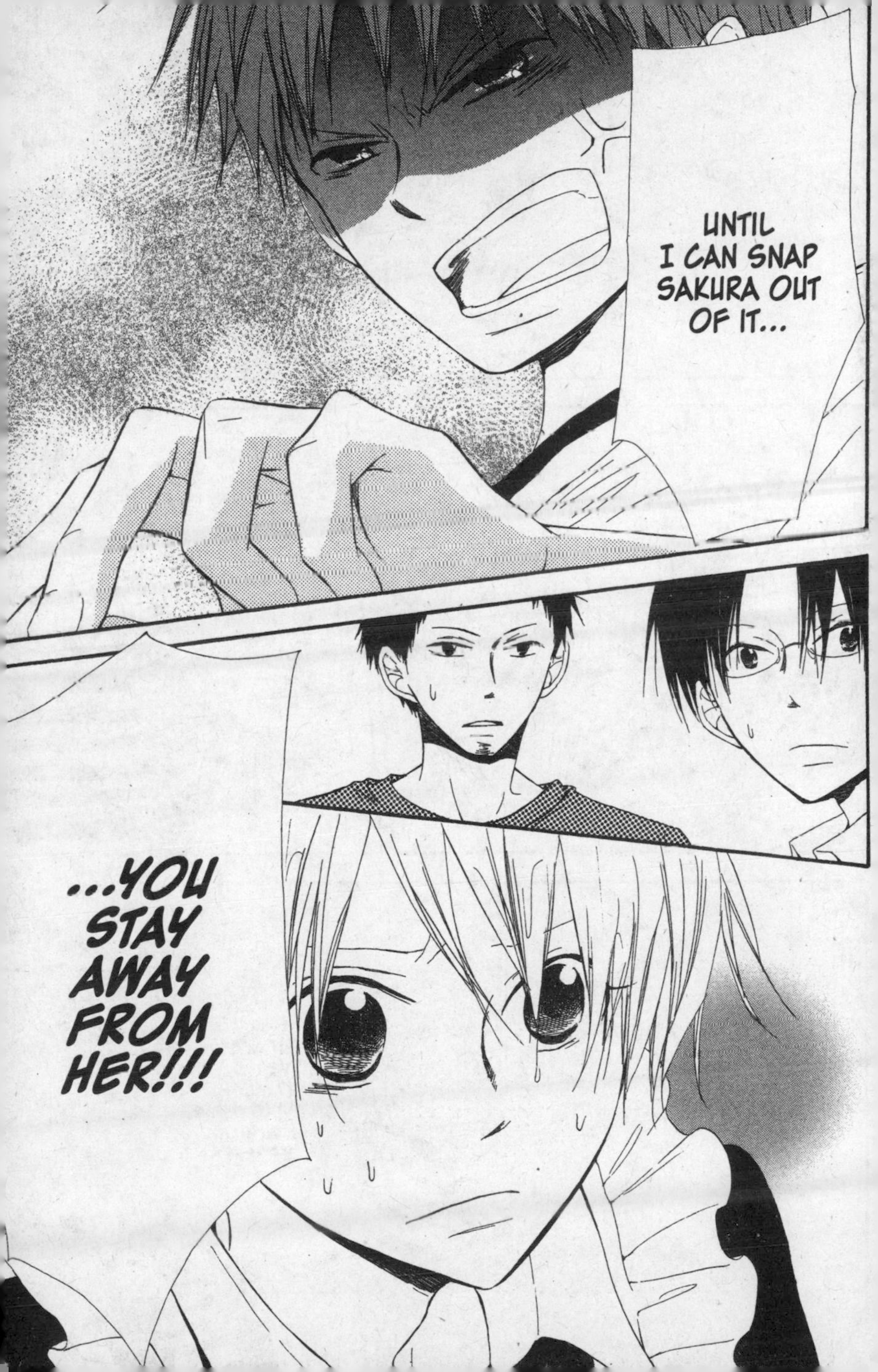
UNTIL I CAN SNAP SAKURA OUT OF IT...
...YOU STAY AWAY FROM HER!!!

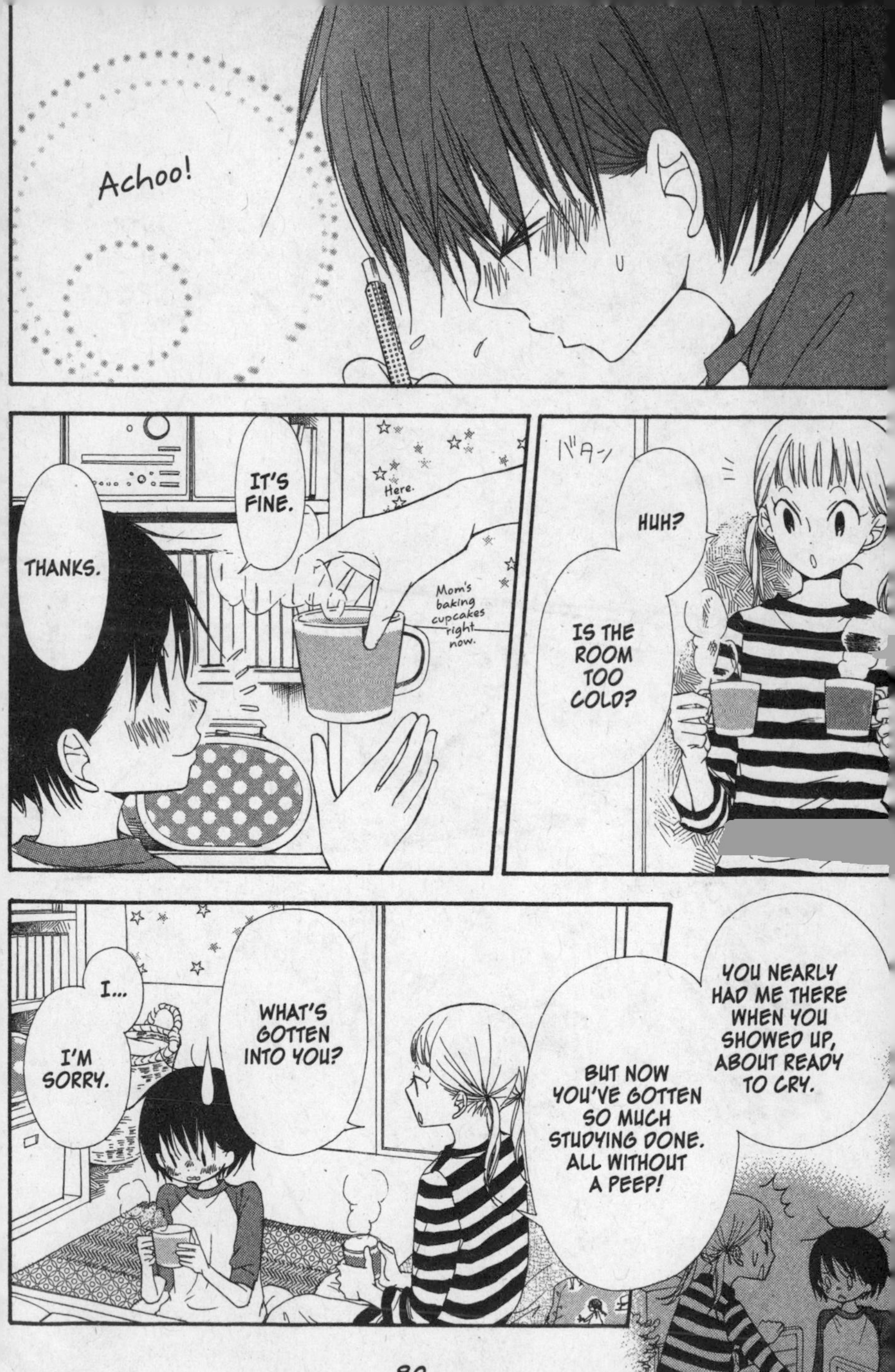

Achoo!
バターン
HUH?
IS THE ROOM TOO COLD?
IT'S FINE.
Here.
Mom's baking cupcakes right now.
THANKS.
YOU NEARLY HAD ME THERE WHEN YOU SHOWED UP, ABOUT READY TO CRY.
BUT NOW YOU'VE GOTTEN SO MUCH STUDYING DONE. ALL WITHOUT A PEEP!
WHAT'S GOTTEN INTO YOU?
I...
I'M SORRY.

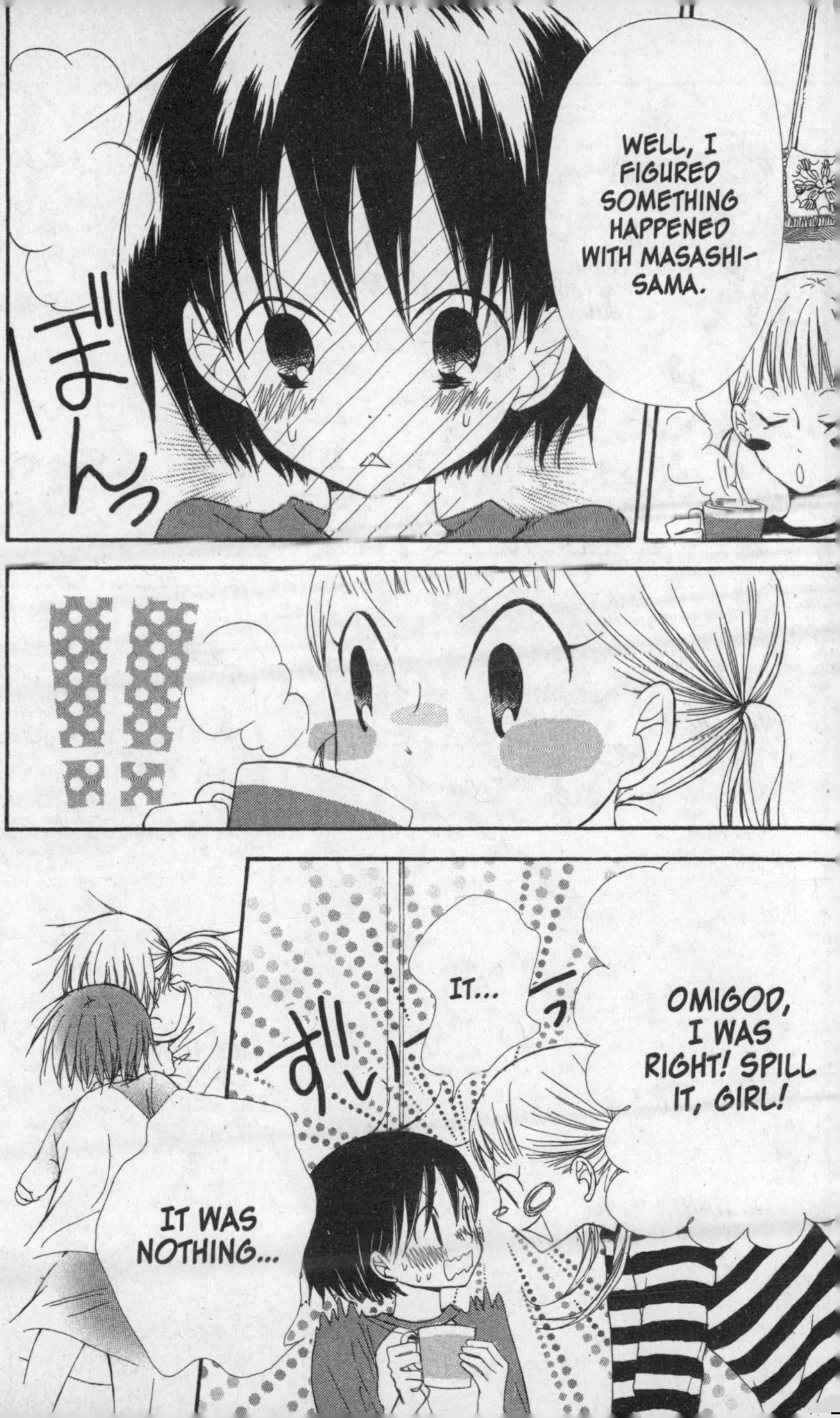
WELL, I FIGURED SOMETHING HAPPENED WITH MASASHI-SAMA.
ぼんっ
OMIGOD, I WAS RIGHT! SPILL IT, GIRL!
IT...
ずいっ
IT WAS NOTHING...

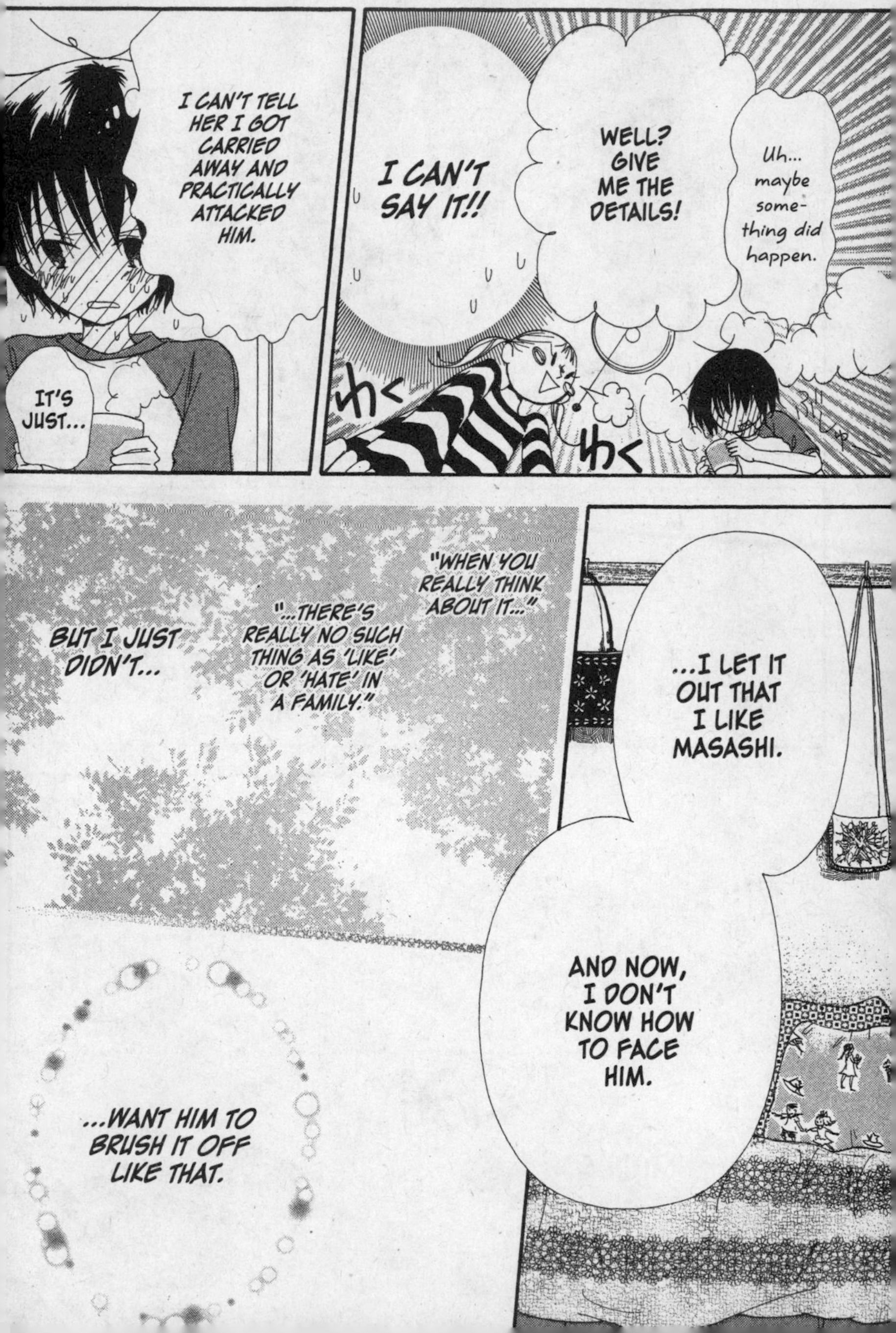
Uh... maybe some-thing did happen.
WELL? GIVE ME THE DETAILS!
I CAN'T SAY IT!!
I CAN'T TELL HER I GOT CARRIED AWAY AND PRACTICALLY ATTACKED HIM.
IT'S JUST...
...I LET IT OUT THAT I LIKE MASASHI.
AND NOW, I DON'T KNOW HOW TO FACE HIM.
"WHEN YOU REALLY THINK ABOUT IT..."
"...THERE'S REALLY NO SUCH THING AS 'LIKE' OR 'HATE' IN A FAMILY."
BUT I JUST DIDN'T...
...WANT HIM TO BRUSH IT OFF LIKE THAT.

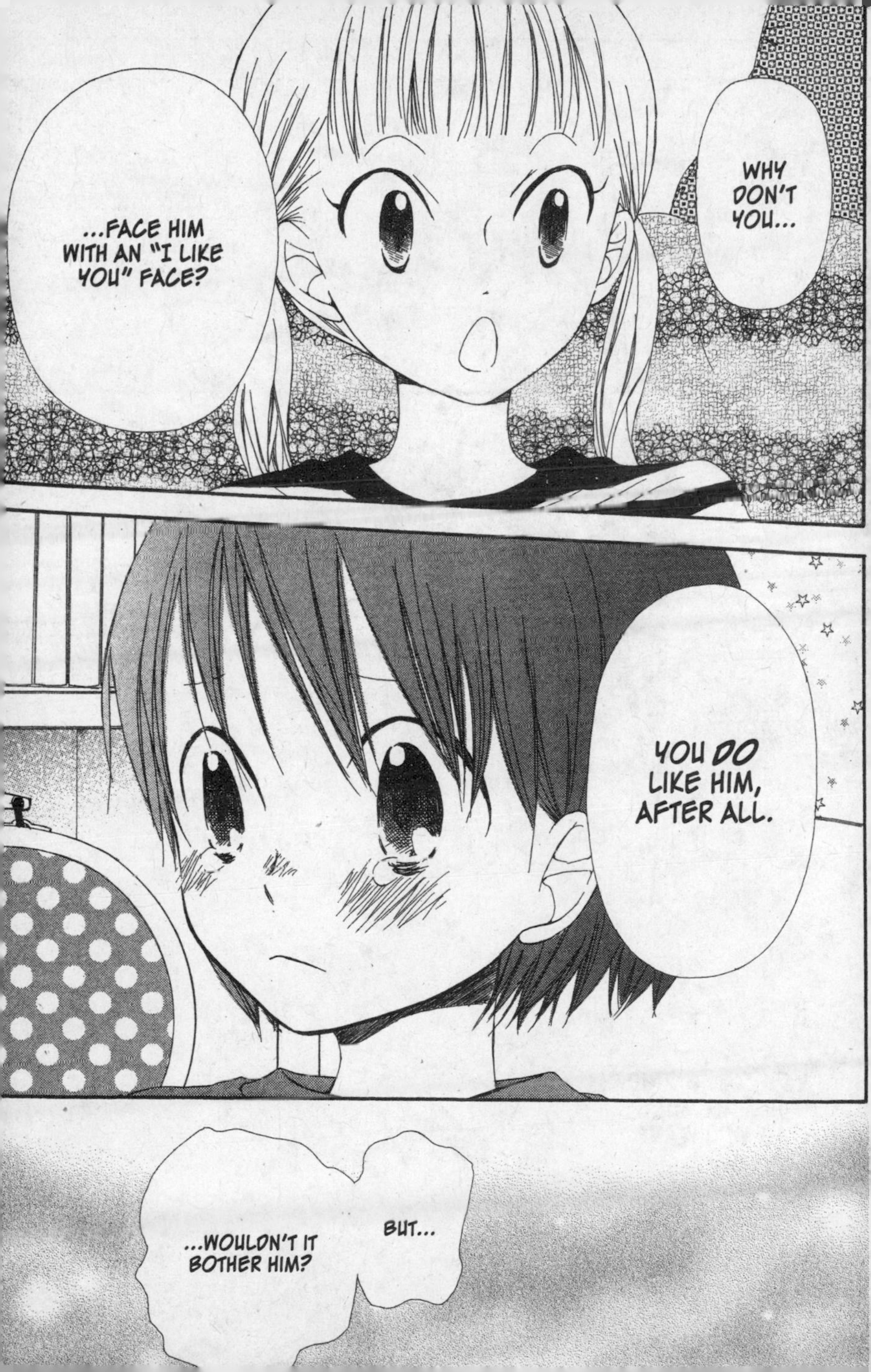
WHY DON'T YOU...
...FACE HIM WITH AN "I LIKE YOU" FACE?
YOU DO LIKE HIM, AFTER ALL.
BUT...
...WOULDN'T IT BOTHER HIM?

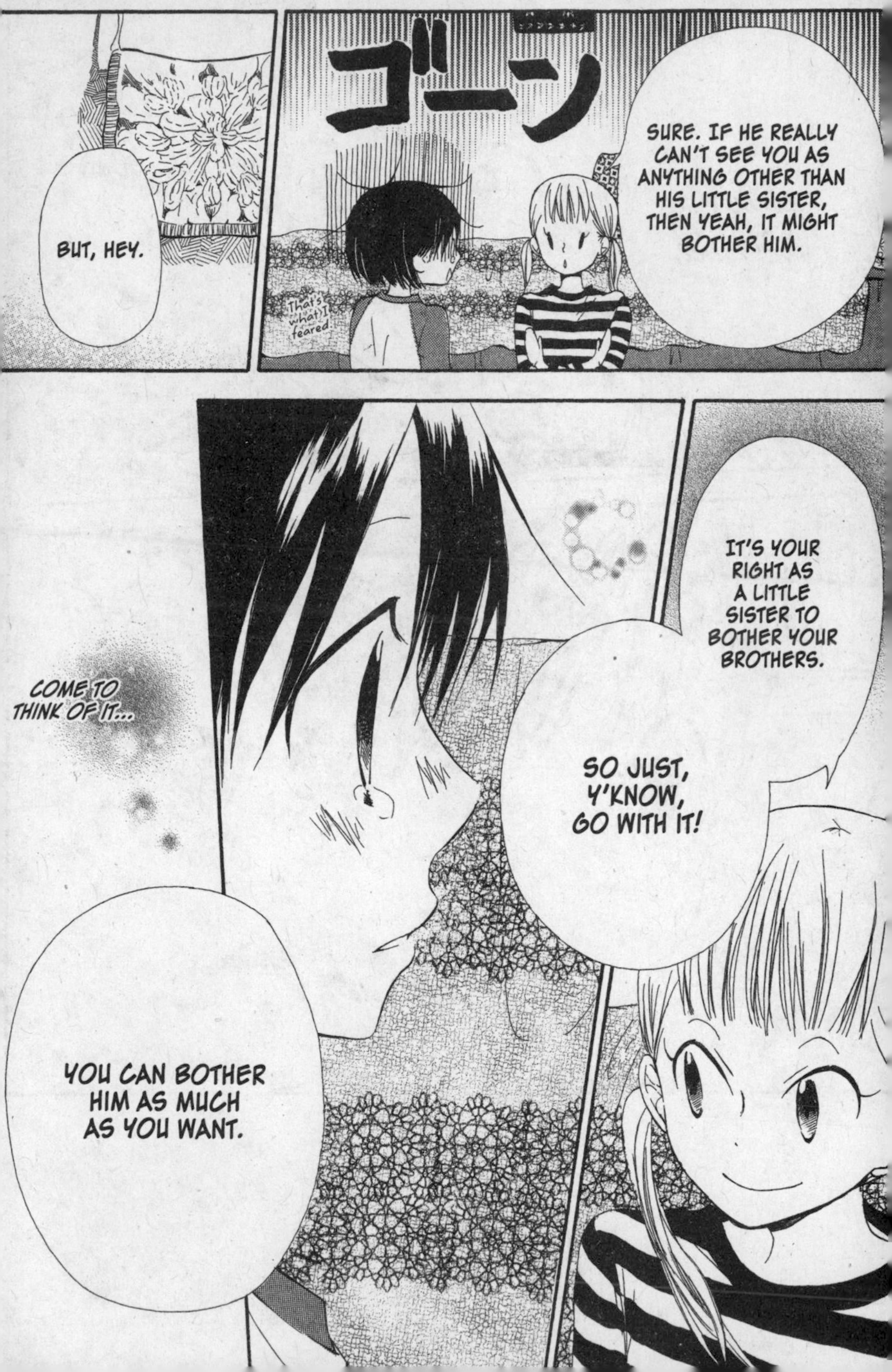
ゴーン
SURE. IF HE REALLY CAN'T SEE YOU AS ANYTHING OTHER THAN HIS LITTLE SISTER, THEN YEAH, IT MIGHT BOTHER HIM.
That's what I feared.
BUT, HEY.
IT'S YOUR RIGHT AS A LITTLE SISTER TO BOTHER YOUR BROTHERS.
SO JUST, Y'KNOW, GO WITH IT!
COME TO THINK OF IT...
YOU CAN BOTHER HIM AS MUCH AS YOU WANT.

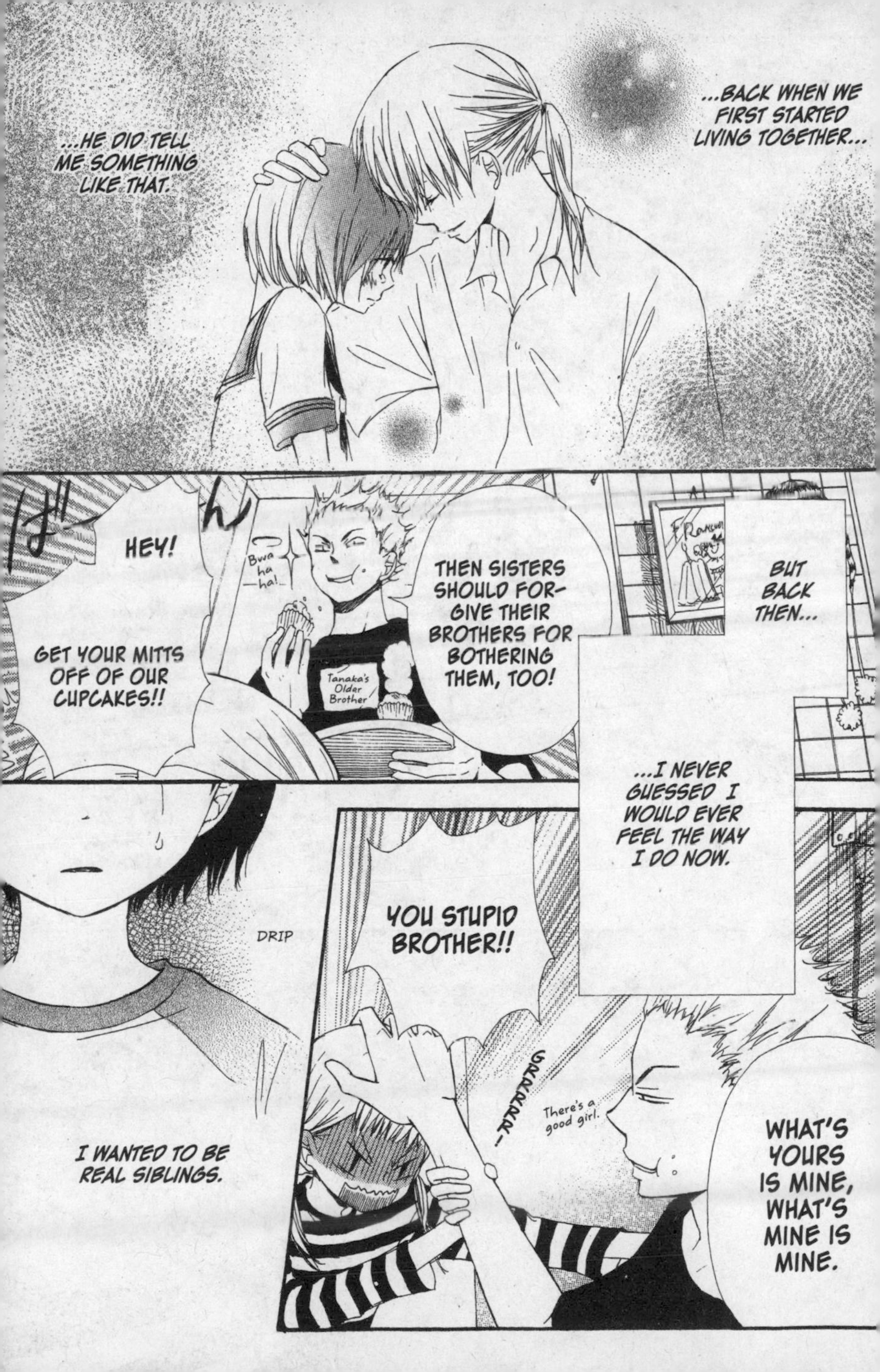
...BACK WHEN WE FIRST STARTED LIVING TOGETHER...
...HE DID TELL ME SOMETHING LIKE THAT.
BUT BACK THEN...
THEN SISTERS SHOULD FOR-GIVE THEIR BROTHERS FOR BOTHERING THEM, TOO!
Bwa ha ha!
Tanaka's Older Brother
HEY!
GET YOUR MITTS OFF OF OUR CUPCAKES!!
...I NEVER GUESSED I WOULD EVER FEEL THE WAY I DO NOW.
WHAT'S YOURS IS MINE, WHAT'S MINE IS MINE.
There's a good girl.
GRRRRRR-
YOU STUPID BROTHER!!
DRIP
I WANTED TO BE REAL SIBLINGS.

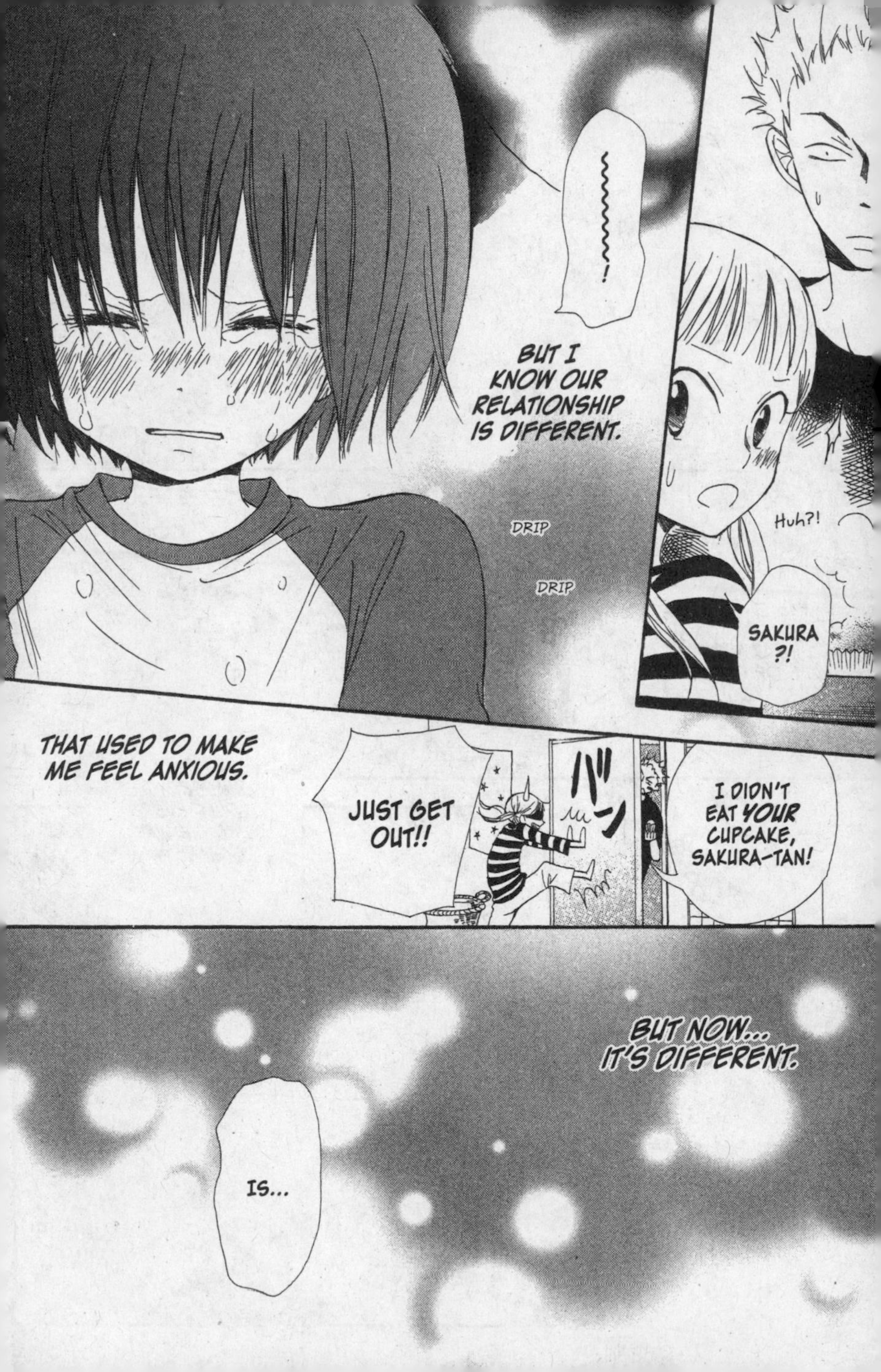

Huh?!
SAKURA ?!
BUT I KNOW OUR RELATIONSHIP IS DIFFERENT.
DRIP
DRIP
I DIDN'T EAT YOUR CUPCAKE, SAKURA-TAN!
バン
JUST GET OUT!!
THAT USED TO MAKE ME FEEL ANXIOUS.
BUT NOW... IT'S DIFFERENT.
IS...

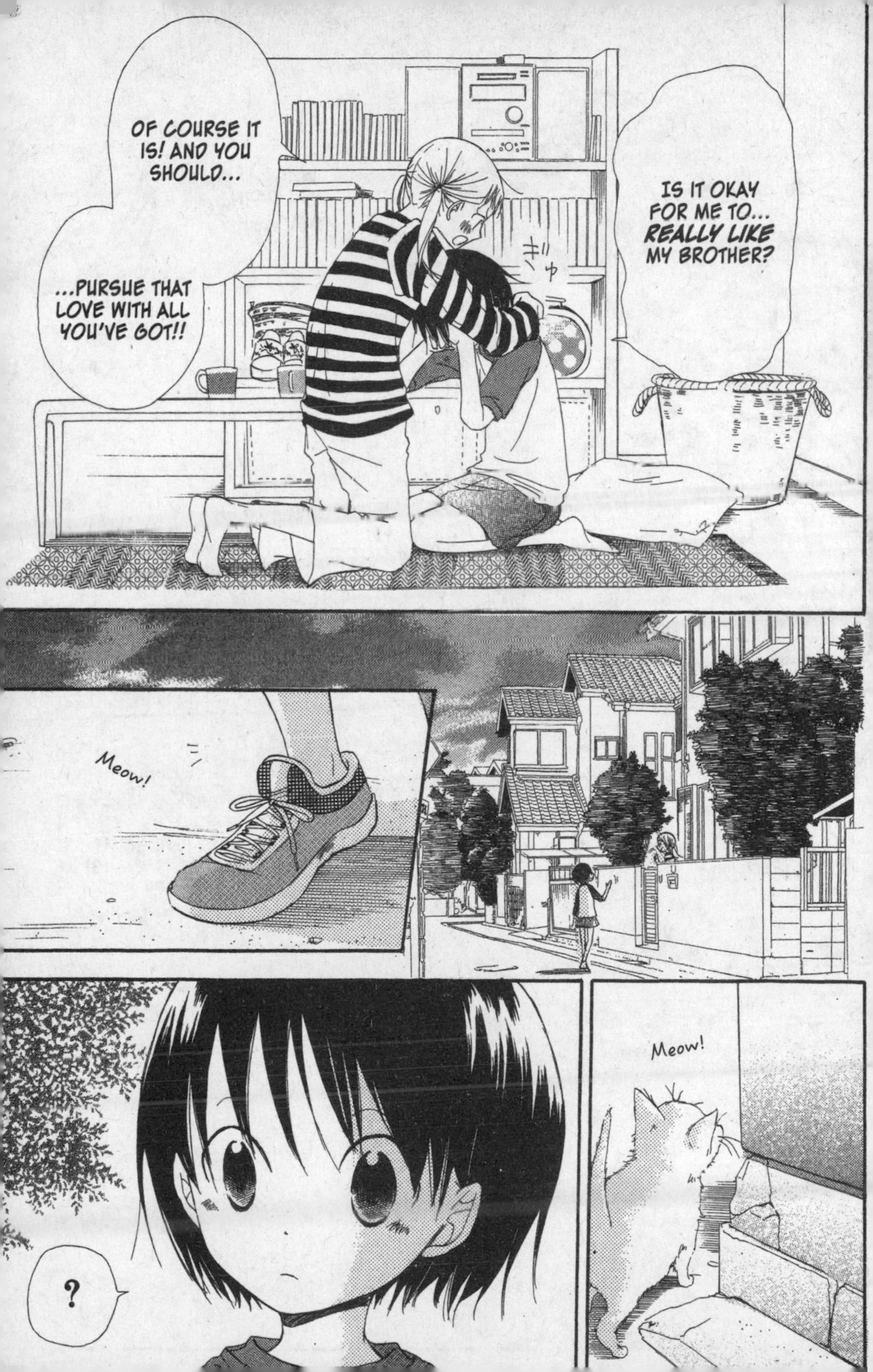
IS IT OKAY FOR ME TO... REALLY LIKE MY BROTHER?
ぎゅ
OF COURSE IT IS! AND YOU SHOULD...
...PURSUE THAT LOVE WITH ALL YOU'VE GOT!!
Meow!
Meow!
?

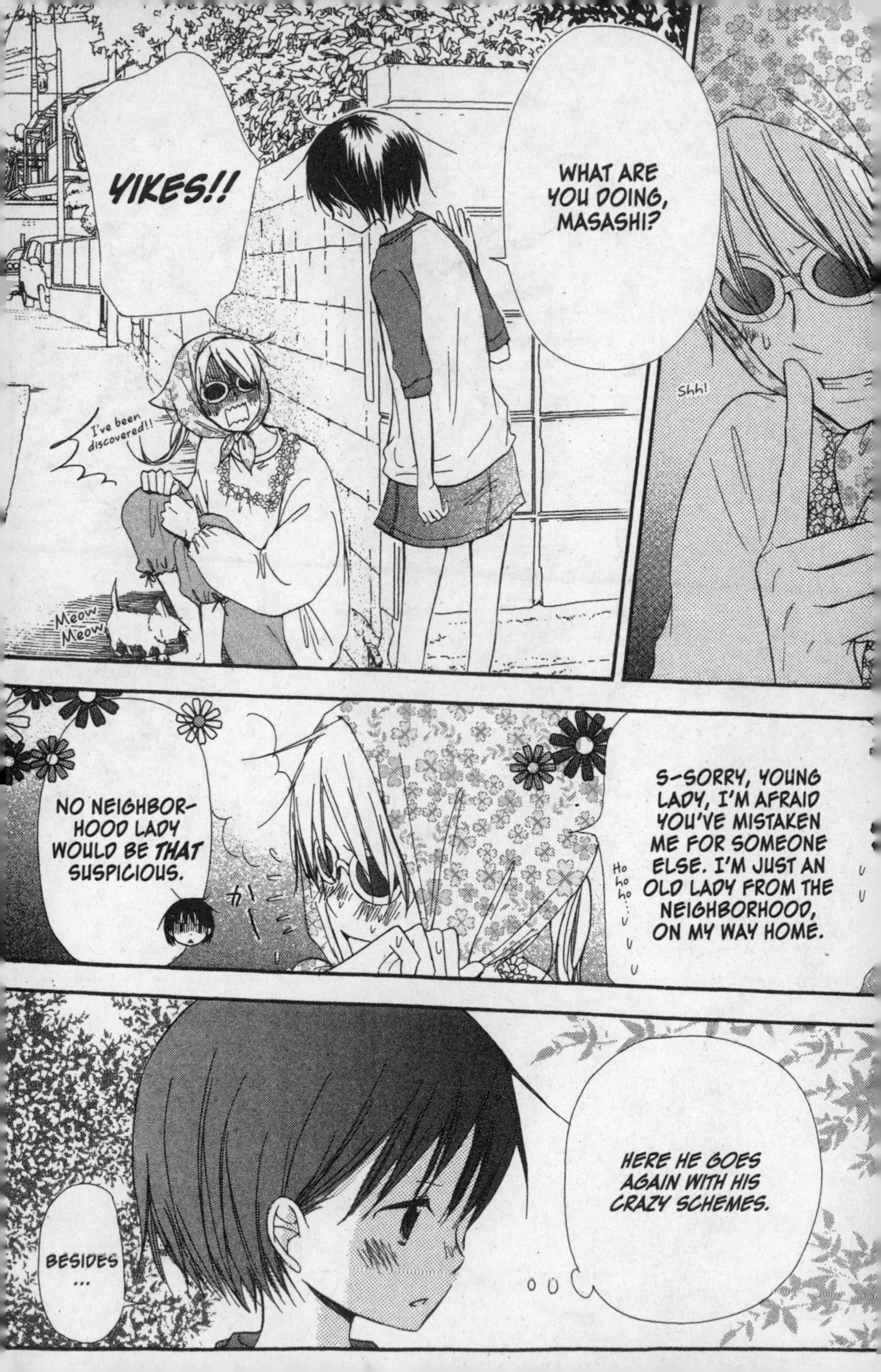

WHAT ARE YOU DOING, MASASHI?
Shh!
YIKES!!
I've been discovered!!
Meow Meow
S-SORRY, YOUNG LADY, I'M AFRAID YOU'VE MISTAKEN ME FOR SOMEONE ELSE. I'M JUST AN OLD LADY FROM THE NEIGHBORHOOD, ON MY WAY HOME.
Ho ho ho...
NO NEIGHBOR-HOOD LADY WOULD BE THAT SUSPICIOUS.
HERE HE GOES AGAIN WITH HIS CRAZY SCHEMES.
BESIDES...

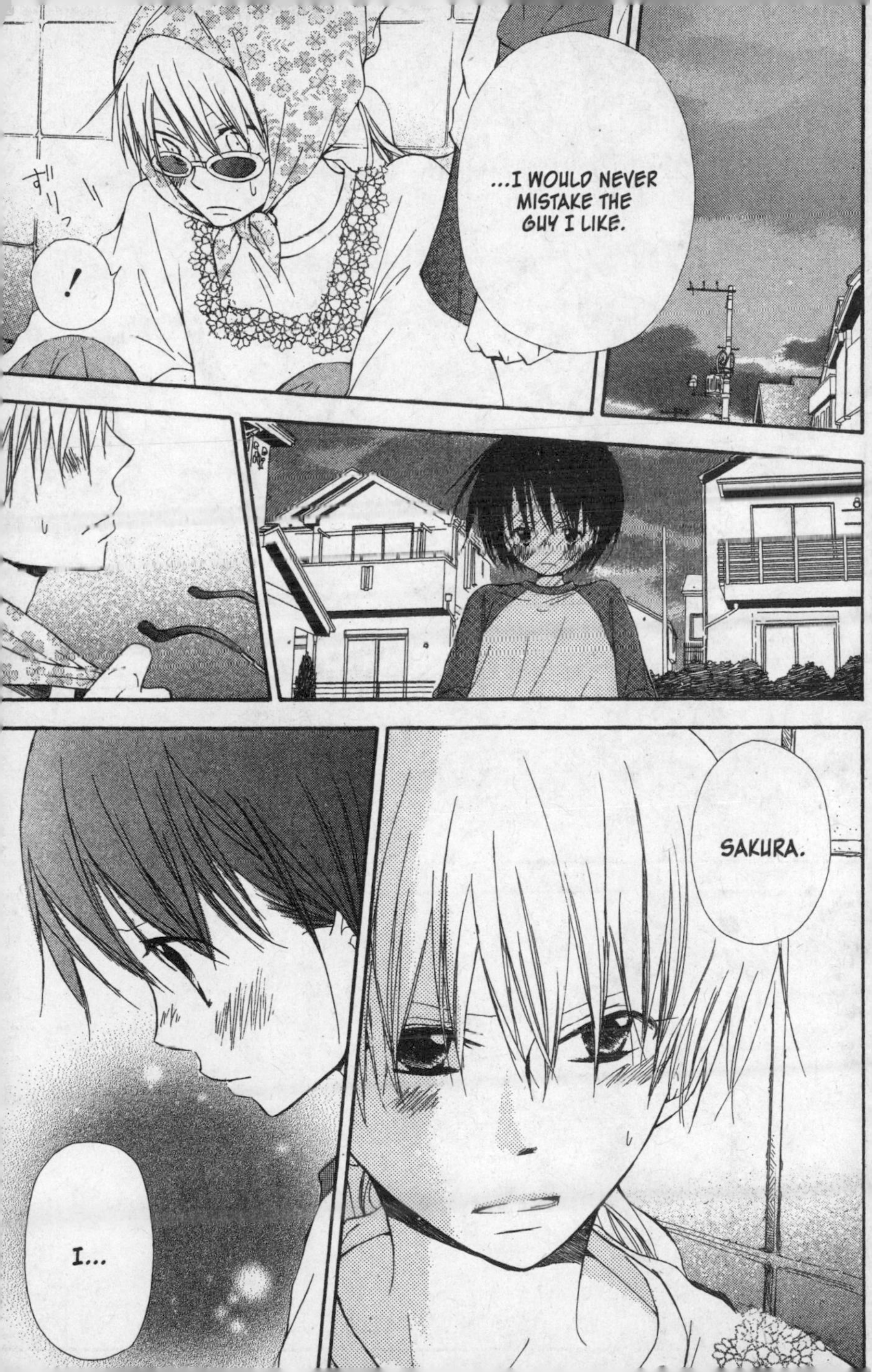
...I WOULD NEVER MISTAKE THE GUY I LIKE.
ずりっ
!
SAKURA.
I...

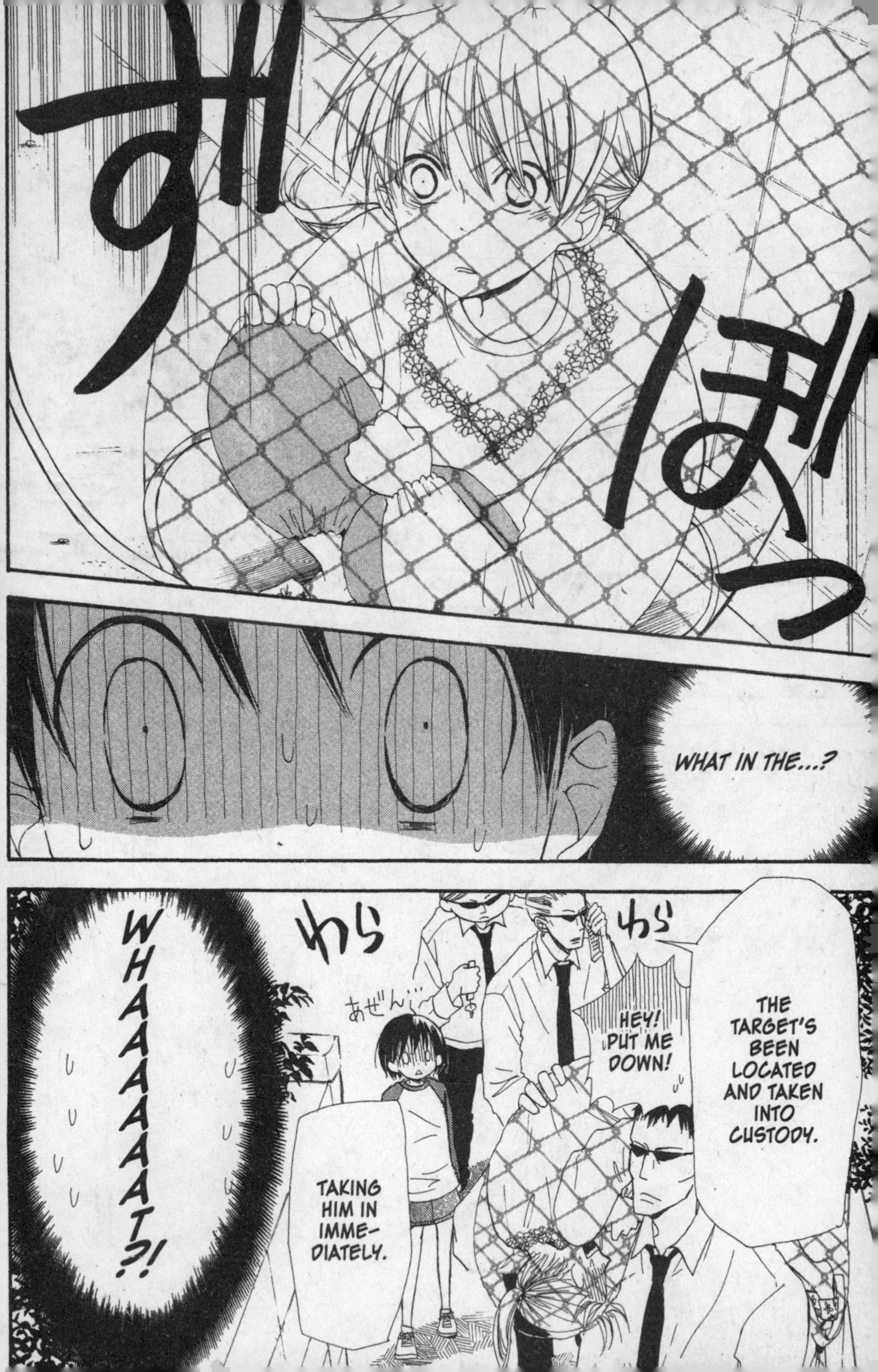
すぽっ
WHAT IN THE...?
THE TARGET'S BEEN LOCATED AND TAKEN INTO CUSTODY.
わら わら
HEY! PUT ME DOWN!
あぜん…
TAKING HIM IN IMME-DIATELY.
WHAAAAAAAT?!

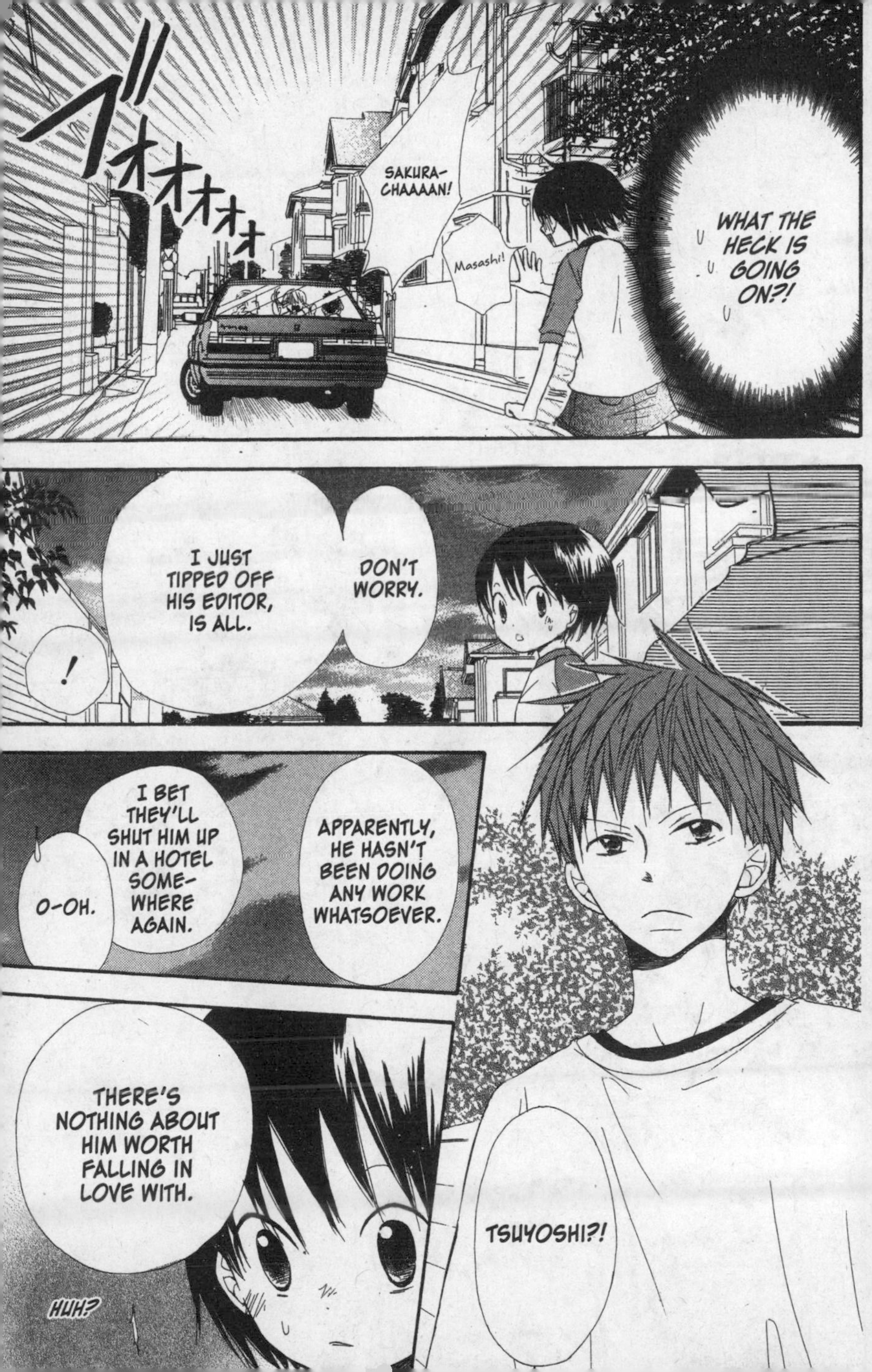
WHAT THE HECK IS GOING ON?!
SAKURA-CHAAAAN!
Masashi!
DON'T WORRY.
I JUST TIPPED OFF HIS EDITOR, IS ALL.
!
TSUYOSHI?!
APPARENTLY, HE HASN'T BEEN DOING ANY WORK WHATSOEVER.
I BET THEY'LL SHUT HIM UP IN A HOTEL SOME-WHERE AGAIN.
O-OH.
THERE'S NOTHING ABOUT HIM WORTH FALLING IN LOVE WITH.
HUH?

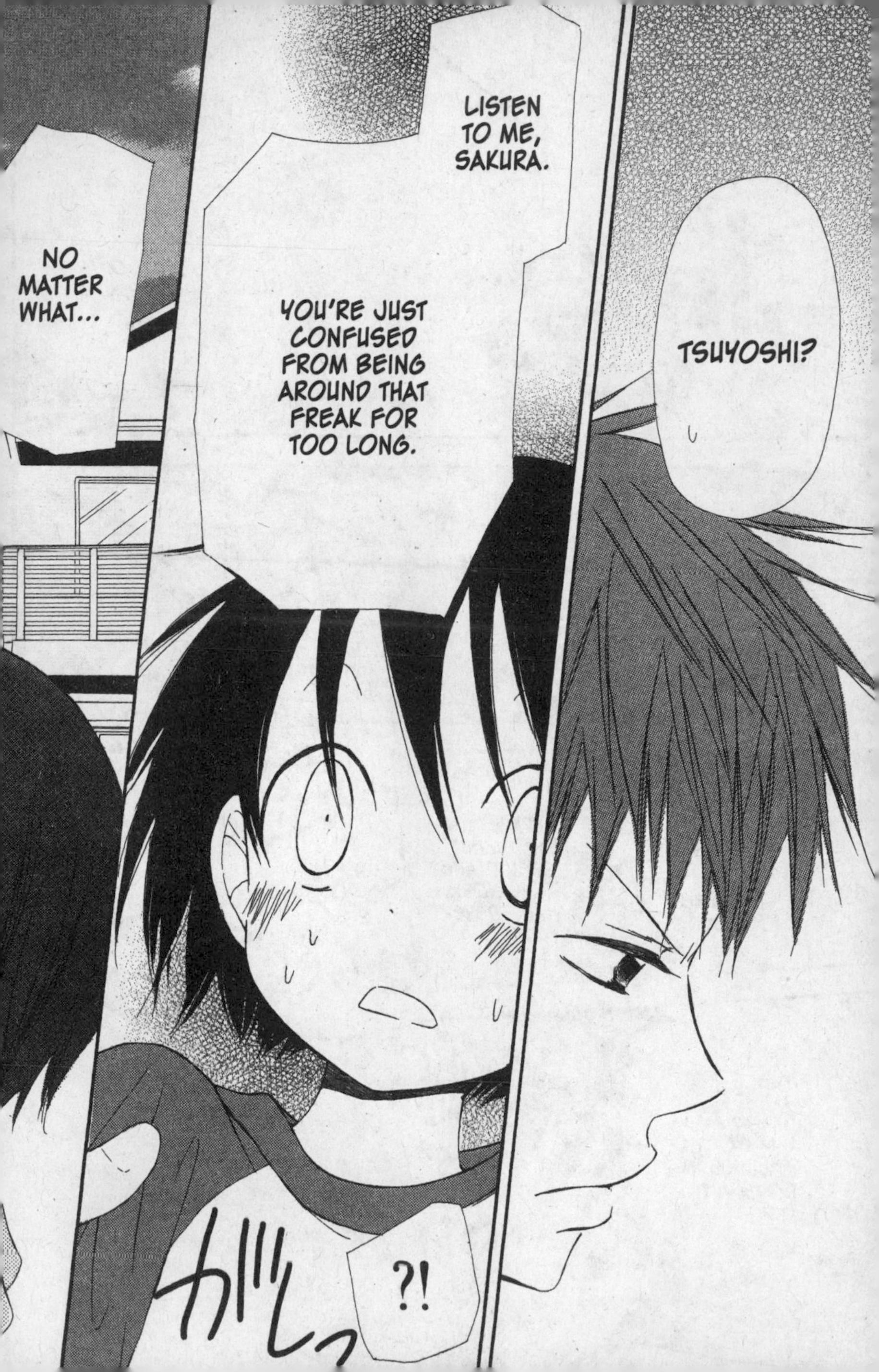
TSUYOSHI?
LISTEN TO ME, SAKURA.
YOU'RE JUST CONFUSED FROM BEING AROUND THAT FREAK FOR TOO LONG.
?!
がしっ
NO MATTER WHAT...

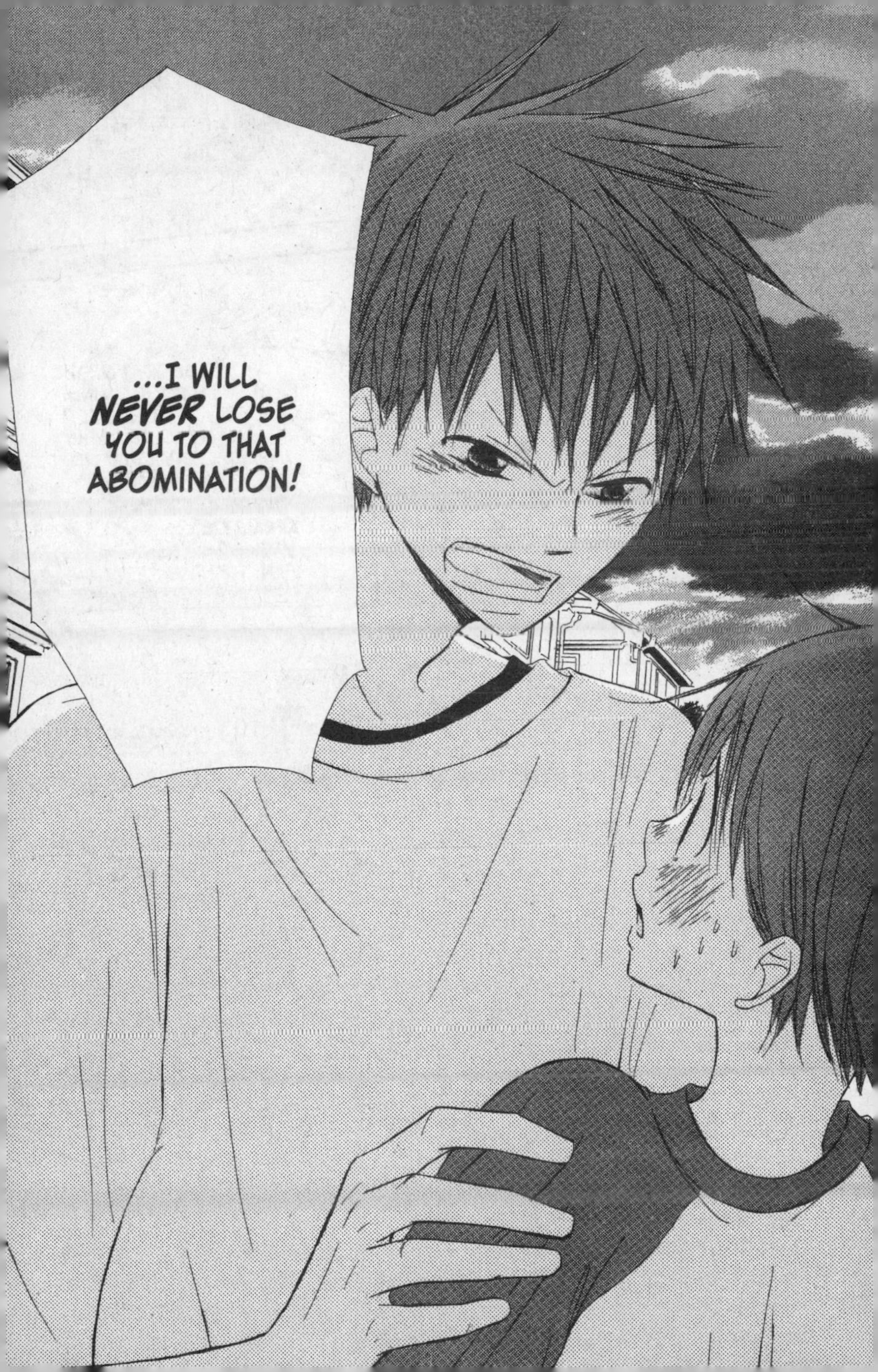
...I WILL **NEVER** LOSE YOU TO THAT ABOMINATION!

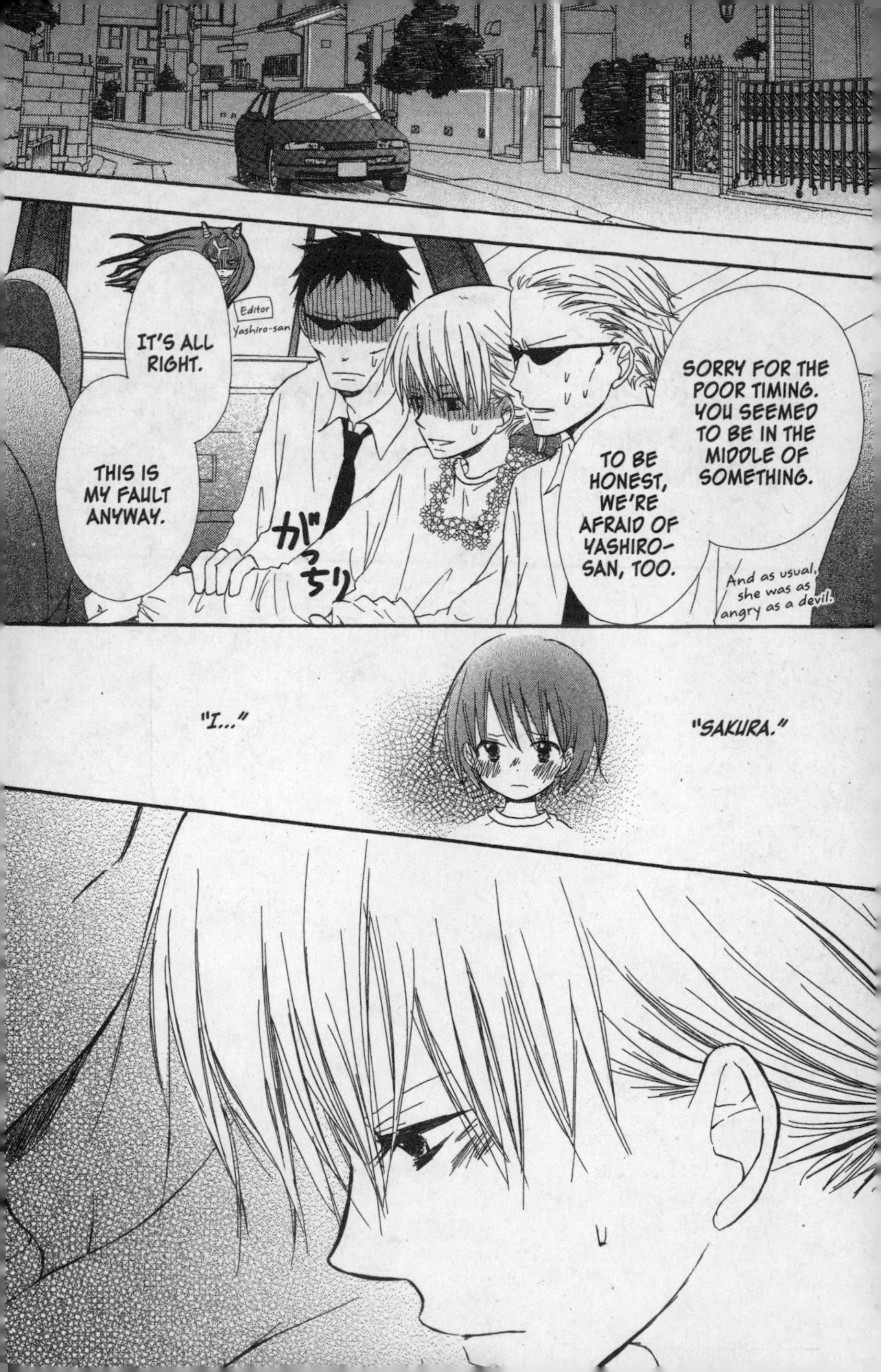
SORRY FOR THE POOR TIMING. YOU SEEMED TO BE IN THE MIDDLE OF SOMETHING.
And as usual, she was as angry as a devil.
TO BE HONEST, WE'RE AFRAID OF YASHIRO-SAN, TOO.
がっちり
Editor
Yashiro-san
IT'S ALL RIGHT.
THIS IS MY FAULT ANYWAY.
"SAKURA."
"I..."

WHAT WAS I GOING TO SAY?
SHE'S MORE PRECIOUS TO ME THAN ANYONE.
I WANT TO PROTECT HER MORE THAN ANYONE.
BUT I DON'T HAVE THE CONFIDENCE TO SAY FOR SURE...
...THAT THOSE ARE MY FEELINGS AS AN OLDER BROTHER.

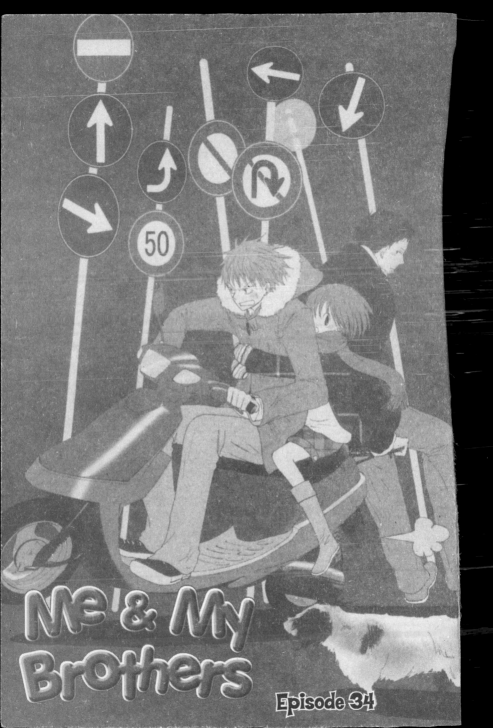

Me & My
Brothers

Episode 34

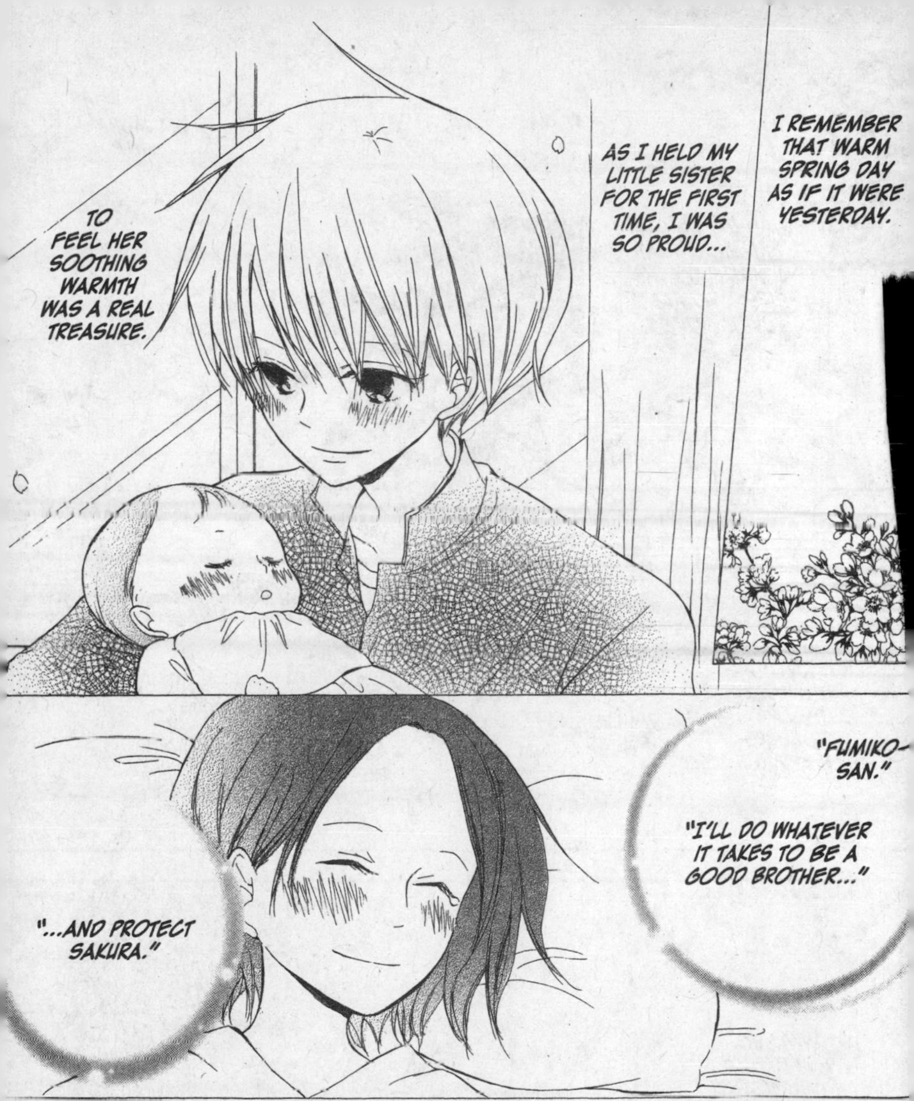
I REMEMBER THAT WARM SPRING DAY AS IF IT WERE YESTERDAY.
AS I HELD MY LITTLE SISTER FOR THE FIRST TIME, I WAS SO PROUD...
TO FEEL HER SOOTHING WARMTH WAS A REAL TREASURE.
"FUMIKO-SAN."
"I'LL DO WHATEVER IT TAKES TO BE A GOOD BROTHER..."
"...AND PROTECT SAKURA."

For those of you who would like to tell me what you think, please direct your letters here:

TOKYOPOP
5900 Wilshire Blvd., #2000
Los Angeles, CA 90036
c/o Hyun Joo Kim

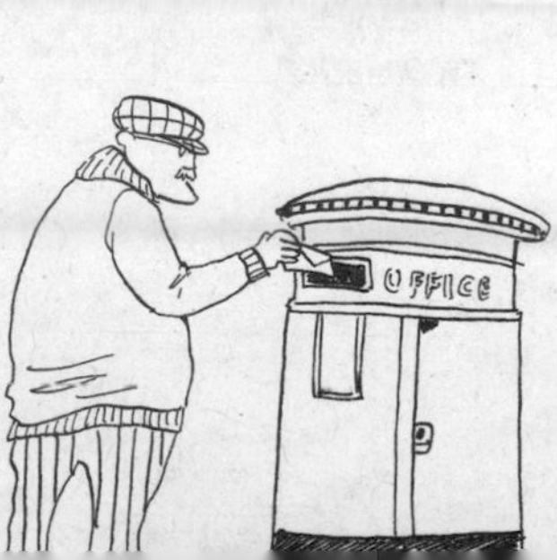

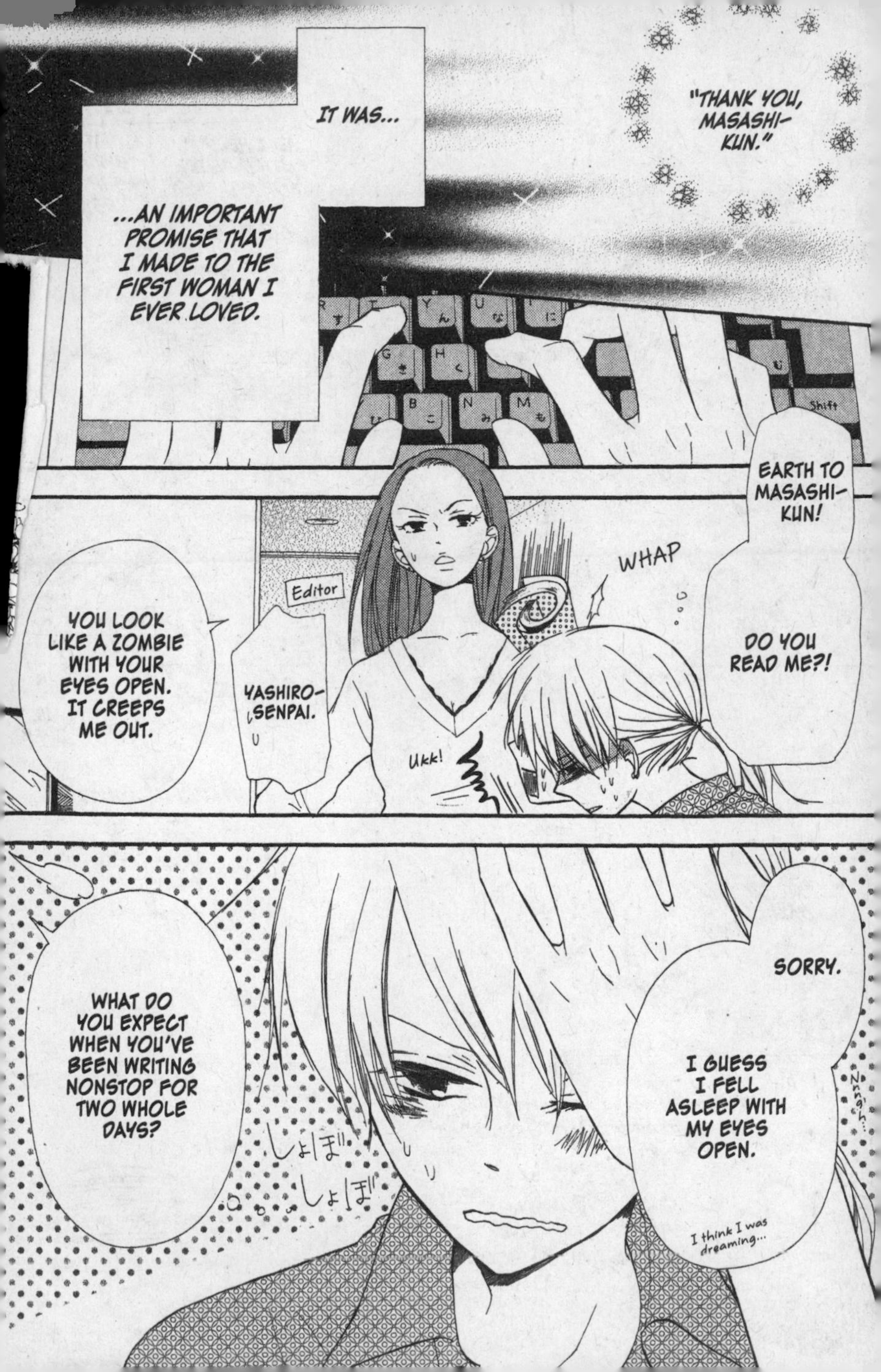
"THANK YOU, MASASHI-KUN."
IT WAS...
...AN IMPORTANT PROMISE THAT I MADE TO THE FIRST WOMAN I EVER LOVED.
EARTH TO MASASHI-KUN!
DO YOU READ ME?!
WHAP
Editor
Ukk!
YASHIRO-SENPAI.
YOU LOOK LIKE A ZOMBIE WITH YOUR EYES OPEN. IT CREEPS ME OUT.
SORRY.
I GUESS I FELL ASLEEP WITH MY EYES OPEN.
I think I was dreaming...
Nnngh...
しょぼ
しょぼ
WHAT DO YOU EXPECT WHEN YOU'VE BEEN WRITING NONSTOP FOR TWO WHOLE DAYS?

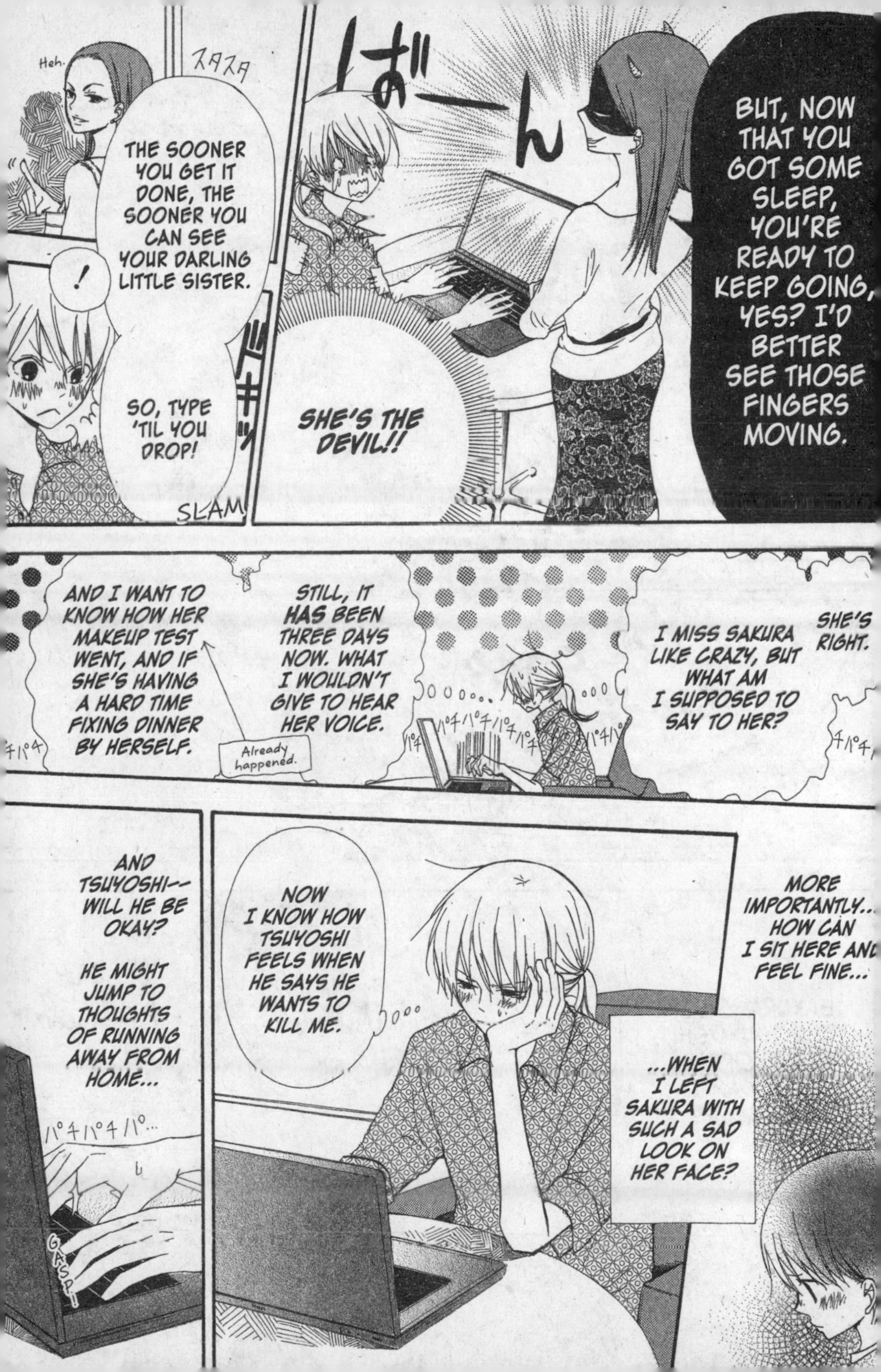
BUT, NOW THAT YOU GOT SOME SLEEP, YOU'RE READY TO KEEP GOING, YES? I'D BETTER SEE THOSE FINGERS MOVING.
ぼーーん
SHE'S THE DEVIL!!
スタスタ
Heh.
THE SOONER YOU GET IT DONE, THE SOONER YOU CAN SEE YOUR DARLING LITTLE SISTER.
!
SO, TYPE 'TIL YOU DROP!
SLAM
SHE'S RIGHT.
I MISS SAKURA LIKE CRAZY, BUT WHAT AM I SUPPOSED TO SAY TO HER?
チパチ
ooo...
パチパチパチパチ
STILL, IT HAS BEEN THREE DAYS NOW. WHAT I WOULDN'T GIVE TO HEAR HER VOICE.
AND I WANT TO KNOW HOW HER MAKEUP TEST WENT, AND IF SHE'S HAVING A HARD TIME FIXING DINNER BY HERSELF.
Already happened.
チパチ
MORE IMPORTANTLY... HOW CAN I SIT HERE AND FEEL FINE...
...WHEN I LEFT SAKURA WITH SUCH A SAD LOOK ON HER FACE?
NOW I KNOW HOW TSUYOSHI FEELS WHEN HE SAYS HE WANTS TO KILL ME.
AND TSUYOSHI-- WILL HE BE OKAY?
HE MIGHT JUMP TO THOUGHTS OF RUNNING AWAY FROM HOME...
パチパチパ…
GASP!

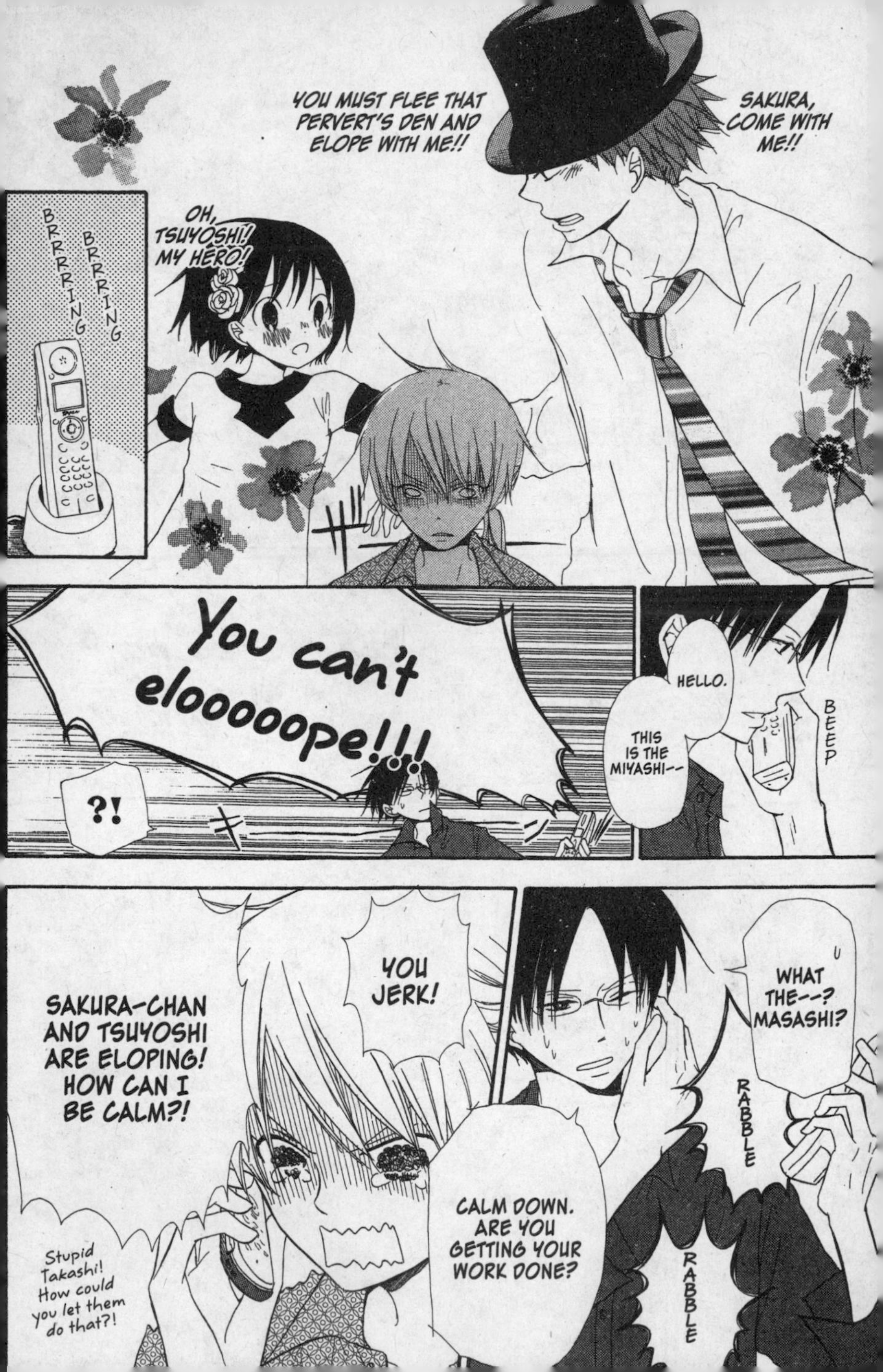
SAKURA, COME WITH ME!!
YOU MUST FLEE THAT PERVERT'S DEN AND ELOPE WITH ME!!
OH, TSUYOSHI! MY HERO!
BRRRING BRRRING
BEEP
HELLO.
THIS IS THE MIYASHI--
You can't eloooooope!!!
?!
WHAT THE--? MASASHI?
RABBLE
YOU JERK!
SAKURA-CHAN AND TSUYOSHI ARE ELOPING! HOW CAN I BE CALM?!
RABBLE
CALM DOWN. ARE YOU GETTING YOUR WORK DONE?
Stupid Takashi! How could you let them do that?!

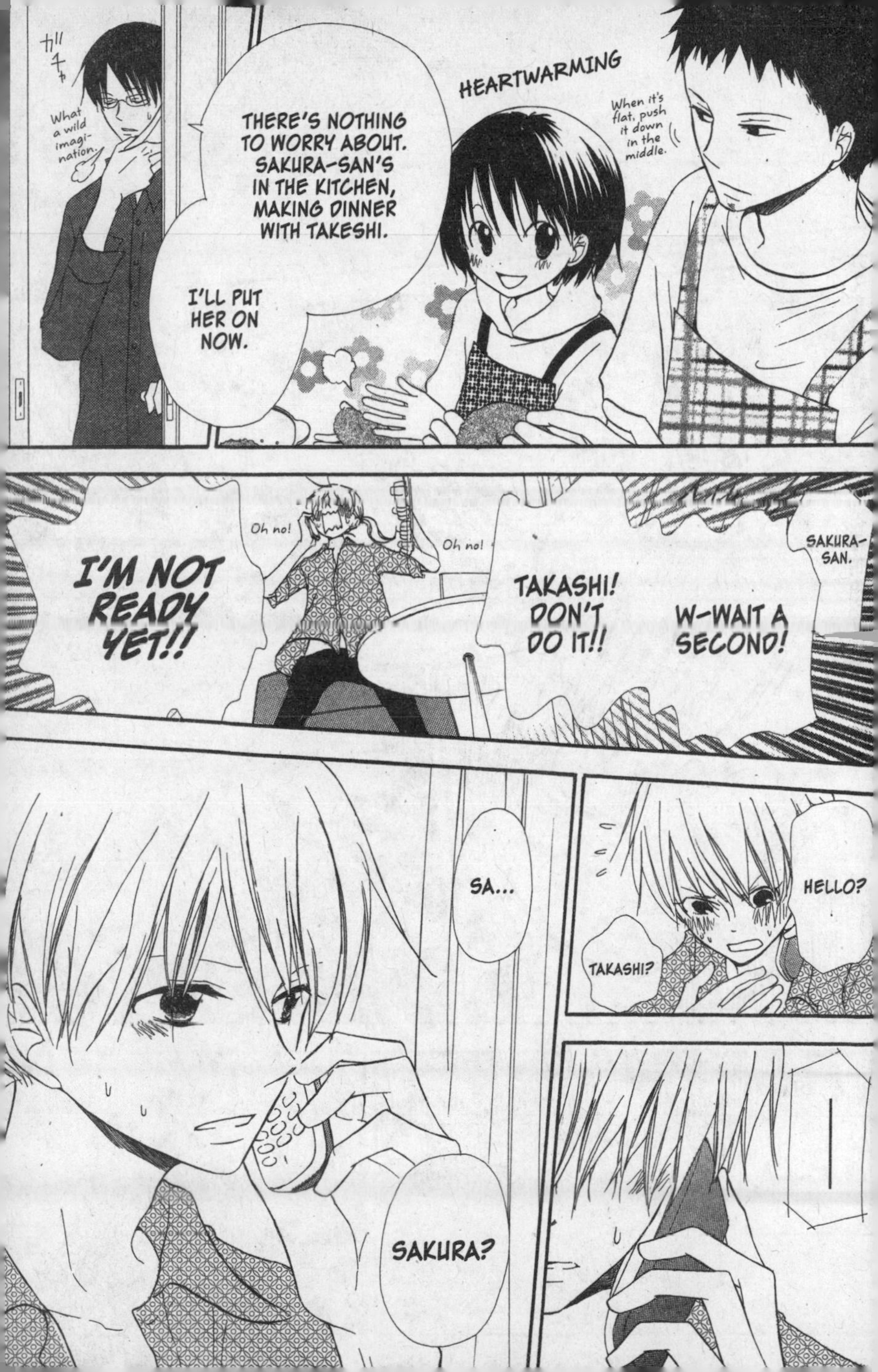
HEARTWARMING
When it's flat, push it down in the middle.
THERE'S NOTHING TO WORRY ABOUT. SAKURA-SAN'S IN THE KITCHEN, MAKING DINNER WITH TAKESHI.
I'LL PUT HER ON NOW.
ガチャ
What a wild imagination.
SAKURA-SAN.
W-WAIT A SECOND!
TAKASHI! DON'T DO IT!!
Oh no!
Oh no!
I'M NOT READY YET!!
HELLO?
TAKASHI?
SA...
SAKURA?

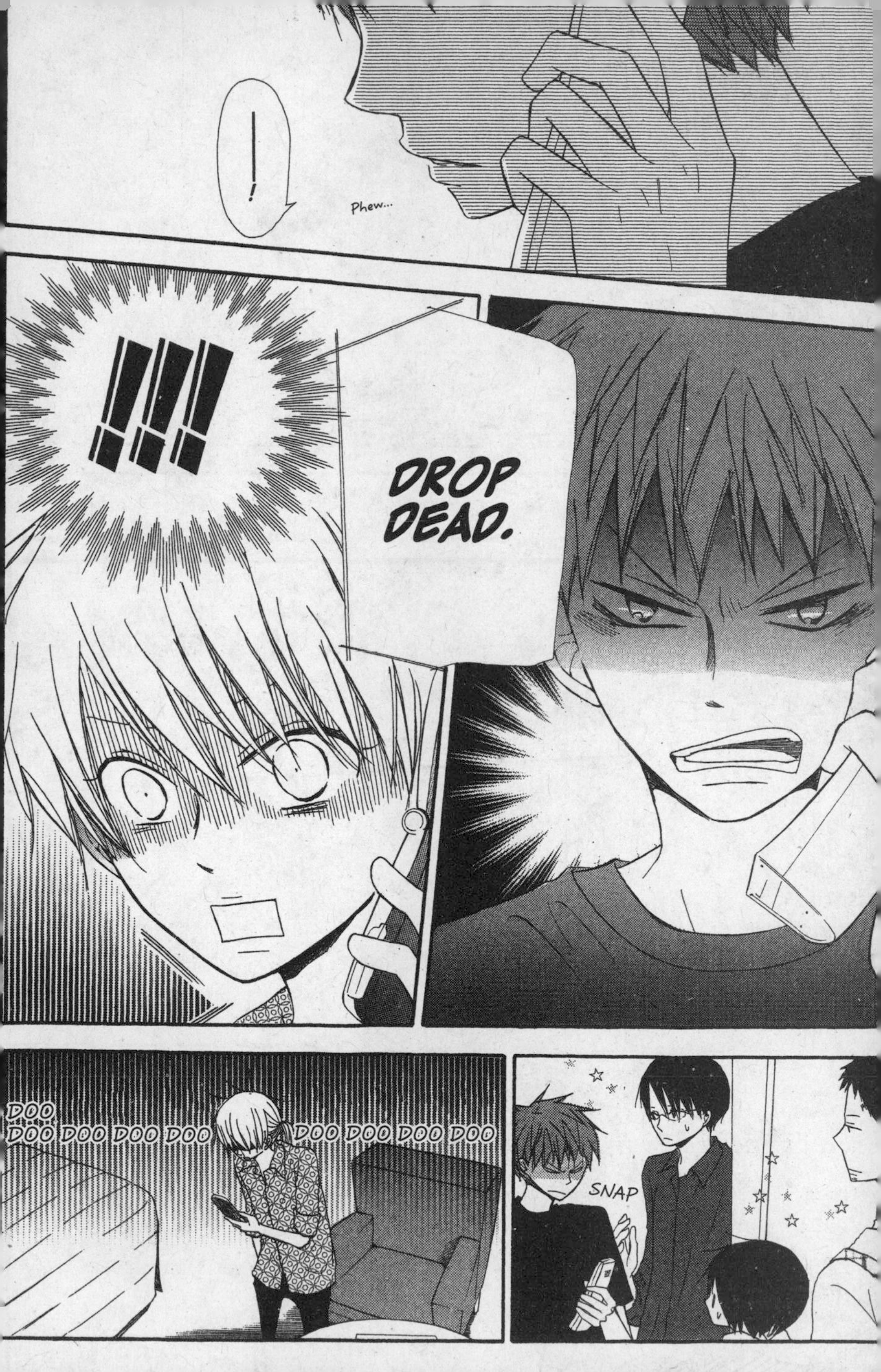
Phew...
!
DROP DEAD.
!!!
SNAP
DOO DOO DOO DOO
DOO
DOO DOO DOO DOO

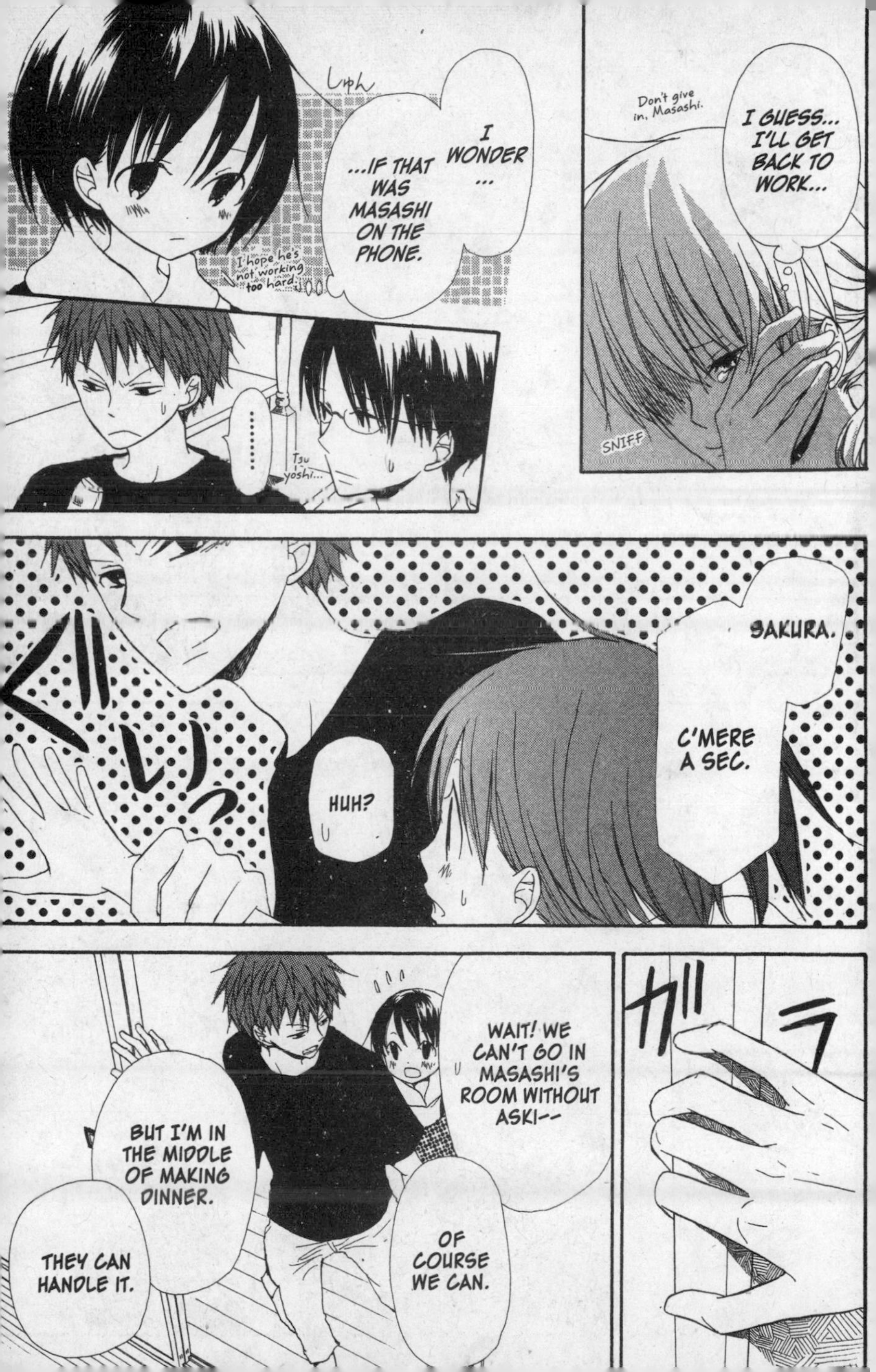
Don't give in, Masashi.
I GUESS... I'LL GET BACK TO WORK...
SNIFF
しゅん
I WONDER...
...IF THAT WAS MASASHI ON THE PHONE.
I hope he's not working too hard.
......
Tsuyoshi...
SAKURA.
C'MERE A SEC.
HUH?
くいっ
ガラ
WAIT! WE CAN'T GO IN MASASHI'S ROOM WITHOUT ASKI--
OF COURSE WE CAN.
BUT I'M IN THE MIDDLE OF MAKING DINNER.
THEY CAN HANDLE IT.

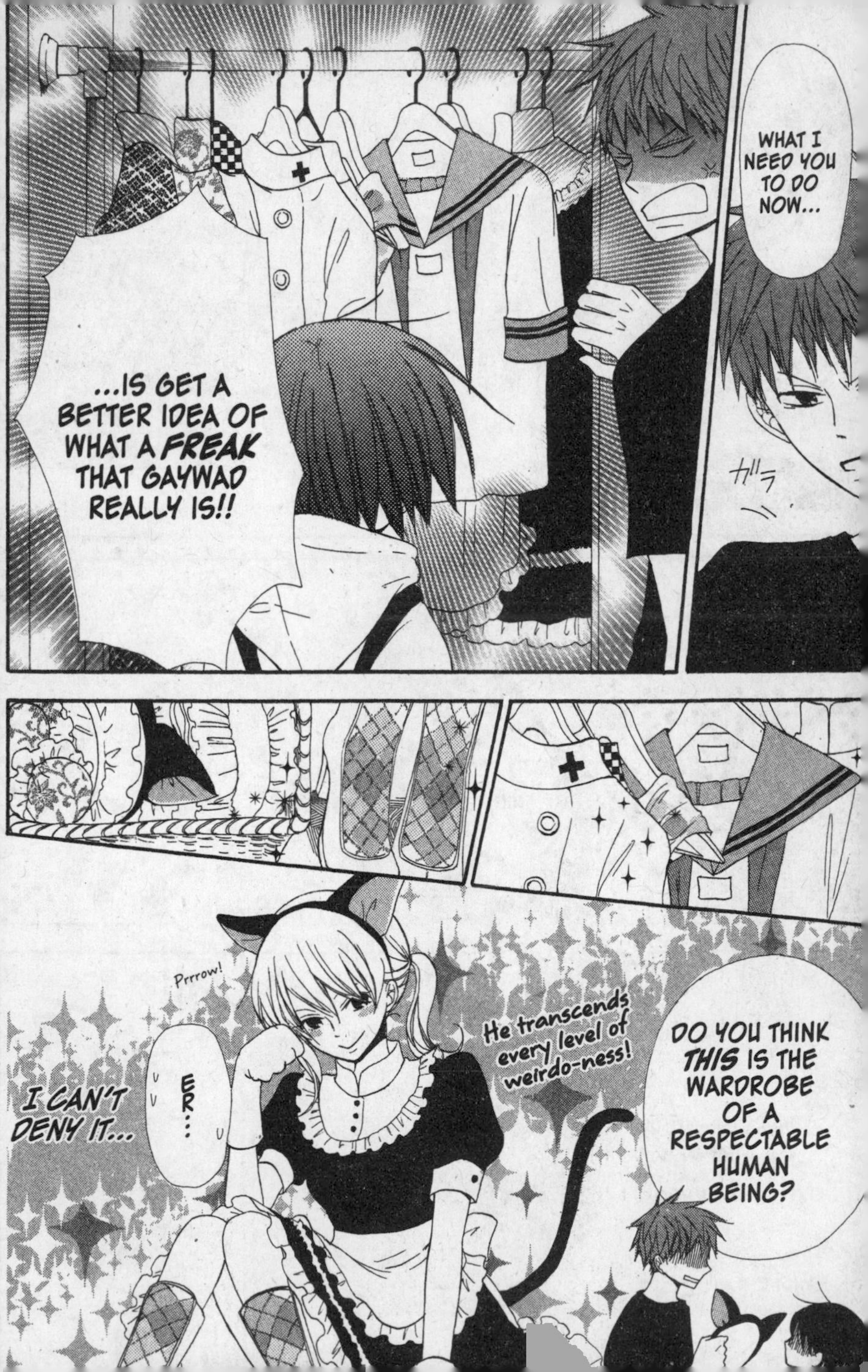
WHAT I NEED YOU TO DO NOW...
ガラ
...IS GET A BETTER IDEA OF WHAT A *FREAK* THAT GAYWAD REALLY IS!!
DO YOU THINK *THIS* IS THE WARDROBE OF A RESPECTABLE HUMAN BEING?
He transcends every level of weirdo-ness!
Prrrow!
ER...
I CAN'T DENY IT...

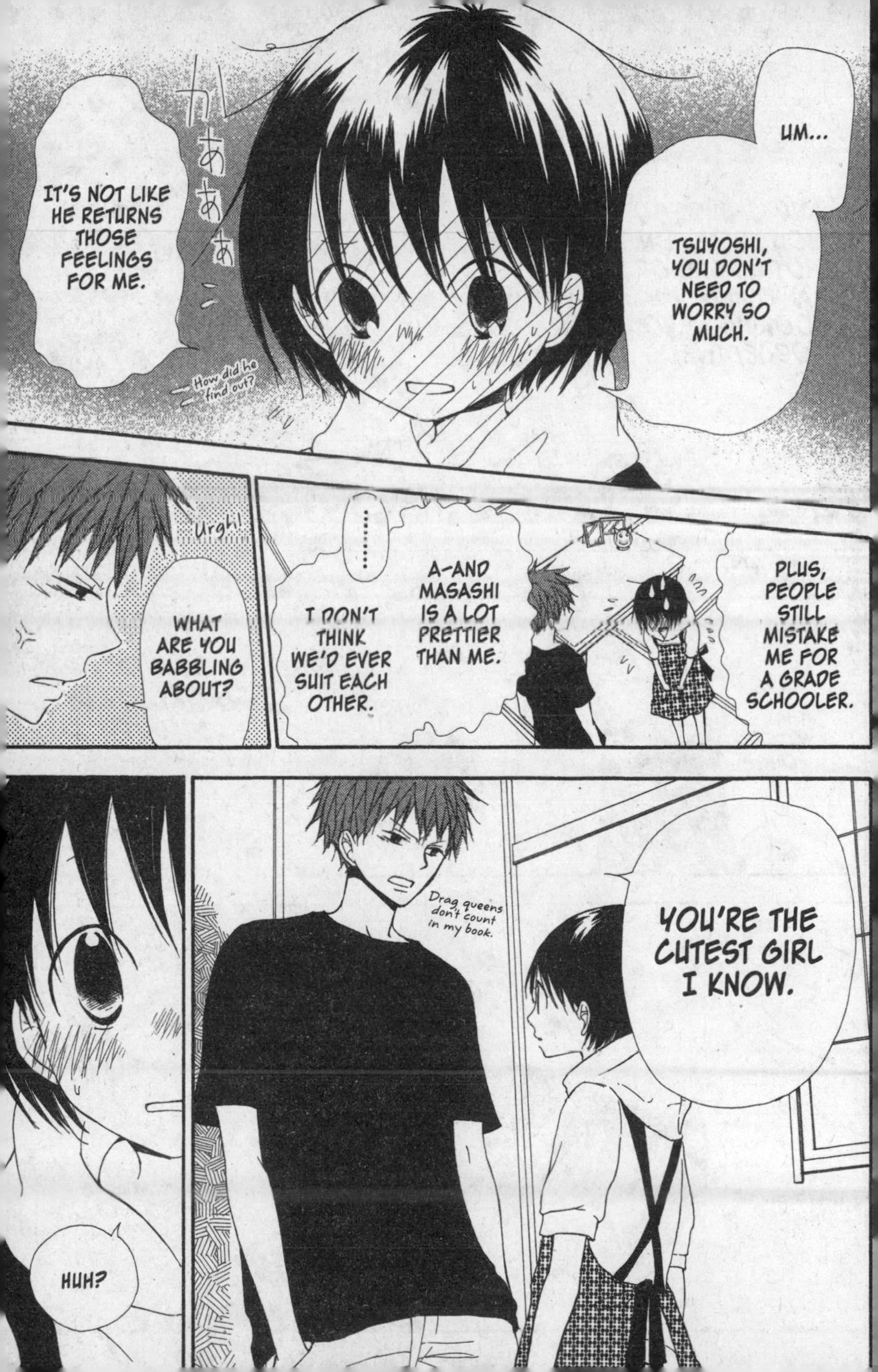
UM...
TSUYOSHI, YOU DON'T NEED TO WORRY SO MUCH.
かあああ
IT'S NOT LIKE HE RETURNS THOSE FEELINGS FOR ME.
How did he find out?
PLUS, PEOPLE STILL MISTAKE ME FOR A GRADE SCHOOLER.
A-AND MASASHI IS A LOT PRETTIER THAN ME.
I DON'T THINK WE'D EVER SUIT EACH OTHER.
......
Urgh!
WHAT ARE YOU BABBLING ABOUT?
YOU'RE THE CUTEST GIRL I KNOW.
Drag queens don't count in my book.
HUH?

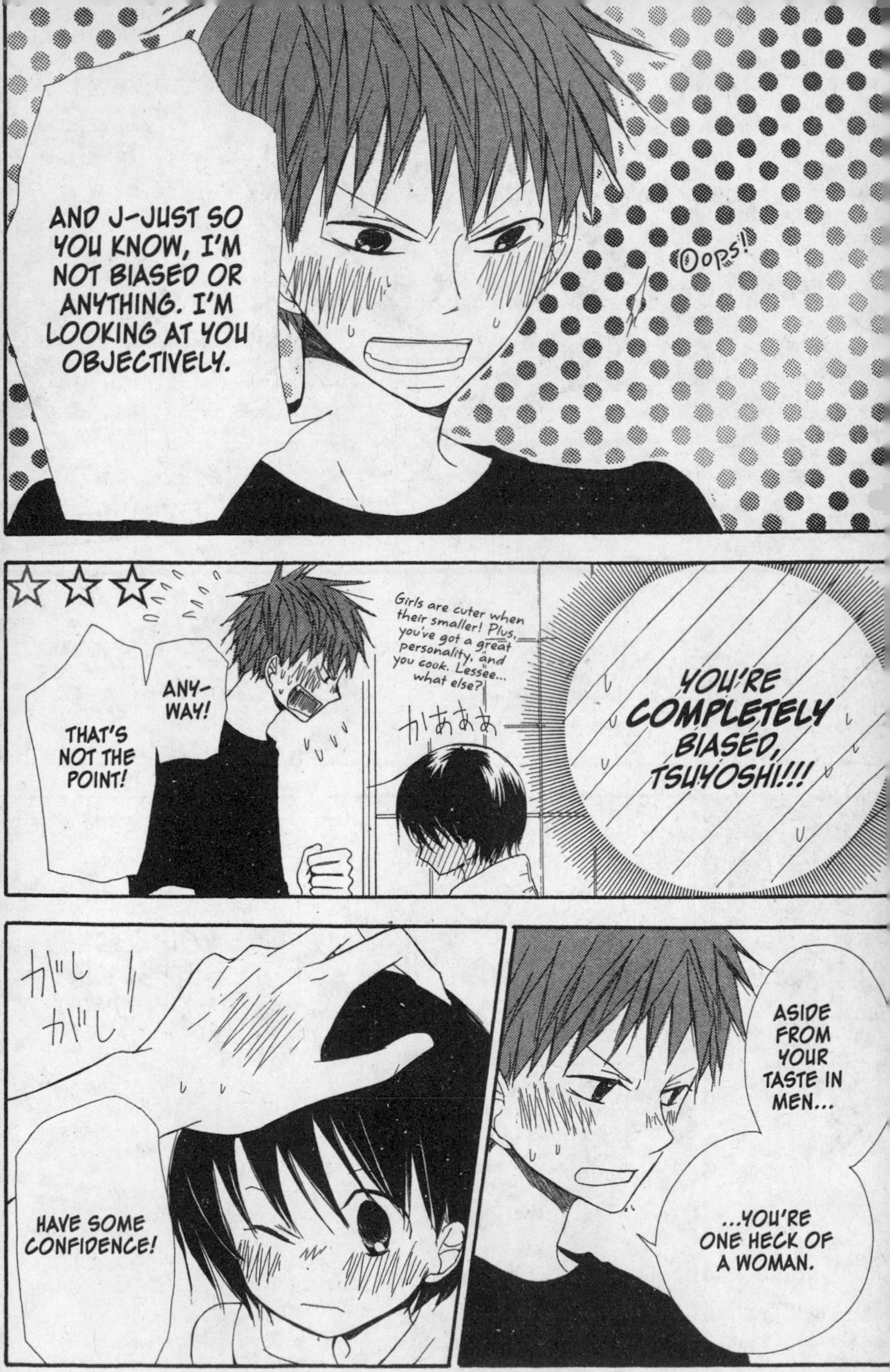
Oops!
AND J-JUST SO YOU KNOW, I'M NOT BIASED OR ANYTHING. I'M LOOKING AT YOU OBJECTIVELY.
YOU'RE COMPLETELY BIASED, TSUYOSHI!!!
Girls are cuter when their smaller! Plus, you've got a great personality, and you cook. Lessee... what else?
ANY-WAY!
THAT'S NOT THE POINT!
かあああ
ASIDE FROM YOUR TASTE IN MEN...
...YOU'RE ONE HECK OF A WOMAN.
ガしガし
HAVE SOME CONFIDENCE!

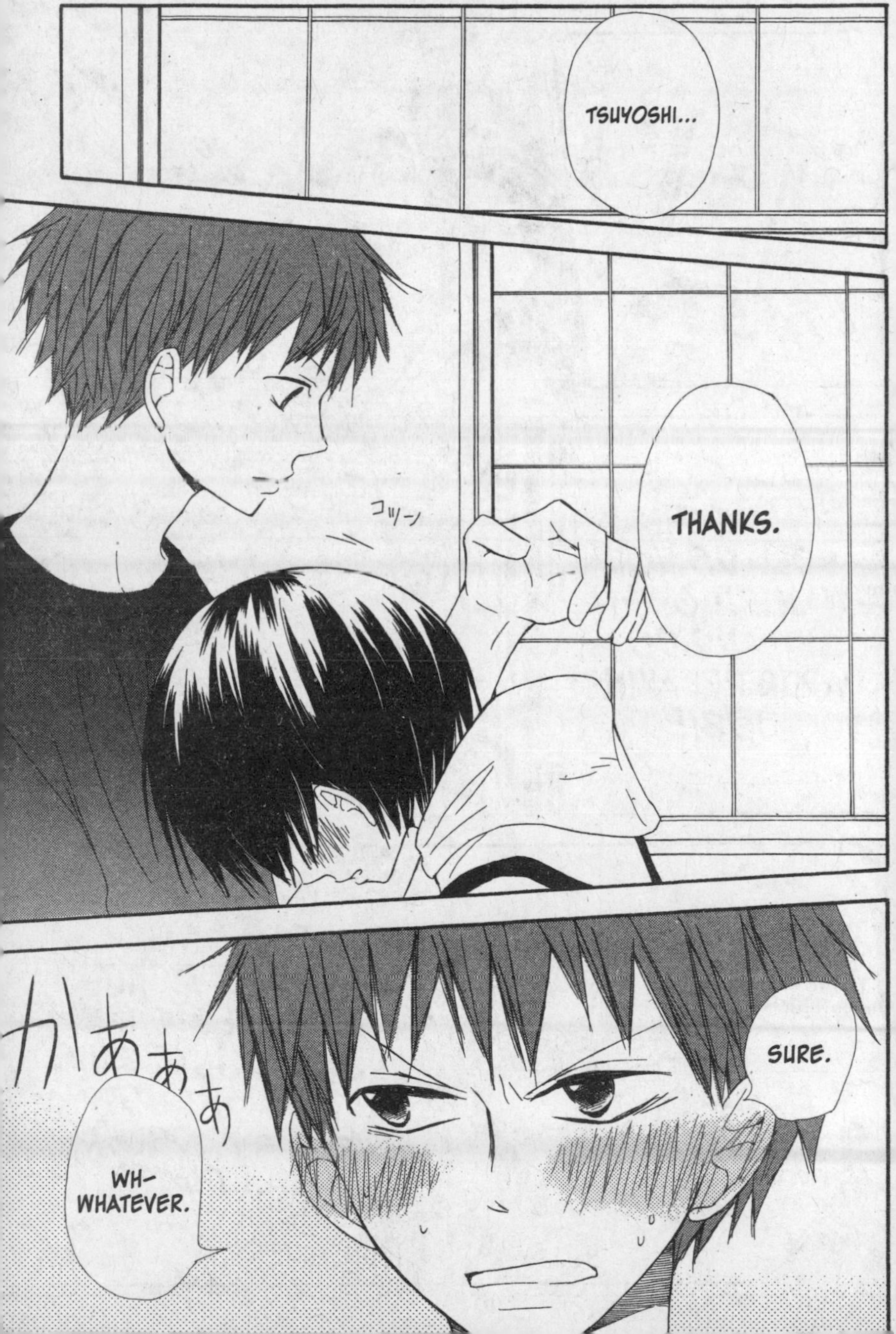
TSUYOSHI...
コツーン
THANKS.
SURE.
かあああ
WH-
WHATEVER.

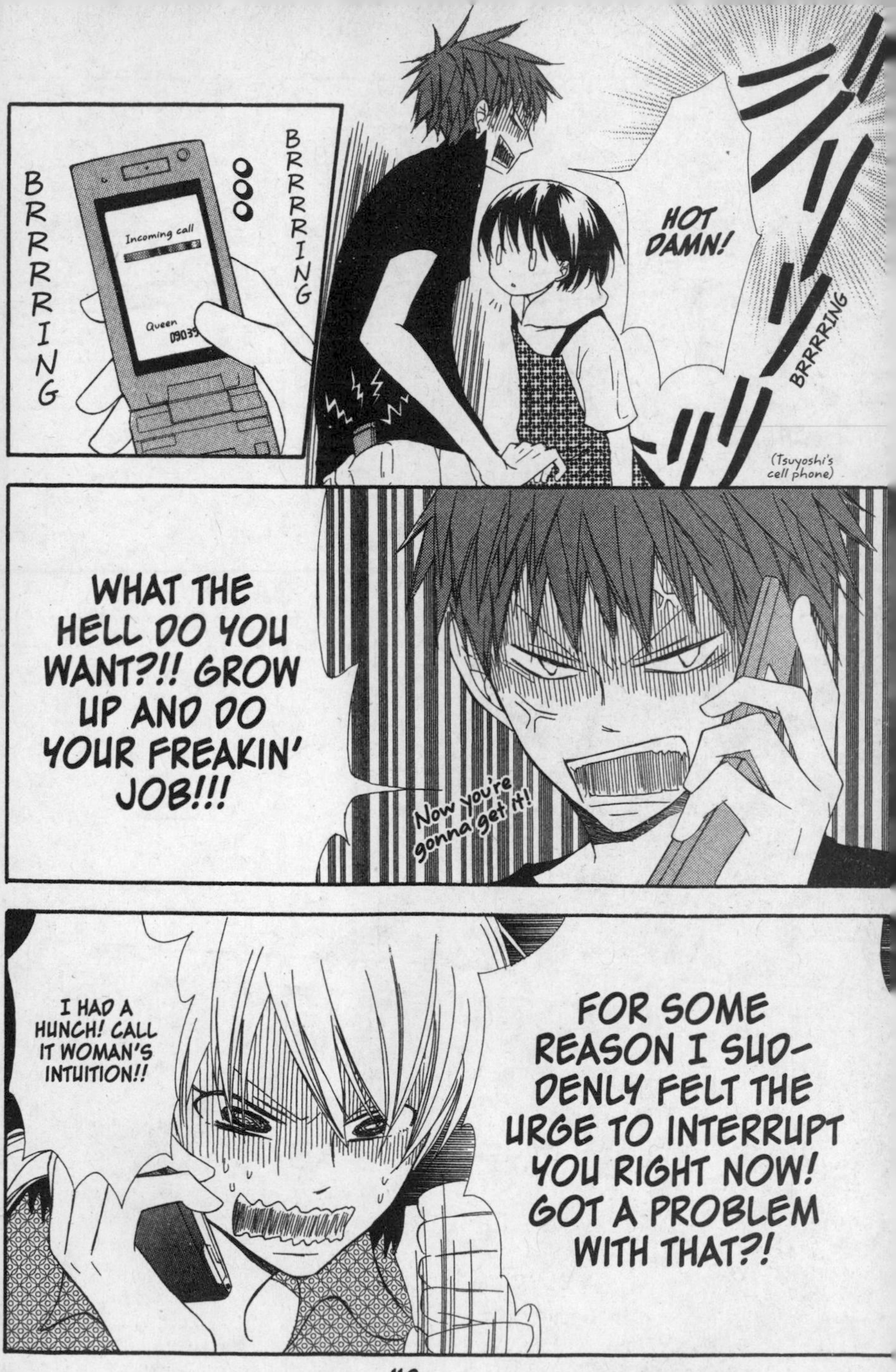
BRRRRING
HOT DAMN!
(Tsuyoshi's cell phone)
BRRRRING
Incoming call
Queen
BRRRRING
WHAT THE HELL DO YOU WANT?!! GROW UP AND DO YOUR FREAKIN' JOB!!!
Now you're gonna get it!
FOR SOME REASON I SUDDENLY FELT THE URGE TO INTERRUPT YOU RIGHT NOW! GOT A PROBLEM WITH THAT?!
I HAD A HUNCH! CALL IT WOMAN'S INTUITION!!

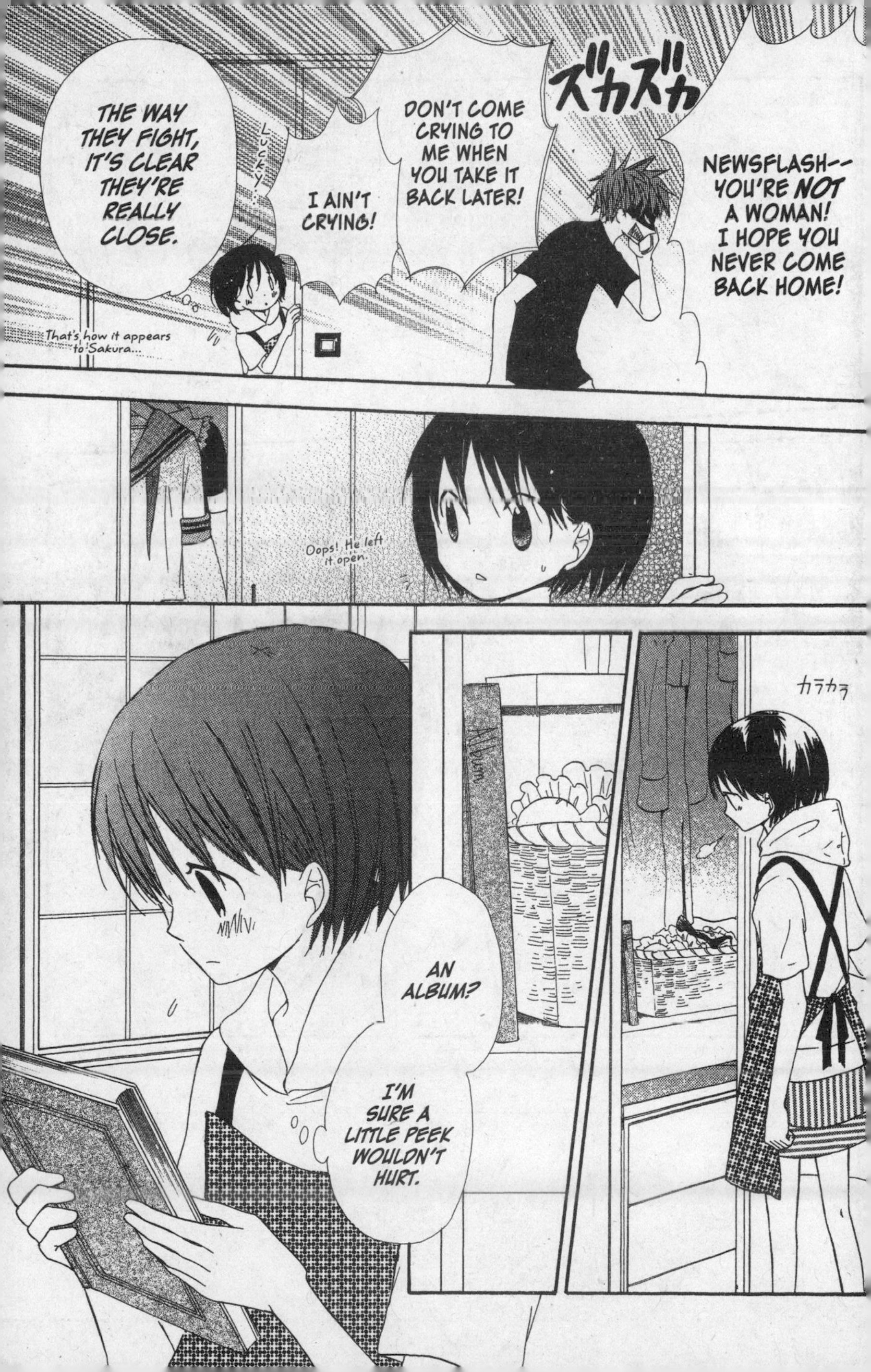

NEWSFLASH-- YOU'RE NOT A WOMAN! I HOPE YOU NEVER COME BACK HOME!
ズカズカ
DON'T COME CRYING TO ME WHEN YOU TAKE IT BACK LATER!
I AIN'T CRYING!
Lucky...
THE WAY THEY FIGHT, IT'S CLEAR THEY'RE REALLY CLOSE.
That's how it appears to Sakura...
Oops! He left it open.
カラカラ
Album
AN ALBUM?
I'M SURE A LITTLE PEEK WOULDN'T HURT.

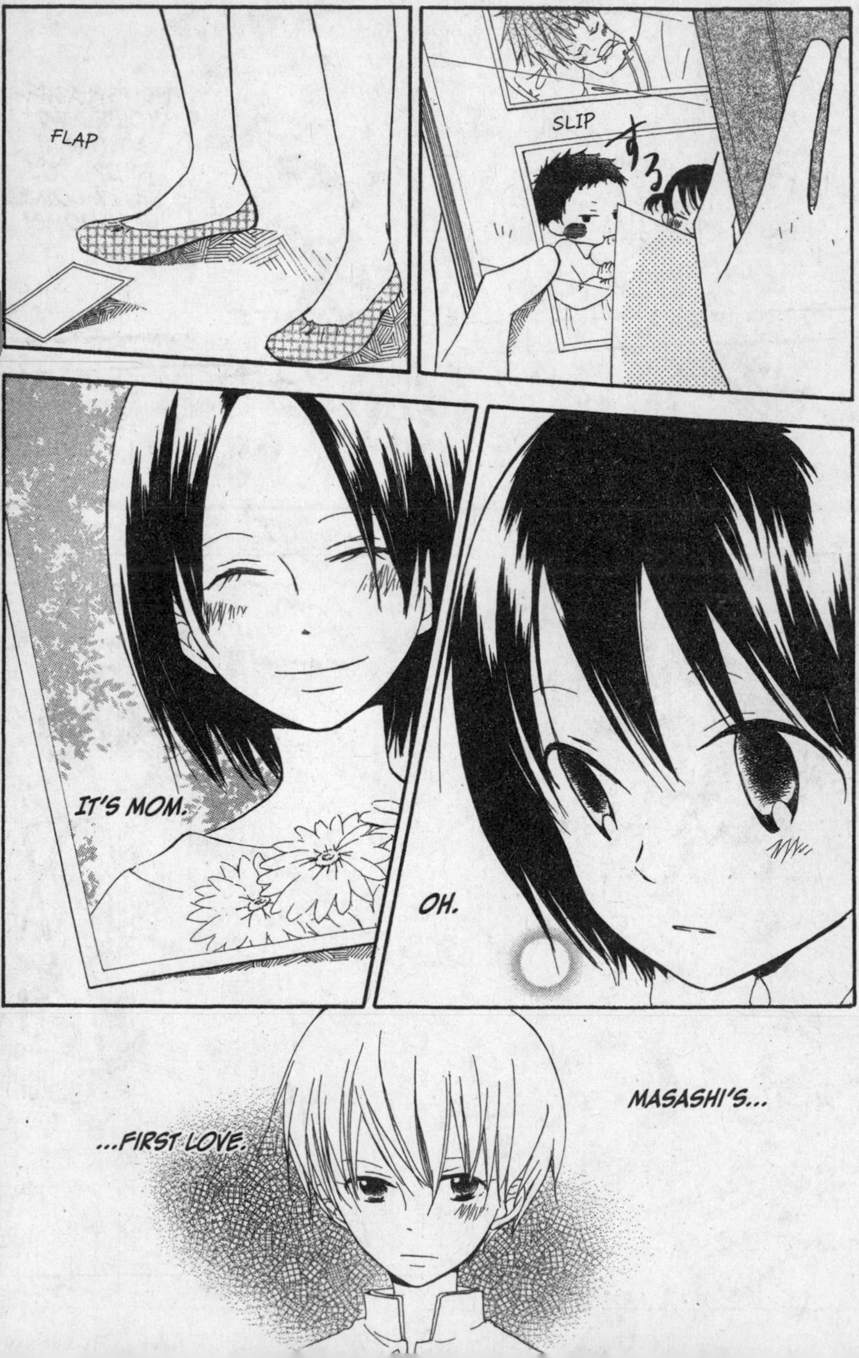
SLIP
する
FLAP
OH.
IT'S MOM.
MASASHI'S...
...FIRST LOVE.

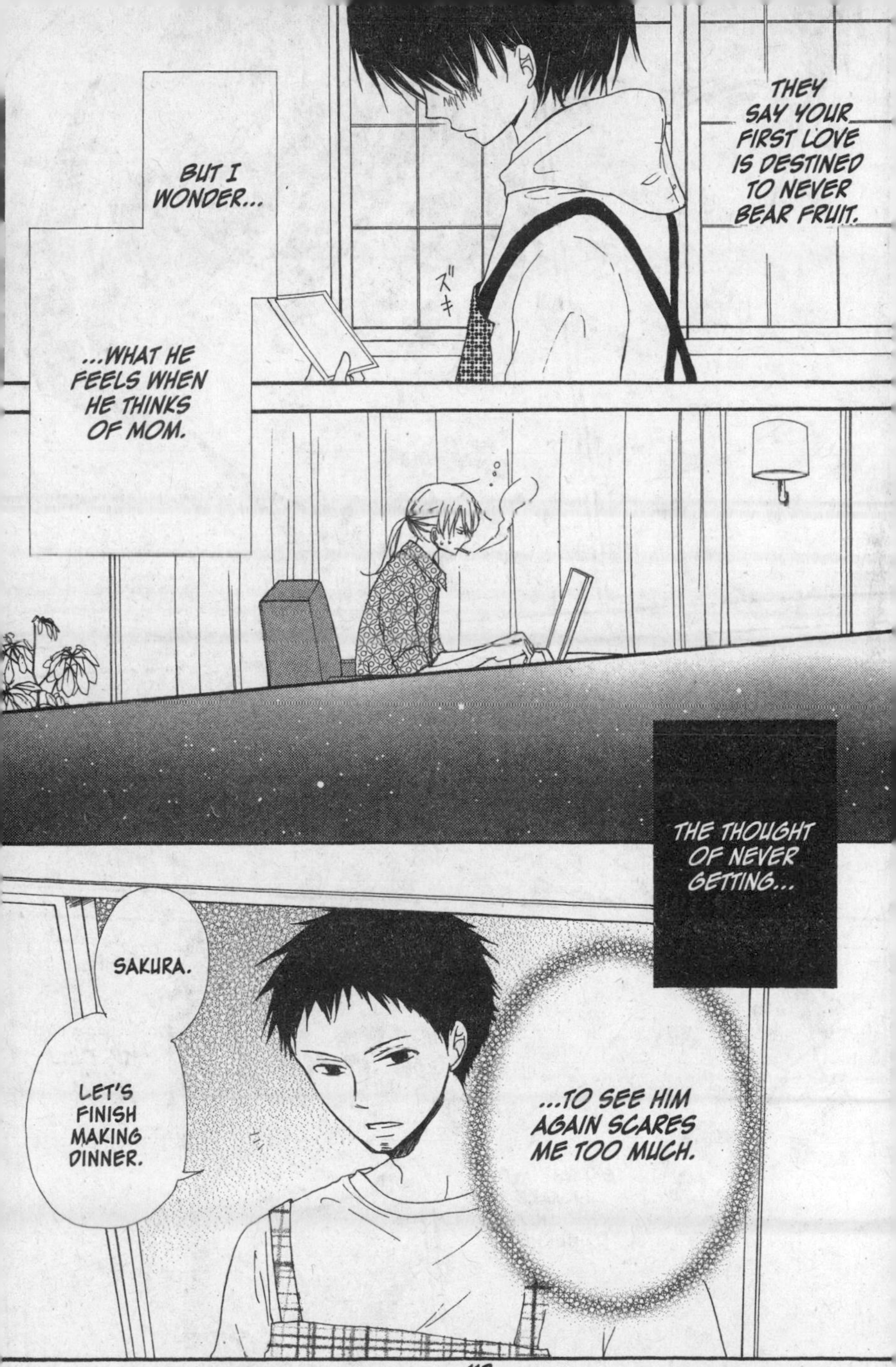
THEY SAY YOUR FIRST LOVE IS DESTINED TO NEVER BEAR FRUIT.
ズキ
BUT I WONDER...
...WHAT HE FEELS WHEN HE THINKS OF MOM.
THE THOUGHT OF NEVER GETTING...
...TO SEE HIM AGAIN SCARES ME TOO MUCH.
SAKURA.
LET'S FINISH MAKING DINNER.

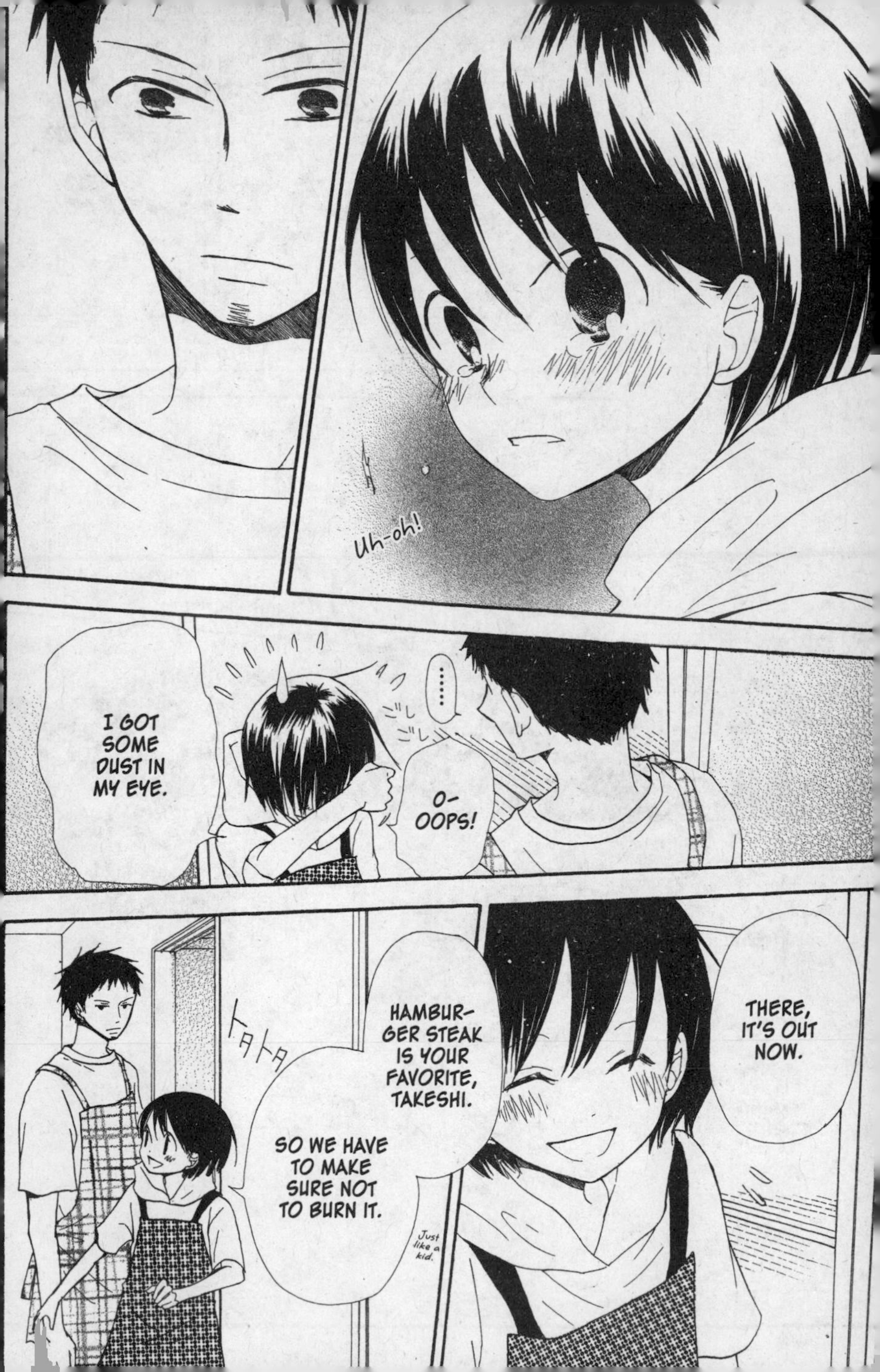
Uh-oh!
......
ゴレ
ゴレ
O-OOPS!
I GOT SOME DUST IN MY EYE.
THERE, IT'S OUT NOW.
HAMBURGER STEAK IS YOUR FAVORITE, TAKESHI.
SO WE HAVE TO MAKE SURE NOT TO BURN IT.
Just like a kid.
トタトタ

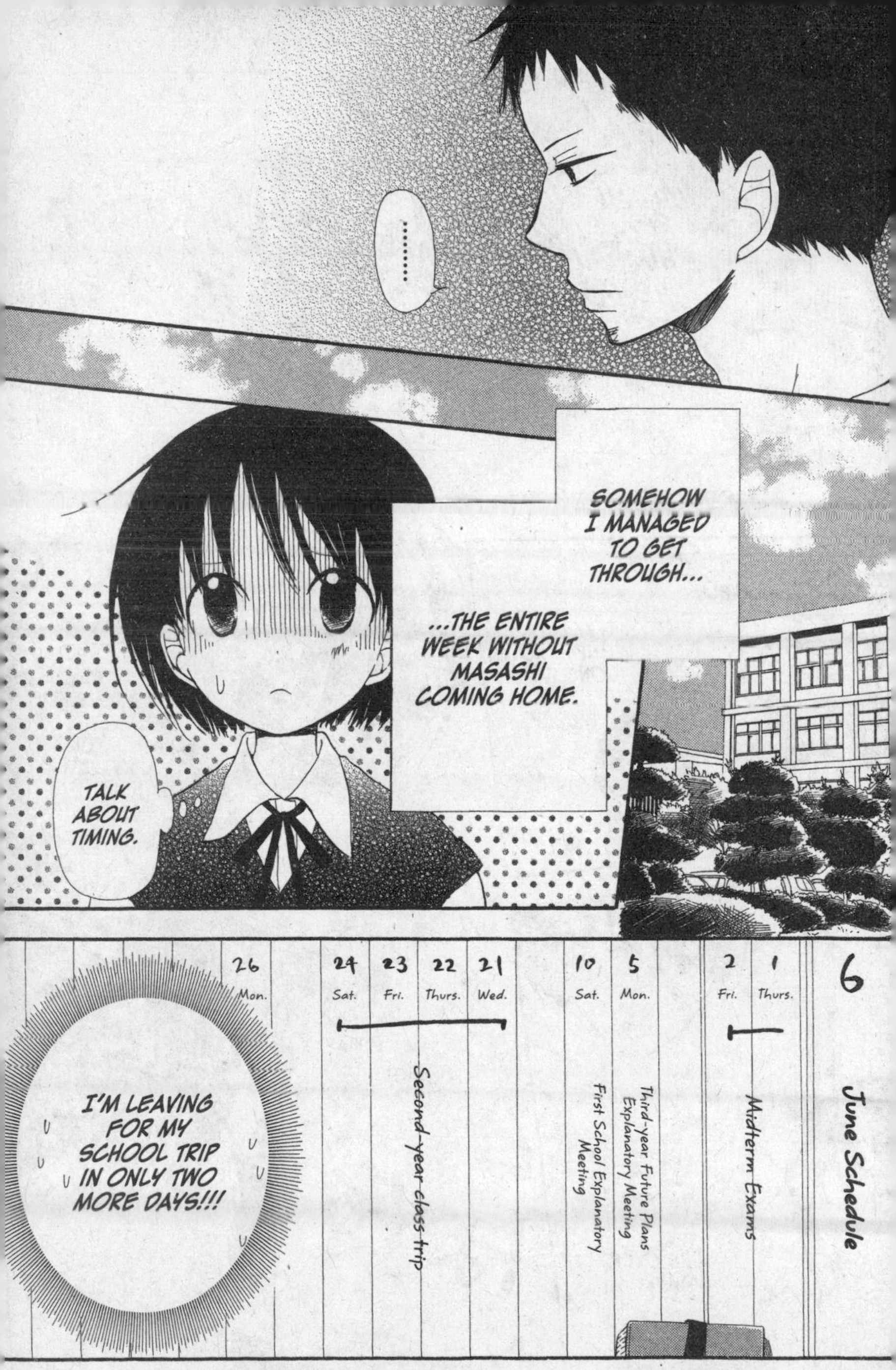
……
SOMEHOW I MANAGED TO GET THROUGH…
…THE ENTIRE WEEK WITHOUT MASASHI COMING HOME.
TALK ABOUT TIMING.
6
June Schedule
1 Thurs.
2 Fri.
Midterm Exams
5 Mon.
Third-year Future Plans Explanatory Meeting
10 Sat.
First School Explanatory Meeting
21 Wed.
22 Thurs.
23 Fri.
24 Sat.
Second-year class trip
26 Mon.
I'M LEAVING FOR MY SCHOOL TRIP IN ONLY TWO MORE DAYS!!!

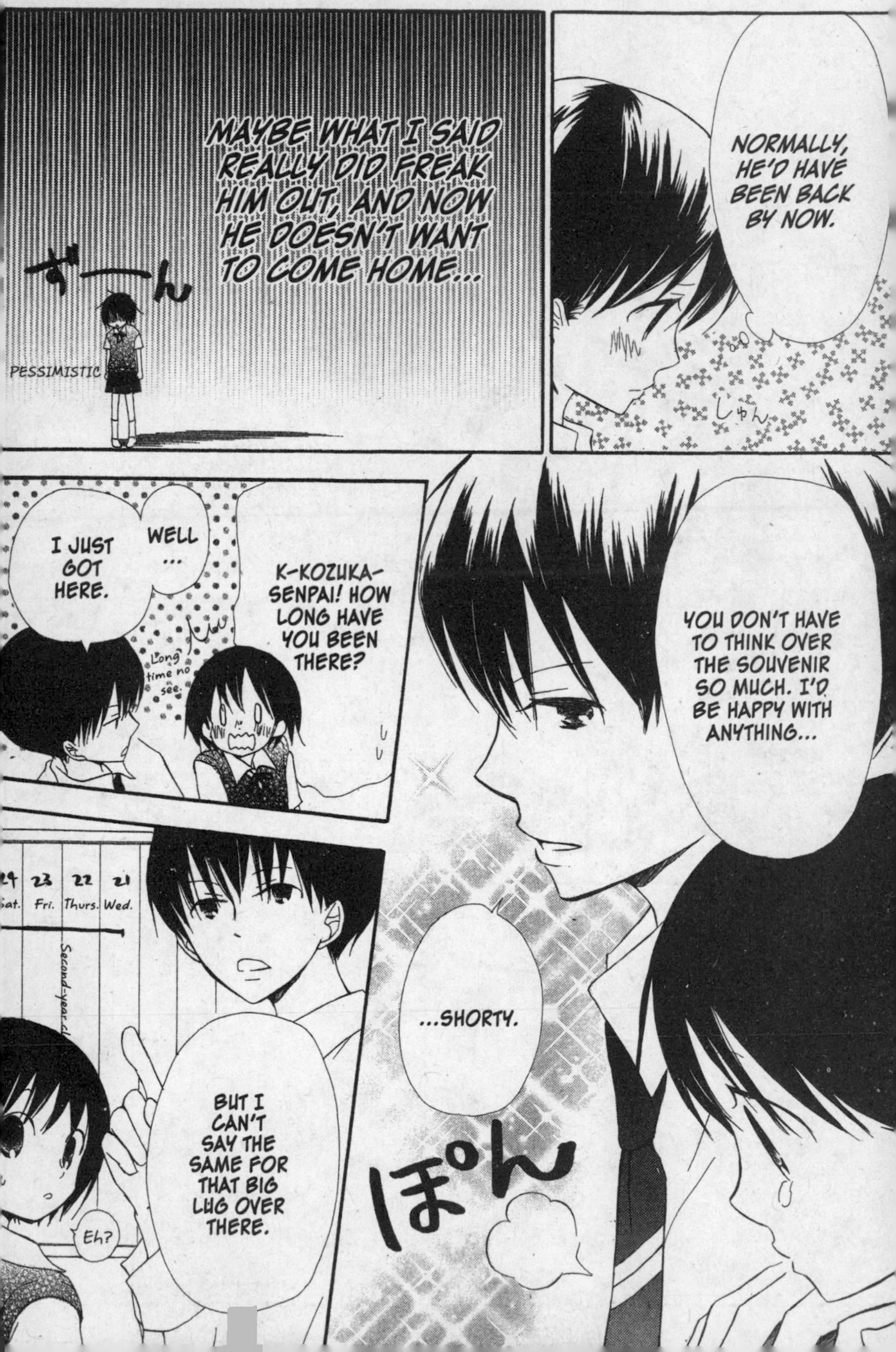

NORMALLY, HE'D HAVE BEEN BACK BY NOW.
しゅん
MAYBE WHAT I SAID REALLY DID FREAK HIM OUT, AND NOW HE DOESN'T WANT TO COME HOME...
ずーん
PESSIMISTIC
YOU DON'T HAVE TO THINK OVER THE SOUVENIR SO MUCH. I'D BE HAPPY WITH ANYTHING...
...SHORTY.
ぽん
K-KOZUKA-SENPAI! HOW LONG HAVE YOU BEEN THERE?
WELL ...
I JUST GOT HERE.
Long time no see.
23 22 21
Fri. Thurs. Wed.
BUT I CAN'T SAY THE SAME FOR THAT BIG LUG OVER THERE.
Eh?

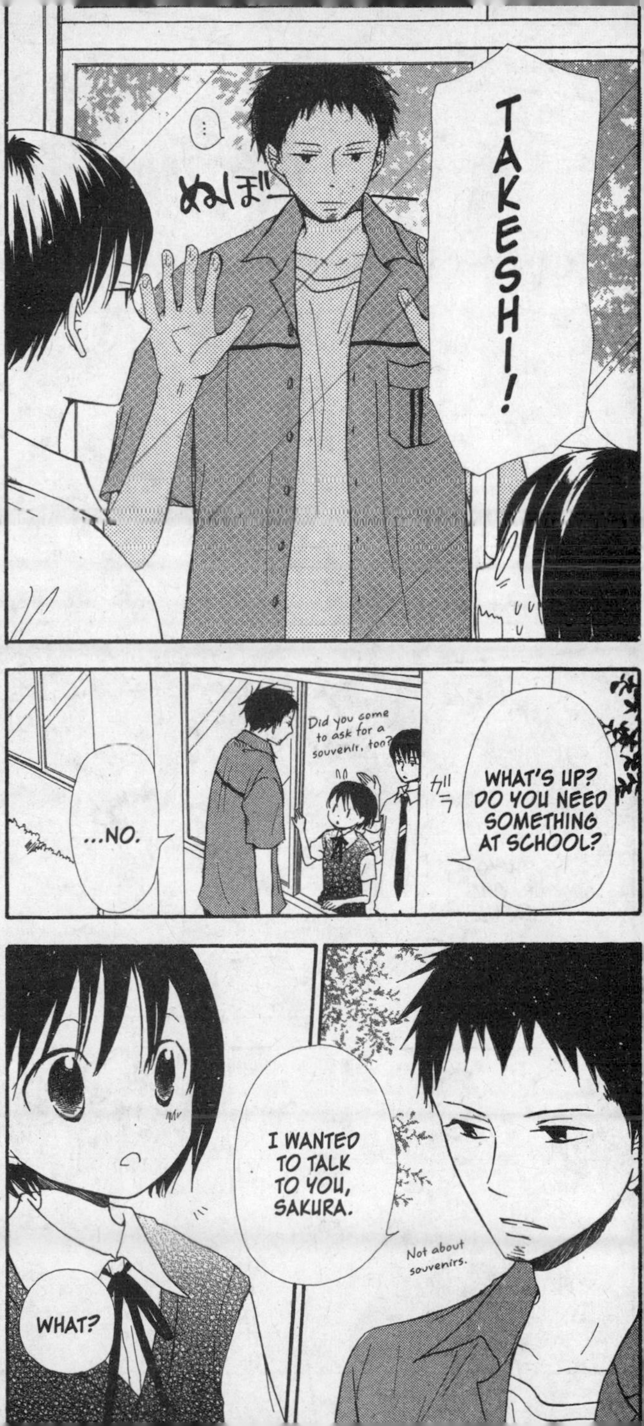
TAKESHI!
…
ぬぼー
WHAT'S UP? DO YOU NEED SOMETHING AT SCHOOL?
ガラ
Did you come to ask for a souvenir, too?
…NO.
I WANTED TO TALK TO YOU, SAKURA.
Not about souvenirs.
WHAT?

4

I also get the energy to work hard from my friends who help me with the manuscript.

First, there's the highly sensible Chito Mikami-chan, who is not only adorable but funny, too!

Then Emiko Nakano-chan. She looks like a princess, but is still goofy and fun on the inside.

They didn't actually work on anything in **this** volume, but I also get help from the smart and cute Shinobu Amano-chan and Mikase Hayashi-sama, who is darling inside and out.

Frankly, this column is turning into an excuse to brag about my friends.

I'd like to thank all the other people who give me energy.

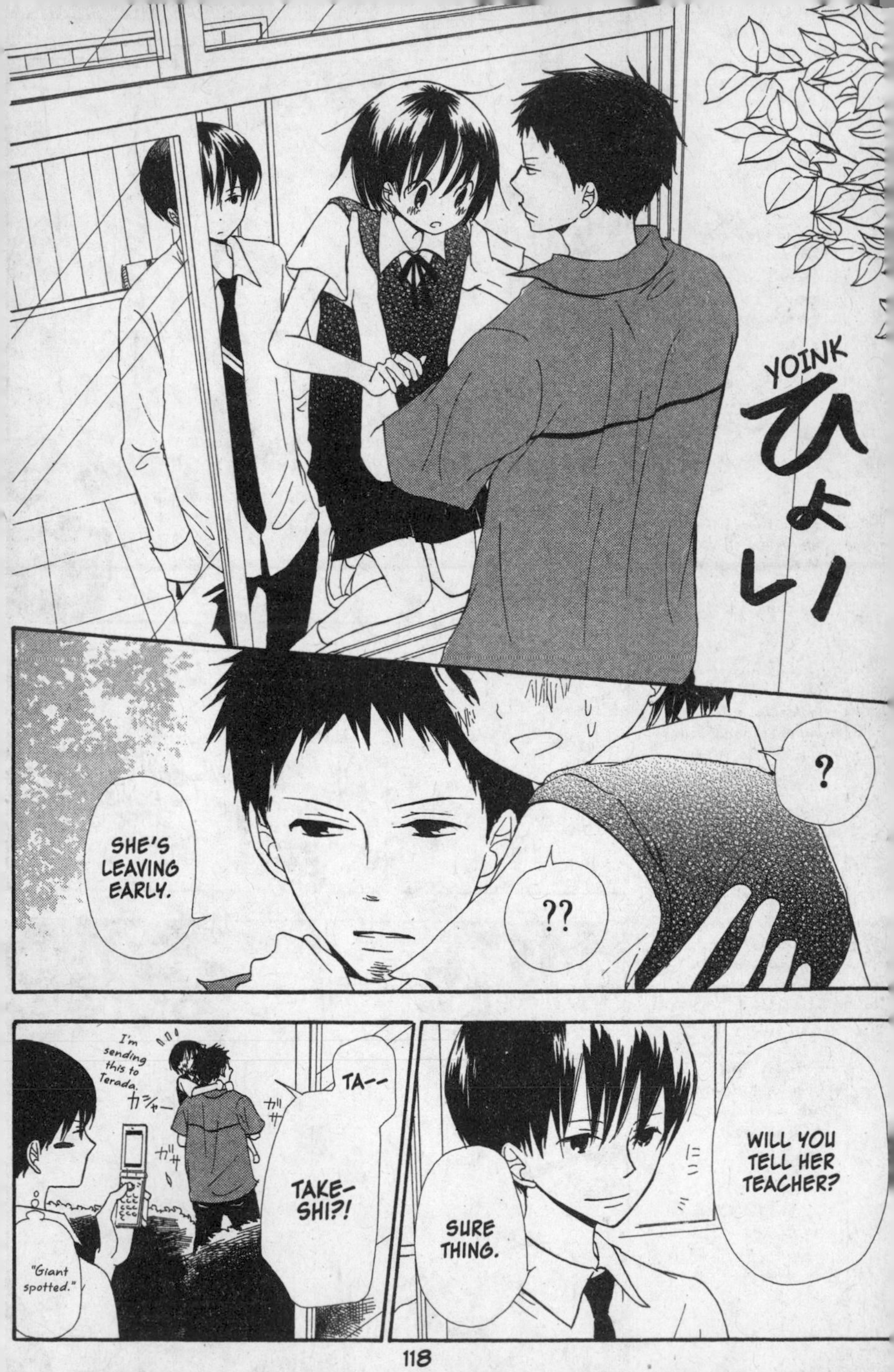
YOINK
ひょい
?
??
SHE'S LEAVING EARLY.
WILL YOU TELL HER TEACHER?
にっ
SURE THING.
TA--
ガサ
TAKE-SHI?!
I'm sending this to Terada.
ガシャー
ガサ
"Giant spotted."

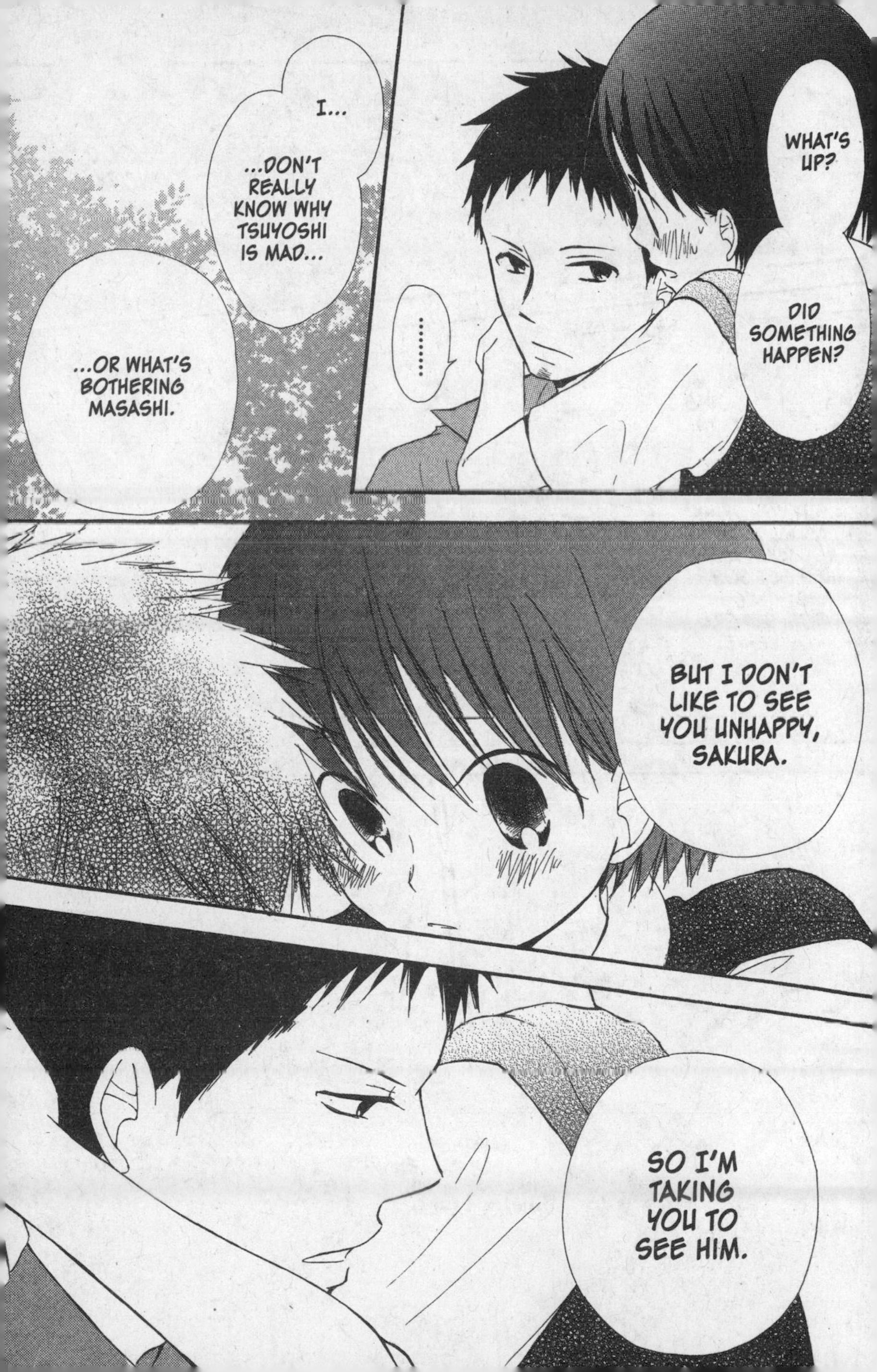
WHAT'S UP?
DID SOMETHING HAPPEN?
......
I...
...DON'T REALLY KNOW WHY TSUYOSHI IS MAD...
...OR WHAT'S BOTHERING MASASHI.
BUT I DON'T LIKE TO SEE YOU UNHAPPY, SAKURA.
SO I'M TAKING YOU TO SEE HIM.

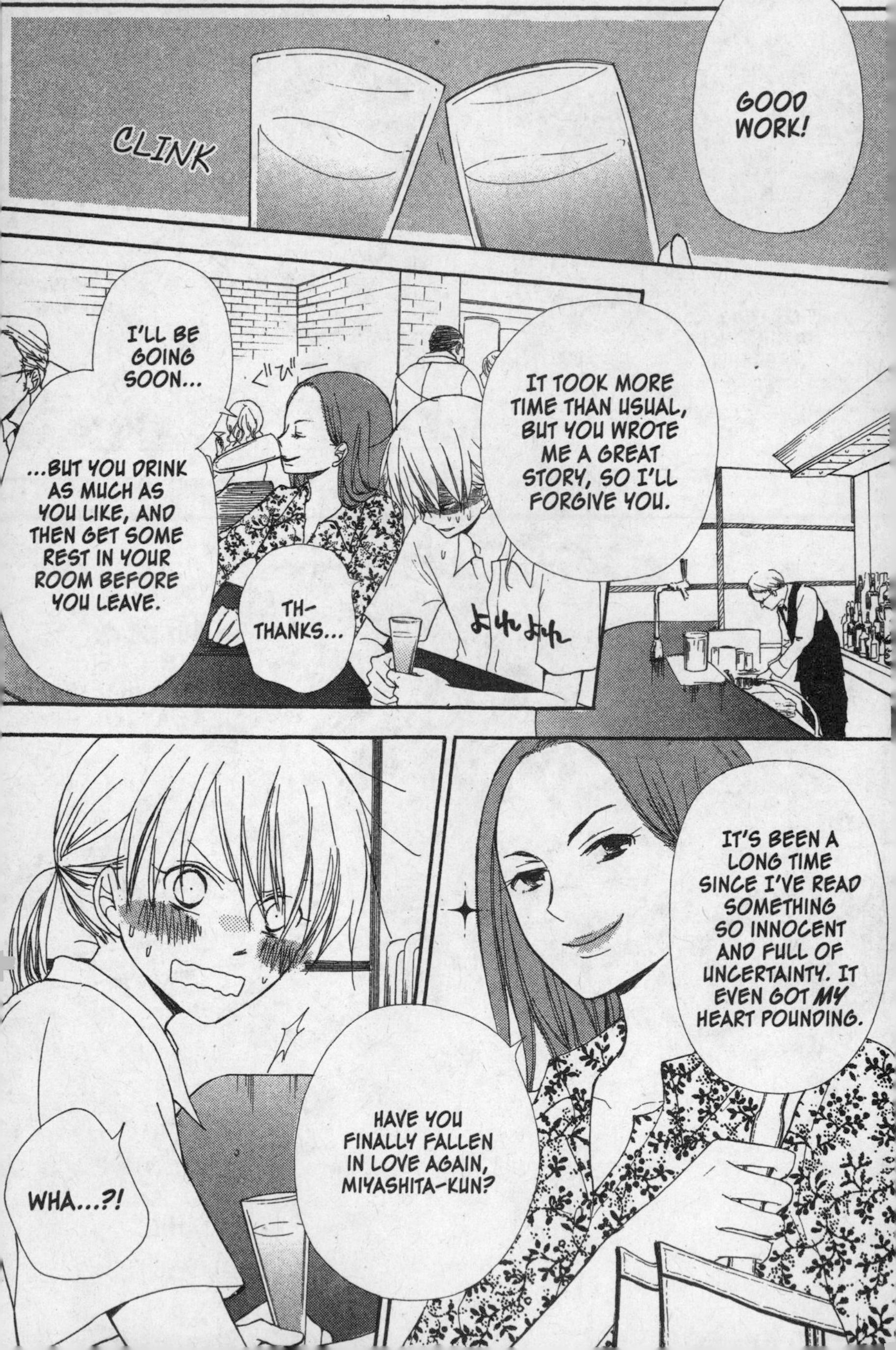
GOOD WORK!
CLINK
IT TOOK MORE TIME THAN USUAL, BUT YOU WROTE ME A GREAT STORY, SO I'LL FORGIVE YOU.
I'LL BE GOING SOON...
...BUT YOU DRINK AS MUCH AS YOU LIKE, AND THEN GET SOME REST IN YOUR ROOM BEFORE YOU LEAVE.
ぐびー
よれよれ
TH- THANKS...
IT'S BEEN A LONG TIME SINCE I'VE READ SOMETHING SO INNOCENT AND FULL OF UNCERTAINTY. IT EVEN GOT MY HEART POUNDING.
HAVE YOU FINALLY FALLEN IN LOVE AGAIN, MIYASHITA-KUN?
WHA...?!

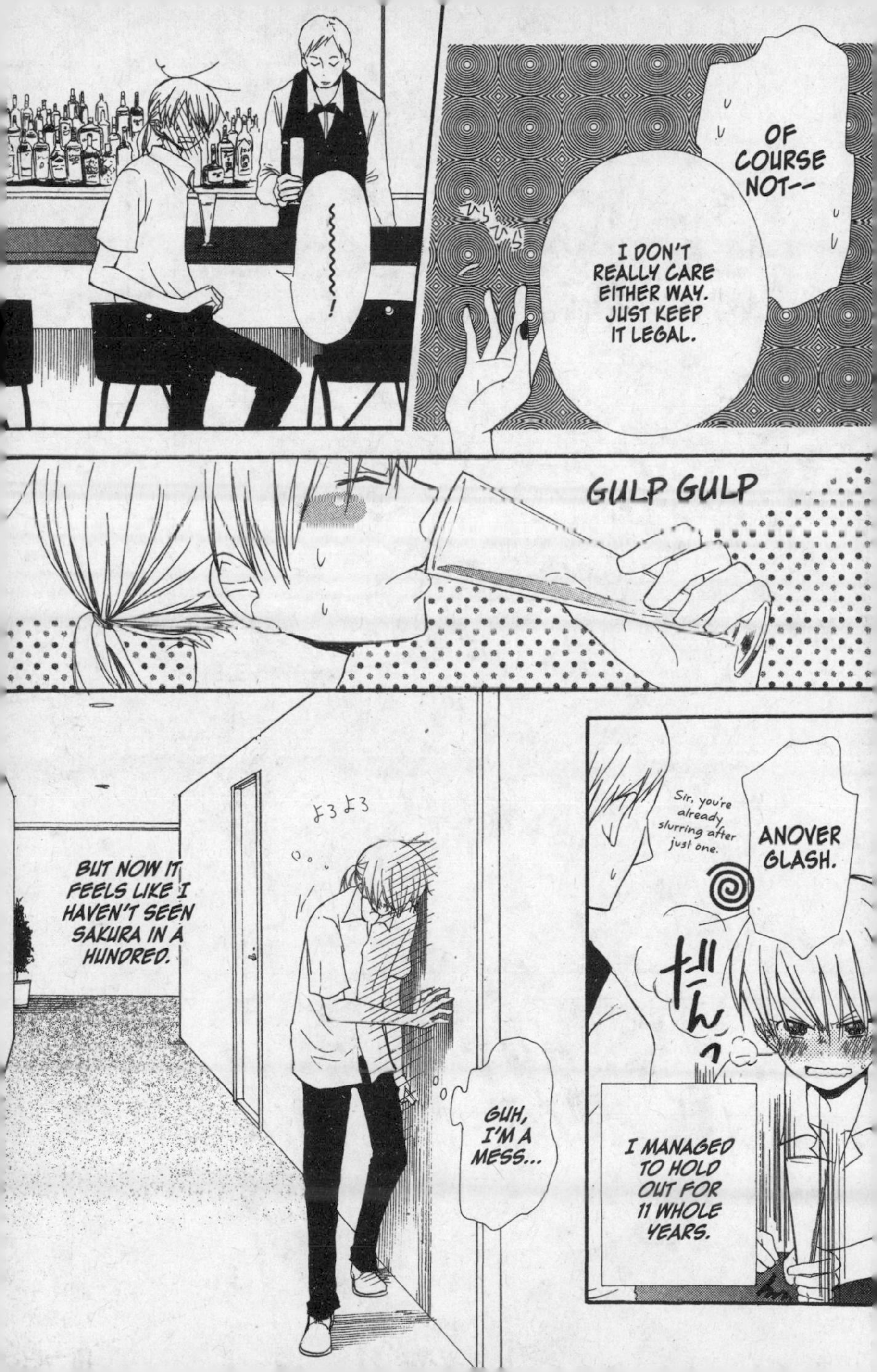
OF COURSE NOT--
I DON'T REALLY CARE EITHER WAY. JUST KEEP IT LEGAL.
GULP GULP
ANOVER GLASH.
Sir, you're already slurring after just one.
I MANAGED TO HOLD OUT FOR 11 WHOLE YEARS.
BUT NOW IT FEELS LIKE I HAVEN'T SEEN SAKURA IN A HUNDRED.
GUH, I'M A MESS...

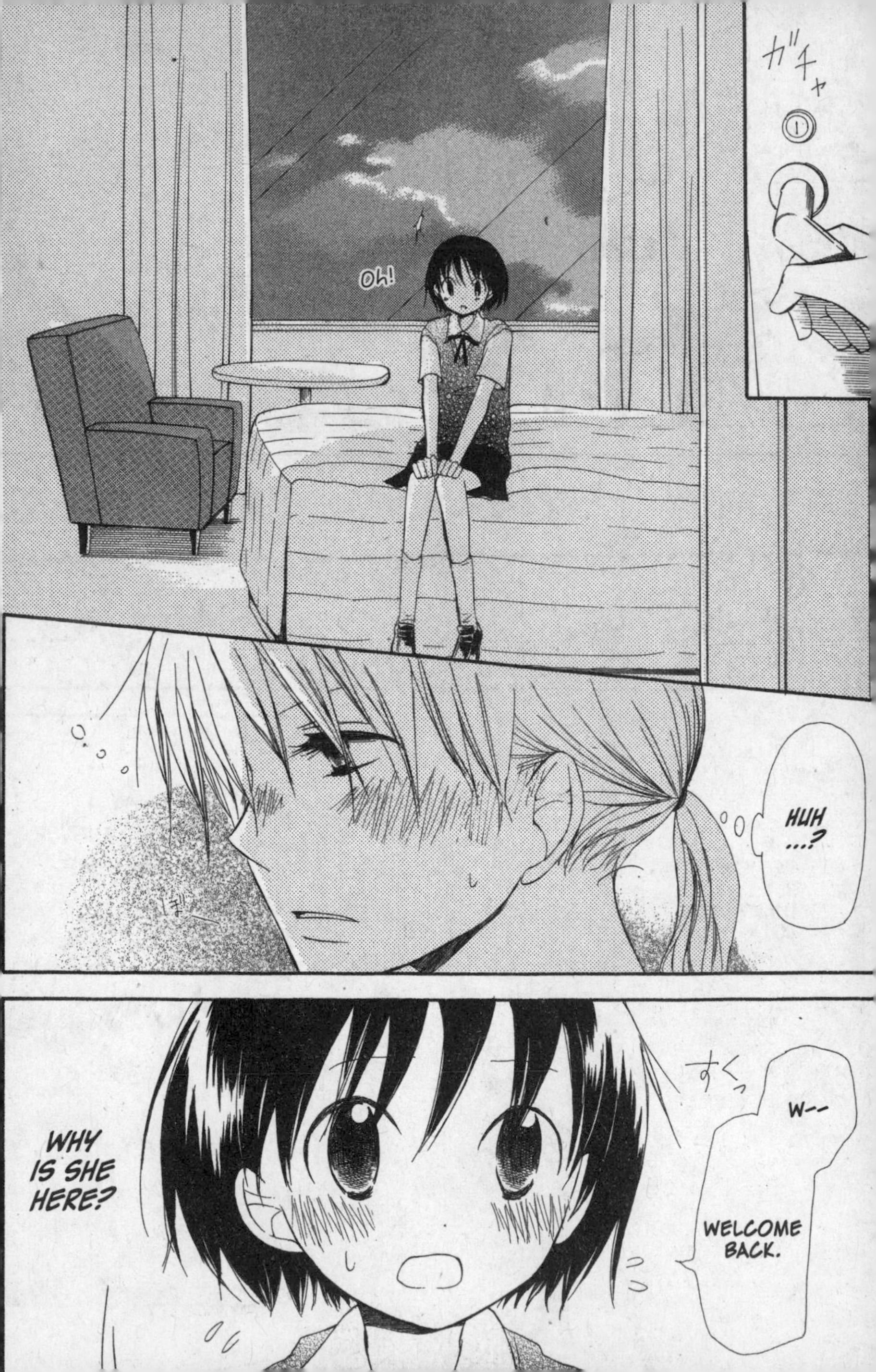
ガチャ
OH!
HUH ....?
すくっ
W-- WELCOME BACK.
WHY IS SHE HERE?

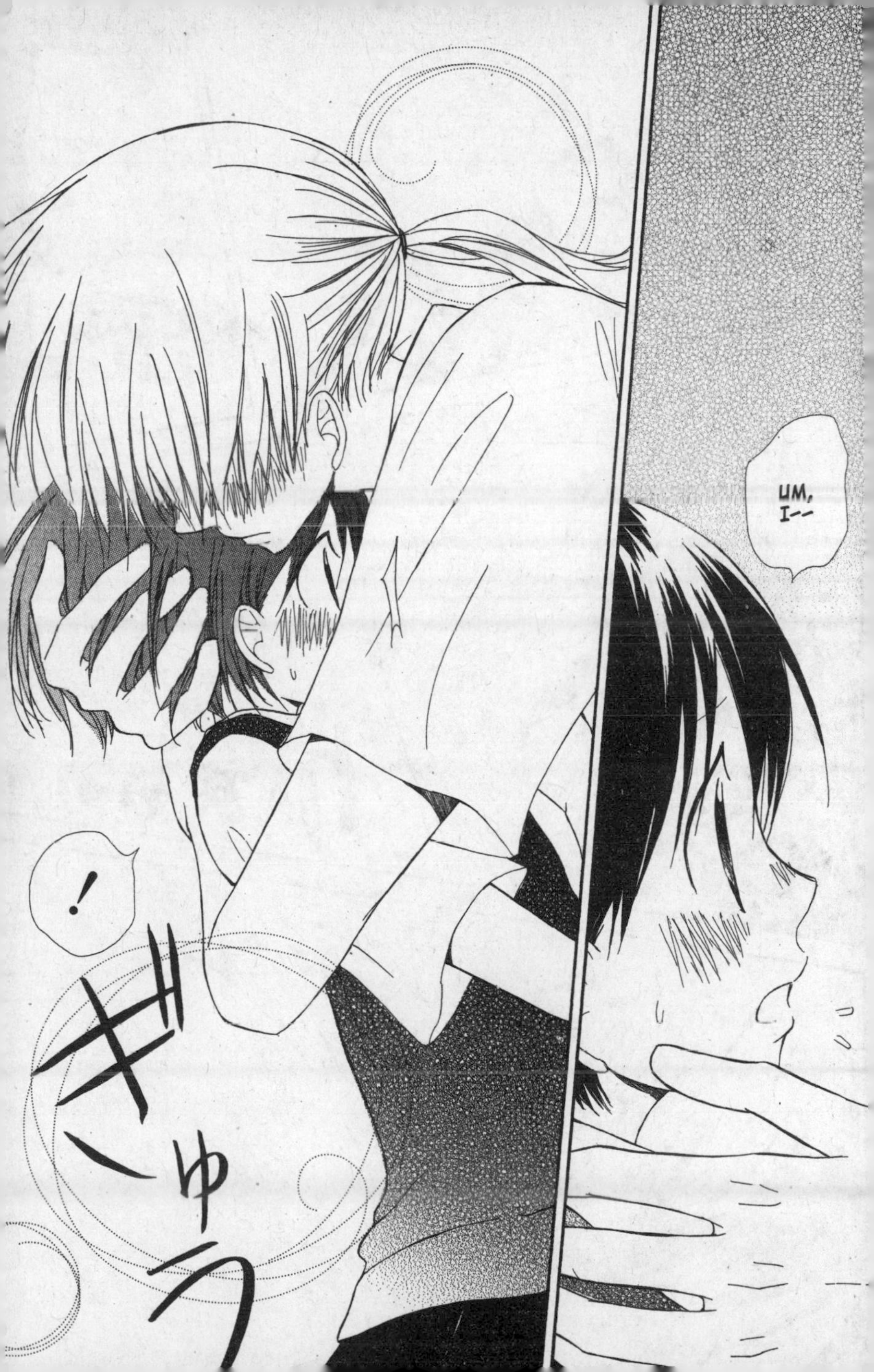
UM, I--
!
ぎゅう

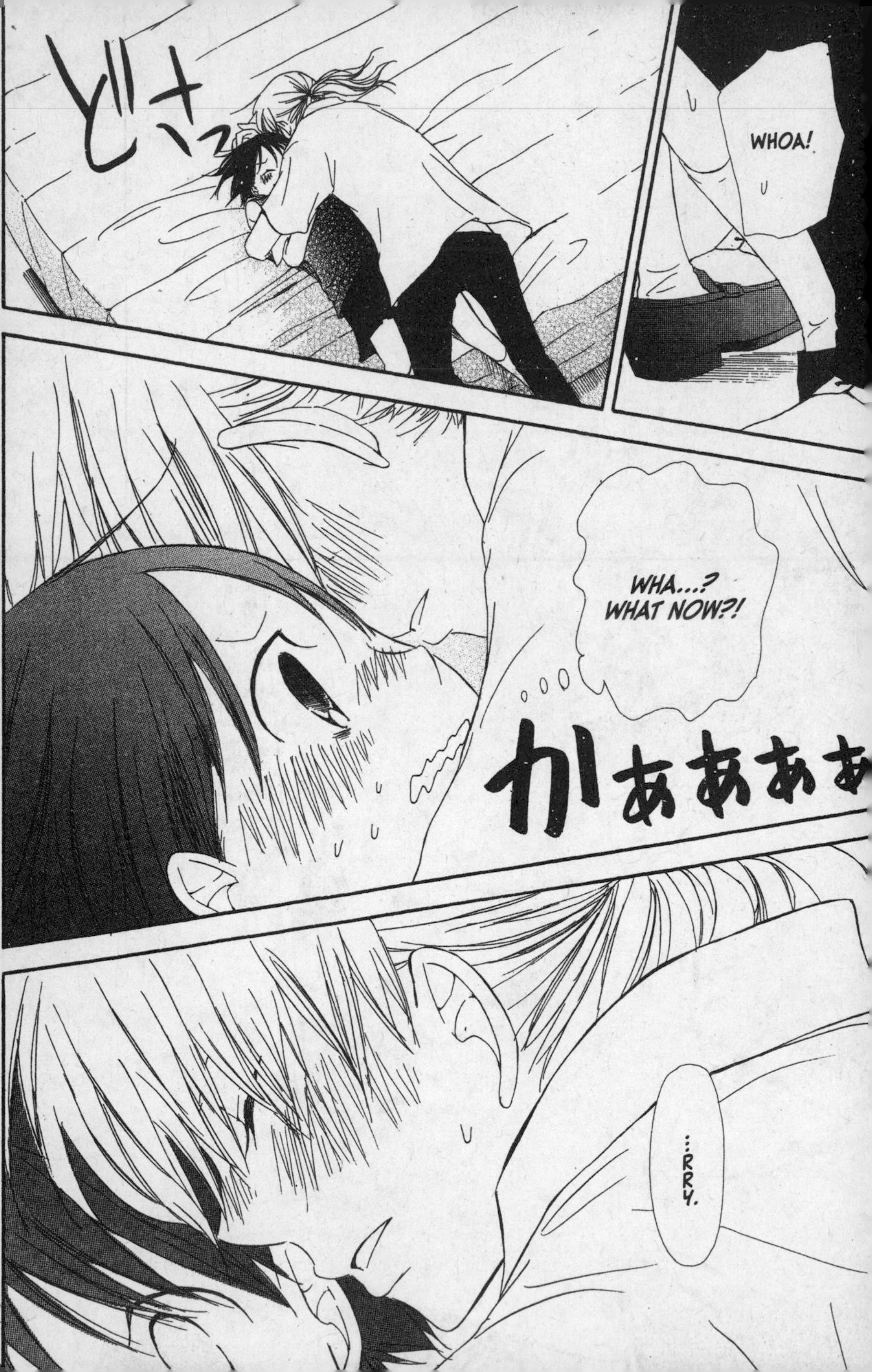
WHOA!
どさっ
WHA...? WHAT NOW?!
かああああ
...RRY.

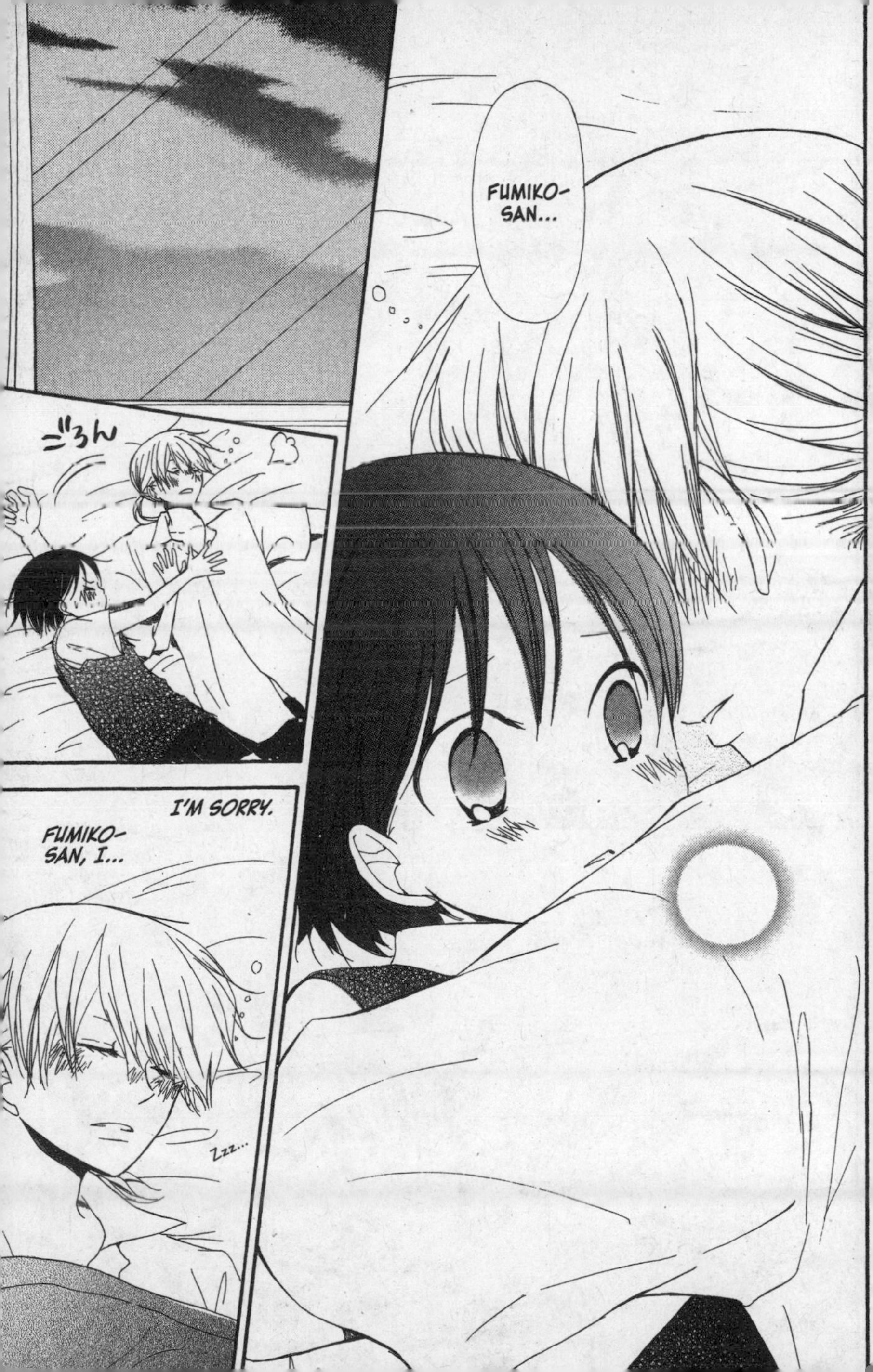
FUMIKO-SAN...
ごろん
I'M SORRY.
FUMIKO-SAN, I...
Zzz...

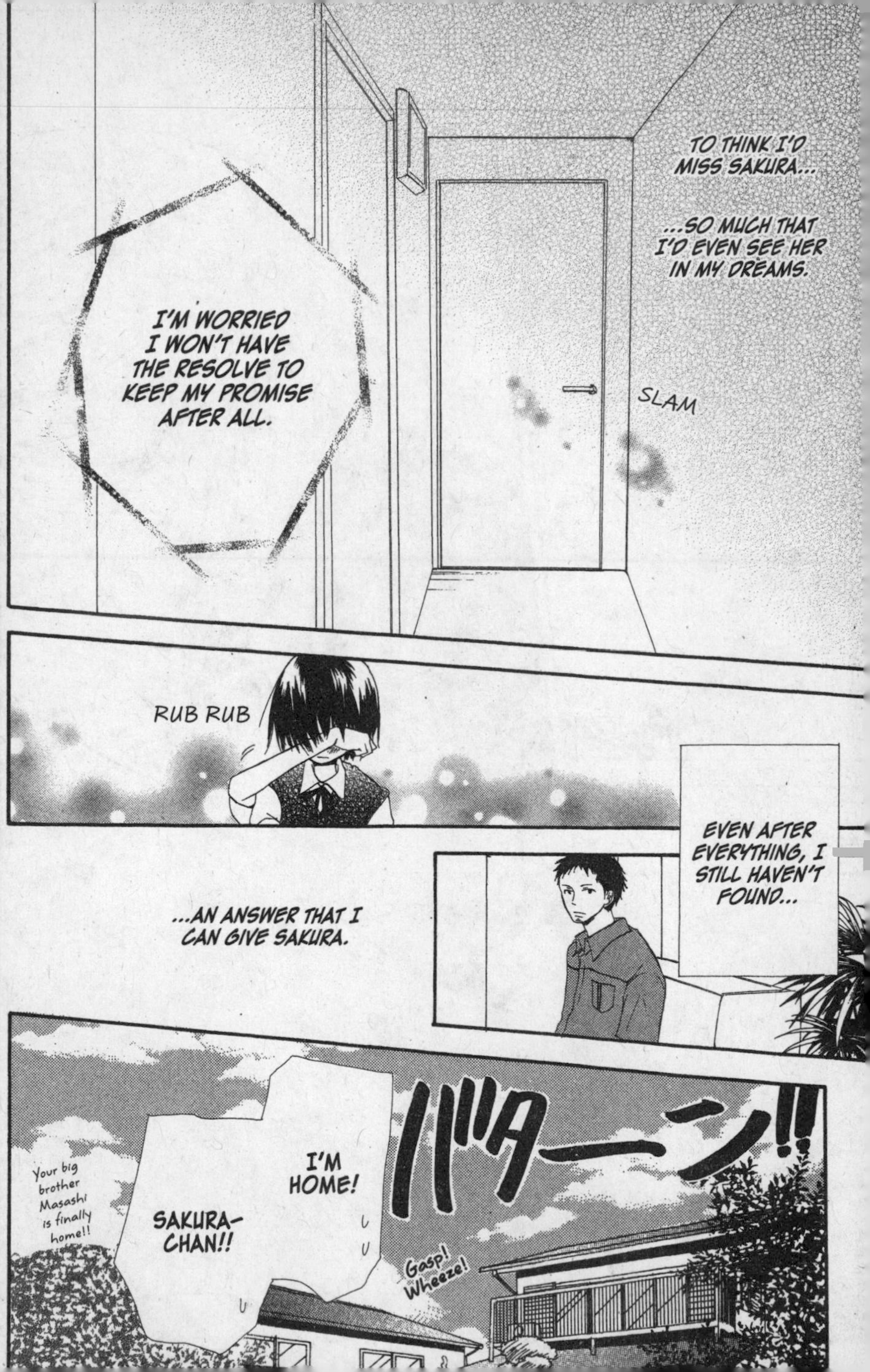
TO THINK I'D MISS SAKURA...
...SO MUCH THAT I'D EVEN SEE HER IN MY DREAMS.
SLAM
I'M WORRIED I WON'T HAVE THE RESOLVE TO KEEP MY PROMISE AFTER ALL.
RUB RUB
EVEN AFTER EVERYTHING, I STILL HAVEN'T FOUND...
...AN ANSWER THAT I CAN GIVE SAKURA.
バターン!!
I'M HOME!
SAKURA-CHAN!!
Gasp! Wheeze!
Your big brother Masashi is finally home!!

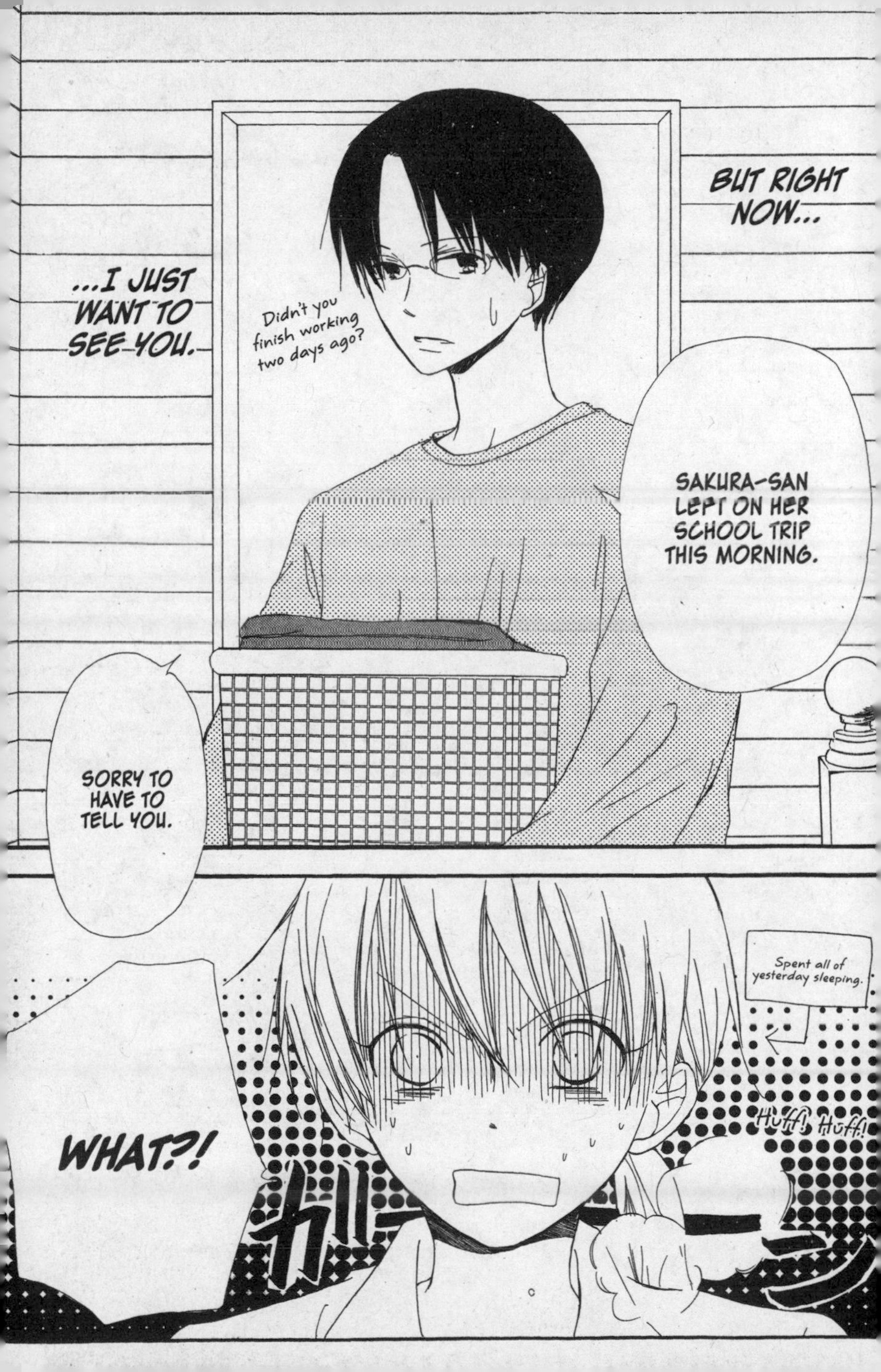
BUT RIGHT NOW...
...I JUST WANT TO SEE YOU.
Didn't you finish working two days ago?
SAKURA-SAN LEFT ON HER SCHOOL TRIP THIS MORNING.
SORRY TO HAVE TO TELL YOU.
Spent all of yesterday sleeping.
Huff! Huff!
WHAT?!

DAJARE Tongue Twisters II

This is a column that appeared in the magazine. I like it a lot, so I'm putting it here. I like puns...

My nose knows nutrition!
This cook can claim any kitchen's cultured cuisine courteously!
While mingling with Mittens might mollify his mind...
...hurling hammers on the harbor...
...hails hordes of herbed squid.
Suddenly the silent sea...
...swiftly swells to a tsunami-sized storm!
Only bountiful blubber bails him out of his embarrassing blunder.
プカプカ
When a squadron of squid swim speedily to his side...
...his store is safe from subsidiaries with steep sales!
How fish can found such flourishing finesse.

HARI

END.

THANKS CHITOCHAN & SUGI.

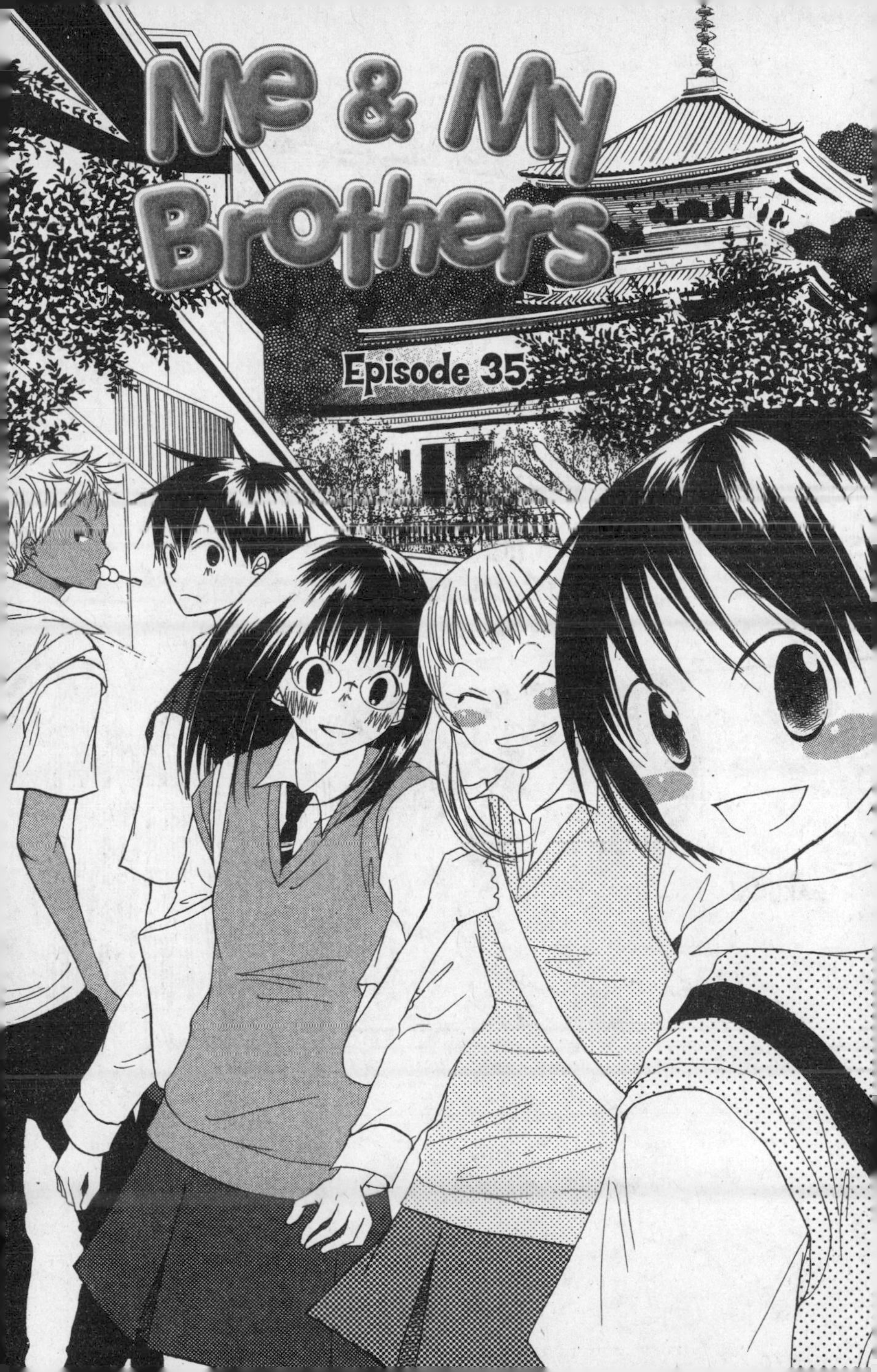
Me & My Brothers
Episode 35

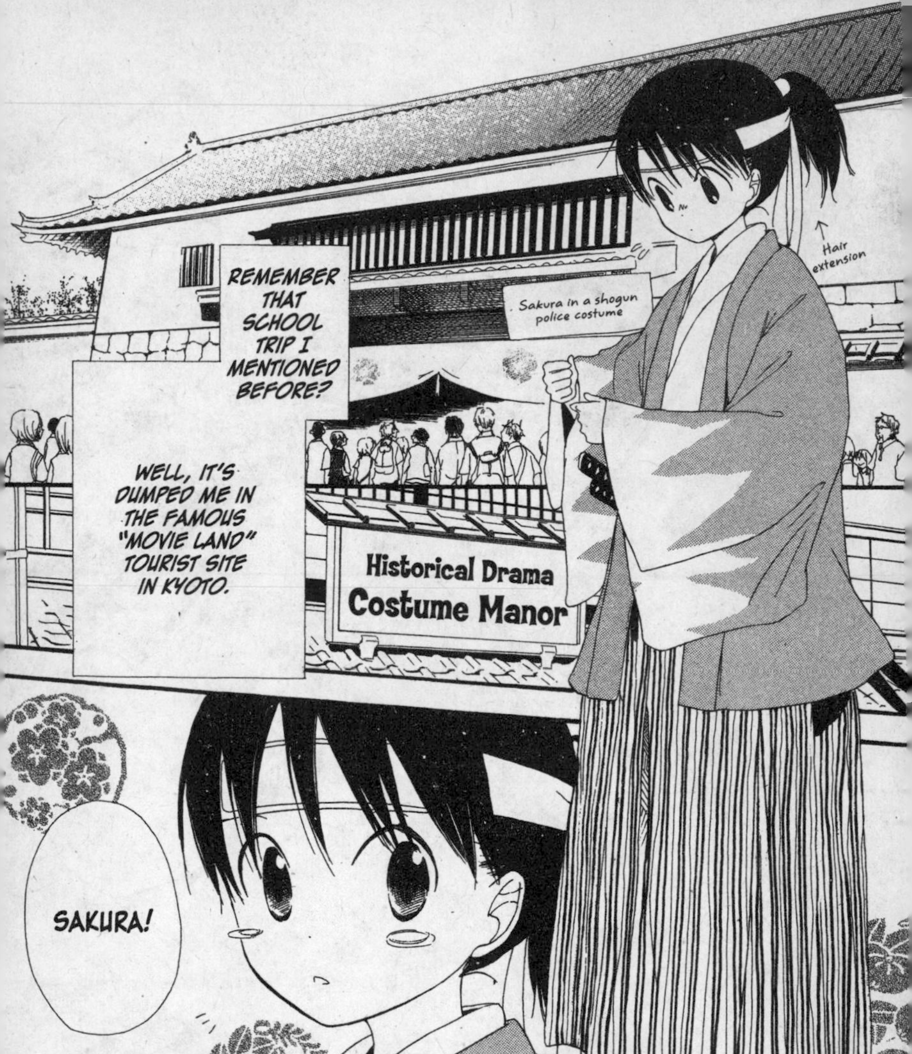
Hair extension
Sakura in a shogun police costume
REMEMBER THAT SCHOOL TRIP I MENTIONED BEFORE?
WELL, IT'S DUMPED ME IN THE FAMOUS "MOVIE LAND" TOURIST SITE IN KYOTO.
Historical Drama Costume Manor
SAKURA!

THANKS

MIKAMI CHITO SAMA
NAKANO EMIKO SAMA
KONDOU SAMA
&
YOU !!

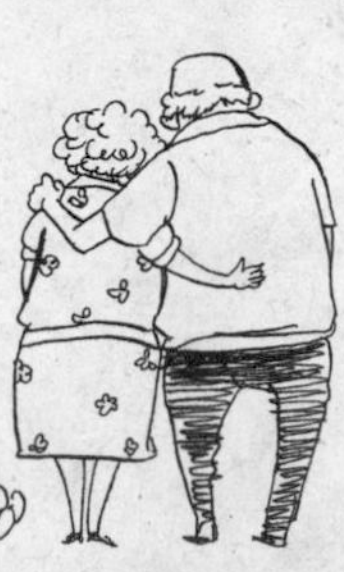

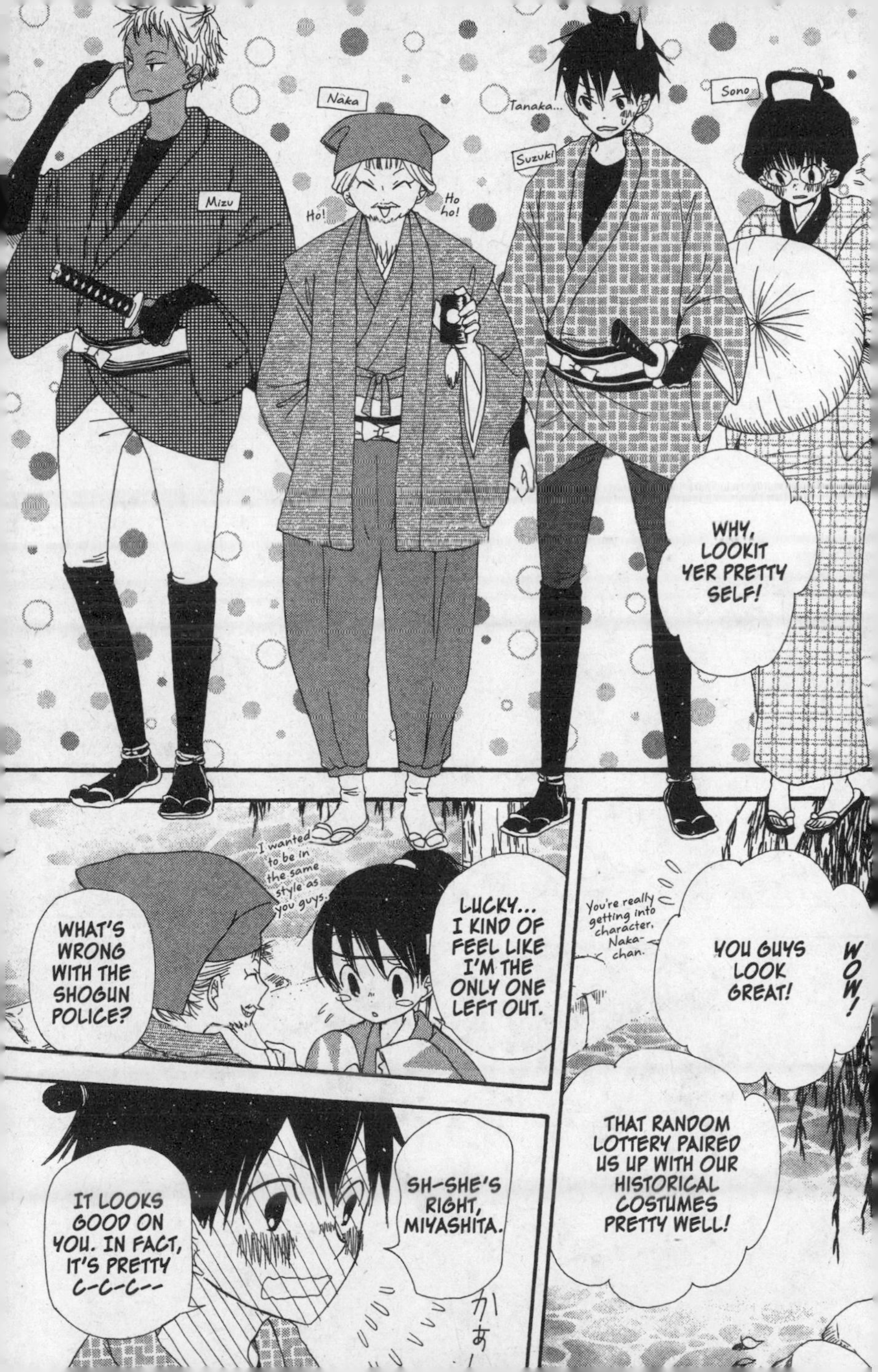
Sono
Tanaka...
Suzuki
WHY, LOOKIT YER PRETTY SELF!
Ho ho!
Naka
Ho!
Mizu
WOW!
YOU GUYS LOOK GREAT!
You're really getting into character, Naka-chan.
THAT RANDOM LOTTERY PAIRED US UP WITH OUR HISTORICAL COSTUMES PRETTY WELL!
LUCKY... I KIND OF FEEL LIKE I'M THE ONLY ONE LEFT OUT.
I wanted to be in the same style as you guys.
WHAT'S WRONG WITH THE SHOGUN POLICE?
SH-SHE'S RIGHT, MIYASHITA.
IT LOOKS GOOD ON YOU. IN FACT, IT'S PRETTY C-C-C--

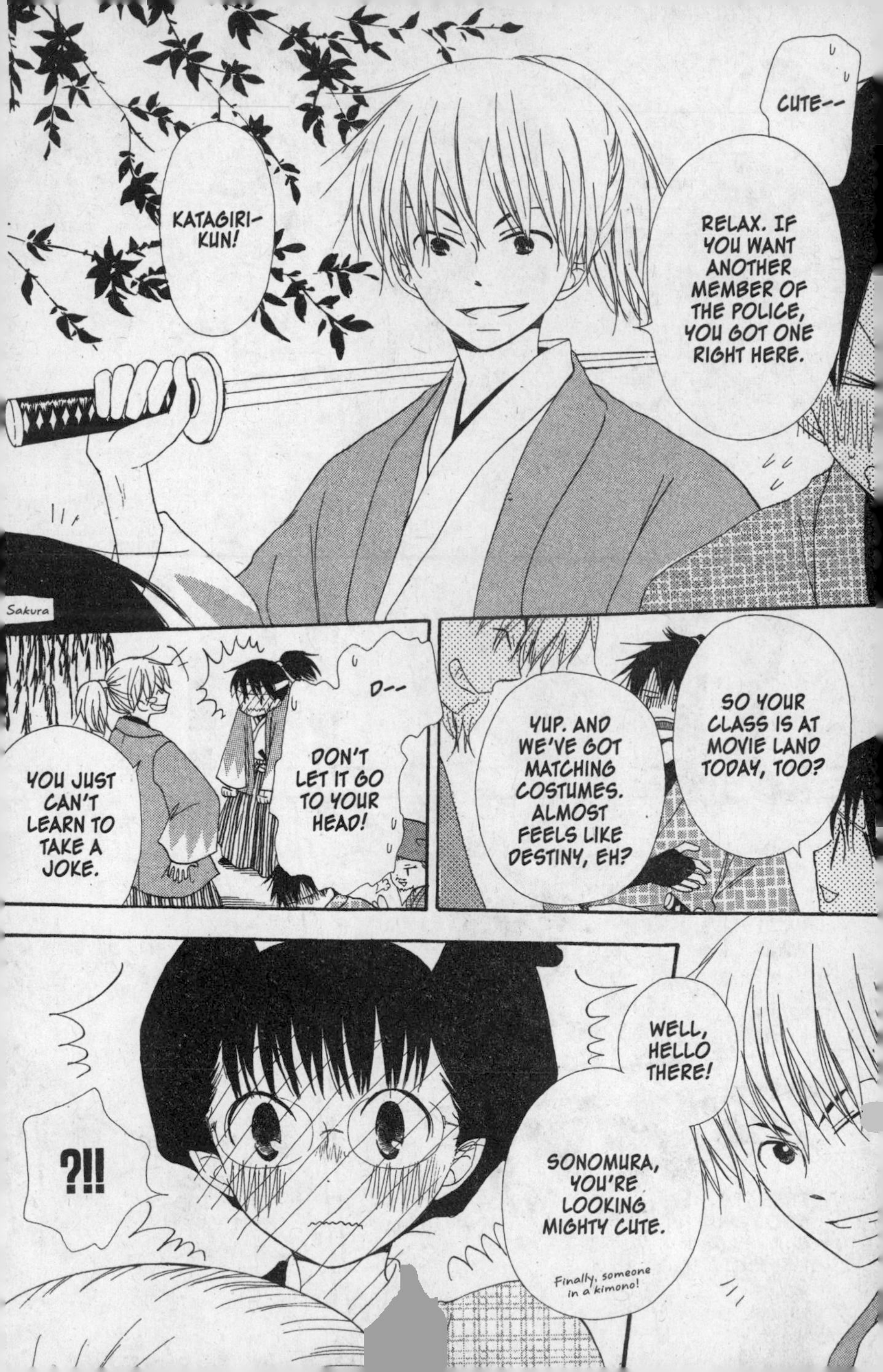
CUTE--
RELAX. IF YOU WANT ANOTHER MEMBER OF THE POLICE, YOU GOT ONE RIGHT HERE.
KATAGIRI-KUN!
Sakura
SO YOUR CLASS IS AT MOVIE LAND TODAY, TOO?
YUP. AND WE'VE GOT MATCHING COSTUMES. ALMOST FEELS LIKE DESTINY, EH?
D--
DON'T LET IT GO TO YOUR HEAD!
YOU JUST CAN'T LEARN TO TAKE A JOKE.
WELL, HELLO THERE!
SONOMURA, YOU'RE LOOKING MIGHTY CUTE.
Finally, someone in a kimono!
?!!

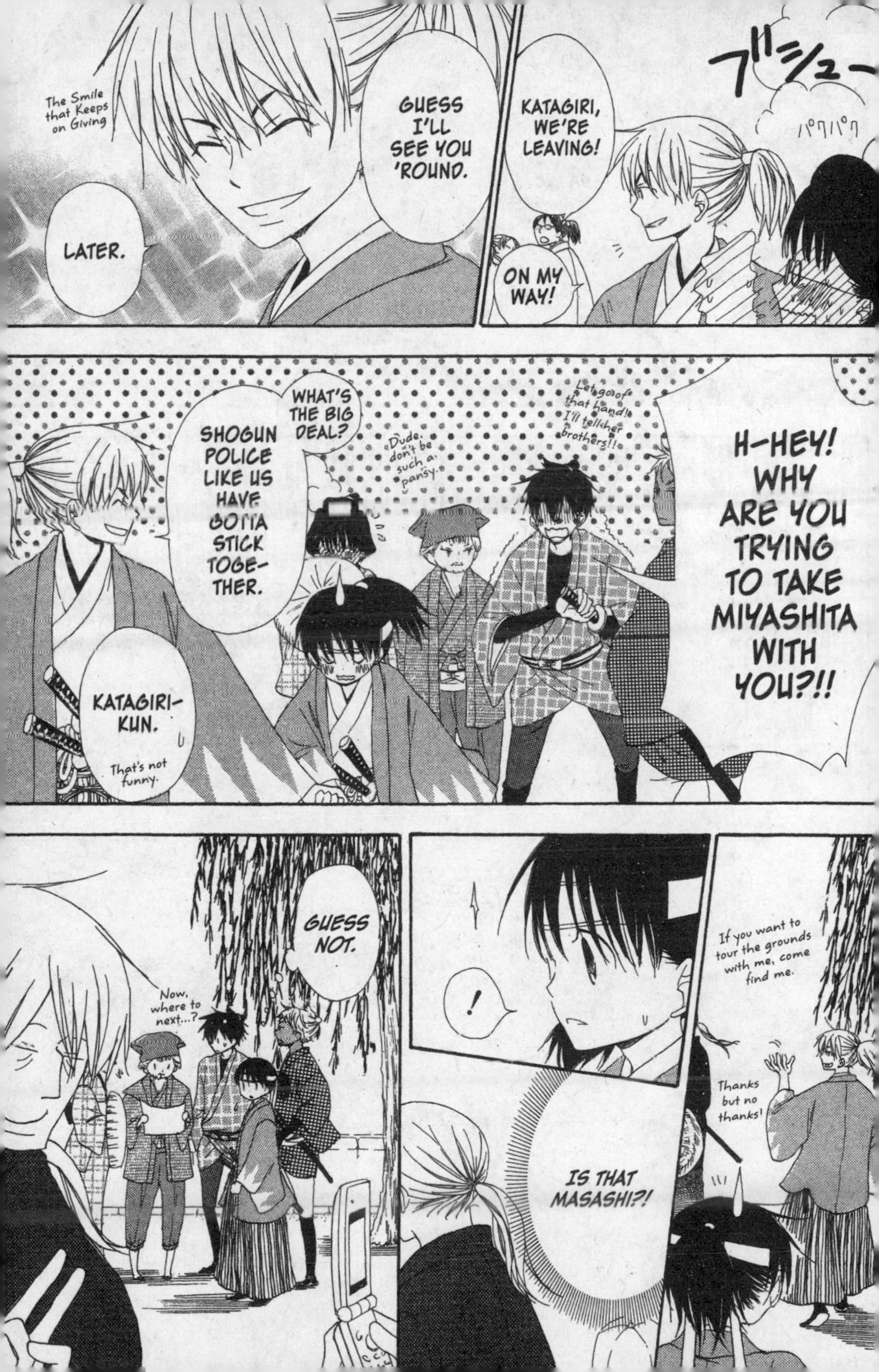
パクパク
KATAGIRI, WE'RE LEAVING!
ON MY WAY!
GUESS I'LL SEE YOU 'ROUND.
The Smile that Keeps on Giving
LATER.
H-HEY! WHY ARE YOU TRYING TO TAKE MIYASHITA WITH YOU?!!
Let go of that hand! I'll tell her brothers!!
Dude, don't be such a pansy.
WHAT'S THE BIG DEAL?
SHOGUN POLICE LIKE US HAVE GOTTA STICK TOGE-THER.
KATAGIRI-KUN.
That's not funny.
If you want to tour the grounds with me, come find me.
Thanks but no thanks!
!
IS THAT MASASHI?!
GUESS NOT.
Now, where to next...?

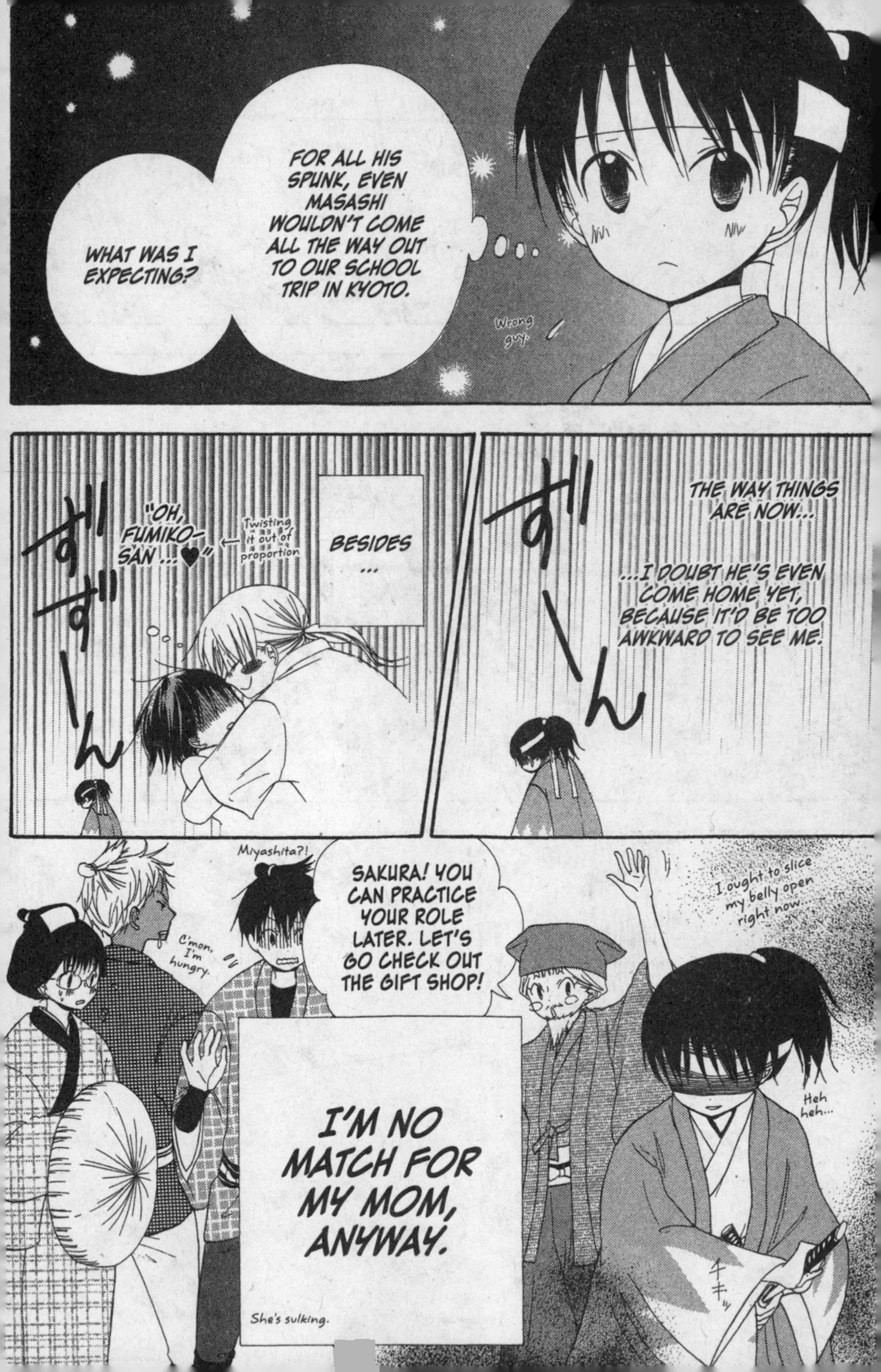
FOR ALL HIS SPUNK, EVEN MASASHI WOULDN'T COME ALL THE WAY OUT TO OUR SCHOOL TRIP IN KYOTO.
WHAT WAS I EXPECTING?
Wrong guy.
THE WAY THINGS ARE NOW...
...I DOUBT HE'S EVEN COME HOME YET, BECAUSE IT'D BE TOO AWKWARD TO SEE ME.
ずーん
BESIDES...
Twisting it out of proportion
"OH, FUMIKO-SAN ...♥"
ずずーん
I ought to slice my belly open right now...
SAKURA! YOU CAN PRACTICE YOUR ROLE LATER. LET'S GO CHECK OUT THE GIFT SHOP!
Miyashita?!
C'mon, I'm hungry.
Heh heh...
I'M NO MATCH FOR MY MOM, ANYWAY.
チキッ
She's sulking.

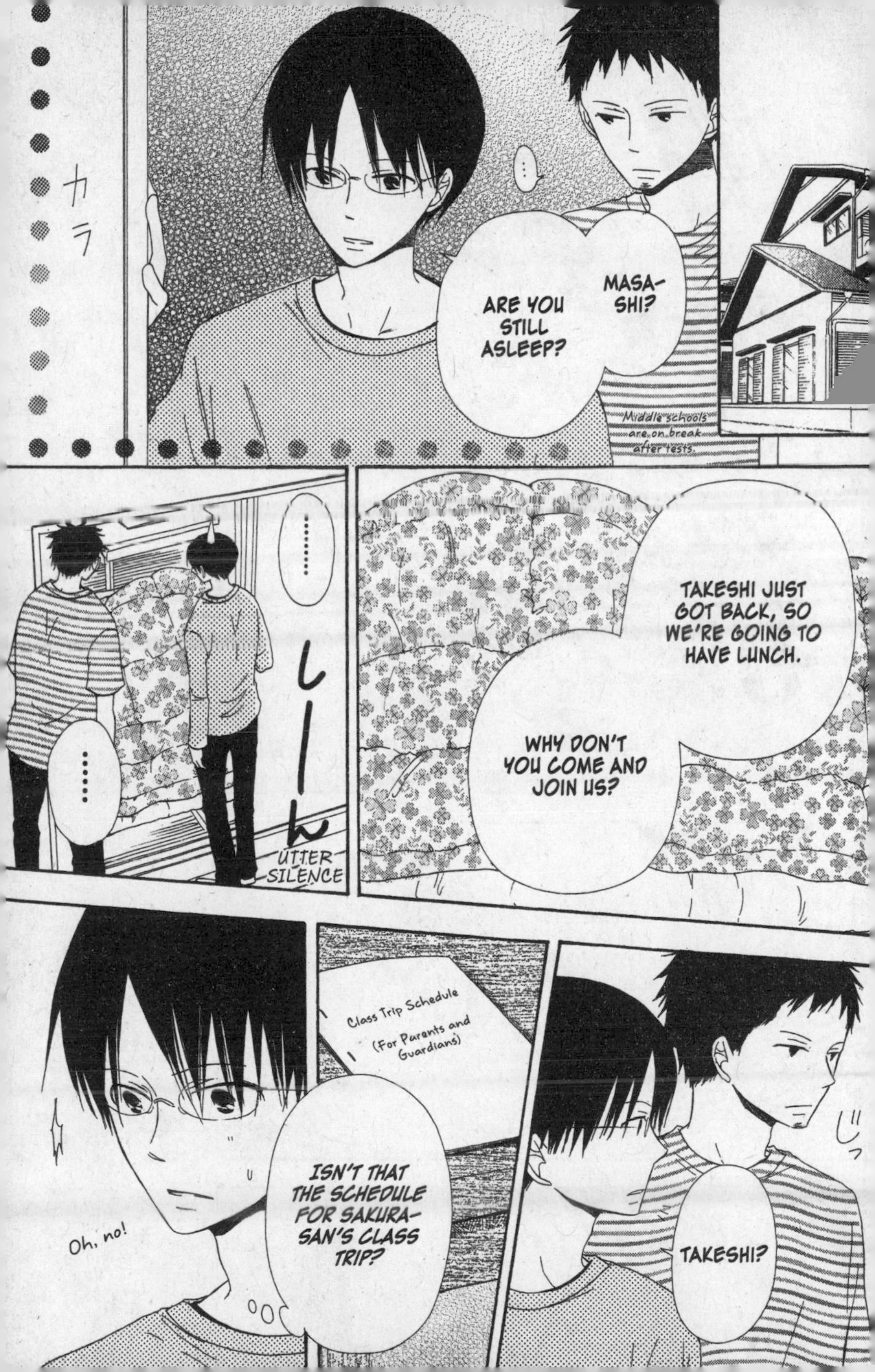
Middle schools are on break after tests.
…
カラ
MASA-SHI?
ARE YOU STILL ASLEEP?
TAKESHI JUST GOT BACK, SO WE'RE GOING TO HAVE LUNCH.
WHY DON'T YOU COME AND JOIN US?
......
しーん
UTTER SILENCE
......
じっ
TAKESHI?
Class Trip Schedule
(For Parents and Guardians)
ISN'T THAT THE SCHEDULE FOR SAKURA-SAN'S CLASS TRIP?
Oh, no!

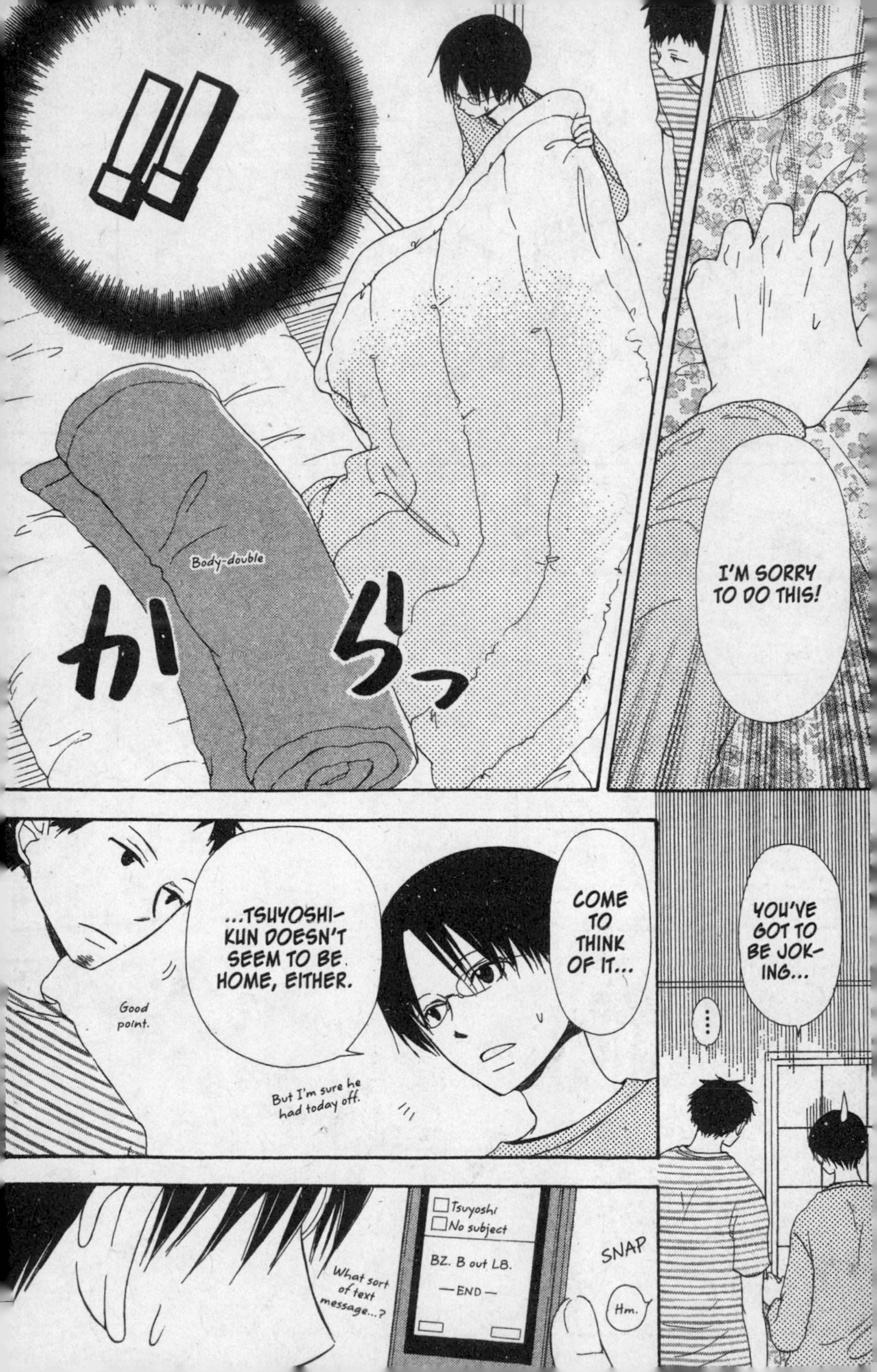

I'M SORRY TO DO THIS!
!!
Body-double
からっ
YOU'VE GOT TO BE JOKING...
...
COME TO THINK OF IT...
...TSUYOSHI-KUN DOESN'T SEEM TO BE HOME, EITHER.
But I'm sure he had today off.
Good point.
SNAP
Hm.
Tsuyoshi
No subject
BZ. B out LB.
—END—
What sort of text message...?

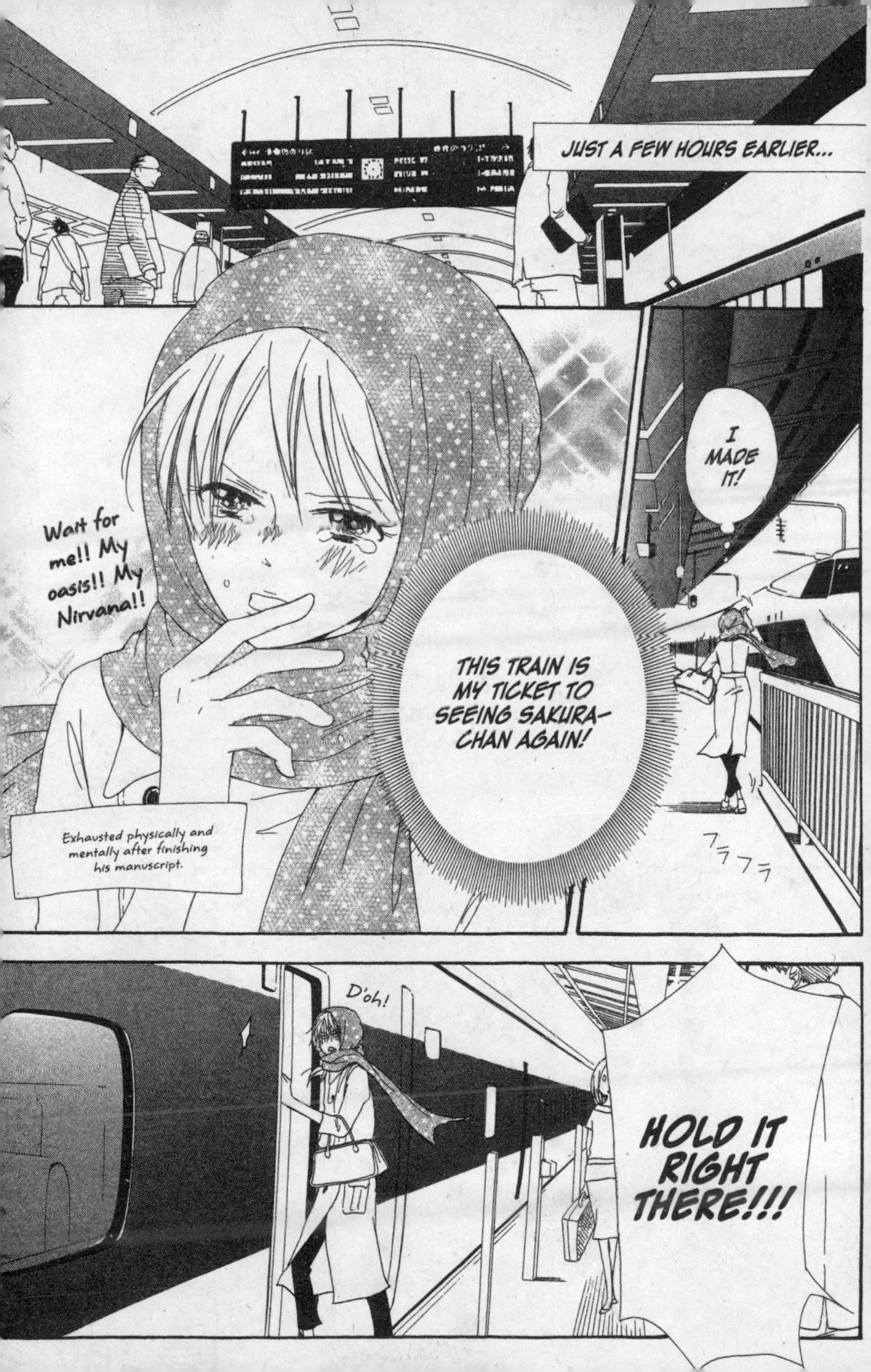
JUST A FEW HOURS EARLIER...
I MADE IT!
フラフラ
THIS TRAIN IS MY TICKET TO SEEING SAKURA-CHAN AGAIN!
Wait for me!! My oasis!! My Nirvana!!
Exhausted physically and mentally after finishing his manuscript.
HOLD IT RIGHT THERE!!!
D'oh!

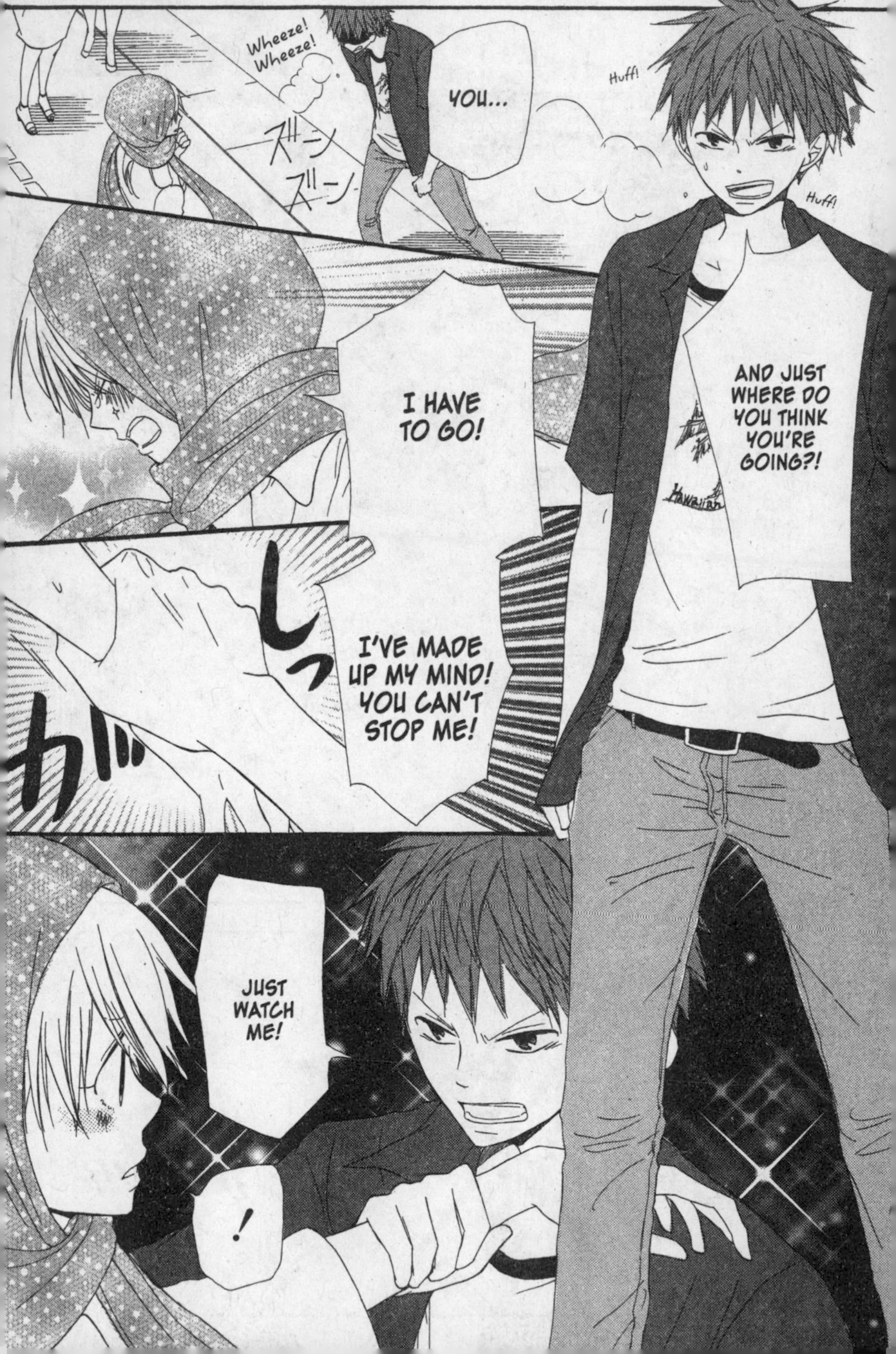
Huff!
Huff!
AND JUST WHERE DO YOU THINK YOU'RE GOING?!
Wheeze! Wheeze!
YOU...
ズーン ズーン
I HAVE TO GO!
しっ
が
I'VE MADE UP MY MIND! YOU CAN'T STOP ME!
JUST WATCH ME!
!

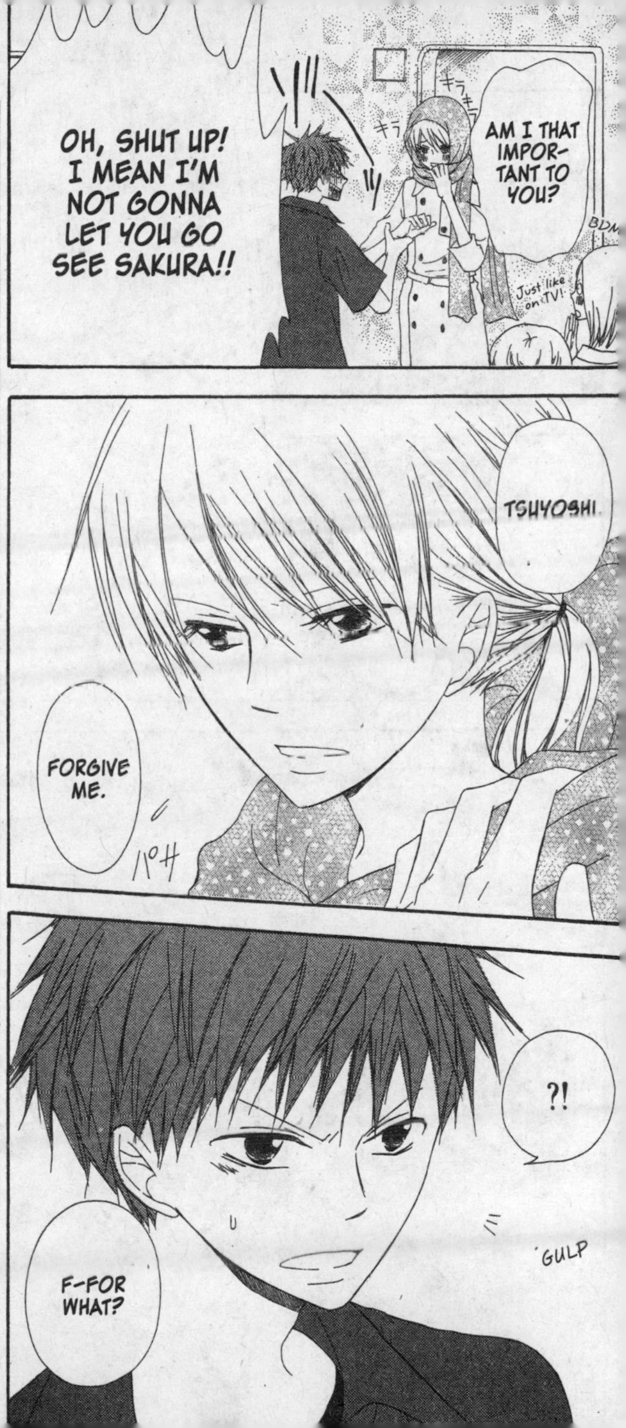
AM I THAT IMPORTANT TO YOU?
Just like on TV!
OH, SHUT UP! I MEAN I'M NOT GONNA LET YOU GO SEE SAKURA!!
TSUYOSHI.
FORGIVE ME.
?!
GULP
F-FOR WHAT?

5

Stay tuned for the short story after this chapter. I have fond memories of it.

It's the work I did after "The Town Where Santa Is," that was published in volume six. This time I didn't make all the corrections I need, so it's pretty embarrassing...

I like to think that I've gotten a lot better since then.

But I aim to get even better...

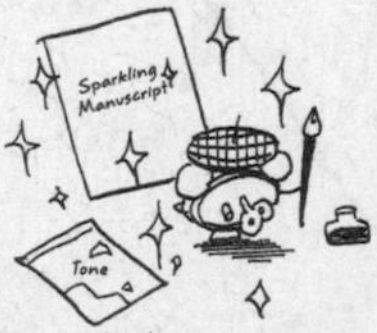
Sparkling Manuscript!
Tone

It would be nice if I could draw with lots of gusto and get really, really good.
No!
I will! (...I hope.)

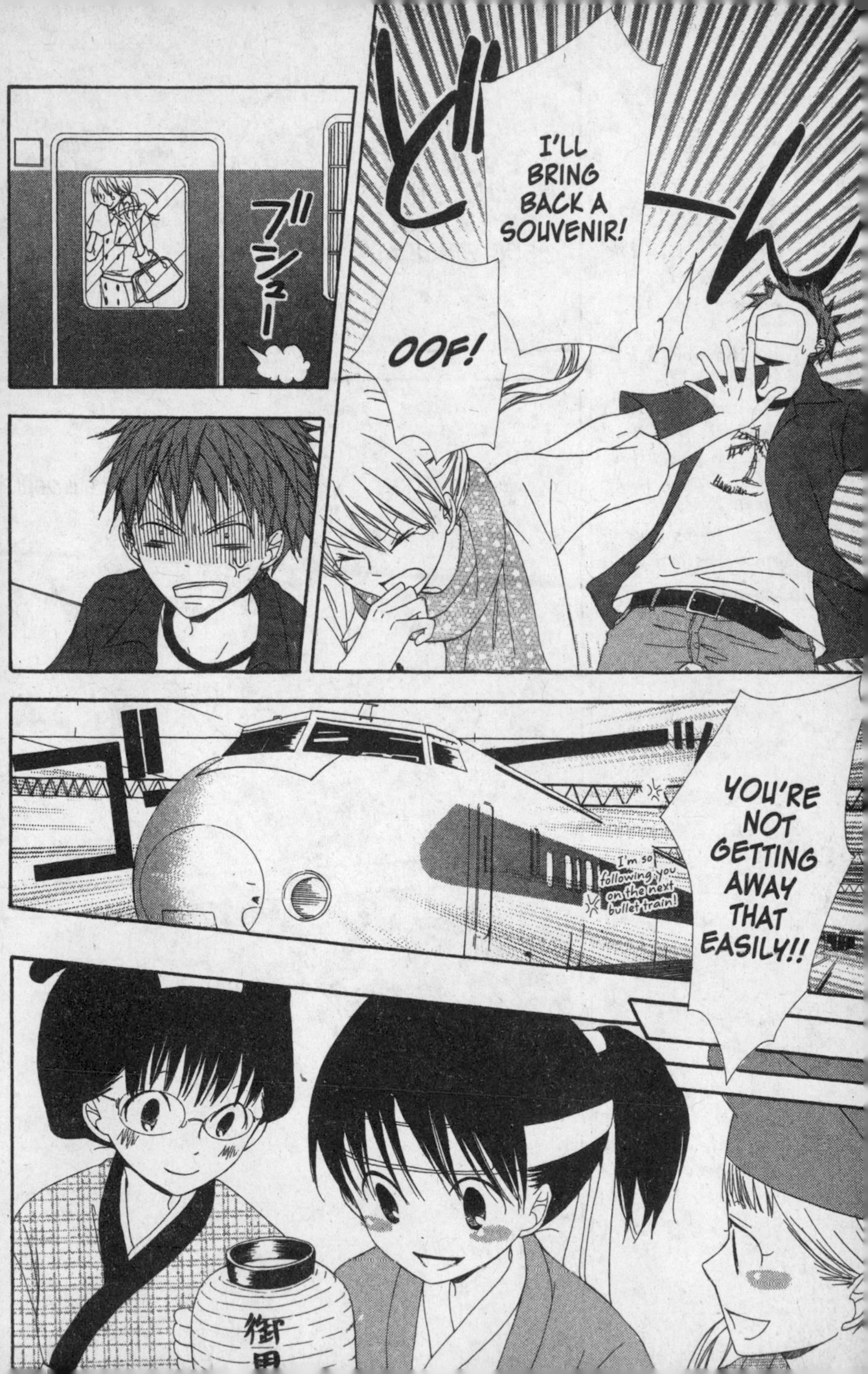
どーん
I'LL BRING BACK A SOUVENIR!
OOF!
ブシュー
YOU'RE NOT GETTING AWAY THAT EASILY!!
I'm so following you on the next bullet train!
ゴー

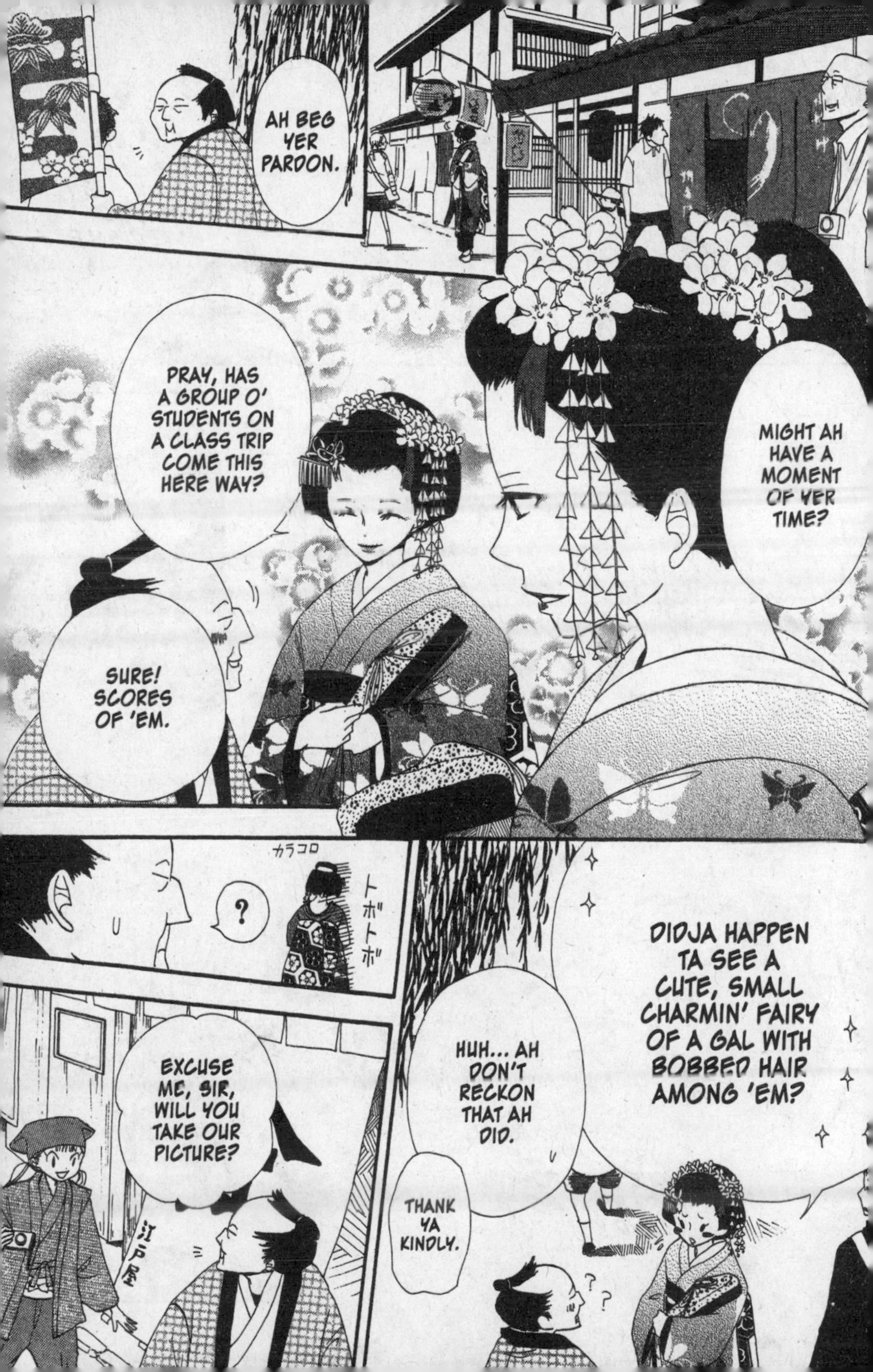
AH BEG YER PARDON.
MIGHT AH HAVE A MOMENT OF YER TIME?
PRAY, HAS A GROUP O' STUDENTS ON A CLASS TRIP COME THIS HERE WAY?
SURE! SCORES OF 'EM.
DIDJA HAPPEN TA SEE A CUTE, SMALL CHARMIN' FAIRY OF A GAL WITH BOBBED HAIR AMONG 'EM?
HUH... AH DON'T RECKON THAT AH DID.
THANK YA KINDLY.
カラコロ
?
トボトボ
EXCUSE ME, SIR, WILL YOU TAKE OUR PICTURE?
江戸屋

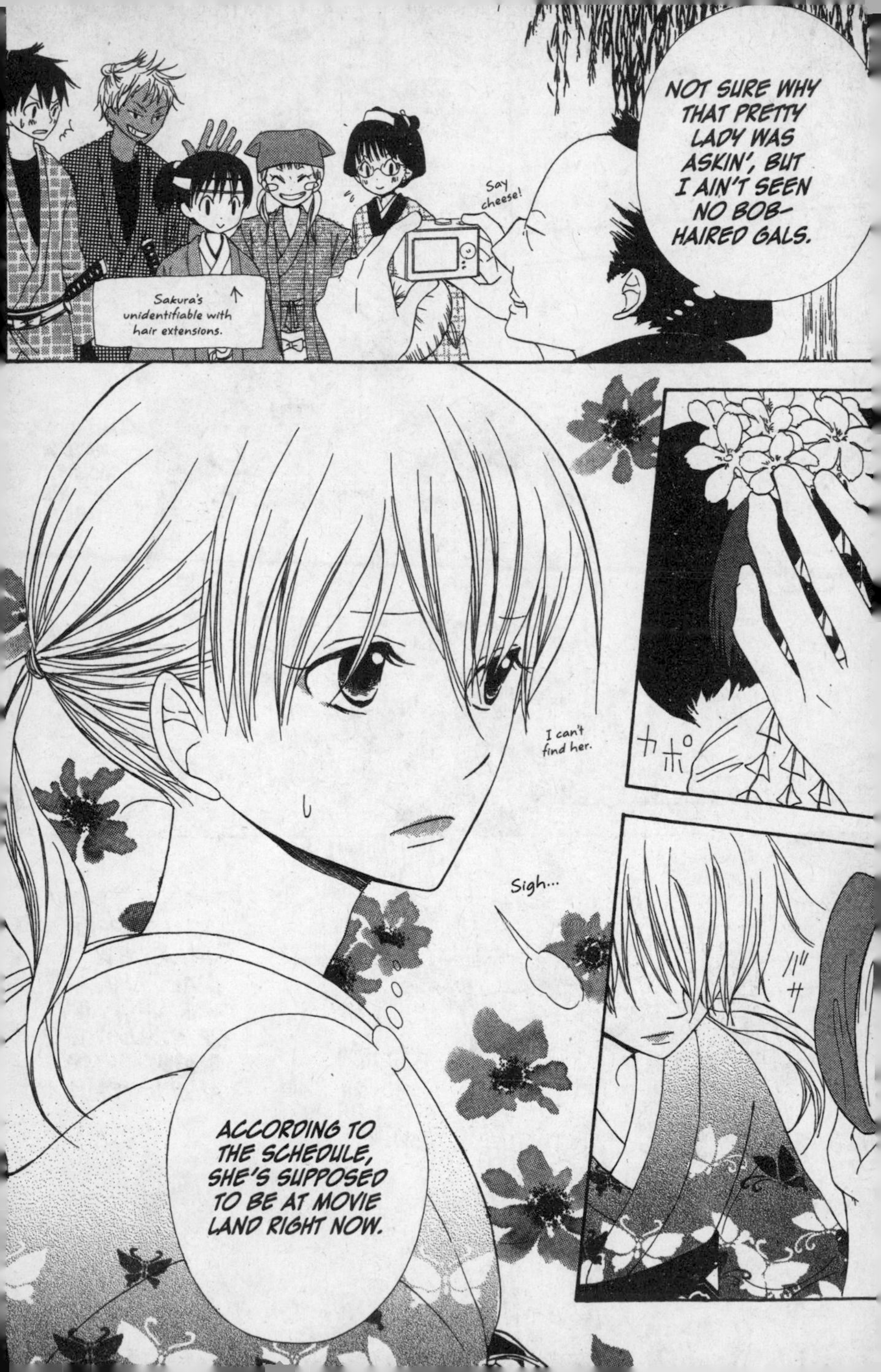
NOT SURE WHY THAT PRETTY LADY WAS ASKIN', BUT I AIN'T SEEN NO BOB-HAIRED GALS.
Say cheese!
Sakura's unidentifiable with hair extensions.
カポ
バサ
Sigh...
I can't find her.
ACCORDING TO THE SCHEDULE, SHE'S SUPPOSED TO BE AT MOVIE LAND RIGHT NOW.

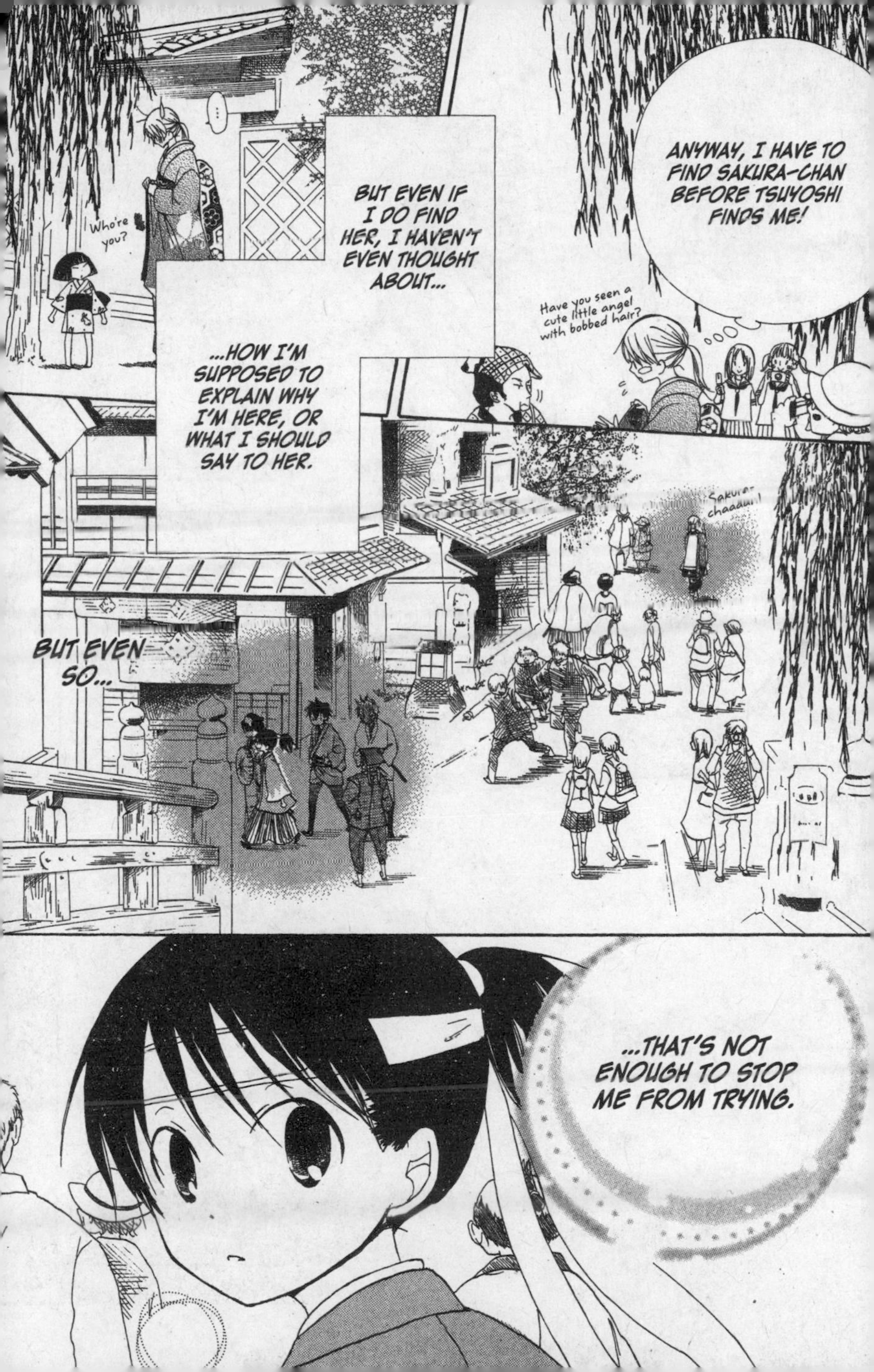
ANYWAY, I HAVE TO FIND SAKURA-CHAN BEFORE TSUYOSHI FINDS ME!
Have you seen a cute little angel with bobbed hair?
...
Who're you?
BUT EVEN IF I DO FIND HER, I HAVEN'T EVEN THOUGHT ABOUT...
...HOW I'M SUPPOSED TO EXPLAIN WHY I'M HERE, OR WHAT I SHOULD SAY TO HER.
Sakura-chaaan!
BUT EVEN SO...
...THAT'S NOT ENOUGH TO STOP ME FROM TRYING.

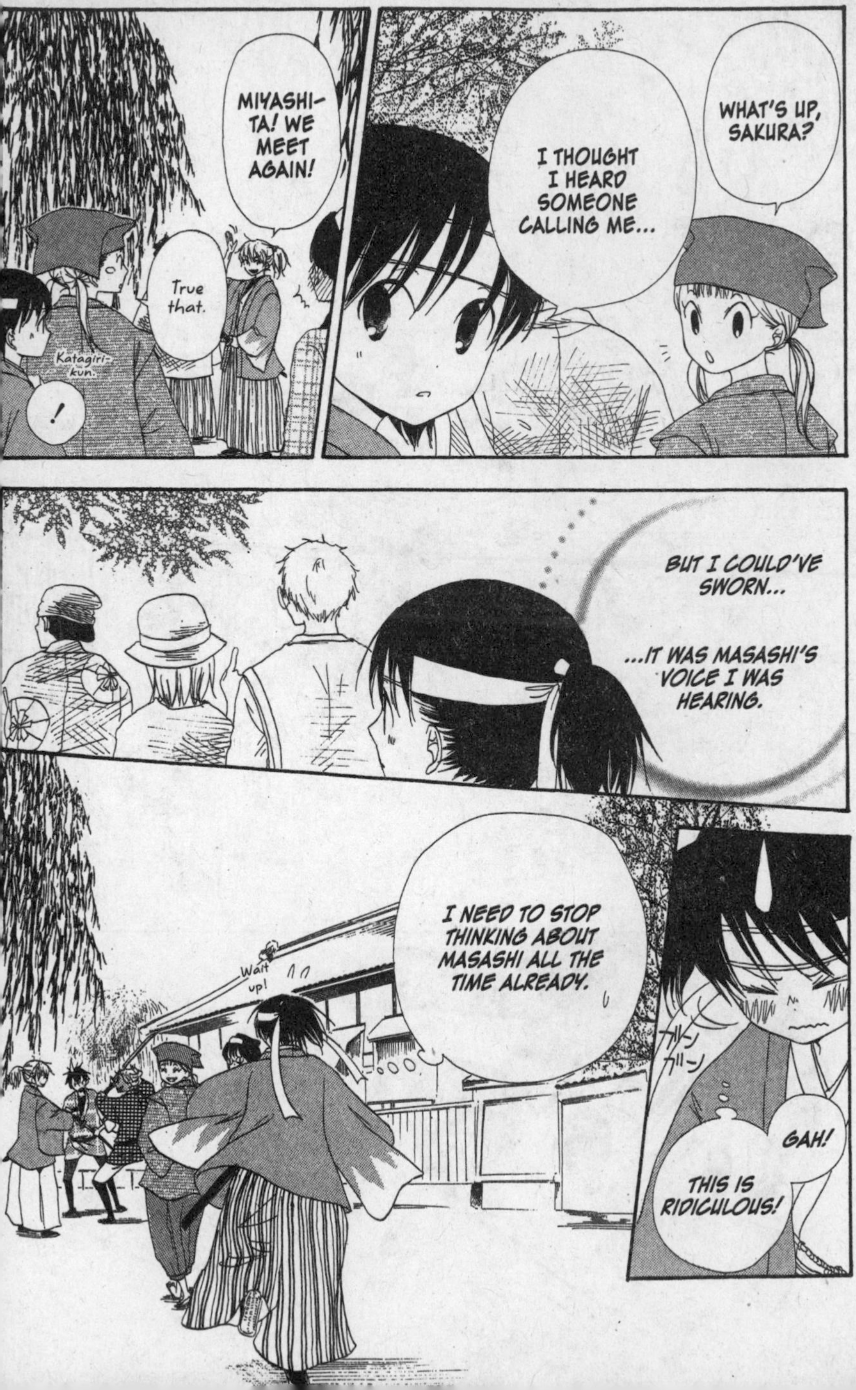
WHAT'S UP, SAKURA?
I THOUGHT I HEARD SOMEONE CALLING ME...
MIYASHITA! WE MEET AGAIN!
True that.
Katagiri-kun.
!
BUT I COULD'VE SWORN...
...IT WAS MASASHI'S VOICE I WAS HEARING.
I NEED TO STOP THINKING ABOUT MASASHI ALL THE TIME ALREADY.
Wait up!
GAH!
THIS IS RIDICULOUS!

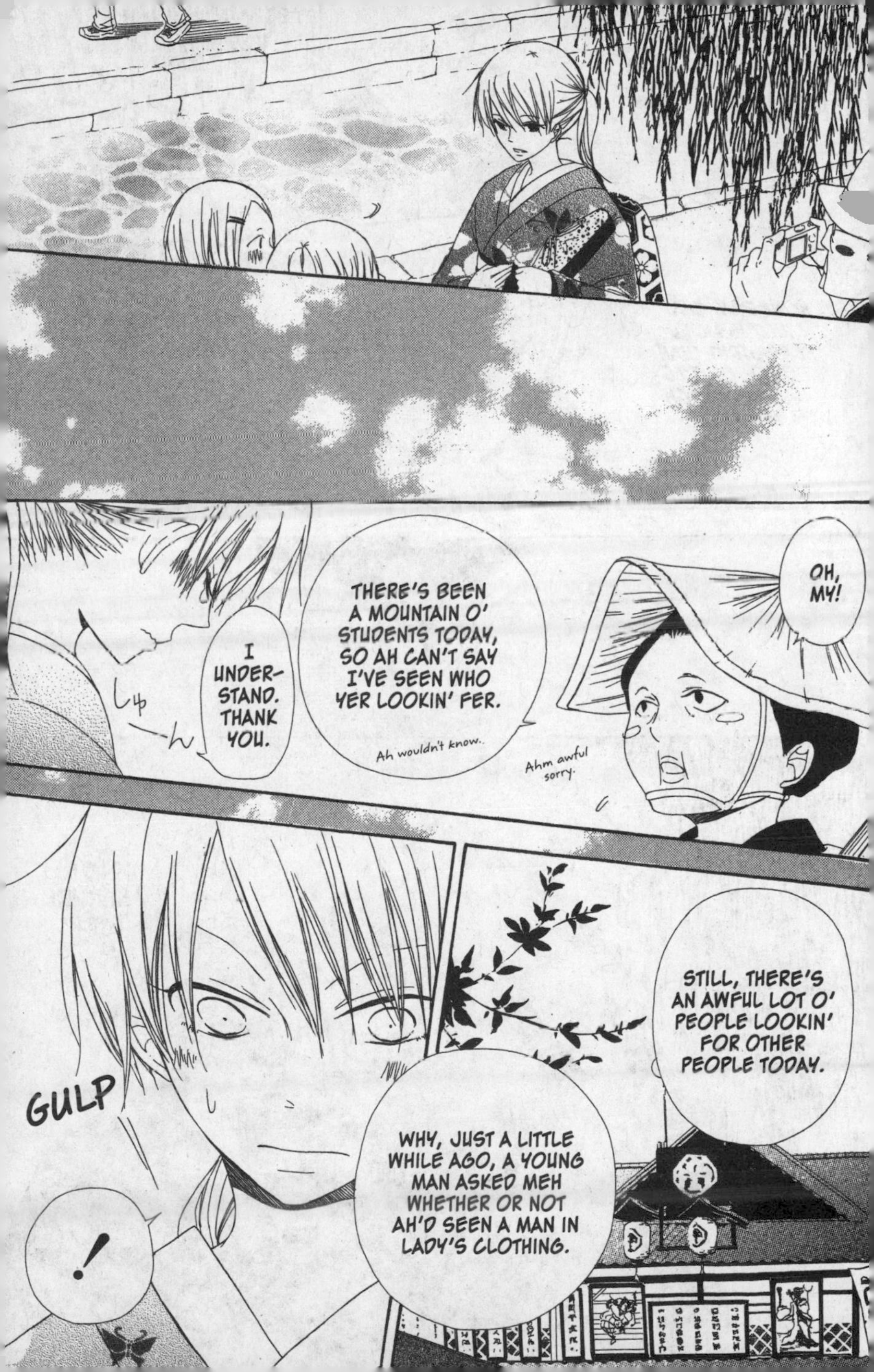
OH, MY!
Ahm awful sorry.
THERE'S BEEN A MOUNTAIN O' STUDENTS TODAY, SO AH CAN'T SAY I'VE SEEN WHO YER LOOKIN' FER.
Ah wouldn't know..
I UNDER-STAND. THANK YOU.
しゅーん
STILL, THERE'S AN AWFUL LOT O' PEOPLE LOOKIN' FOR OTHER PEOPLE TODAY.
WHY, JUST A LITTLE WHILE AGO, A YOUNG MAN ASKED MEH WHETHER OR NOT AH'D SEEN A MAN IN LADY'S CLOTHING.
GULP
!

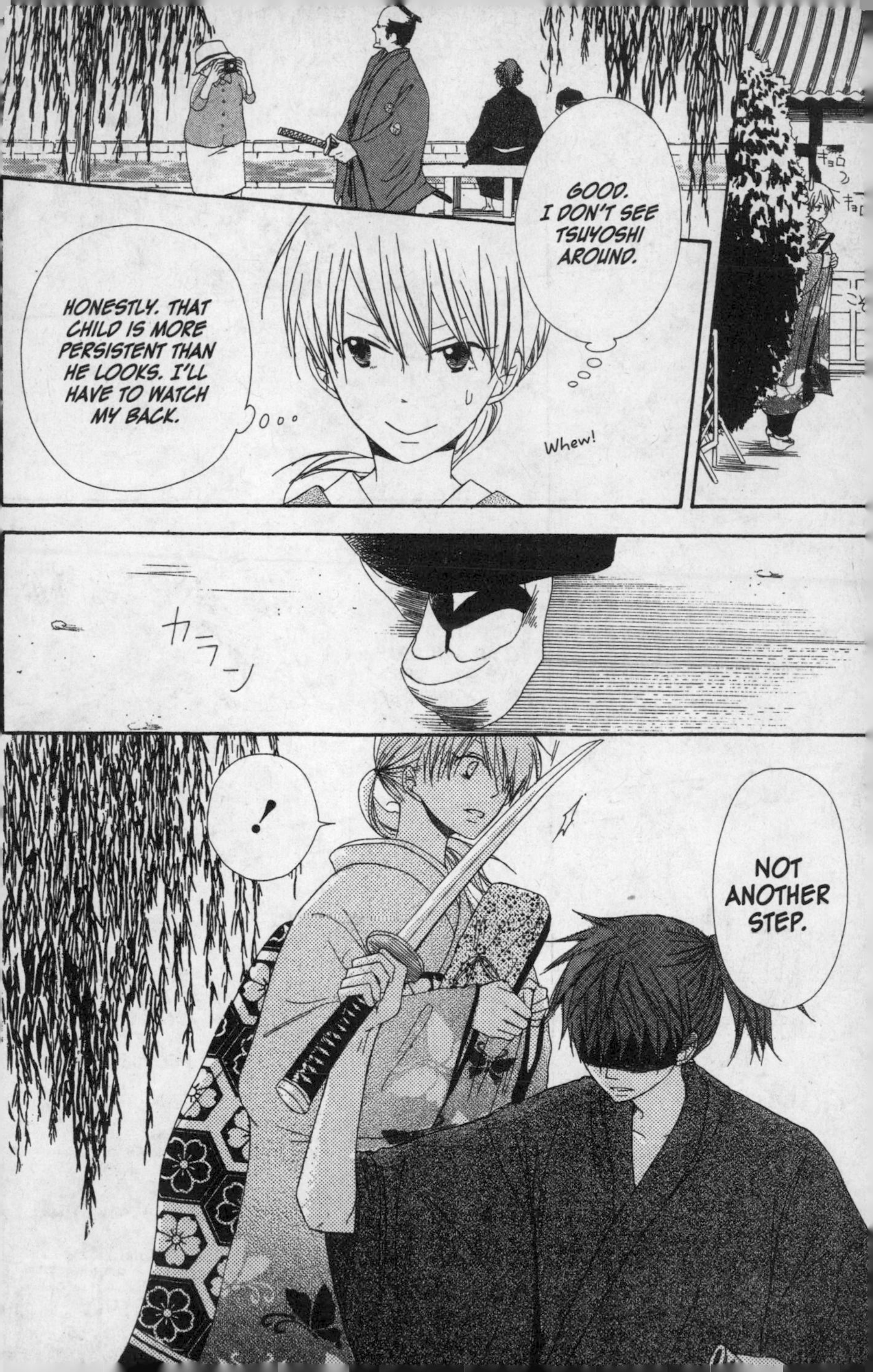
キョロ
キョロ
GOOD. I DON'T SEE TSUYOSHI AROUND.
Whew!
HONESTLY. THAT CHILD IS MORE PERSISTENT THAN HE LOOKS. I'LL HAVE TO WATCH MY BACK.
カラーン
NOT ANOTHER STEP.
!

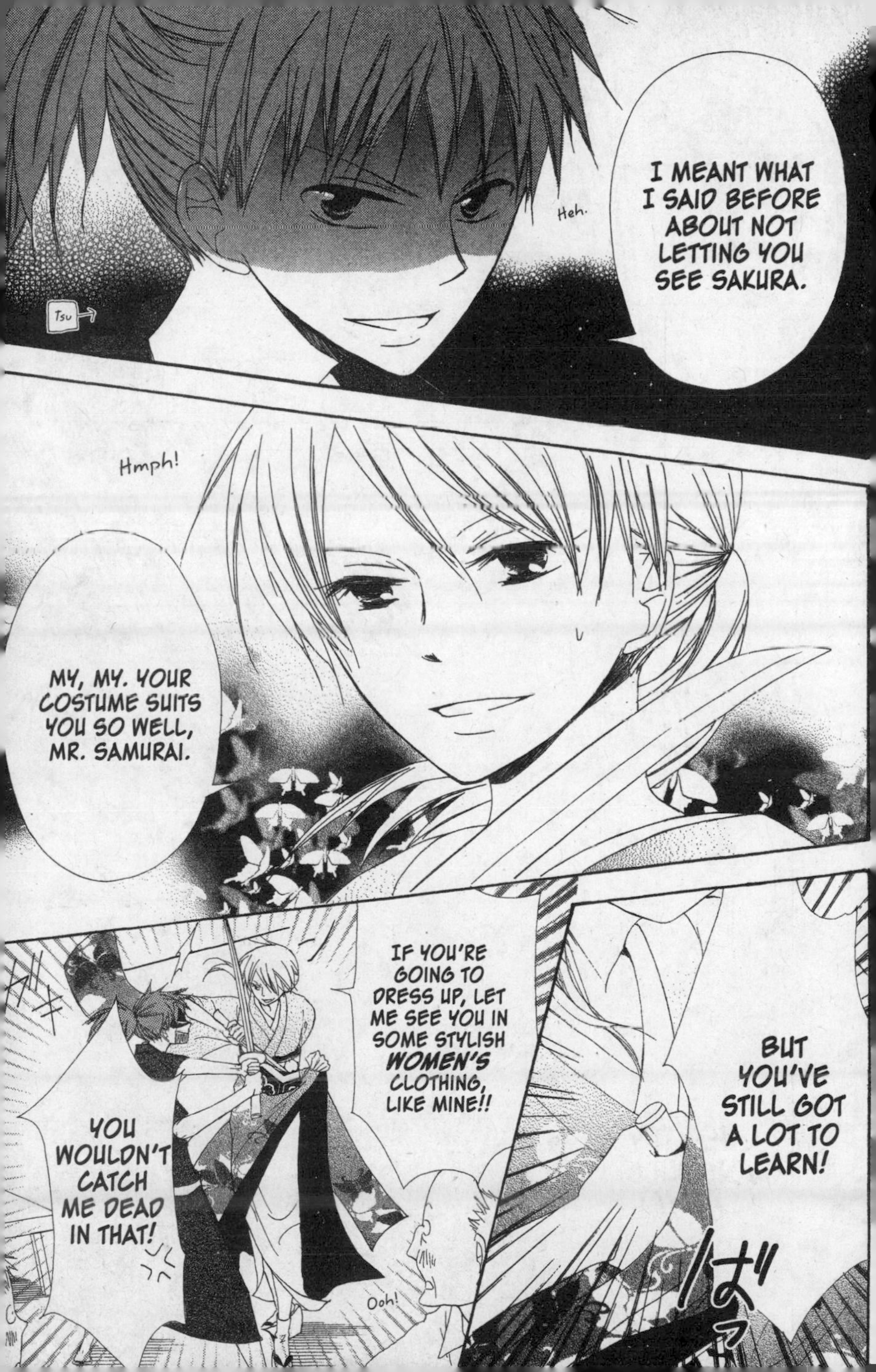

I MEANT WHAT I SAID BEFORE ABOUT NOT LETTING YOU SEE SAKURA.
Heh.
Tsu
Hmph!
MY, MY. YOUR COSTUME SUITS YOU SO WELL, MR. SAMURAI.
BUT YOU'VE STILL GOT A LOT TO LEARN!
ばっ
IF YOU'RE GOING TO DRESS UP, LET ME SEE YOU IN SOME STYLISH *WOMEN'S* CLOTHING, LIKE MINE!!
YOU WOULDN'T CATCH ME DEAD IN THAT!
Ooh!

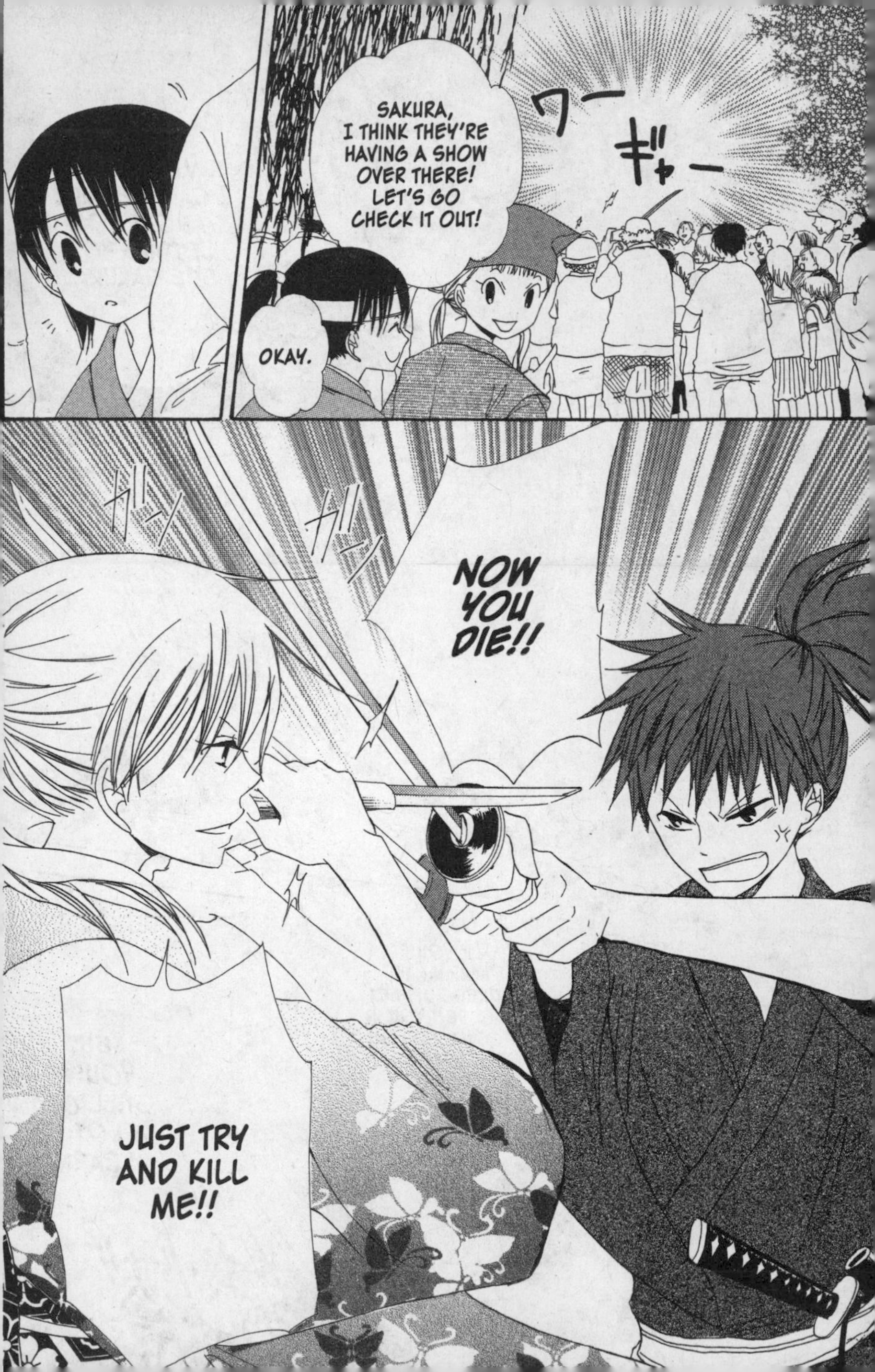
ワー
ギャー
SAKURA, I THINK THEY'RE HAVING A SHOW OVER THERE! LET'S GO CHECK IT OUT!
OKAY.
NOW YOU DIE!!
JUST TRY AND KILL ME!!

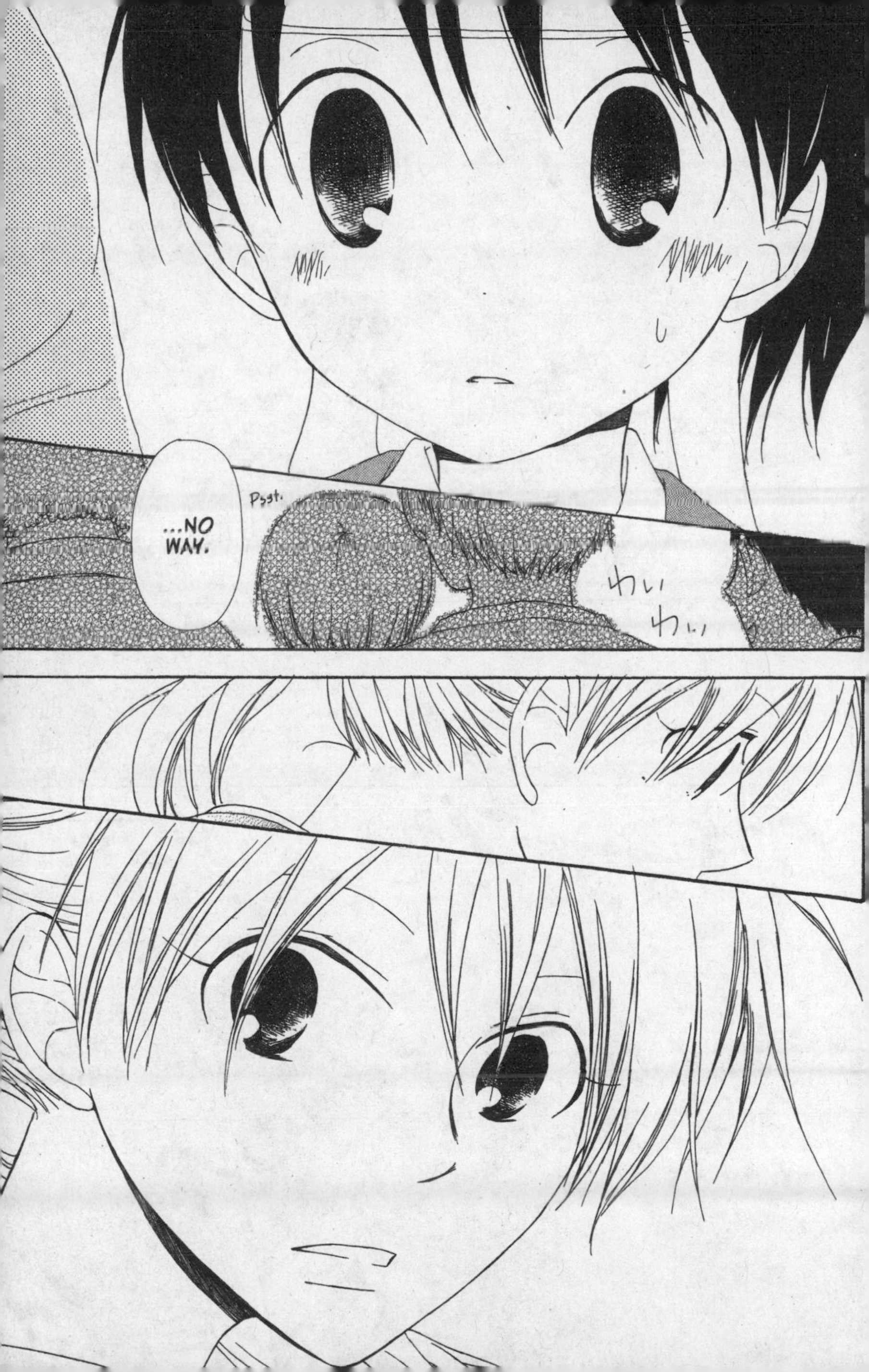
わい わい
Psst.
...NO WAY.

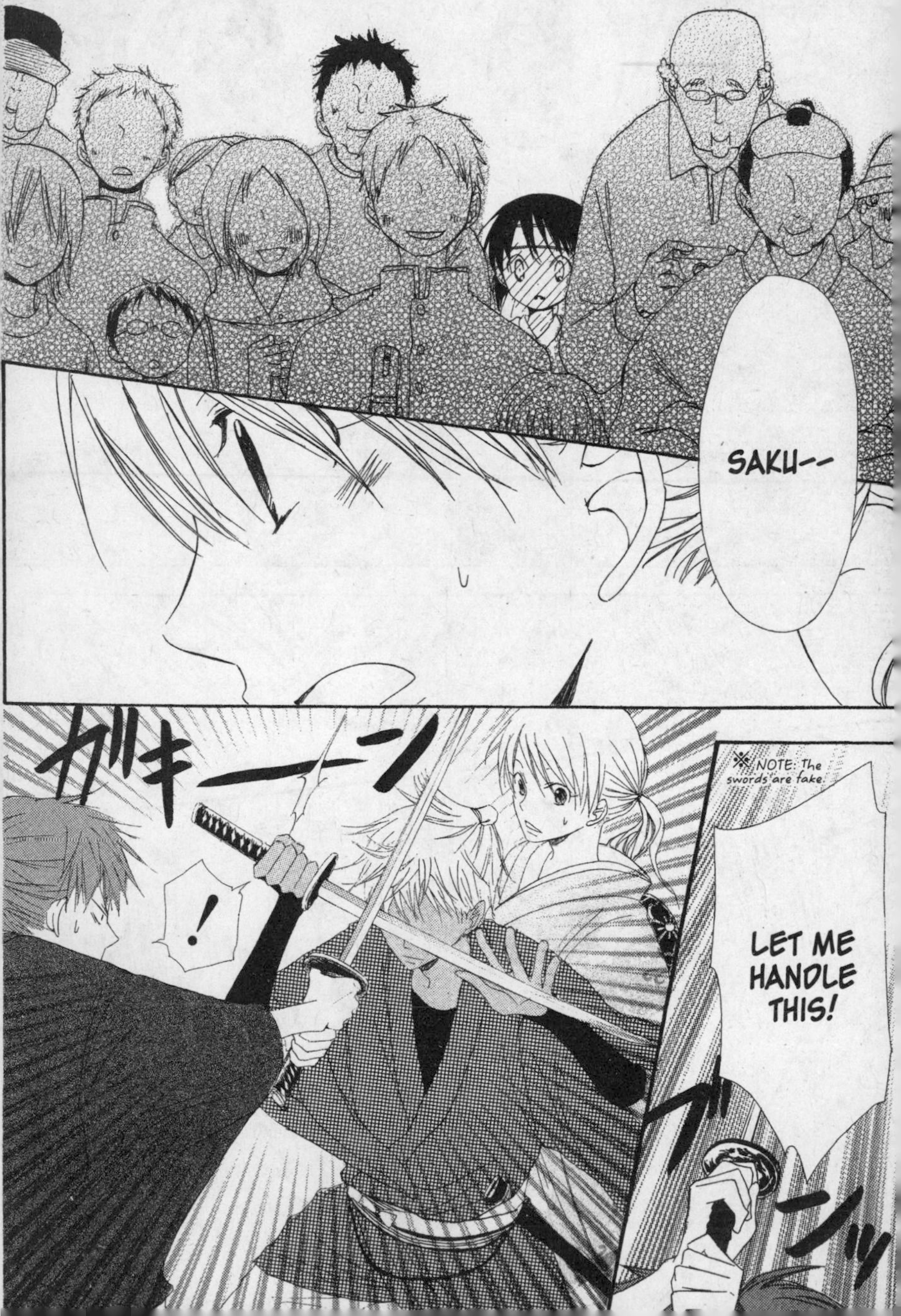
SAKU--
※NOTE: The swords are fake.
LET ME HANDLE THIS!
ガキーーン
!

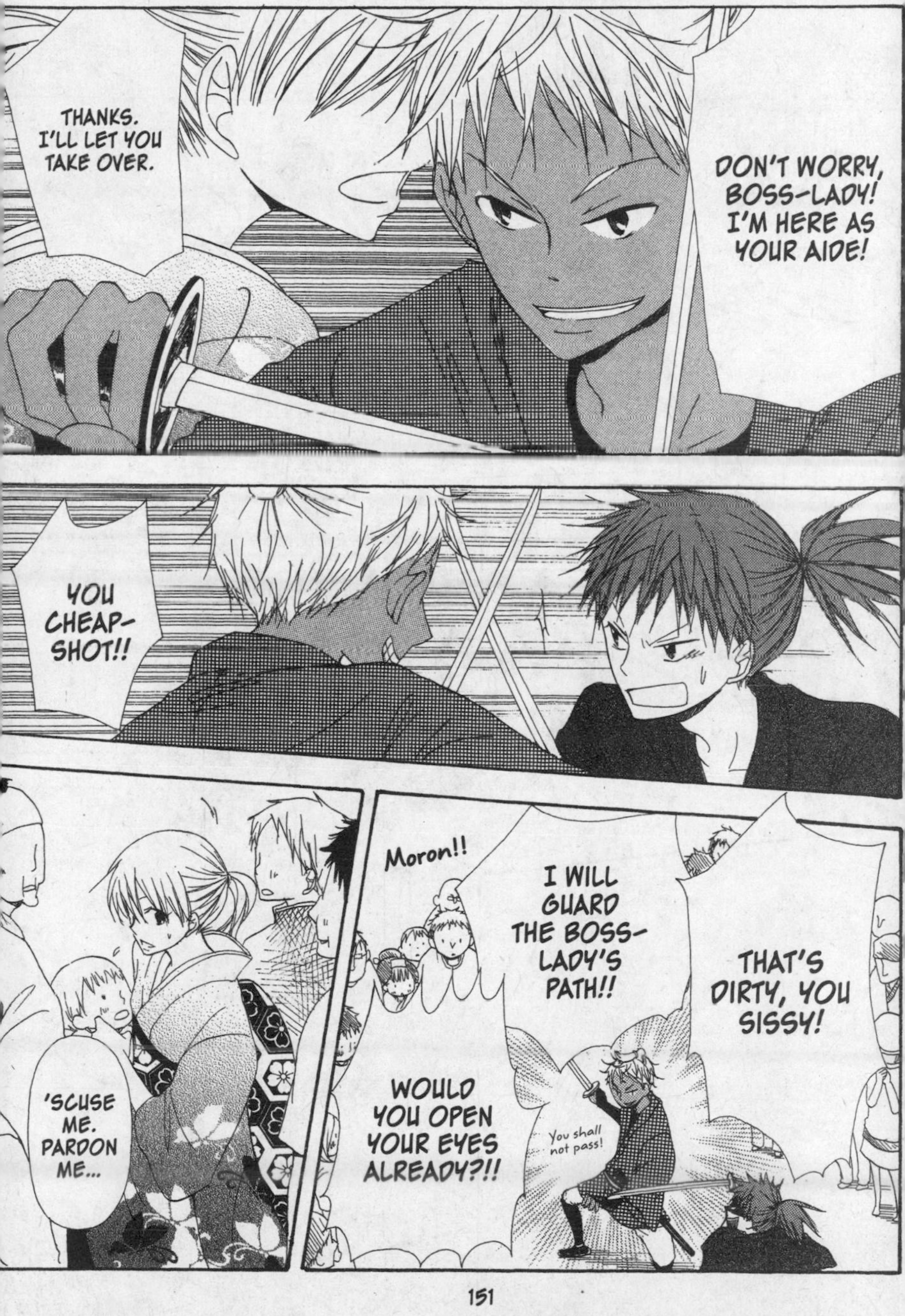
DON'T WORRY, BOSS-LADY! I'M HERE AS YOUR AIDE!
THANKS. I'LL LET YOU TAKE OVER.
YOU CHEAP-SHOT!!
THAT'S DIRTY, YOU SISSY!
I WILL GUARD THE BOSS-LADY'S PATH!!
Moron!!
WOULD YOU OPEN YOUR EYES ALREADY?!!
You shall not pass!
'SCUSE ME. PARDON ME...

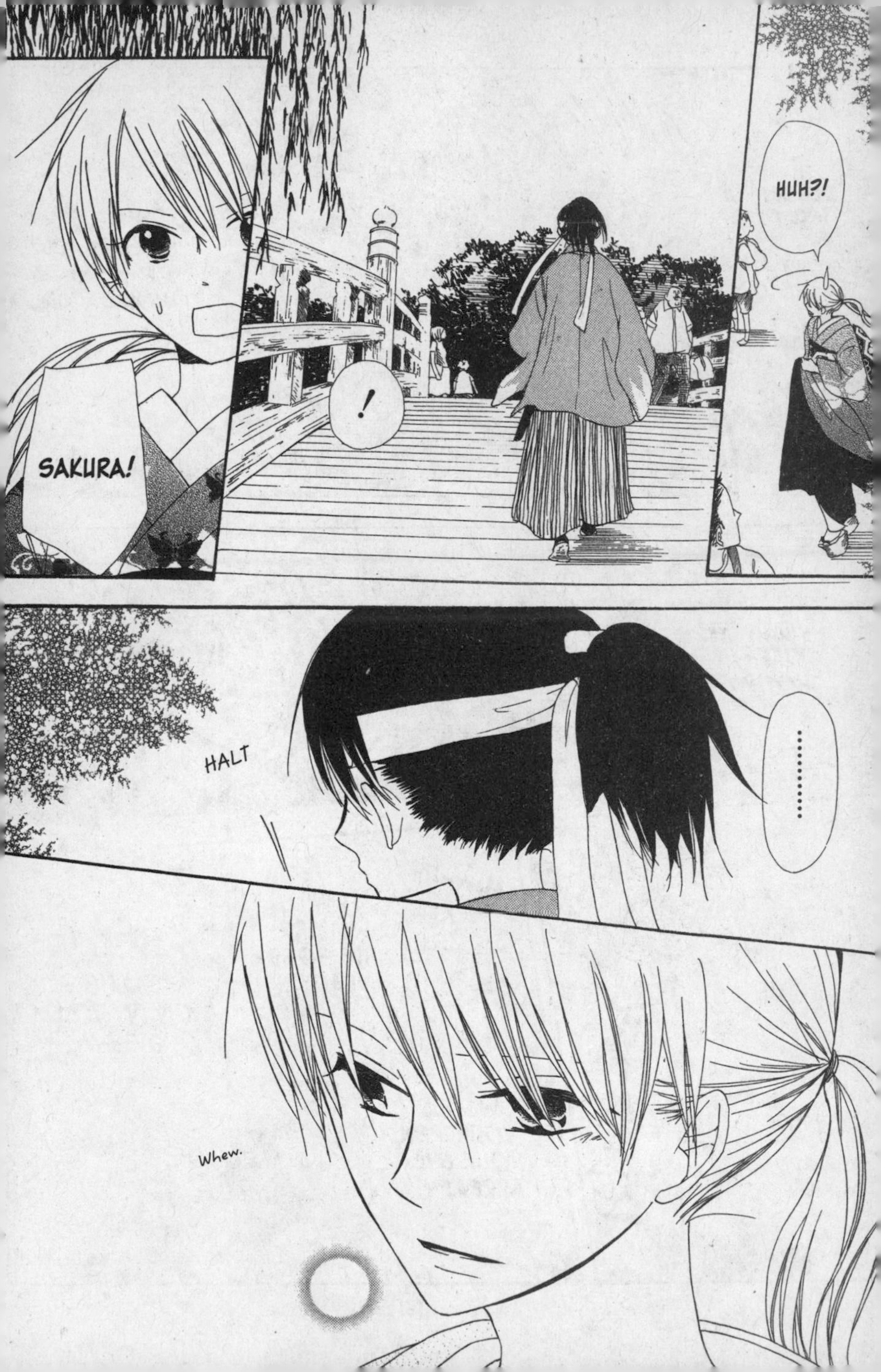
HUH?!
!
SAKURA!
......
HALT
Whew.

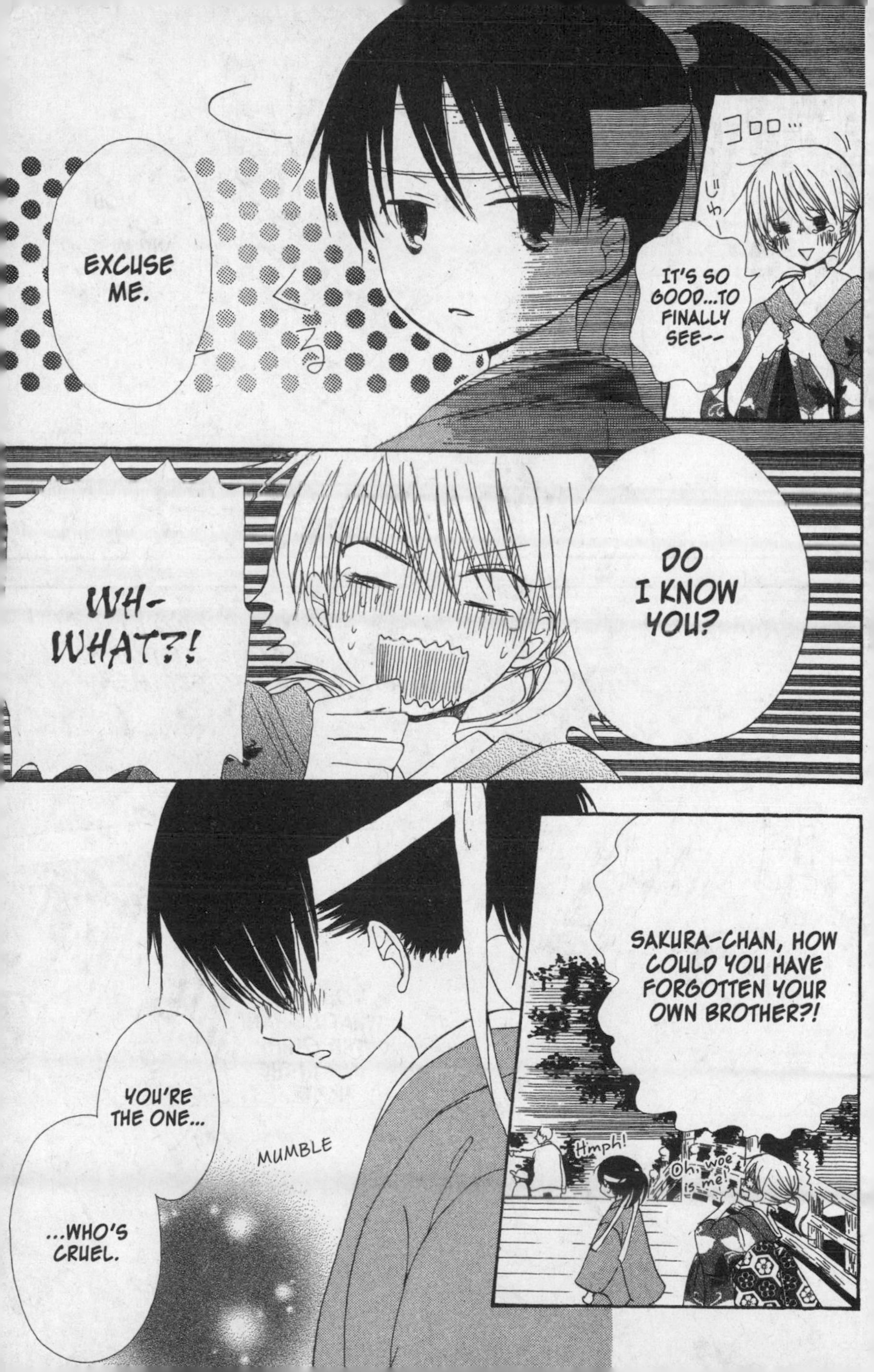
IT'S SO GOOD...TO FINALLY SEE--
EXCUSE ME.
DO I KNOW YOU?
WH-WHAT?!
SAKURA-CHAN, HOW COULD YOU HAVE FORGOTTEN YOUR OWN BROTHER?!
Oh, woe is me!
Hmph!
YOU'RE THE ONE...
MUMBLE
...WHO'S CRUEL.

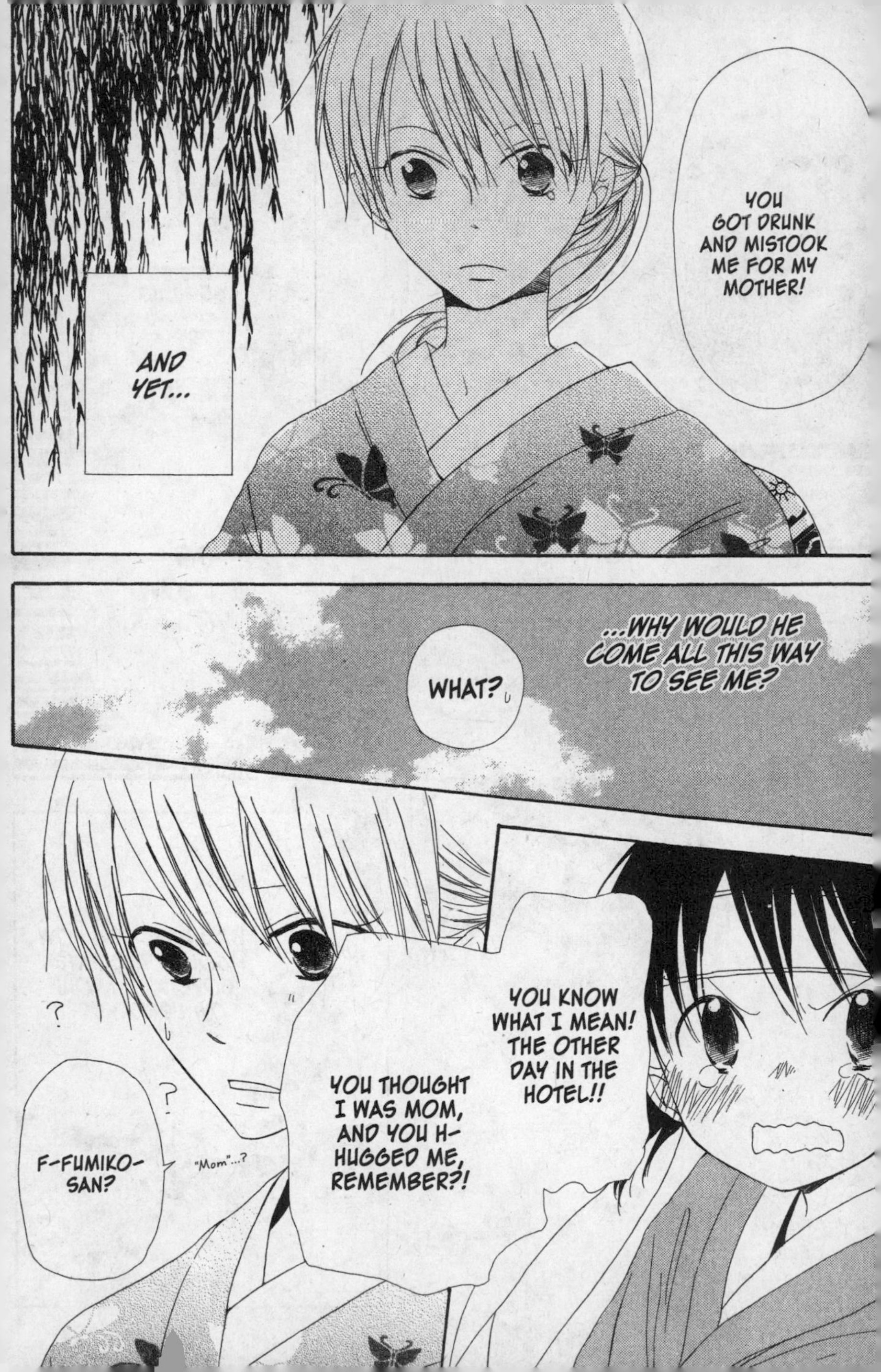
YOU GOT DRUNK AND MISTOOK ME FOR MY MOTHER!
AND YET...
...WHY WOULD HE COME ALL THIS WAY TO SEE ME?
WHAT?
YOU KNOW WHAT I MEAN! THE OTHER DAY IN THE HOTEL!!
YOU THOUGHT I WAS MOM, AND YOU H-HUGGED ME, REMEMBER?!
"Mom"...?
F-FUMIKO-SAN?

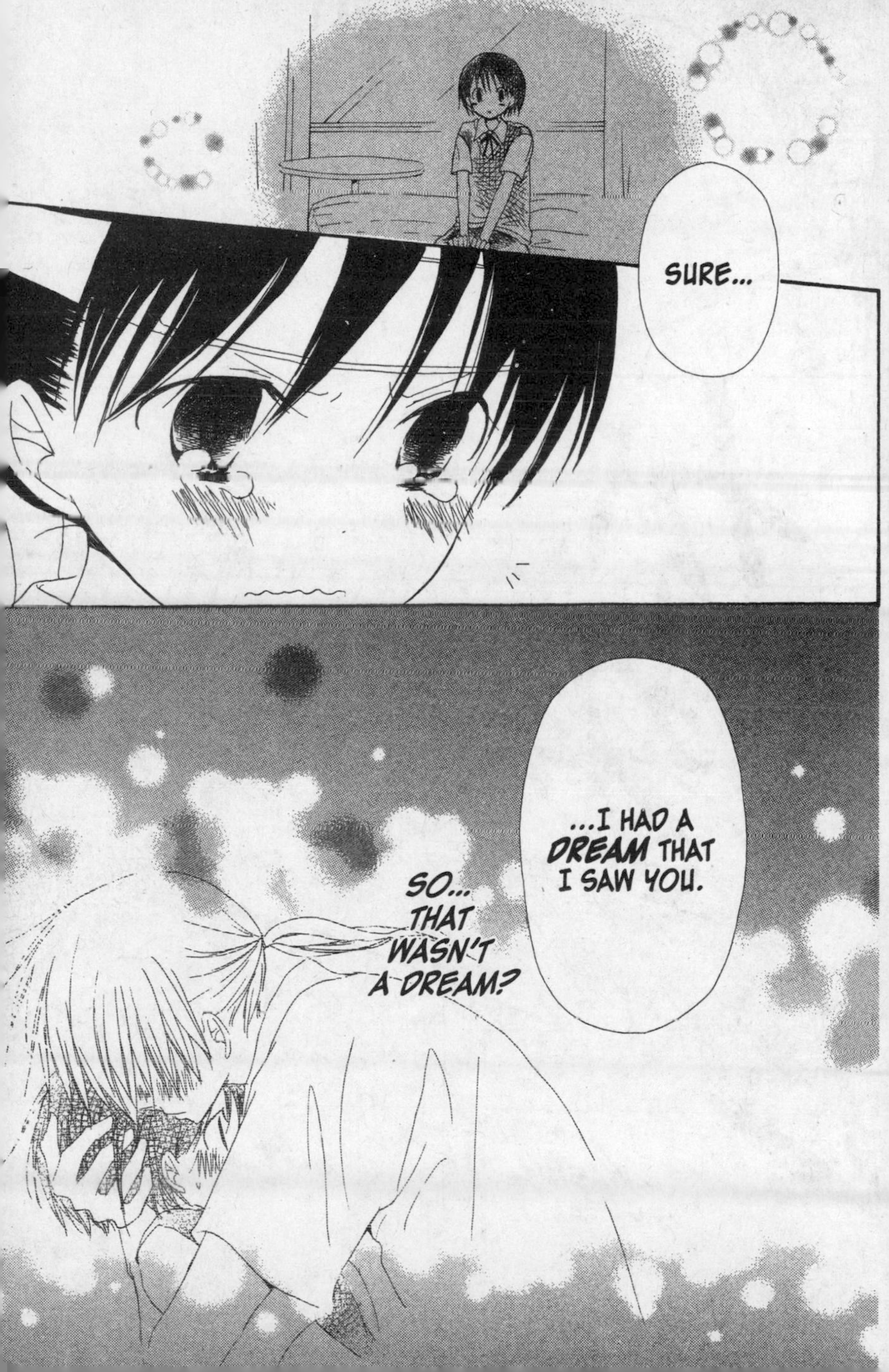
SURE...
...I HAD A DREAM THAT I SAW YOU.
SO... THAT WASN'T A DREAM?

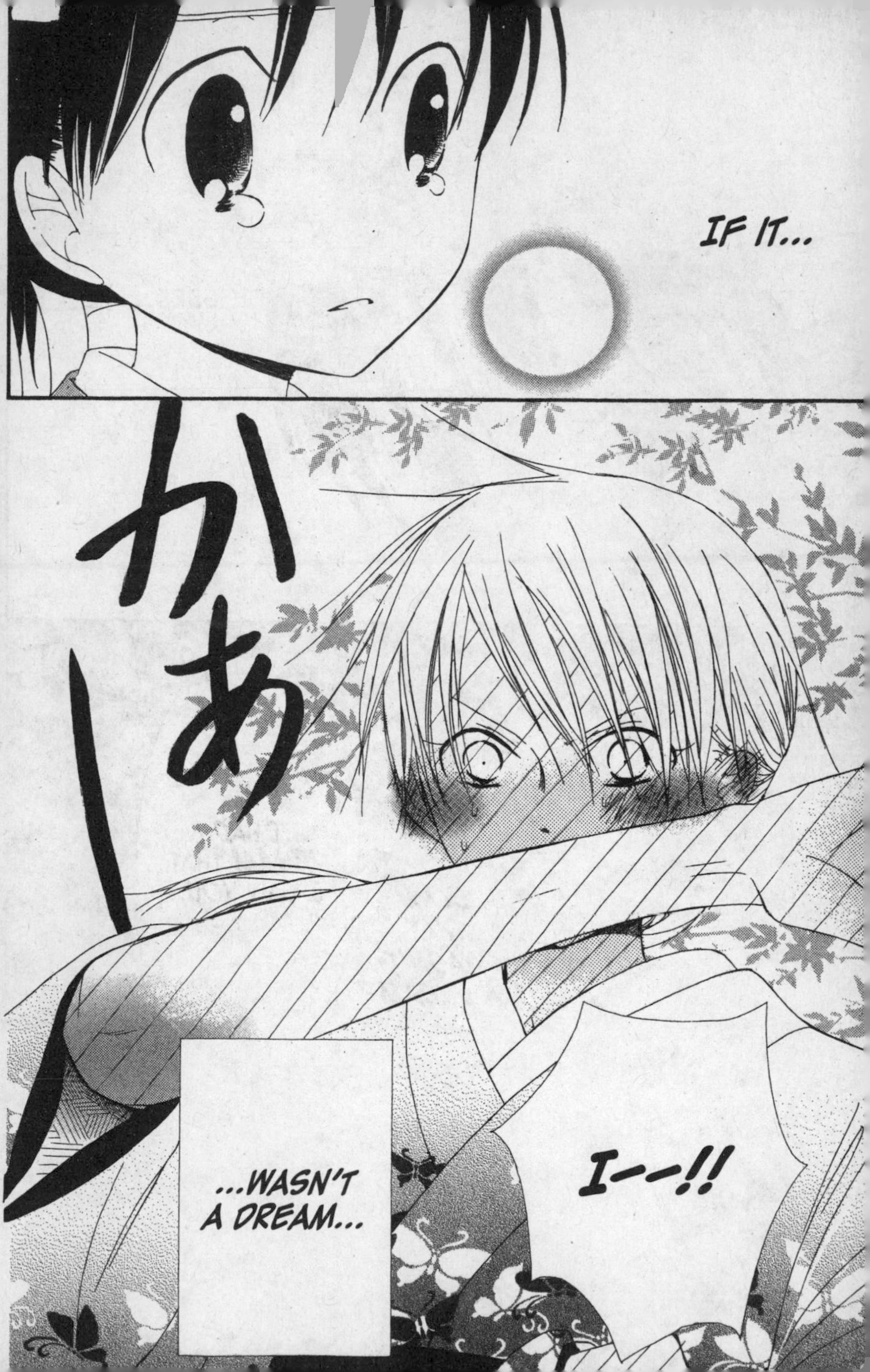
IF IT...
かあー
...WASN'T A DREAM...
I--!!

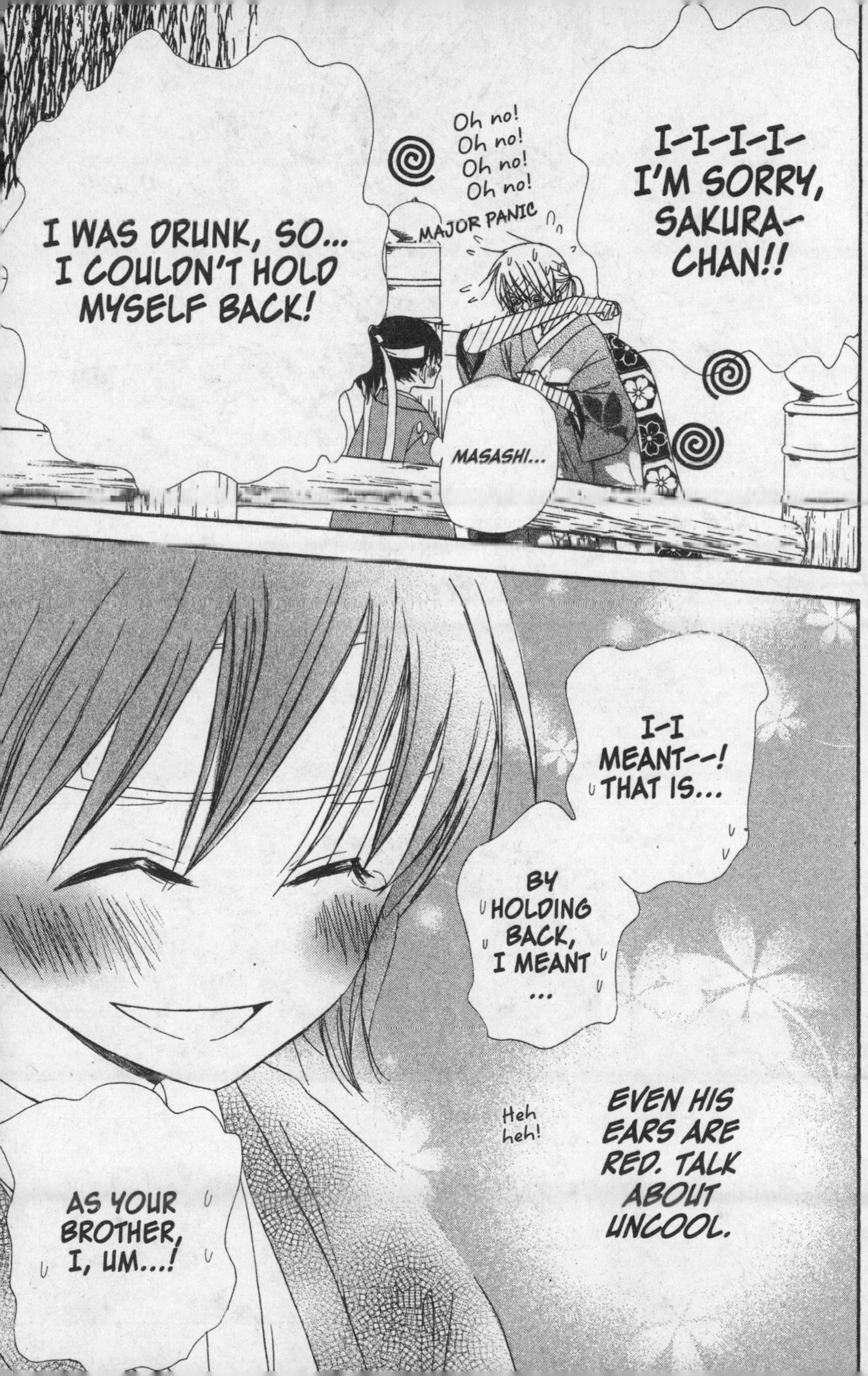
I-I-I-I- I'M SORRY, SAKURA-CHAN!!
Oh no! Oh no! Oh no! Oh no!
MAJOR PANIC
I WAS DRUNK, SO... I COULDN'T HOLD MYSELF BACK!
MASASHI...
I-I MEANT--! THAT IS...
BY HOLDING BACK, I MEANT ...
EVEN HIS EARS ARE RED. TALK ABOUT UNCOOL.
Heh heh!
AS YOUR BROTHER, I, UM...!

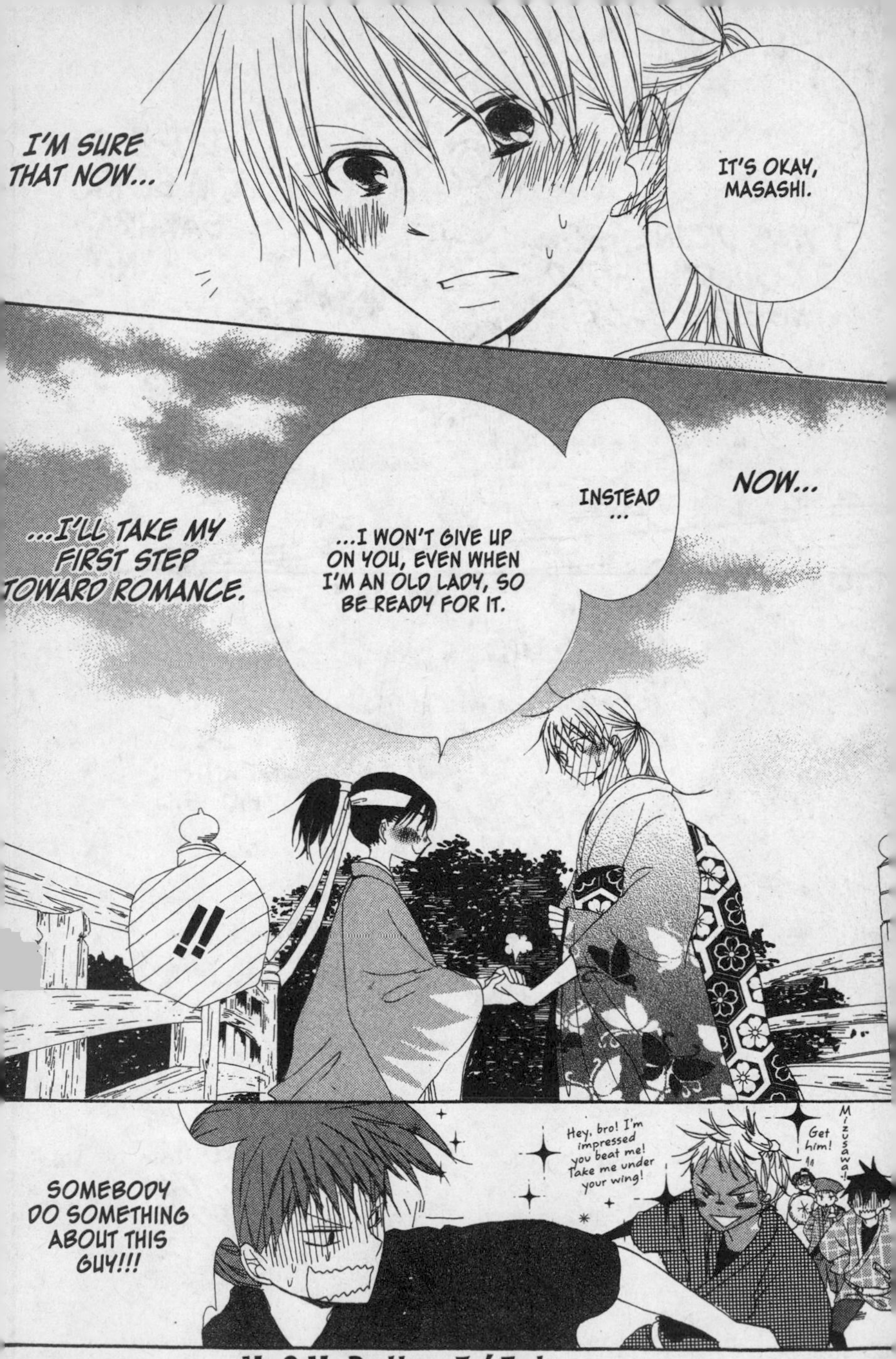
IT'S OKAY, MASASHI.
I'M SURE THAT NOW...
NOW...
INSTEAD...
...I WON'T GIVE UP ON YOU, EVEN WHEN I'M AN OLD LADY, SO BE READY FOR IT.
...I'LL TAKE MY FIRST STEP TOWARD ROMANCE.
!!
Mizusawa-!
Get him!
Hey, bro! I'm impressed you beat me! Take me under your wing!
SOMEBODY DO SOMETHING ABOUT THIS GUY!!!

Me & My Brothers 7 / End

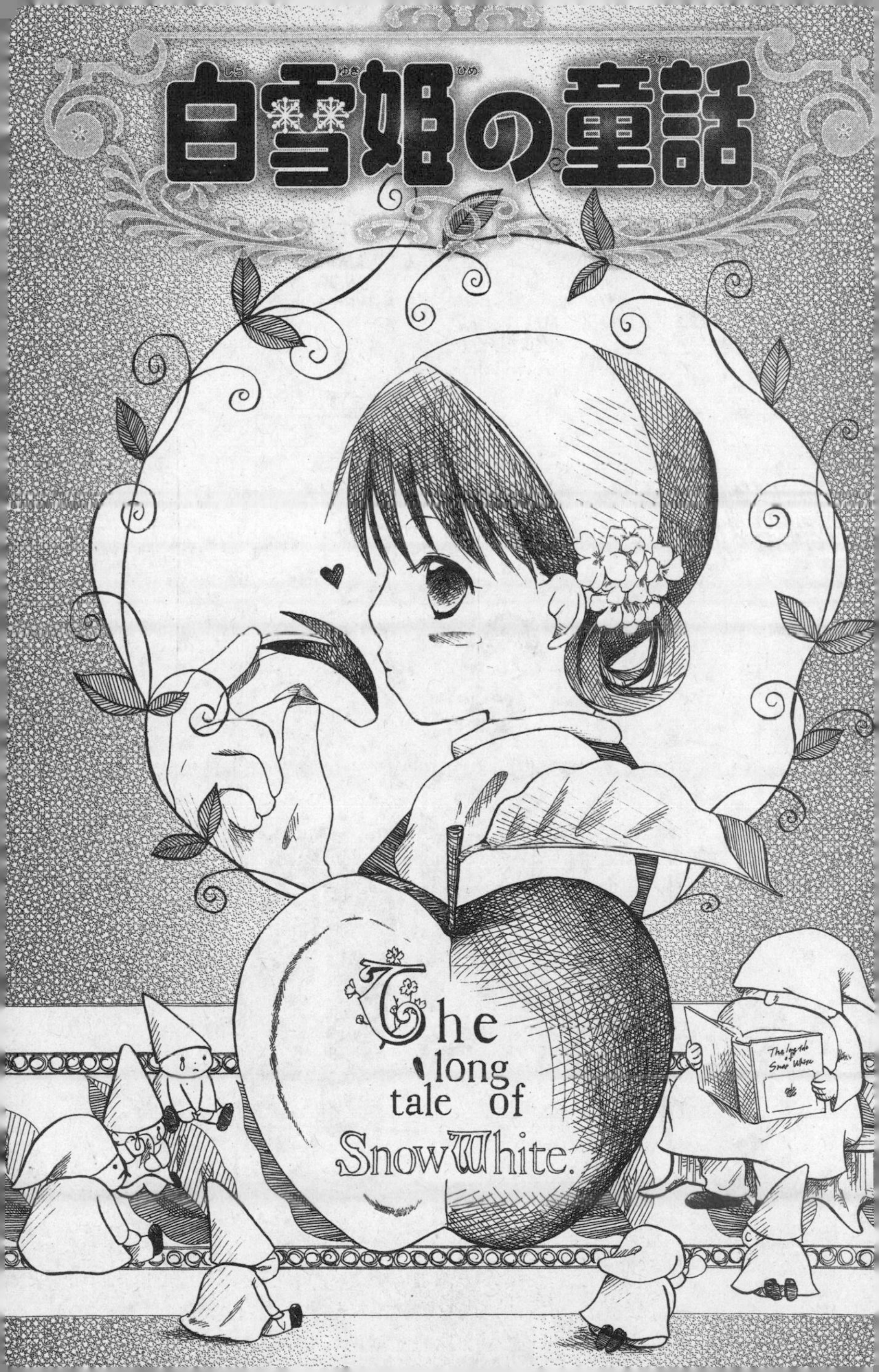
白雪姫の童話
The long tale of Snow White.

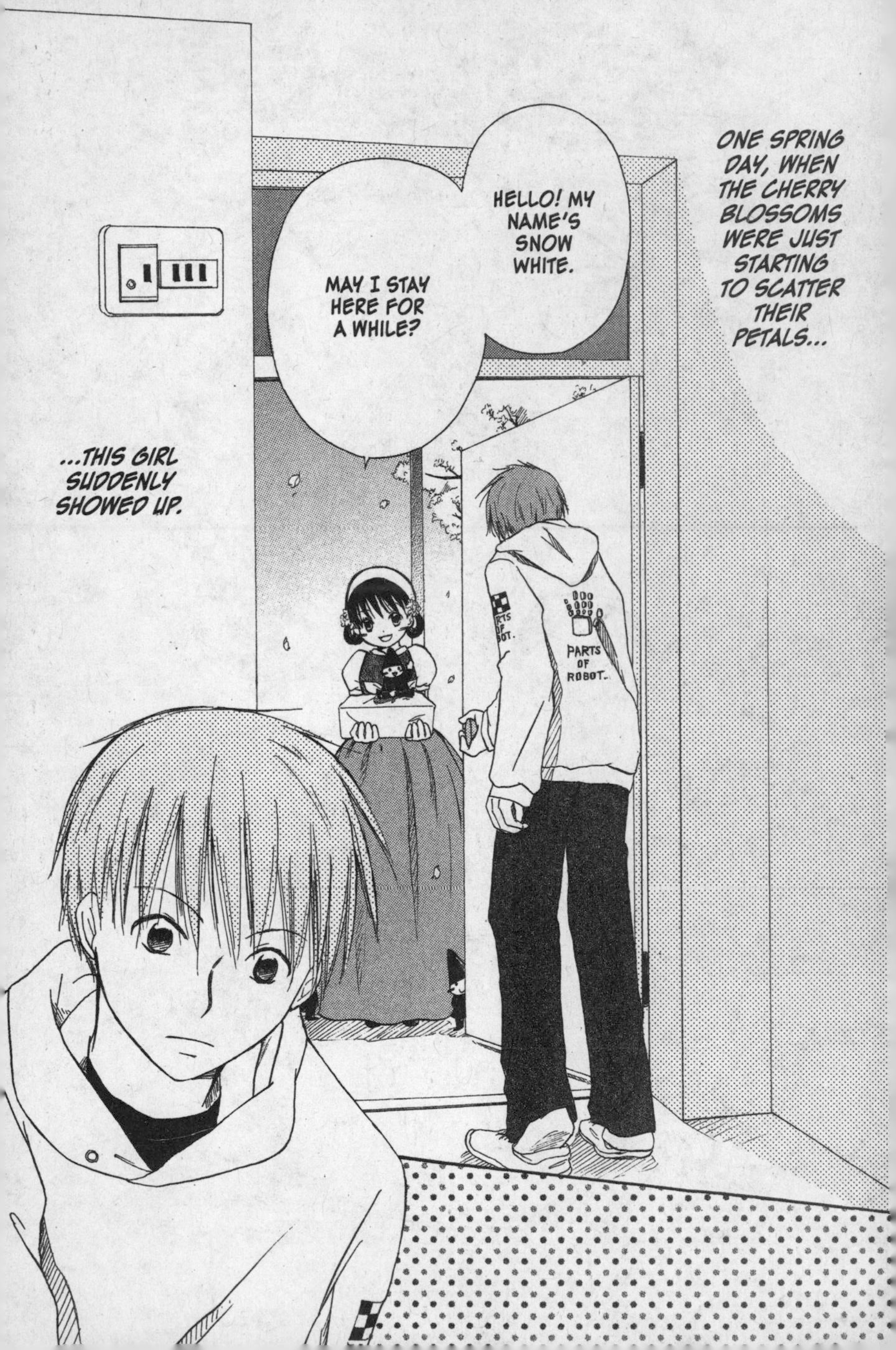
ONE SPRING DAY, WHEN THE CHERRY BLOSSOMS WERE JUST STARTING TO SCATTER THEIR PETALS...
HELLO! MY NAME'S SNOW WHITE.
MAY I STAY HERE FOR A WHILE?
PARTS OF ROBOT.
...THIS GIRL SUDDENLY SHOWED UP.

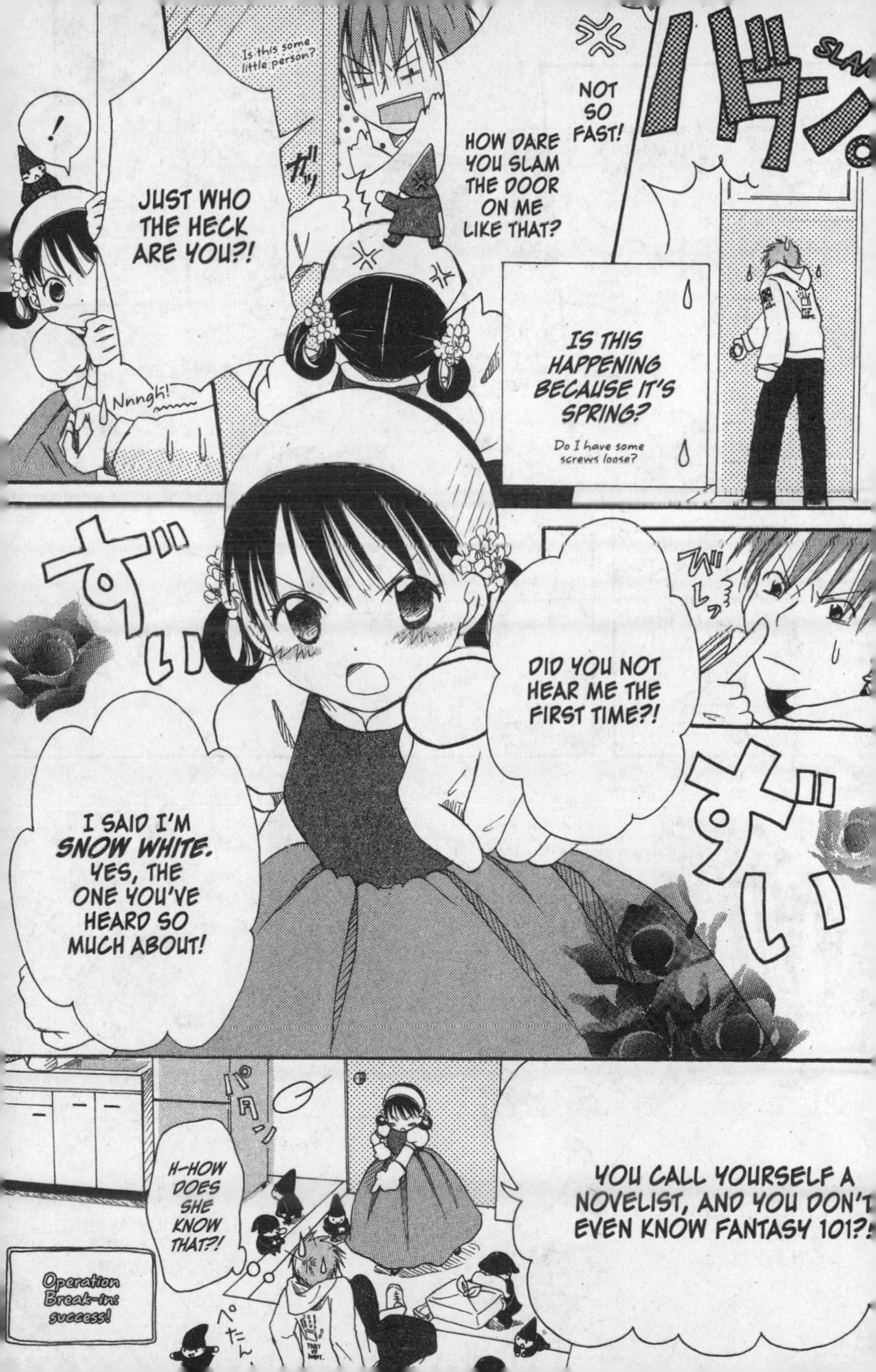
SLAM
IS THIS HAPPENING BECAUSE IT'S SPRING?
Do I have some screws loose?
NOT SO FAST!
HOW DARE YOU SLAM THE DOOR ON ME LIKE THAT?
Is this some little person?
!
JUST WHO THE HECK ARE YOU?!
Nnngh!
DID YOU NOT HEAR ME THE FIRST TIME?!
I SAID I'M ***SNOW WHITE.*** YES, THE ONE YOU'VE HEARD SO MUCH ABOUT!
YOU CALL YOURSELF A NOVELIST, AND YOU DON'T EVEN KNOW FANTASY 101?!
H-HOW DOES SHE KNOW THAT?!
Operation Break-in: success!

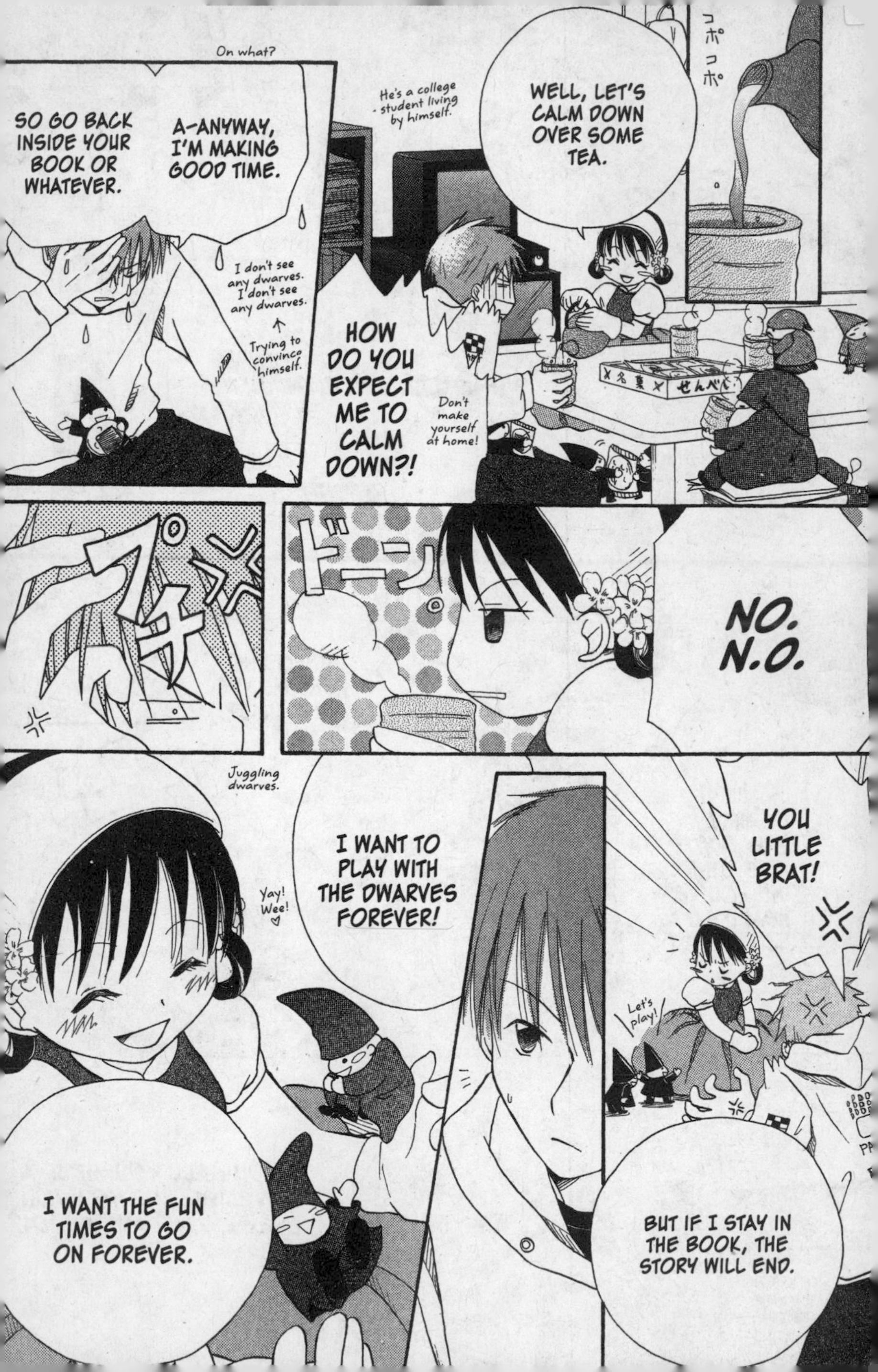
コポコポ
WELL, LET'S CALM DOWN OVER SOME TEA.
He's a college student living by himself.
HOW DO YOU EXPECT ME TO CALM DOWN?!
Don't make yourself at home!
名菓
せんべい
On what?
A-ANYWAY, I'M MAKING GOOD TIME.
SO GO BACK INSIDE YOUR BOOK OR WHATEVER.
I don't see any dwarves. I don't see any dwarves.
Trying to convinco himself.
NO. N.O.
ドーン
プチ
YOU LITTLE BRAT!
Let's play!
BUT IF I STAY IN THE BOOK, THE STORY WILL END.
I WANT TO PLAY WITH THE DWARVES FOREVER!
Juggling dwarves.
Yay! Wee! ♡
I WANT THE FUN TIMES TO GO ON FOREVER.

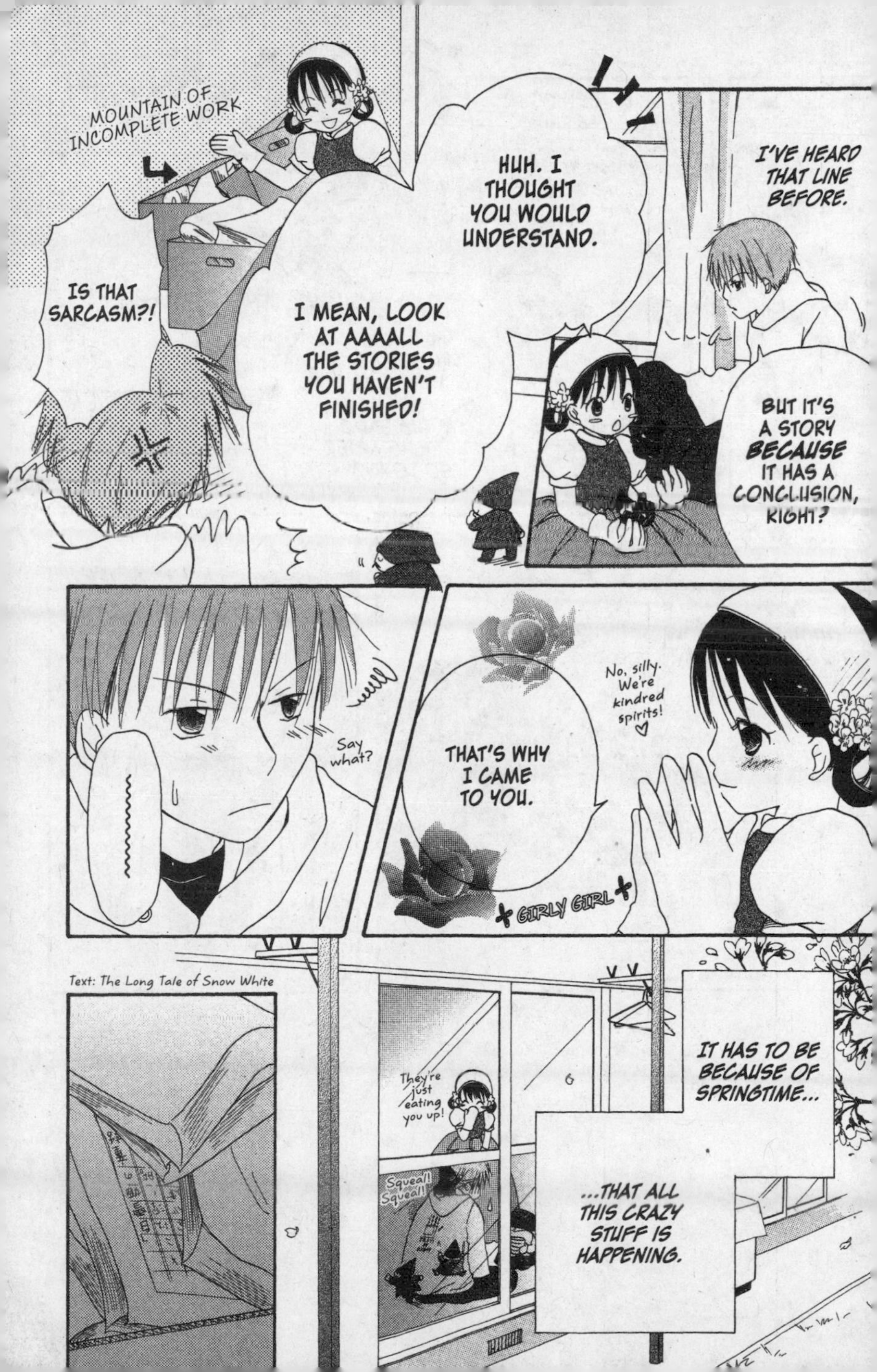
HUH. I THOUGHT YOU WOULD UNDERSTAND.
I'VE HEARD THAT LINE BEFORE.
BUT IT'S A STORY BECAUSE IT HAS A CONCLUSION, RIGHT?
I MEAN, LOOK AT AAAALL THE STORIES YOU HAVEN'T FINISHED!
MOUNTAIN OF INCOMPLETE WORK
IS THAT SARCASM?!
No, silly. We're kindred spirits! ♡
THAT'S WHY I CAME TO YOU.
GIRLY GIRL
Say what?
IT HAS TO BE BECAUSE OF SPRINGTIME...
...THAT ALL THIS CRAZY STUFF IS HAPPENING.
They're just eating you up!
Squeal! Squeal!
Text: The Long Tale of Snow White

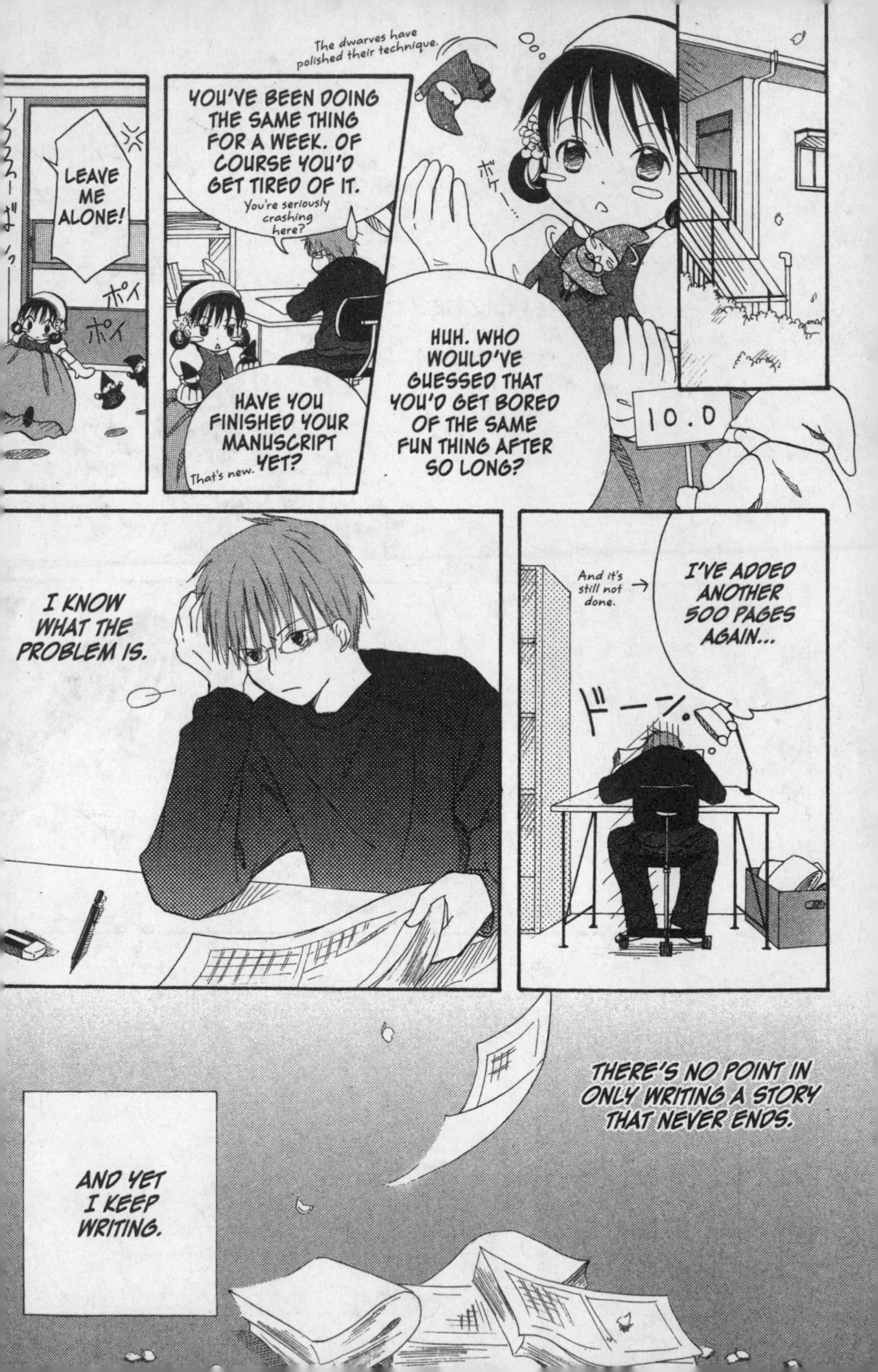
The dwarves have polished their technique.
ボケー…
HUH. WHO WOULD'VE GUESSED THAT YOU'D GET BORED OF THE SAME FUN THING AFTER SO LONG?
10.0
YOU'VE BEEN DOING THE SAME THING FOR A WEEK. OF COURSE YOU'D GET TIRED OF IT.
You're seriously crashing here?
HAVE YOU FINISHED YOUR MANUSCRIPT YET?
That's new.
LEAVE ME ALONE!
ポイ
ポイ
And it's still not done. →
I'VE ADDED ANOTHER 500 PAGES AGAIN...
ドーン。
I KNOW WHAT THE PROBLEM IS.
THERE'S NO POINT IN ONLY WRITING A STORY THAT NEVER ENDS.
AND YET I KEEP WRITING.

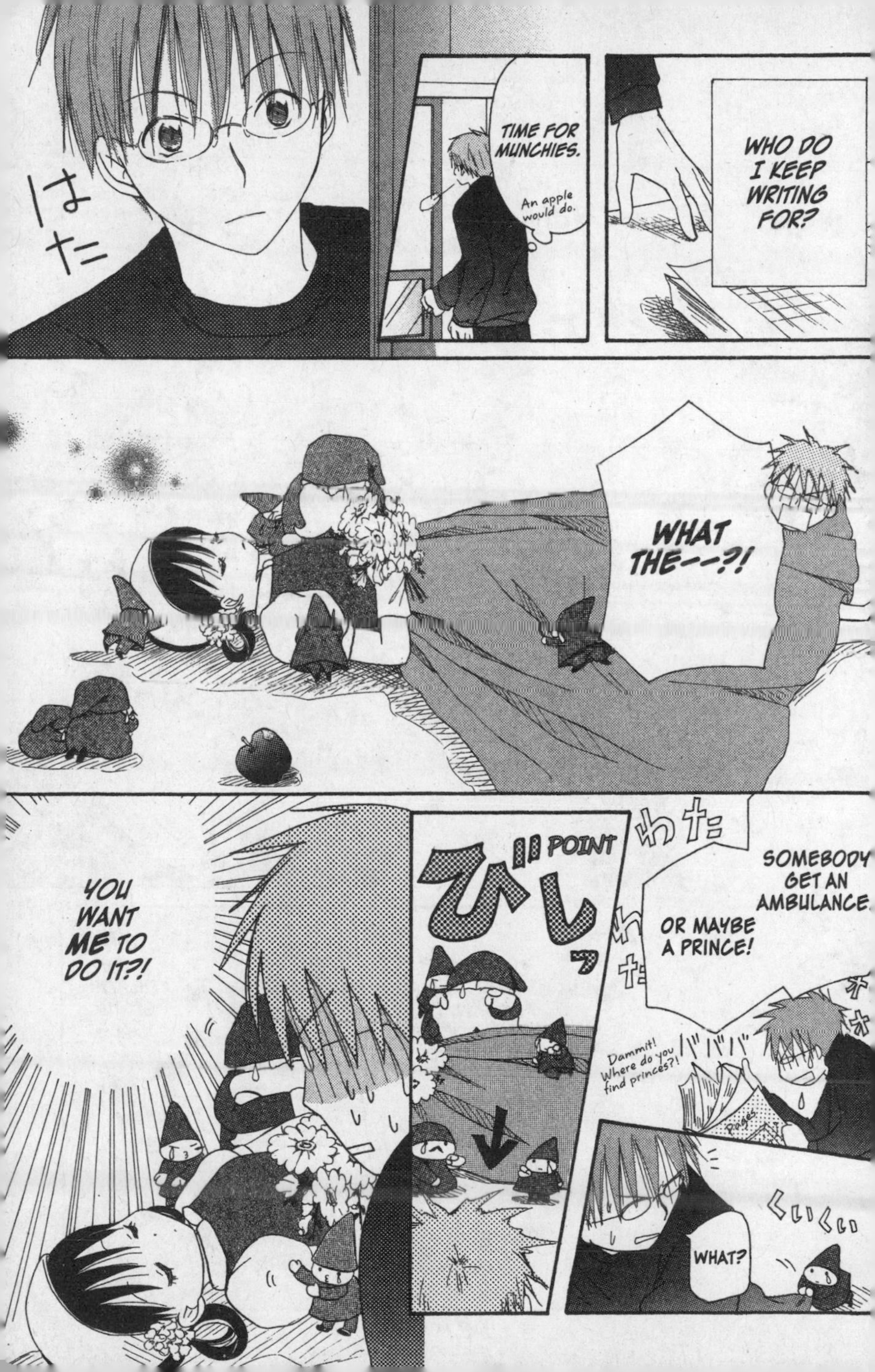
WHO DO I KEEP WRITING FOR?
TIME FOR MUNCHIES.
An apple would do.
はた
WHAT THE--?!
SOMEBODY GET AN AMBULANCE.
OR MAYBE A PRINCE!
わたわた
Dammit! Where do you find princes?!
バババ
Pages
くいくい
WHAT?
POINT
ひしっ
YOU WANT ME TO DO IT?!

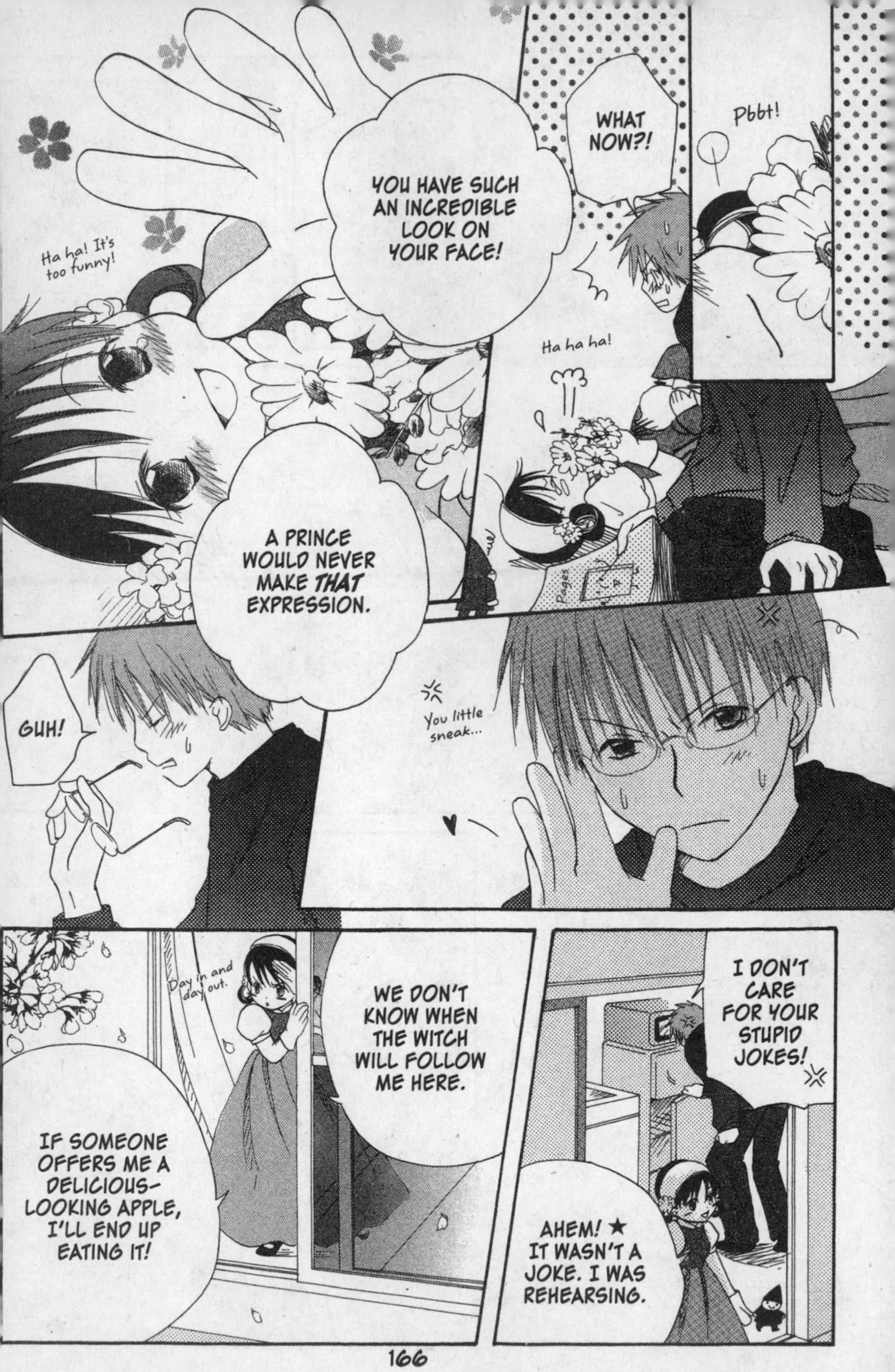
Pbbt!
WHAT NOW?!
Ha ha ha!
YOU HAVE SUCH AN INCREDIBLE LOOK ON YOUR FACE!
Ha ha! It's too funny!
A PRINCE WOULD NEVER MAKE *THAT* EXPRESSION.
Pages
You little sneak...
GUH!
I DON'T CARE FOR YOUR STUPID JOKES!
AHEM! ★ IT WASN'T A JOKE. I WAS REHEARSING.
Day in and day out.
WE DON'T KNOW WHEN THE WITCH WILL FOLLOW ME HERE.
IF SOMEONE OFFERS ME A DELICIOUS-LOOKING APPLE, I'LL END UP EATING IT!

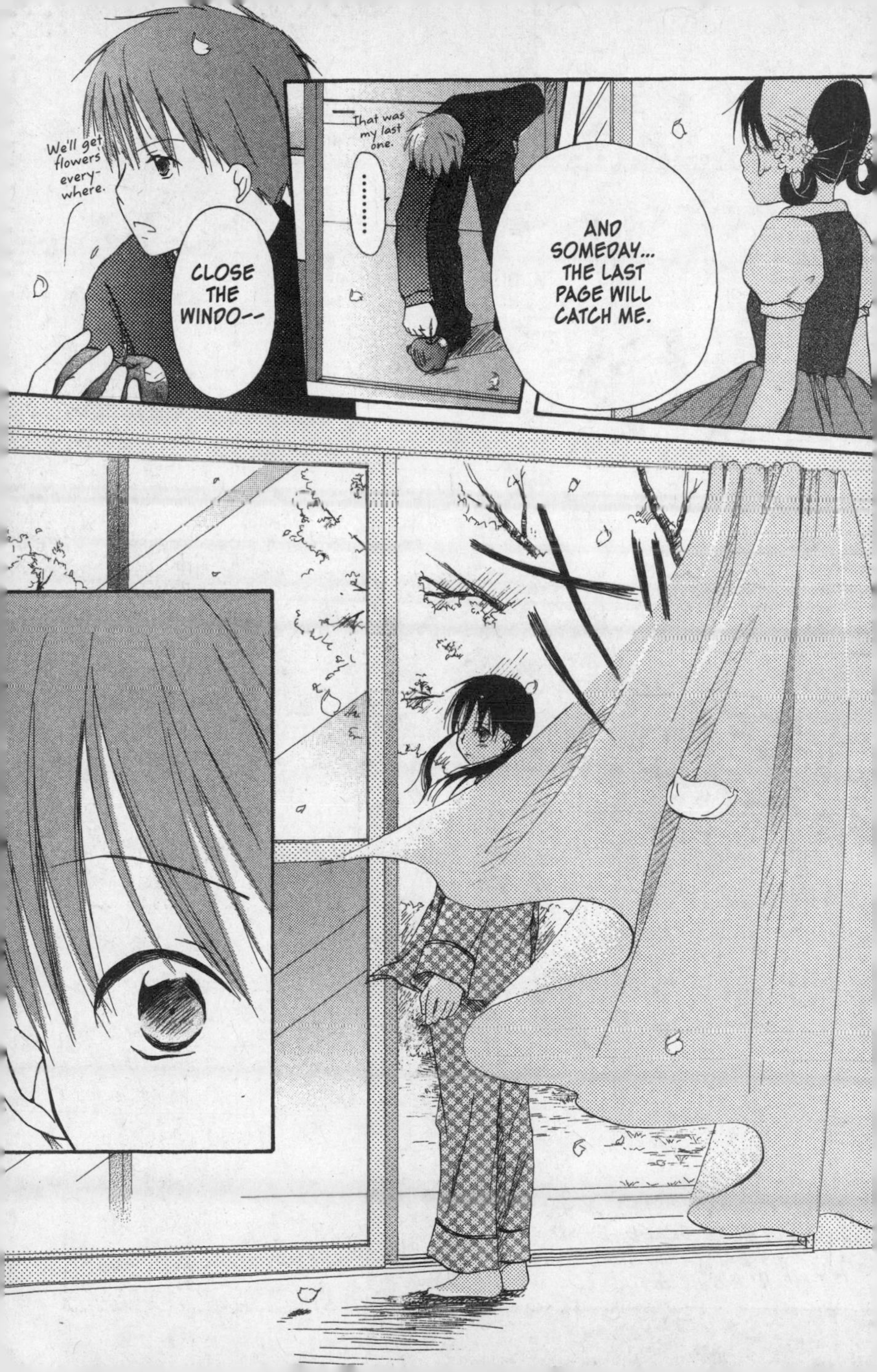
AND SOMEDAY... THE LAST PAGE WILL CATCH ME.
That was my last one.
......
CLOSE THE WINDO--
We'll get flowers every-where.

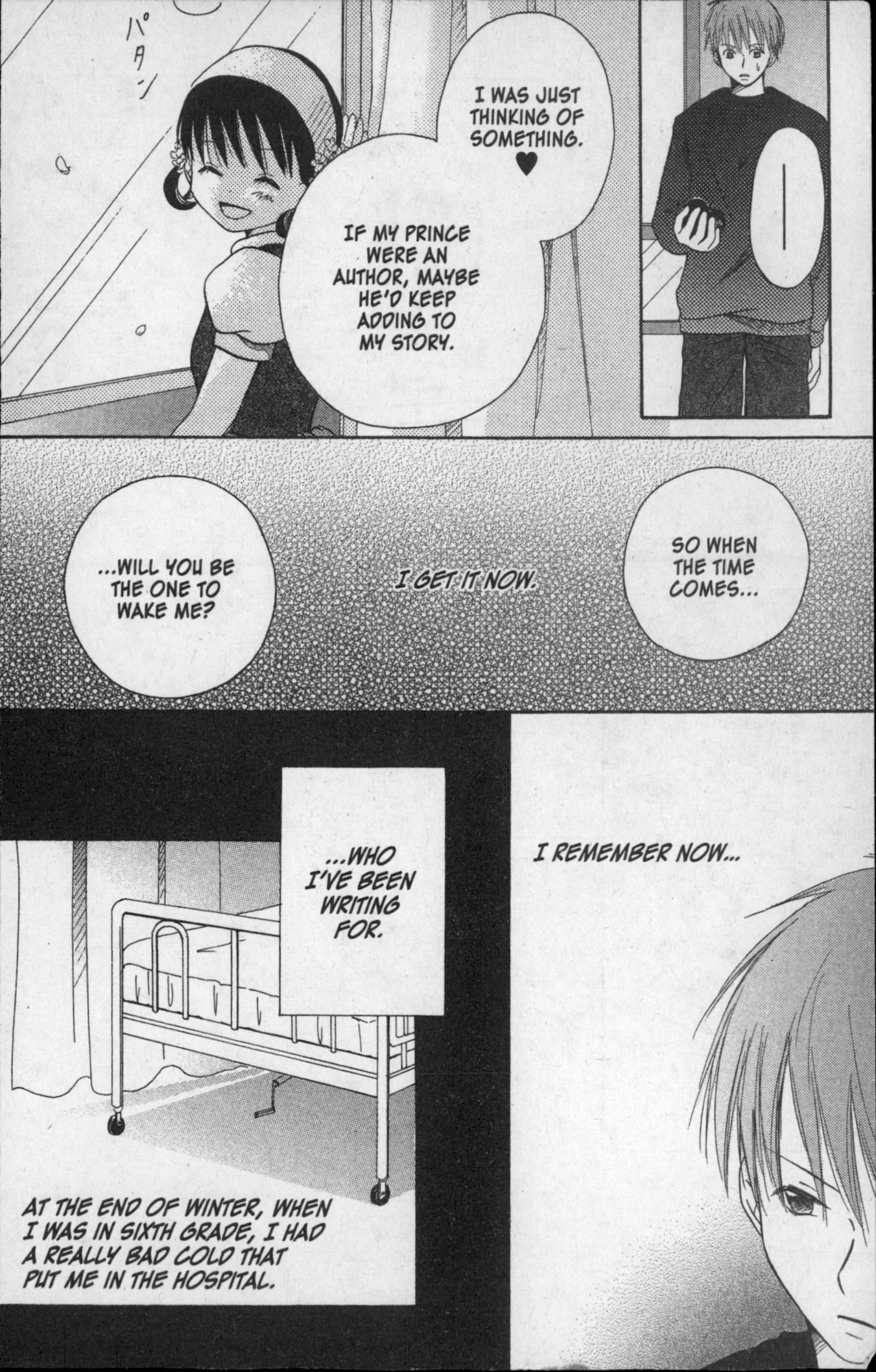
I WAS JUST THINKING OF SOMETHING. ♥
IF MY PRINCE WERE AN AUTHOR, MAYBE HE'D KEEP ADDING TO MY STORY.
パタン
SO WHEN THE TIME COMES...
I GET IT NOW.
...WILL YOU BE THE ONE TO WAKE ME?
I REMEMBER NOW...
...WHO I'VE BEEN WRITING FOR.
AT THE END OF WINTER, WHEN I WAS IN SIXTH GRADE, I HAD A REALLY BAD COLD THAT PUT ME IN THE HOSPITAL.

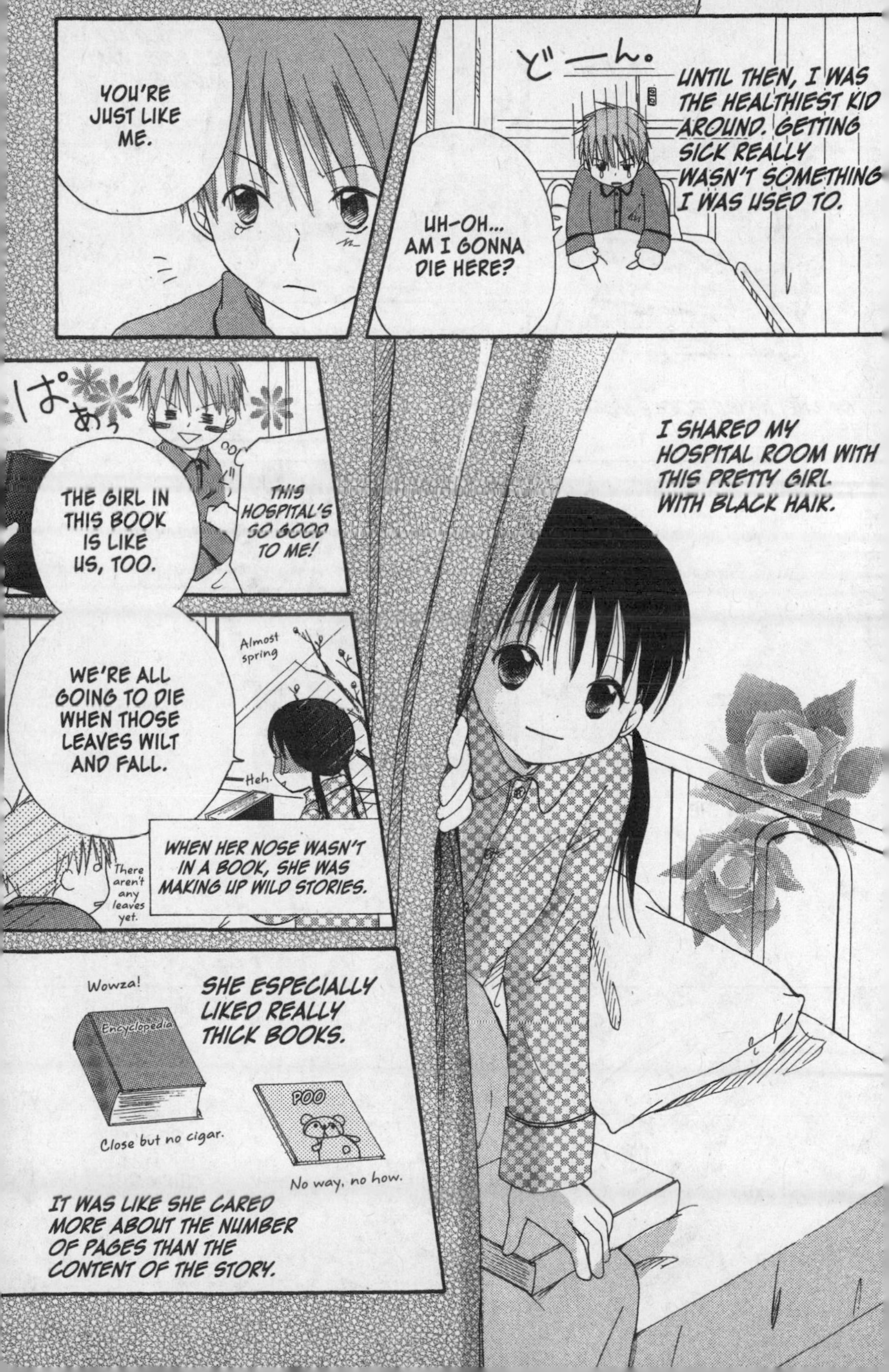
UNTIL THEN, I WAS THE HEALTHIEST KID AROUND. GETTING SICK REALLY WASN'T SOMETHING I WAS USED TO.
どーん。
UH-OH... AM I GONNA DIE HERE?
YOU'RE JUST LIKE ME.
I SHARED MY HOSPITAL ROOM WITH THIS PRETTY GIRL WITH BLACK HAIR.
ぱあっ
THIS HOSPITAL'S SO GOOD TO ME!
THE GIRL IN THIS BOOK IS LIKE US, TOO.
Almost spring
WE'RE ALL GOING TO DIE WHEN THOSE LEAVES WILT AND FALL.
Heh.
There aren't any leaves yet.
WHEN HER NOSE WASN'T IN A BOOK, SHE WAS MAKING UP WILD STORIES.
SHE ESPECIALLY LIKED REALLY THICK BOOKS.
Wowza!
Encyclopedia
Close but no cigar.
POO
No way, no how.
IT WAS LIKE SHE CARED MORE ABOUT THE NUMBER OF PAGES THAN THE CONTENT OF THE STORY.

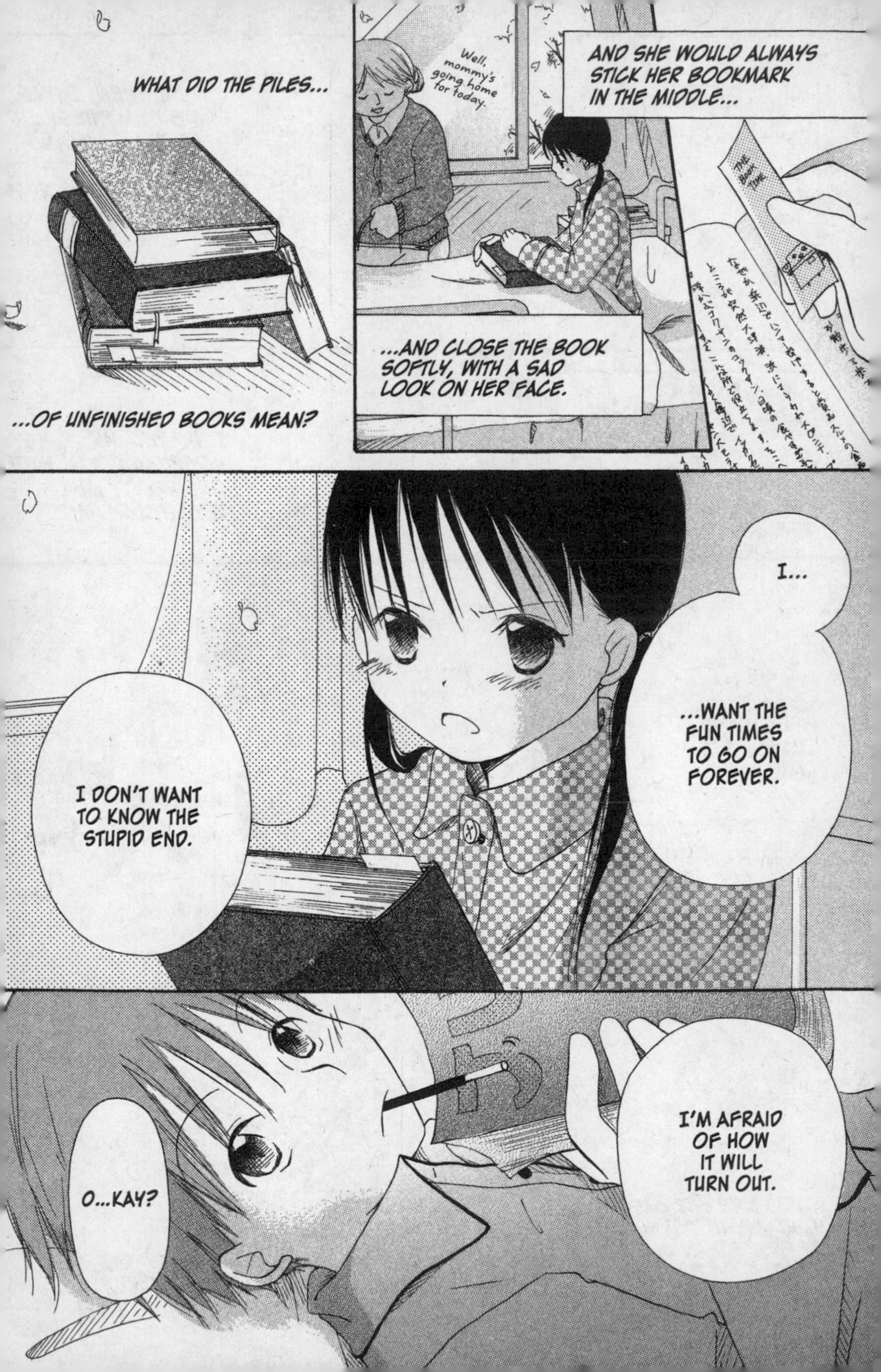
AND SHE WOULD ALWAYS STICK HER BOOKMARK IN THE MIDDLE...
Well, mommy's going home for today.
...AND CLOSE THE BOOK SOFTLY, WITH A SAD LOOK ON HER FACE.
WHAT DID THE PILES...
...OF UNFINISHED BOOKS MEAN?
I...
...WANT THE FUN TIMES TO GO ON FOREVER.
I DON'T WANT TO KNOW THE STUPID END.
I'M AFRAID OF HOW IT WILL TURN OUT.
O...KAY?

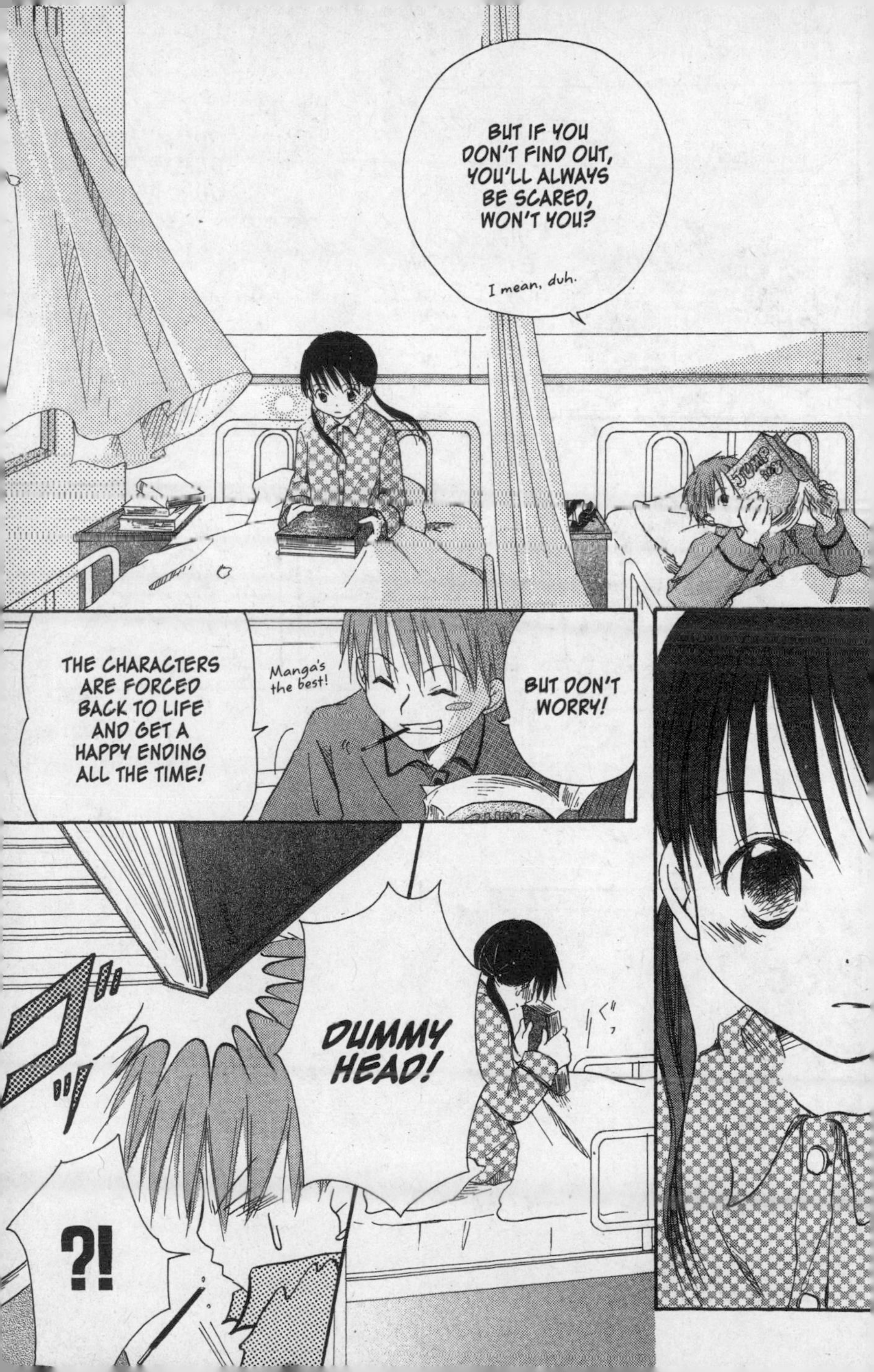
BUT IF YOU DON'T FIND OUT, YOU'LL ALWAYS BE SCARED, WON'T YOU?
I mean, duh.
BUT DON'T WORRY!
Manga's the best!
THE CHARACTERS ARE FORCED BACK TO LIFE AND GET A HAPPY ENDING ALL THE TIME!
DUMMY HEAD!
?!

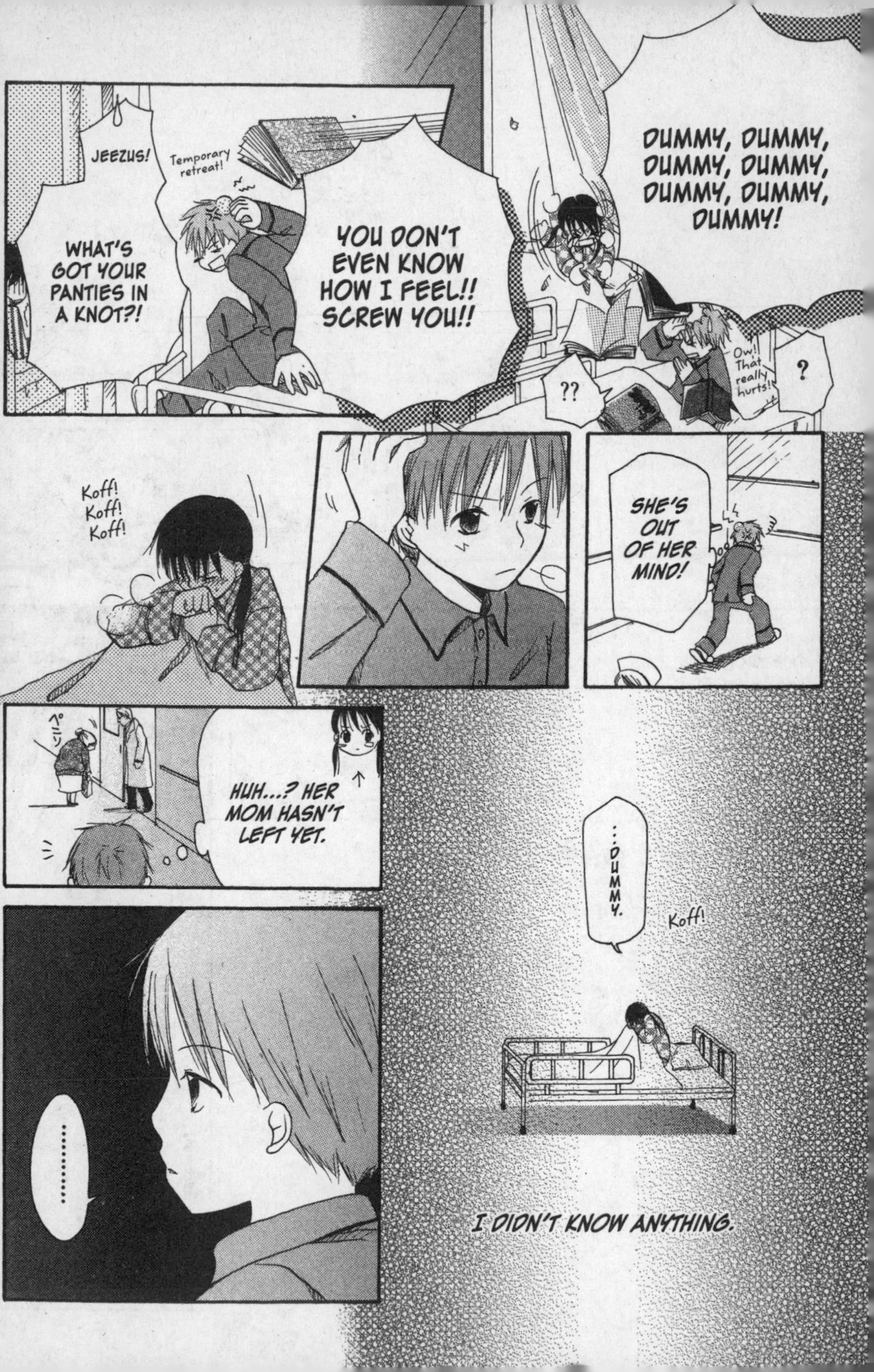

DUMMY, DUMMY, DUMMY, DUMMY, DUMMY, DUMMY, DUMMY!
?
Ow! That really hurts!
??
YOU DON'T EVEN KNOW HOW I FEEL!! SCREW YOU!!
Temporary retreat!
JEEZUS!
WHAT'S GOT YOUR PANTIES IN A KNOT?!
SHE'S OUT OF HER MIND!
Koff! Koff! Koff!
...DUMMY.
Koff!
I DIDN'T KNOW ANYTHING.
HUH...? HER MOM HASN'T LEFT YET.
....

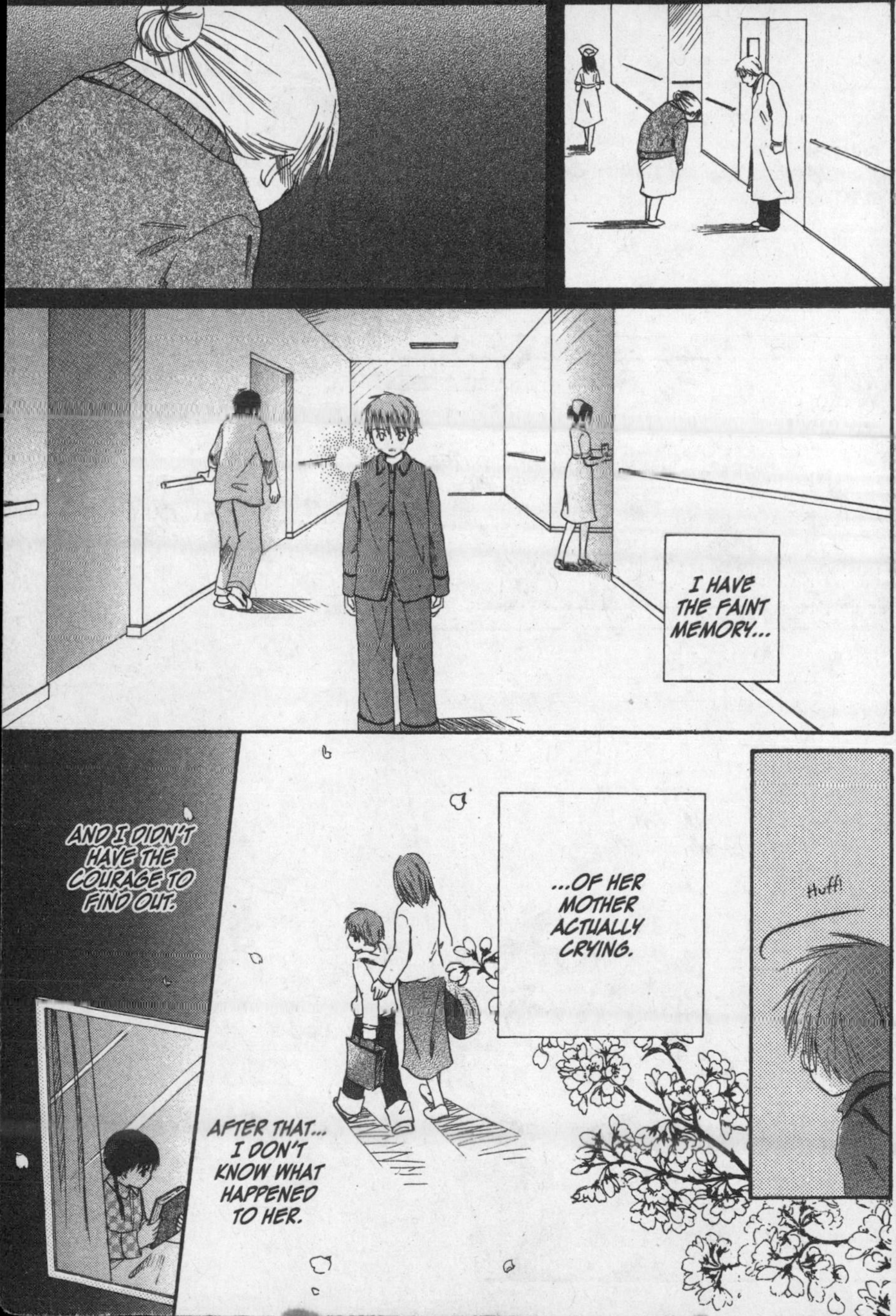
I HAVE THE FAINT MEMORY...
Huff!
...OF HER MOTHER ACTUALLY CRYING.
AFTER THAT... I DON'T KNOW WHAT HAPPENED TO HER.
AND I DIDN'T HAVE THE COURAGE TO FIND OUT.

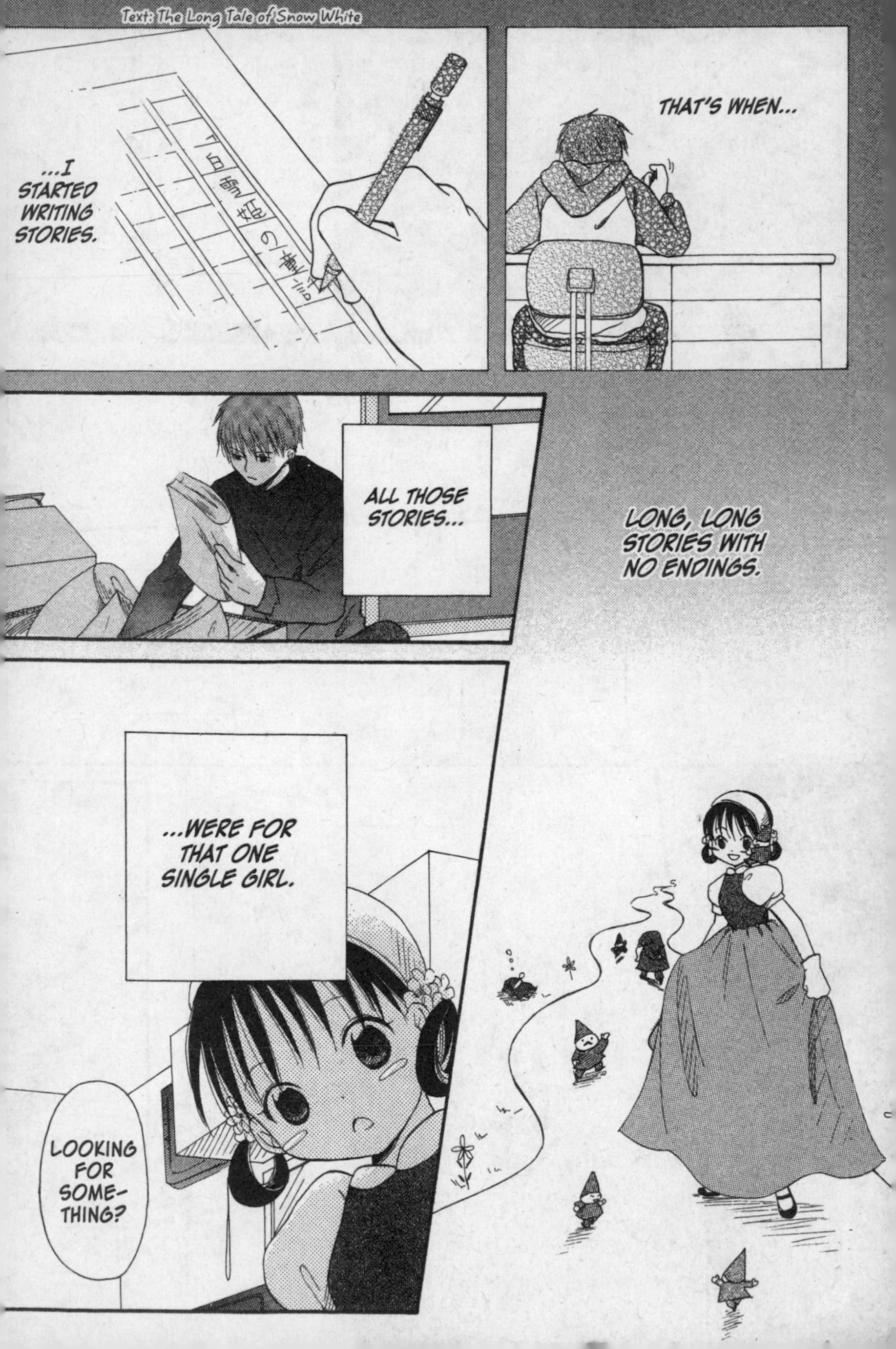
Text: The Long Tale of Snow White
THAT'S WHEN...
...I STARTED WRITING STORIES.
LONG, LONG STORIES WITH NO ENDINGS.
ALL THOSE STORIES...
...WERE FOR THAT ONE SINGLE GIRL.
LOOKING FOR SOME-THING?

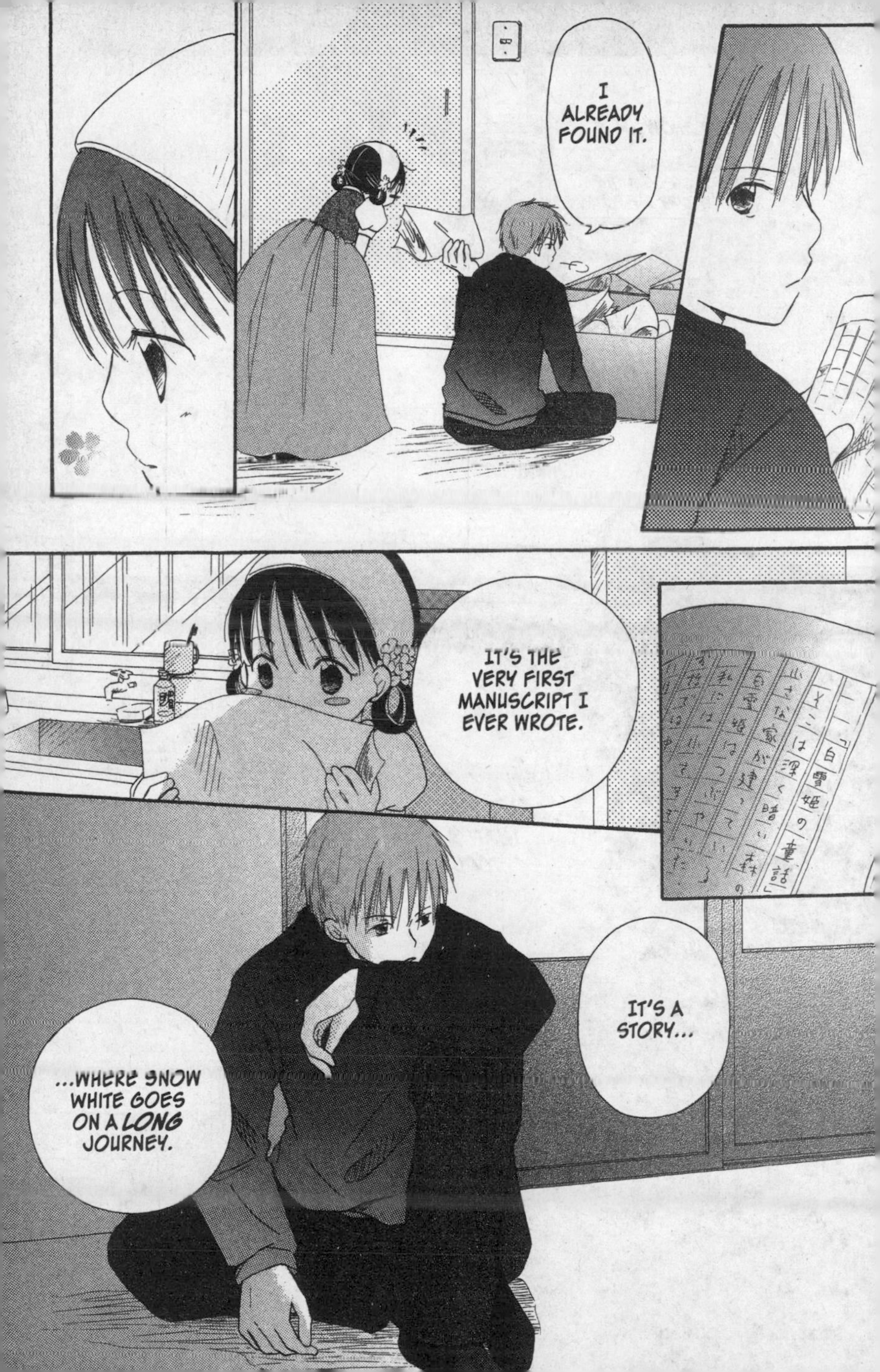
I ALREADY FOUND IT.
IT'S THE VERY FIRST MANUSCRIPT I EVER WROTE.
IT'S A STORY...
...WHERE SNOW WHITE GOES ON A *LONG* JOURNEY.

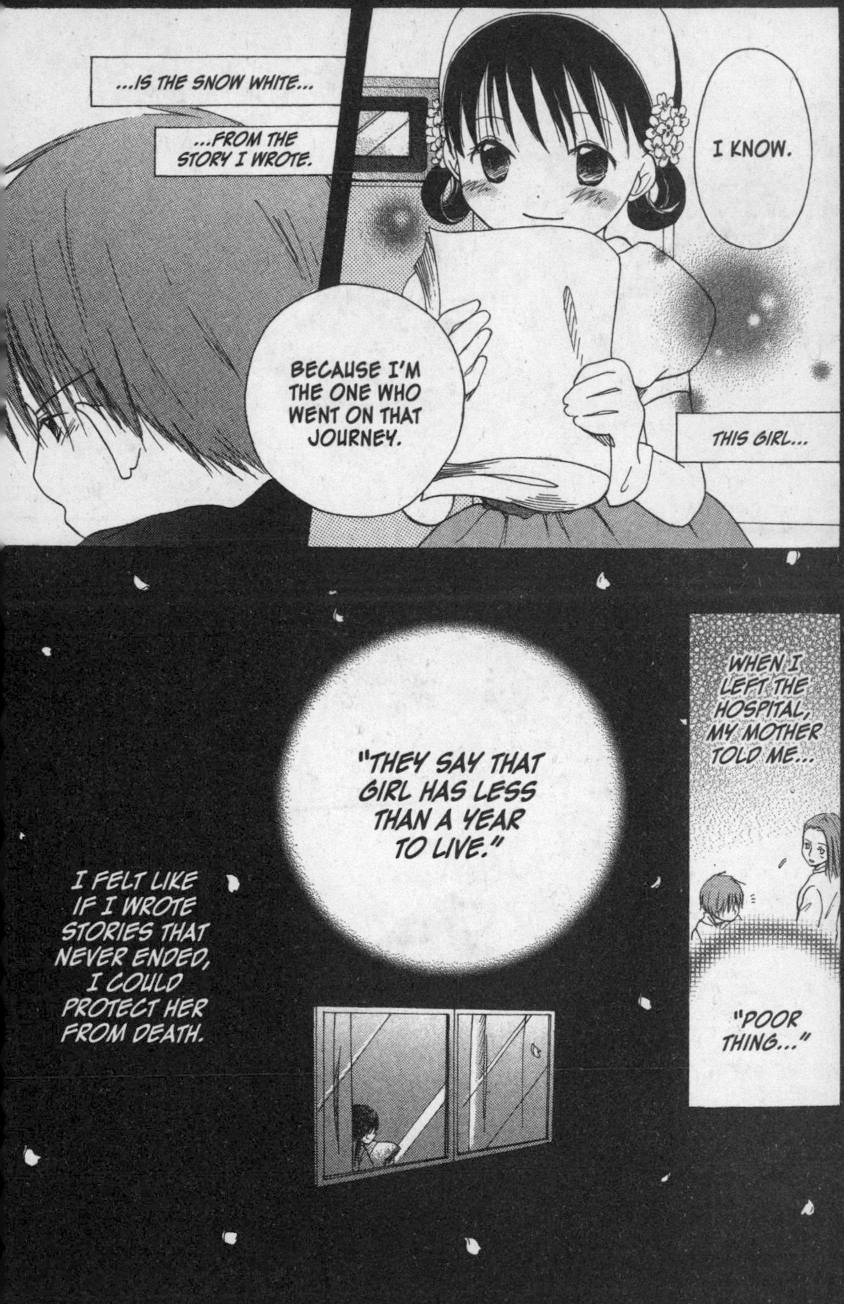
I KNOW.
...IS THE SNOW WHITE...
...FROM THE STORY I WROTE.
BECAUSE I'M THE ONE WHO WENT ON THAT JOURNEY.
THIS GIRL...
WHEN I LEFT THE HOSPITAL, MY MOTHER TOLD ME...
"POOR THING..."
"THEY SAY THAT GIRL HAS LESS THAN A YEAR TO LIVE."
I FELT LIKE IF I WROTE STORIES THAT NEVER ENDED, I COULD PROTECT HER FROM DEATH.

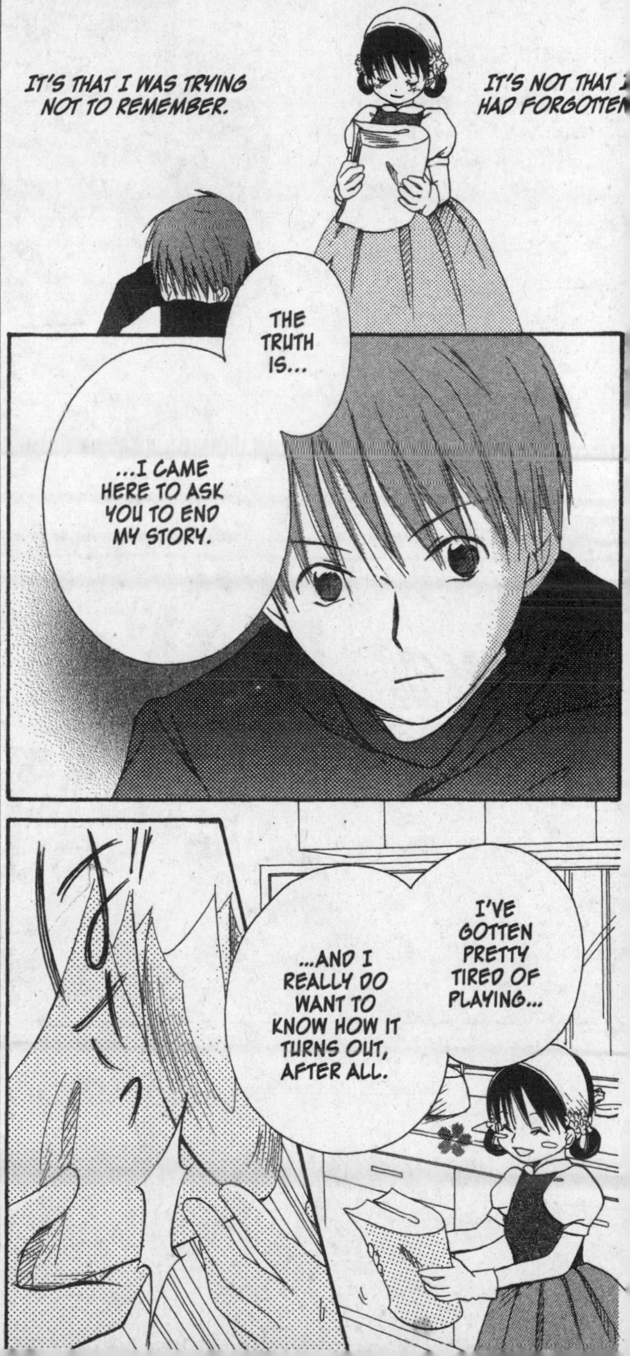
IT'S NOT THAT I HAD FORGOTTEN
IT'S THAT I WAS TRYING NOT TO REMEMBER.
THE TRUTH IS...
...I CAME HERE TO ASK YOU TO END MY STORY.
I'VE GOTTEN PRETTY TIRED OF PLAYING...
...AND I REALLY DO WANT TO KNOW HOW IT TURNS OUT, AFTER ALL.

6

Thanks for reading. *Me & My Brothers* volume seven is just about at its end.

I myself have no idea how long this story can go on, but I want to work hard on it as far as I can, so if it's all right, please stay with me a little longer.

Well then, I hope that we can meet again in volume eight.

Thank you very much.

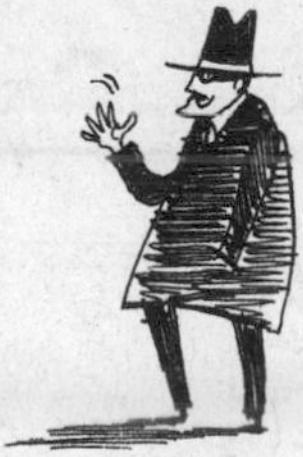

Hari Tokeino

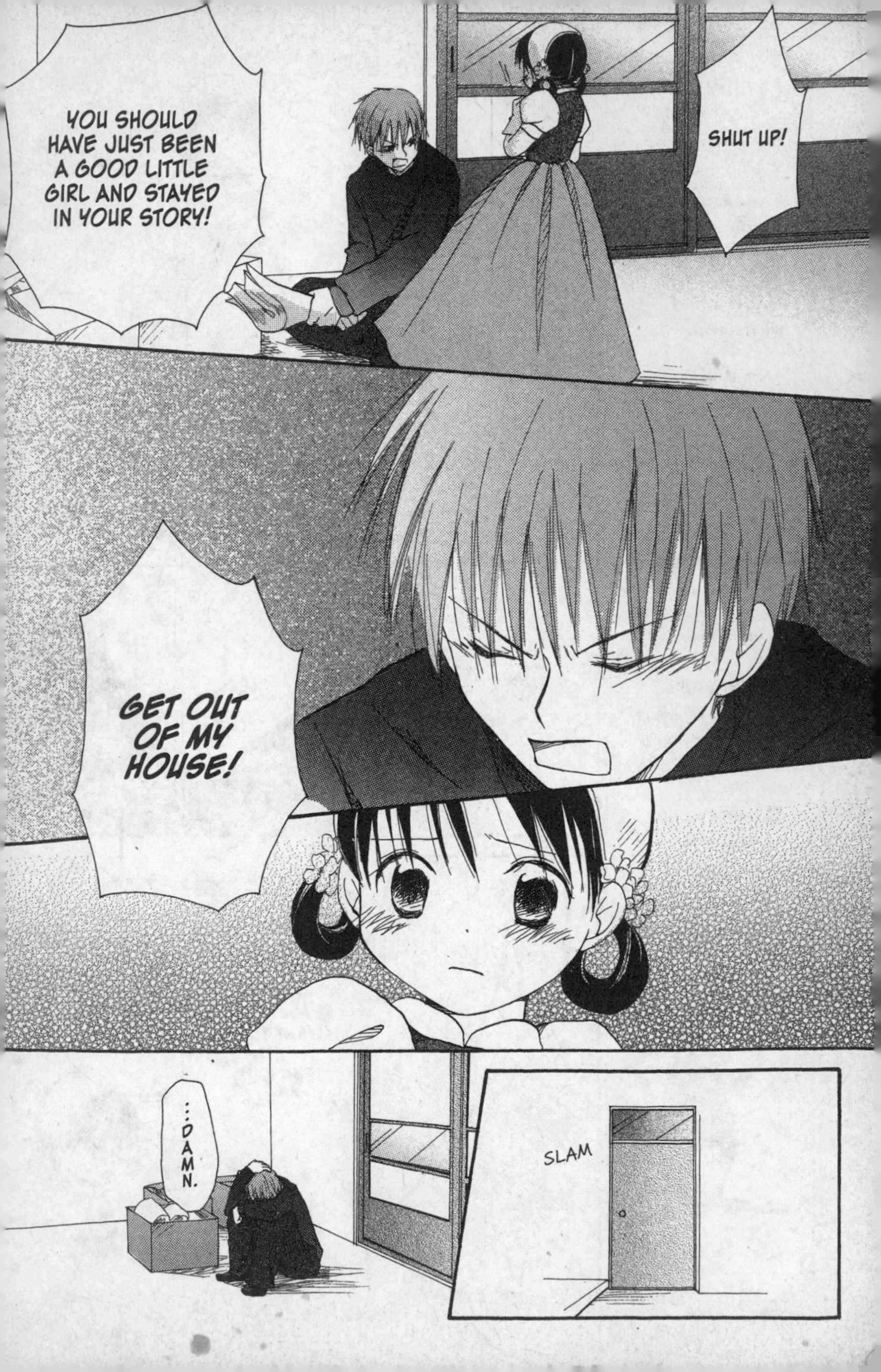
YOU SHOULD HAVE JUST BEEN A GOOD LITTLE GIRL AND STAYED IN YOUR STORY!
SHUT UP!
GET OUT OF MY HOUSE!
SLAM
...DAMN.

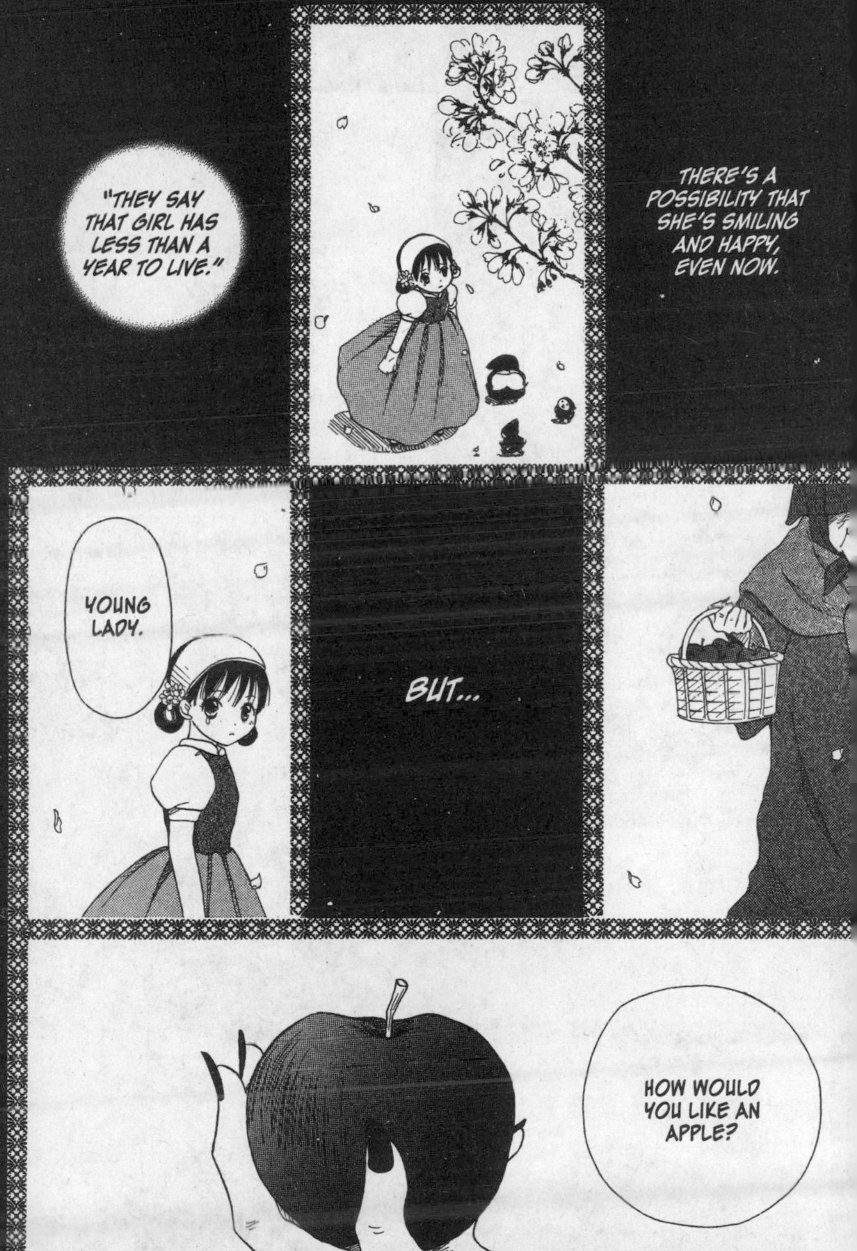
THERE'S A POSSIBILITY THAT SHE'S SMILING AND HAPPY, EVEN NOW.
"THEY SAY THAT GIRL HAS LESS THAN A YEAR TO LIVE."
BUT...
YOUNG LADY.
HOW WOULD YOU LIKE AN APPLE?

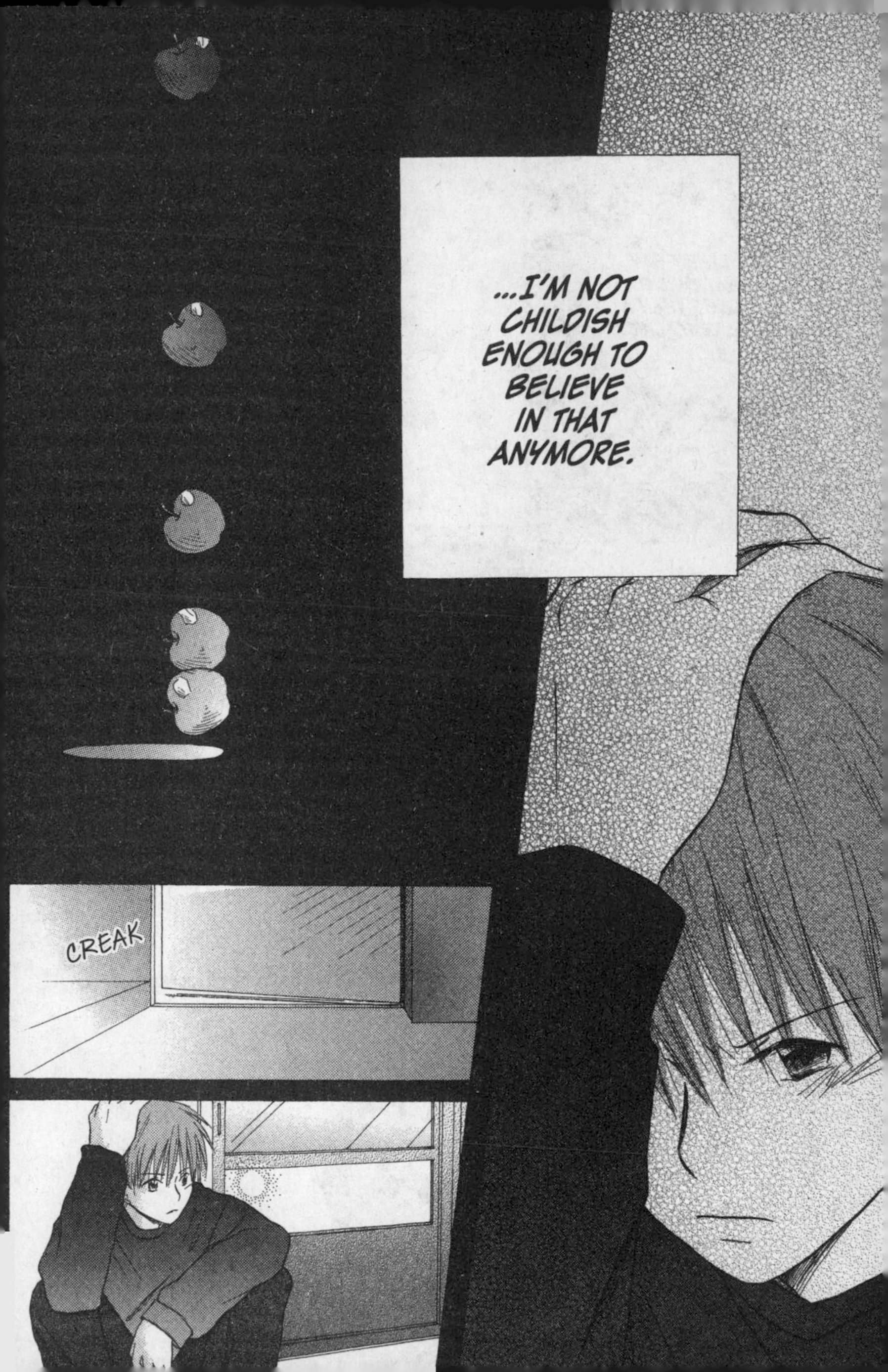
...I'M NOT CHILDISH ENOUGH TO BELIEVE IN THAT ANYMORE.
CREAK

HER STORY...

...THAT I WROTE FOR HER...

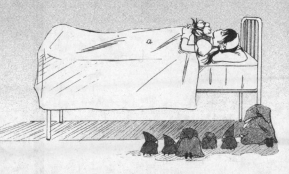

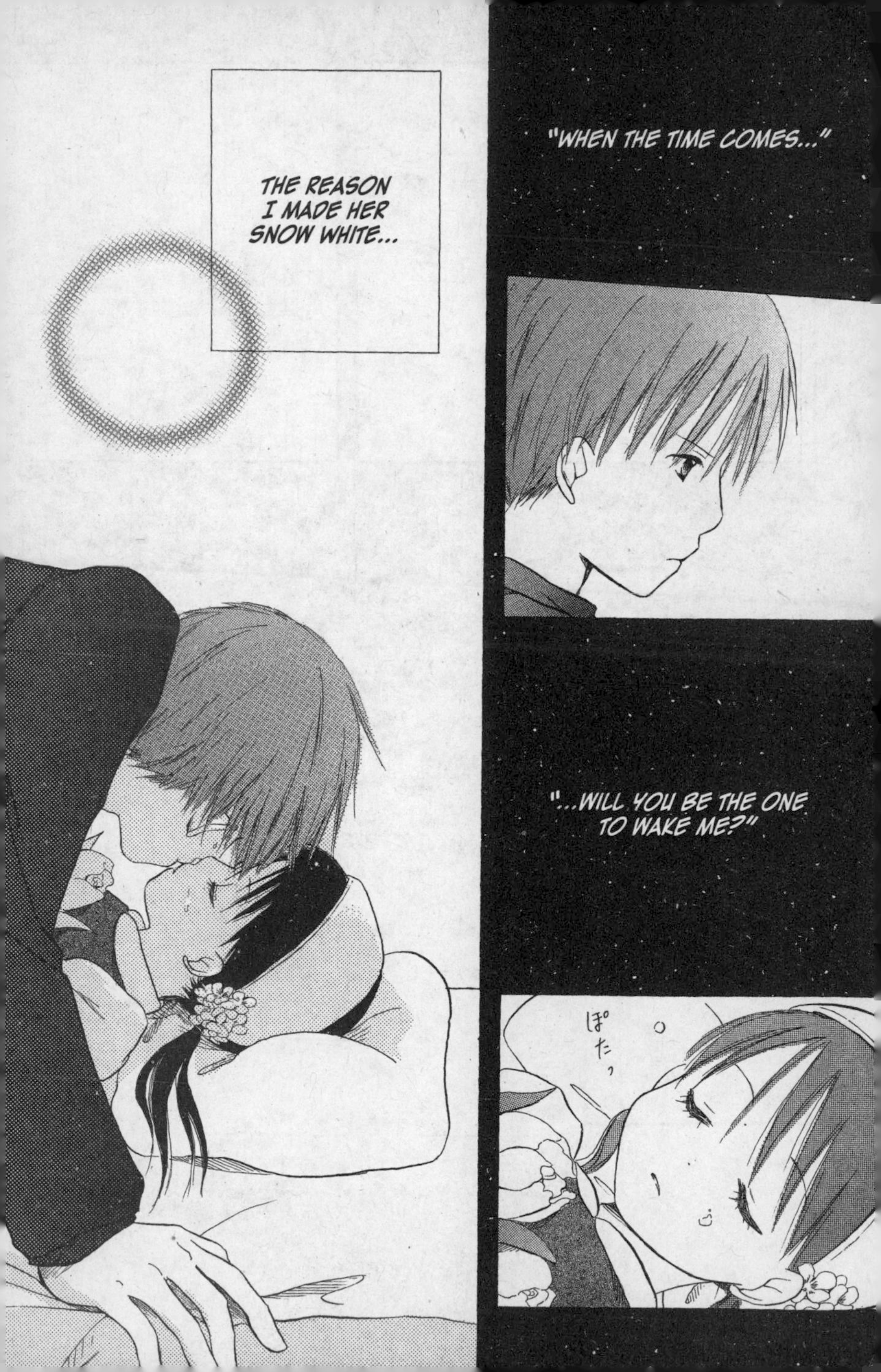
"WHEN THE TIME COMES..."
"...WILL YOU BE THE ONE TO WAKE ME?"
ぽたっ
THE REASON I MADE HER SNOW WHITE...

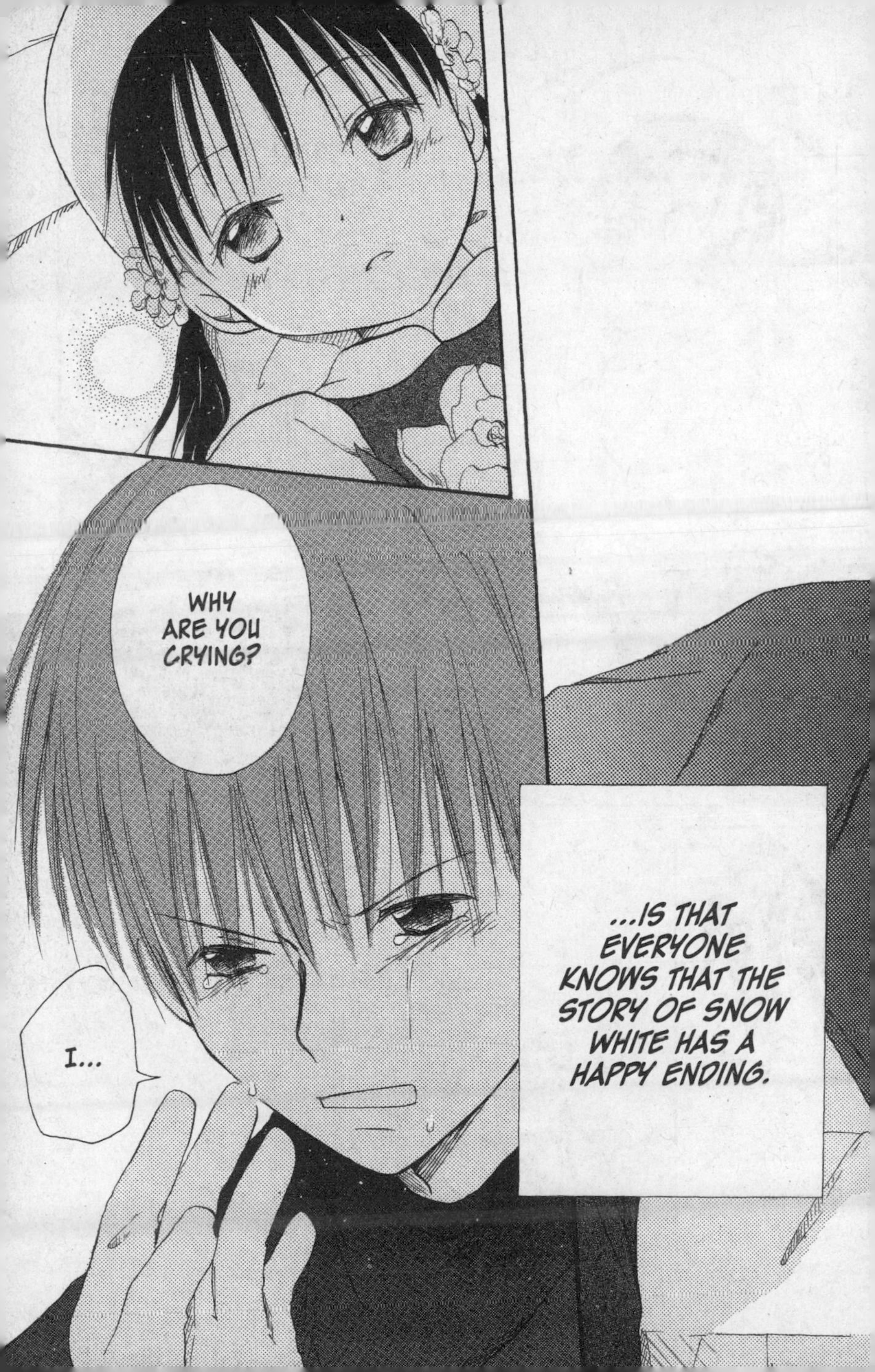
WHY ARE YOU CRYING?
...IS THAT EVERYONE KNOWS THAT THE STORY OF SNOW WHITE HAS A HAPPY ENDING.
I...

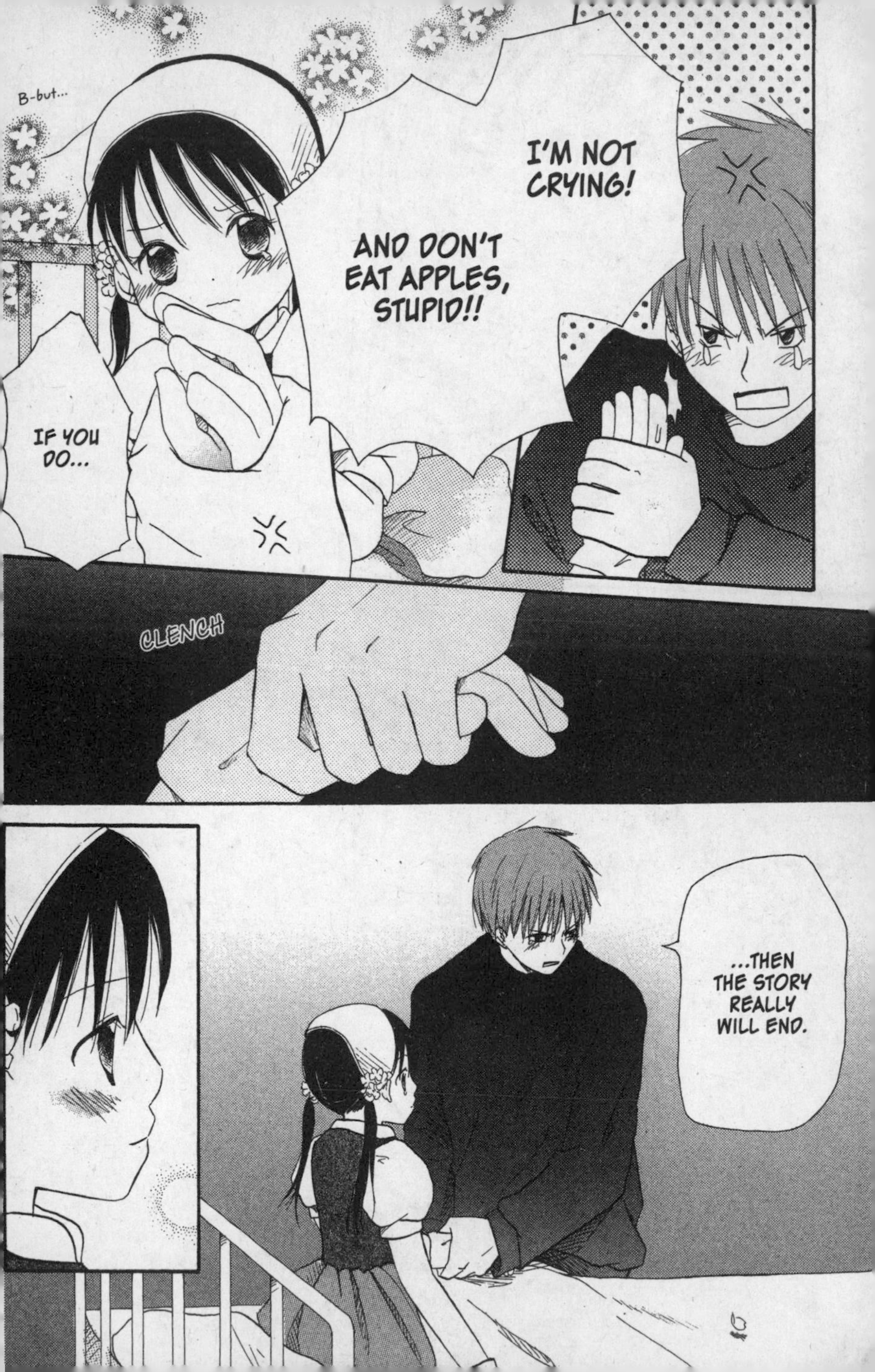
I'M NOT CRYING!
AND DON'T EAT APPLES, STUPID!!
B-but...
IF YOU DO...
CLENCH
...THEN THE STORY REALLY WILL END.

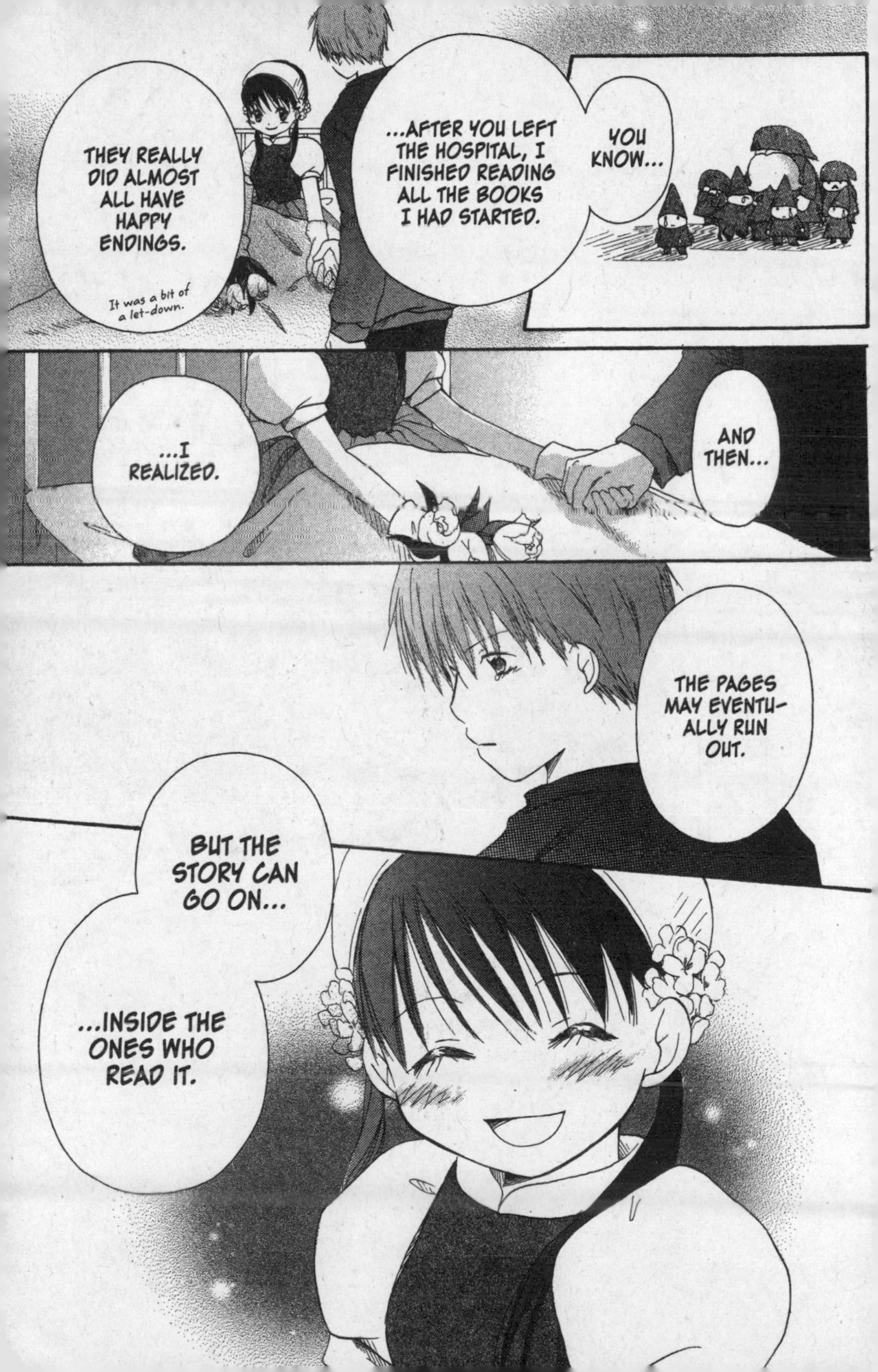
YOU KNOW...
...AFTER YOU LEFT THE HOSPITAL, I FINISHED READING ALL THE BOOKS I HAD STARTED.
THEY REALLY DID ALMOST ALL HAVE HAPPY ENDINGS.
It was a bit of a let-down.
AND THEN...
...I REALIZED.
THE PAGES MAY EVENTU-ALLY RUN OUT.
BUT THE STORY CAN GO ON...
...INSIDE THE ONES WHO READ IT.

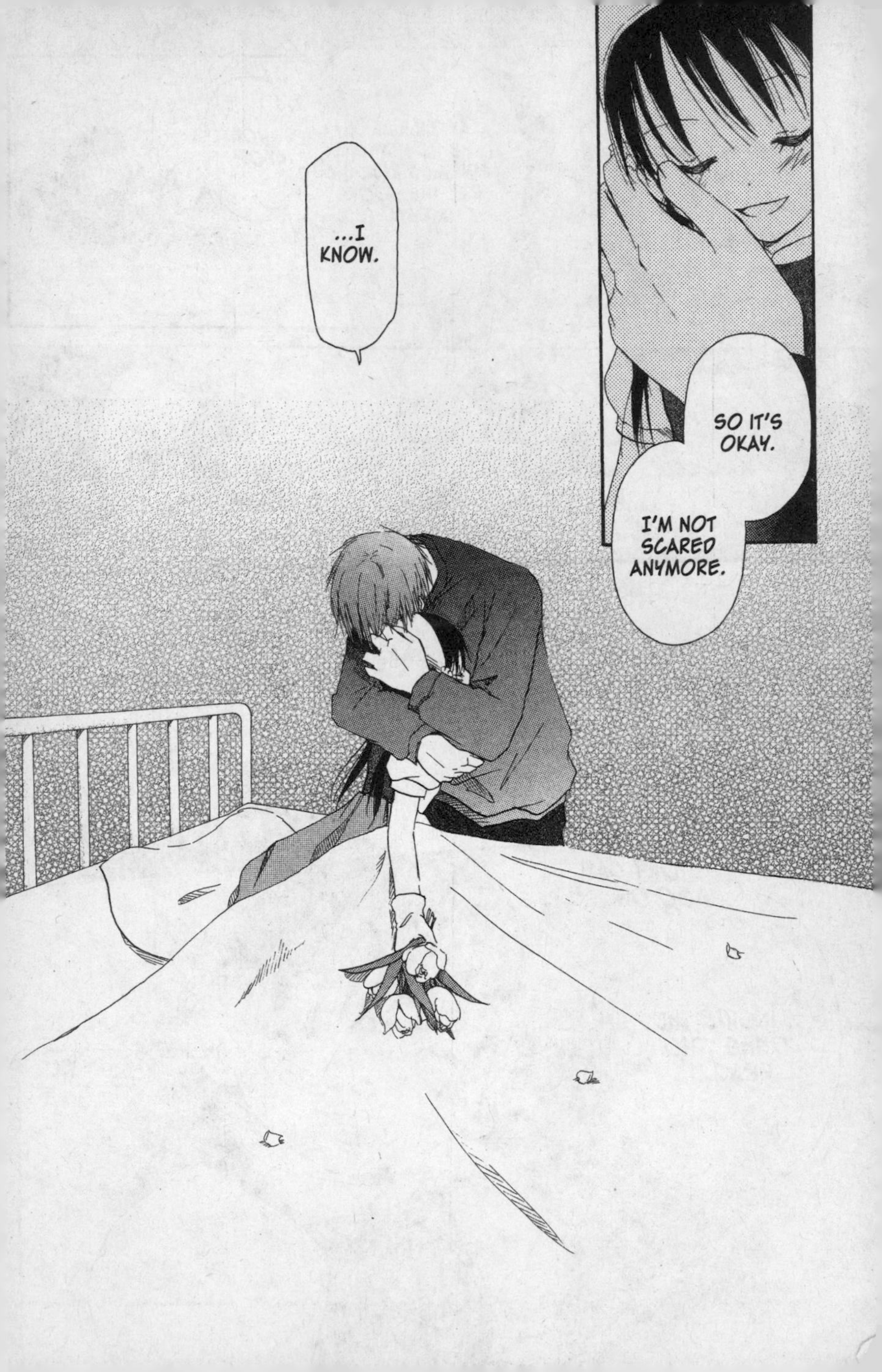
SO IT'S OKAY.
I'M NOT SCARED ANYMORE.
...I KNOW.

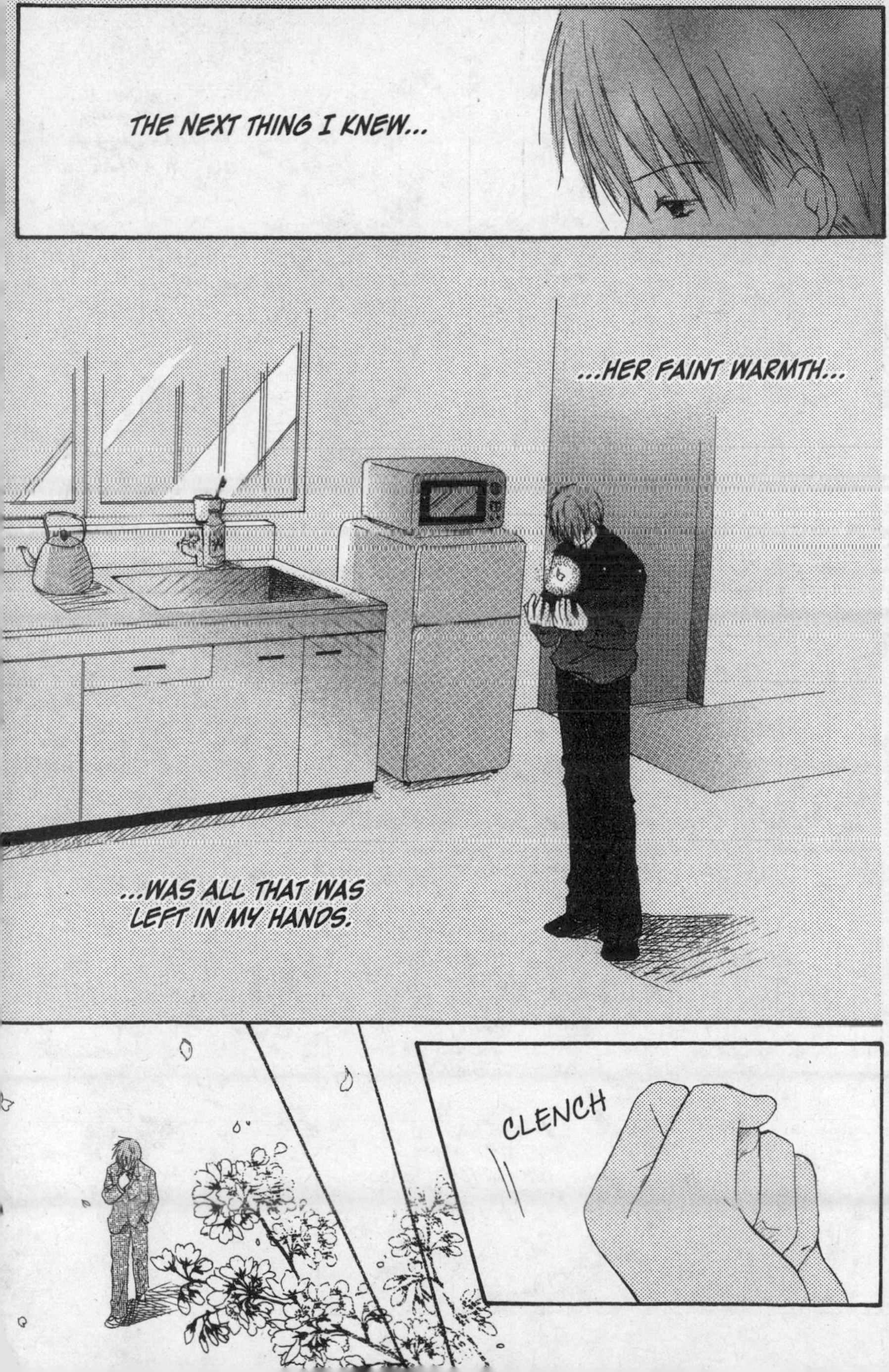
THE NEXT THING I KNEW...
...HER FAINT WARMTH...
...WAS ALL THAT WAS LEFT IN MY HANDS.
CLENCH

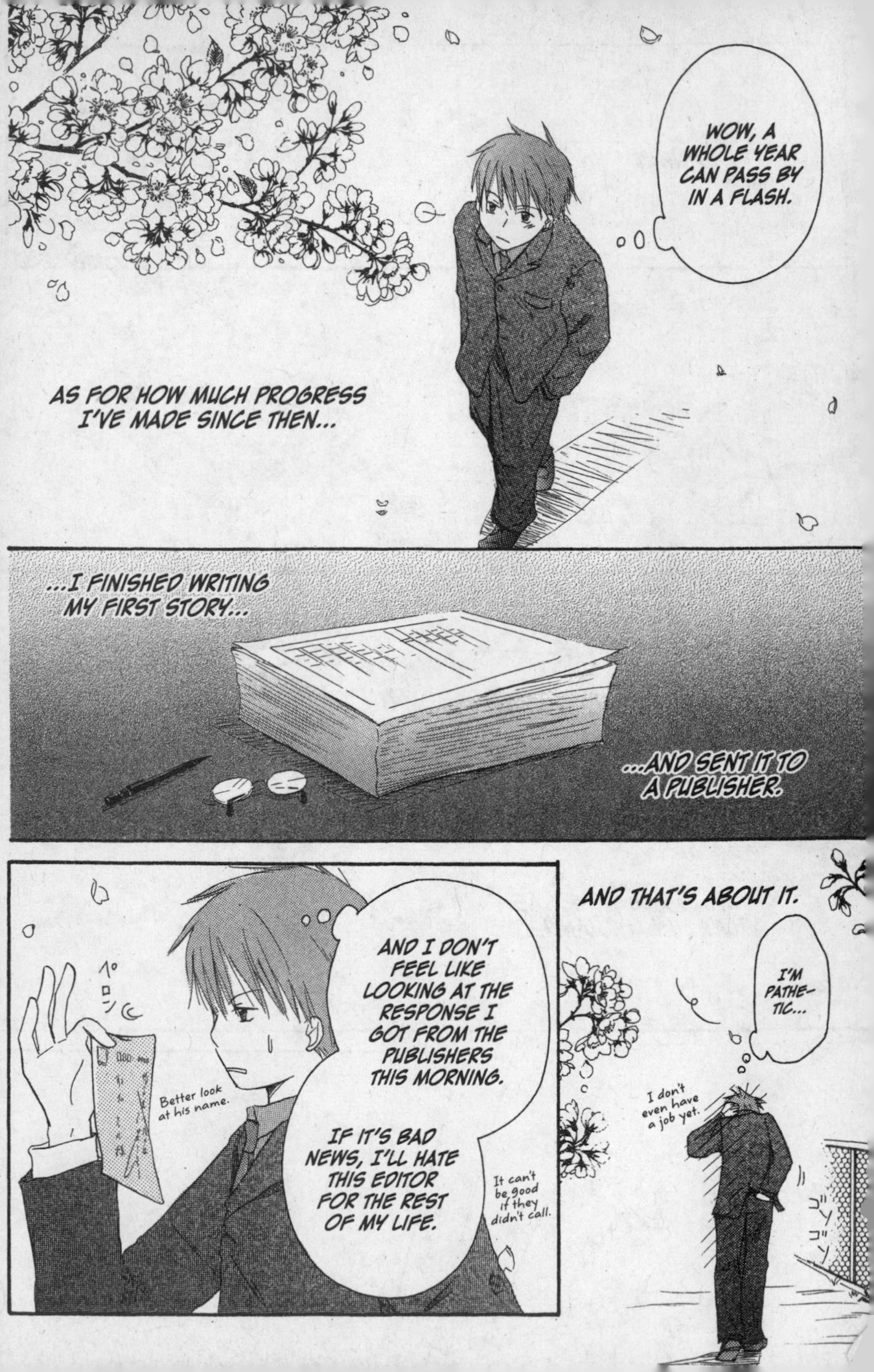
WOW, A WHOLE YEAR CAN PASS BY IN A FLASH.
AS FOR HOW MUCH PROGRESS I'VE MADE SINCE THEN...
...I FINISHED WRITING MY FIRST STORY...
...AND SENT IT TO A PUBLISHER.
AND THAT'S ABOUT IT.
I'M PATHETIC...
I don't even have a job yet.
ゴソゴソ
AND I DON'T FEEL LIKE LOOKING AT THE RESPONSE I GOT FROM THE PUBLISHERS THIS MORNING.
IF IT'S BAD NEWS, I'LL HATE THIS EDITOR FOR THE REST OF MY LIFE.
It can't be good if they didn't call.
Better look at his name.
ペロン

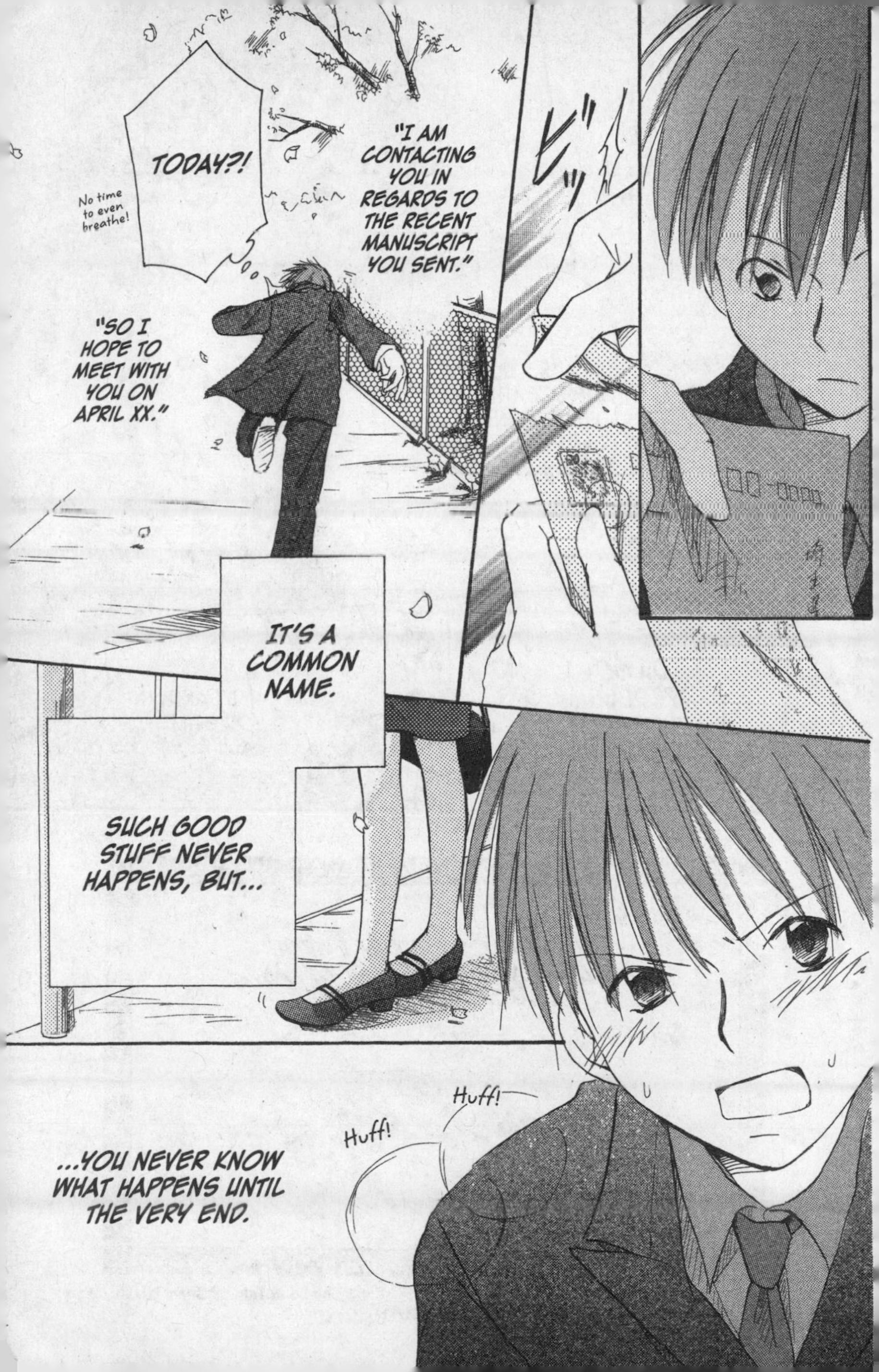
"I AM CONTACTING YOU IN REGARDS TO THE RECENT MANUSCRIPT YOU SENT."
TODAY?!
No time to even breathe!
"SO I HOPE TO MEET WITH YOU ON APRIL XX."
IT'S A COMMON NAME.
SUCH GOOD STUFF NEVER HAPPENS, BUT...
Huff!
Huff!
...YOU NEVER KNOW WHAT HAPPENS UNTIL THE VERY END.

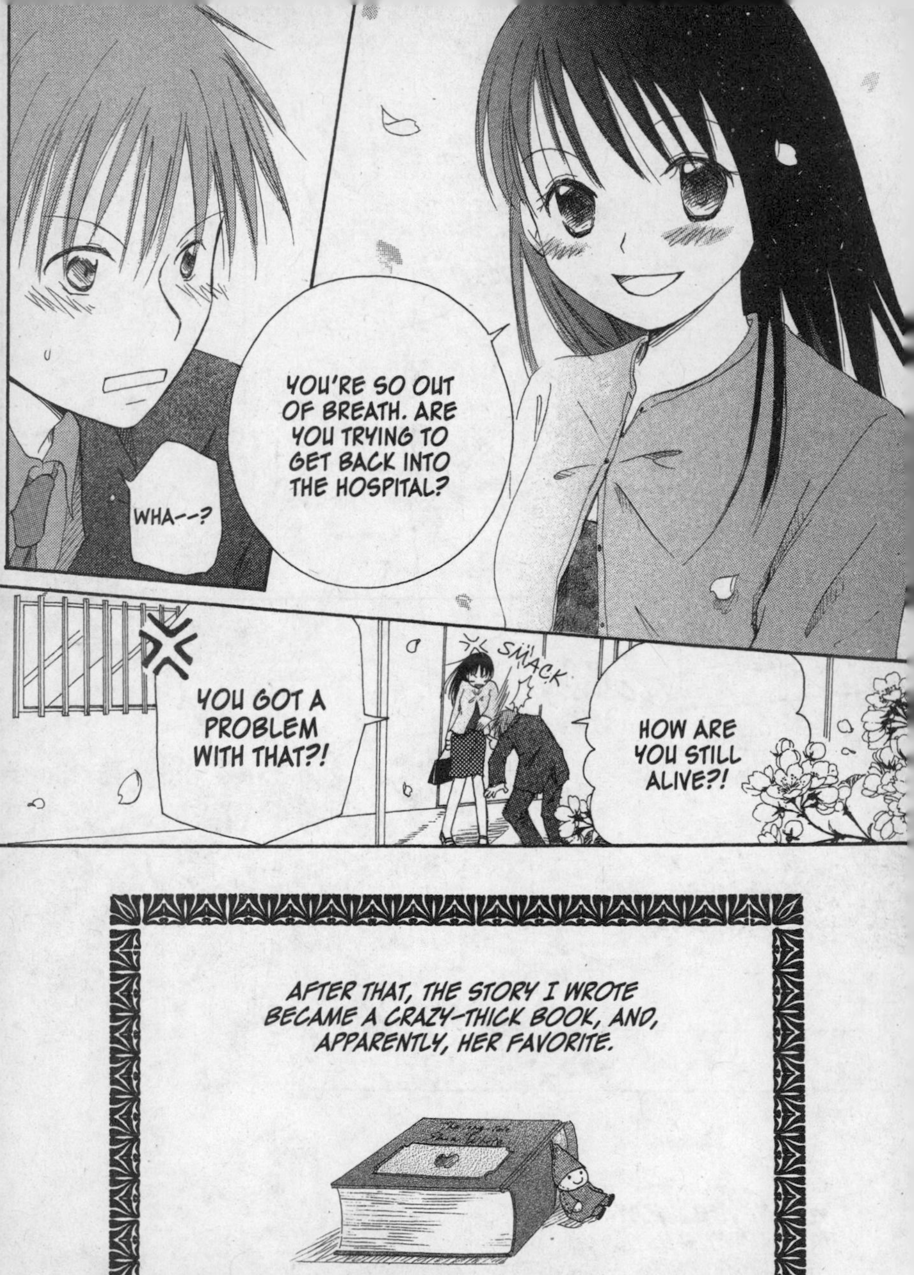
YOU'RE SO OUT OF BREATH. ARE YOU TRYING TO GET BACK INTO THE HOSPITAL?
WHA--?
HOW ARE YOU STILL ALIVE?!
SMACK
YOU GOT A PROBLEM WITH THAT?!
AFTER THAT, THE STORY I WROTE BECAME A CRAZY-THICK BOOK, AND, APPARENTLY, HER FAVORITE.

The Long Tale of Snow White / End

Happy end....

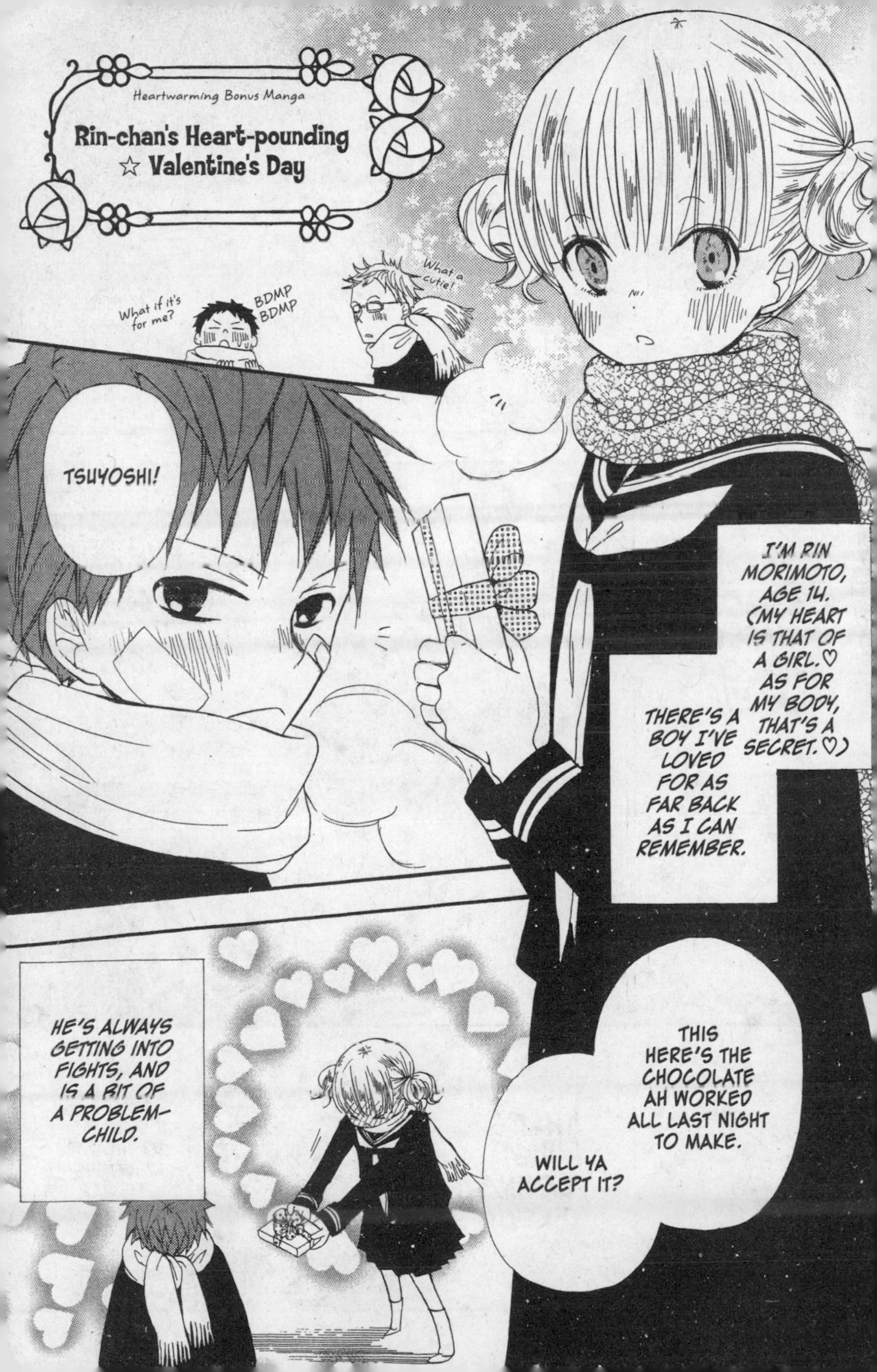
Heartwarming Bonus Manga
Rin-chan's Heart-pounding ☆ Valentine's Day
What a cutie!
BDMP BDMP
What if it's for me?
I'M RIN MORIMOTO, AGE 14. (MY HEART IS THAT OF A GIRL. ♡ AS FOR MY BODY, THAT'S A SECRET. ♡)
THERE'S A BOY I'VE LOVED FOR AS FAR BACK AS I CAN REMEMBER.
TSUYOSHI!
THIS HERE'S THE CHOCOLATE AH WORKED ALL LAST NIGHT TO MAKE.
WILL YA ACCEPT IT?
HE'S ALWAYS GETTING INTO FIGHTS, AND IS A BIT OF A PROBLEM-CHILD.

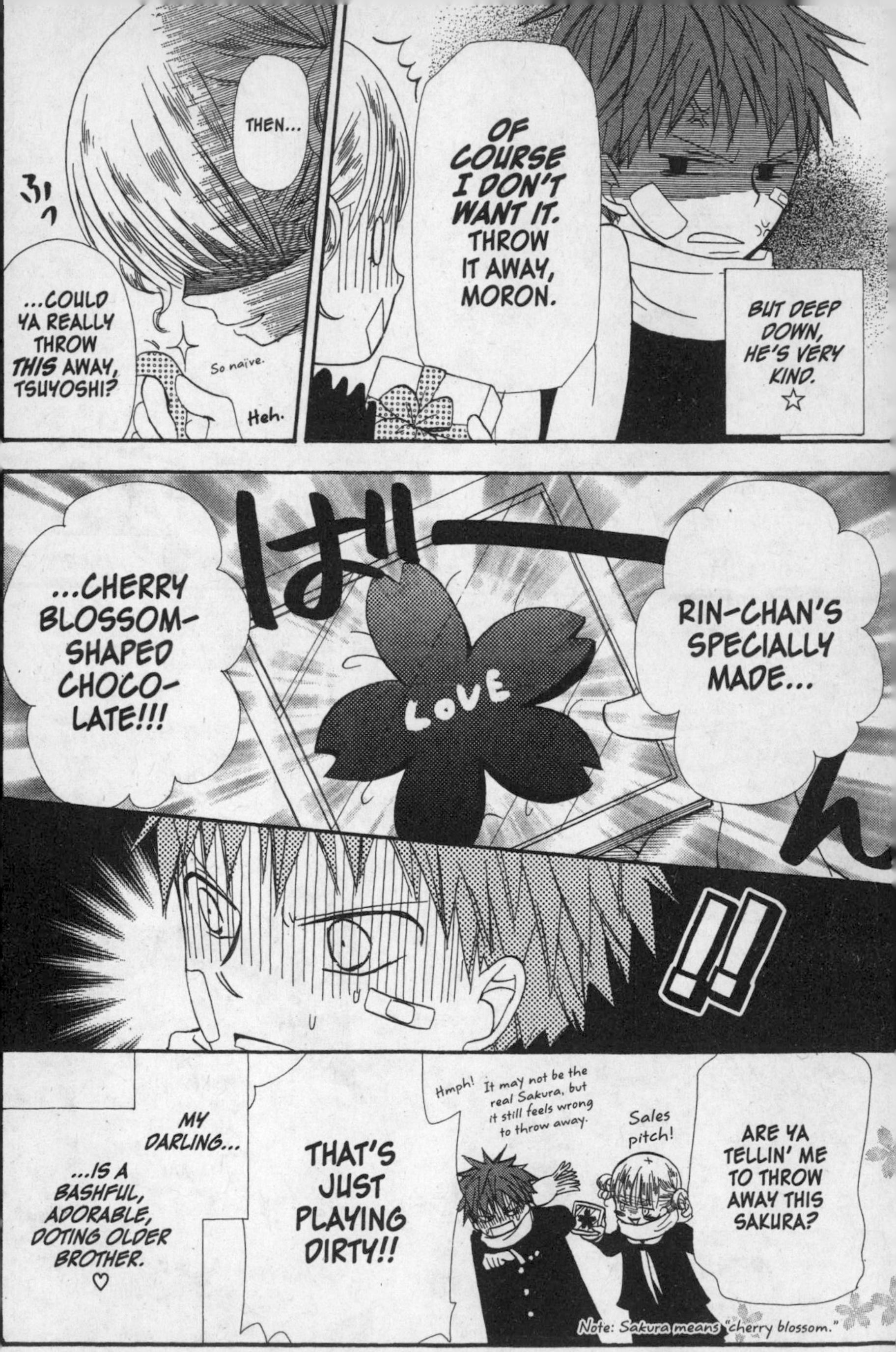
OF COURSE I DON'T WANT IT. THROW IT AWAY, MORON.
BUT DEEP DOWN, HE'S VERY KIND. ☆
THEN...
ふっ
...COULD YA REALLY THROW THIS AWAY, TSUYOSHI?
So naïve.
Heh.
RIN-CHAN'S SPECIALLY MADE...
はーん
...CHERRY BLOSSOM-SHAPED CHOCO-LATE!!!
LOVE
!!
ARE YA TELLIN' ME TO THROW AWAY THIS SAKURA?
Sales pitch!
Hmph! It may not be the real Sakura, but it still feels wrong to throw away.
Note: Sakura means "cherry blossom."
THAT'S JUST PLAYING DIRTY!!
MY DARLING...
...IS A BASHFUL, ADORABLE, DOTING OLDER BROTHER. ♡

End

Me & My Brothers

Preview of the next volume!

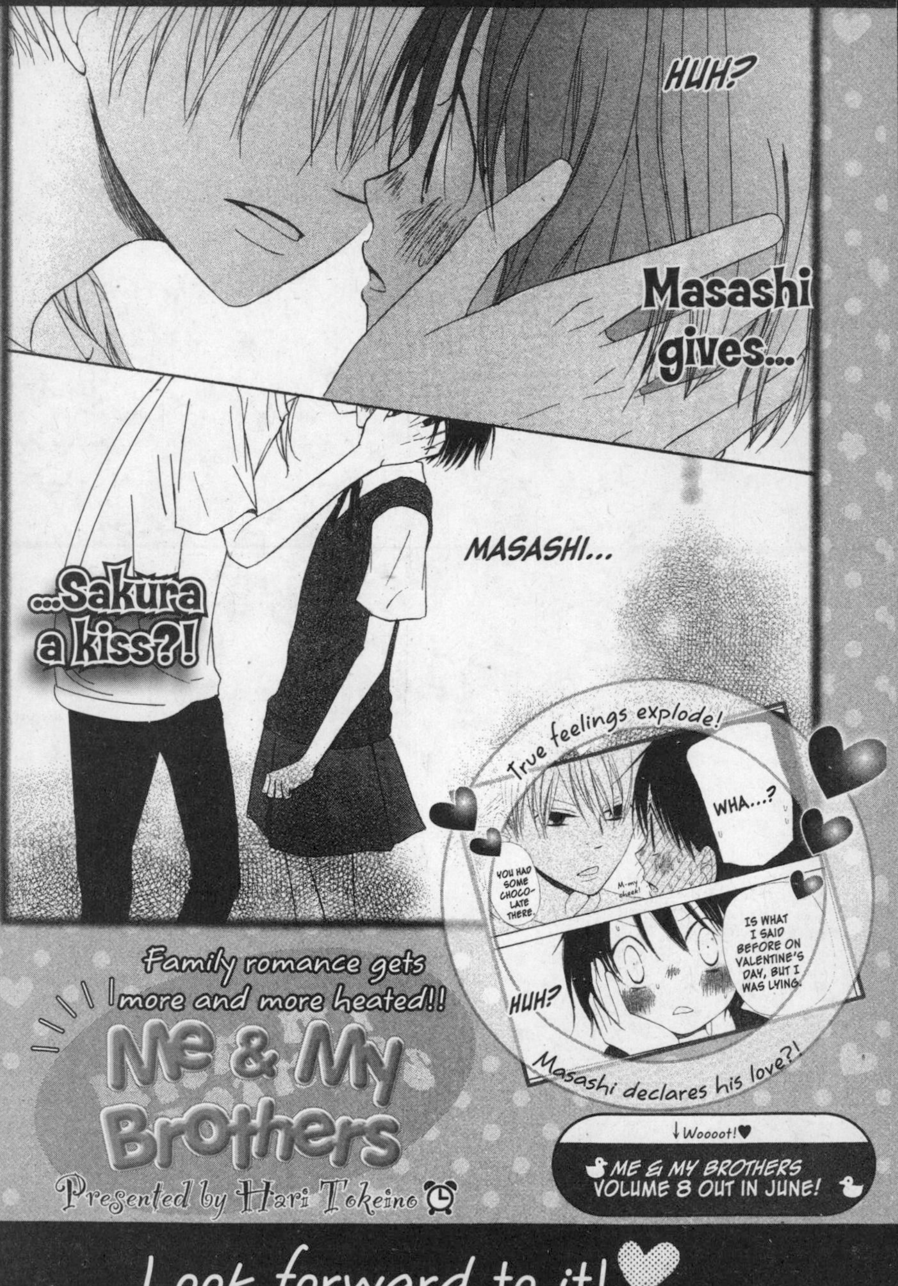
HUH?
Masashi gives...
MASASHI...
...Sakura a kiss?!
True feelings explode!
WHA...?
YOU HAD SOME CHOCO-LATE THERE.
M-my cheek!
IS WHAT I SAID BEFORE ON VALENTINE'S DAY, BUT I WAS LYING.
HUH?
Masashi declares his love?!
Family romance gets more and more heated!!
Me & My Brothers
Presented by Hari Tokeino
↓Woooot!
ME & MY BROTHERS VOLUME 8 OUT IN JUNE!

Look forward to it!

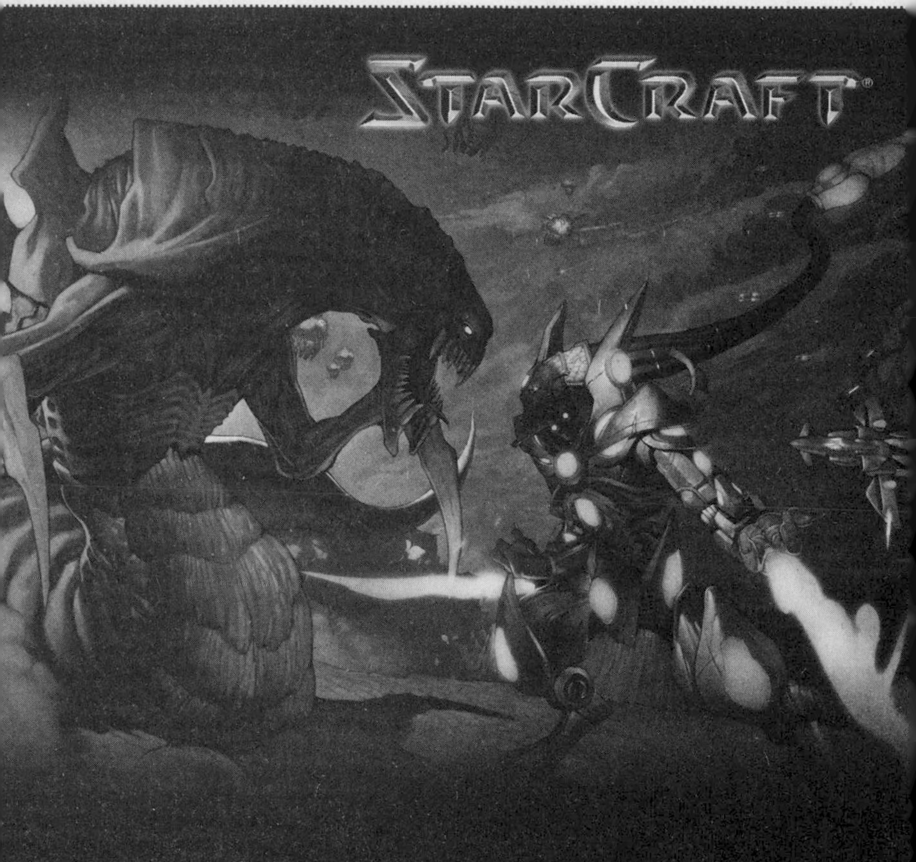
StarCraft®

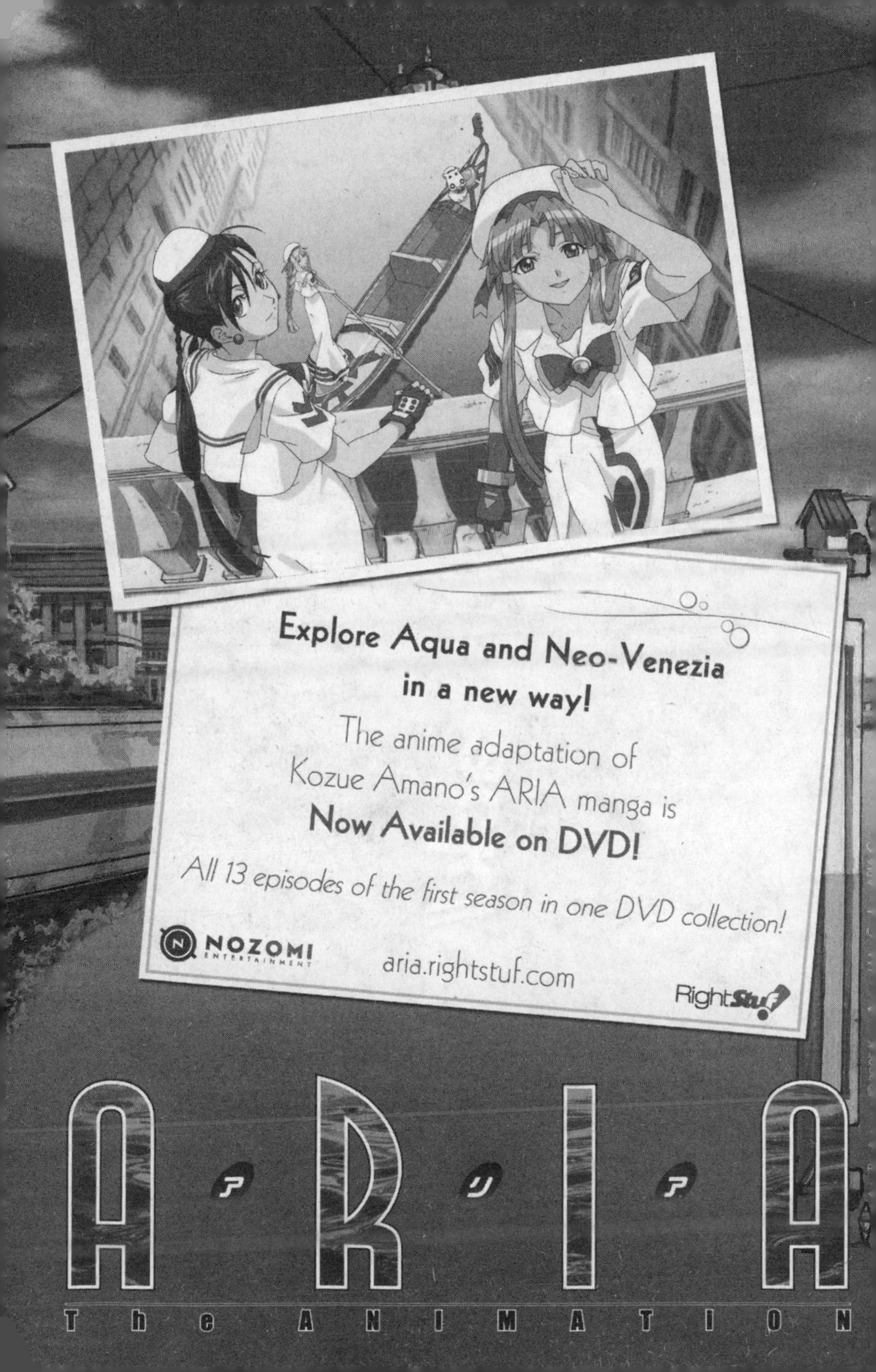
Explore Aqua and Neo-Venezia
in a new way!
The anime adaptation of
Kozue Amano's ARIA manga is
Now Available on DVD!
All 13 episodes of the first season in one DVD collection!
NOZOMI ENTERTAINMENT
aria.rightstuf.com
RightStuf
ARIA
アリア
The ANIMATION

NEVER

SEEN IT BEFORE!

.hack//G.U.+

.hack//
AI buster
Volume 1-2

Story by Tatsuya Hamazaki // Art By Yuzuka Morita

P.COM

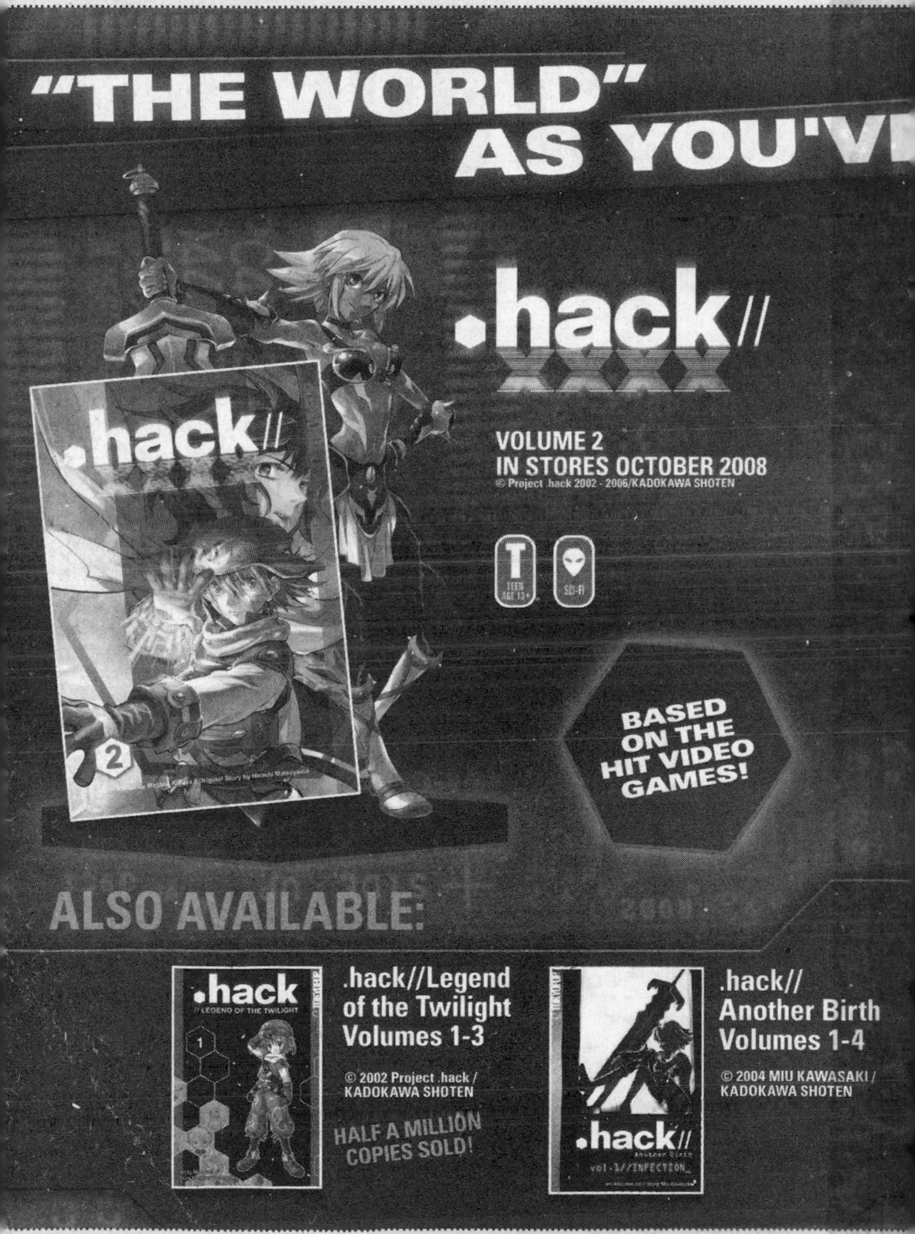
"THE WORLD" AS YOU'VE
.hack//XXXX
VOLUME 2
IN STORES OCTOBER 2008
© Project .hack 2002 - 2006/KADOKAWA SHOTEN
T TEEN AGE 13+
SCI-FI
BASED ON THE HIT VIDEO GAMES!
.hack//
2
ALSO AVAILABLE:
.hack // LEGEND OF THE TWILIGHT
.hack//Legend of the Twilight Volumes 1-3
© 2002 Project .hack / KADOKAWA SHOTEN
HALF A MILLION COPIES SOLD!
.hack// Another Birth
.hack// Another Birth Volumes 1-4
© 2004 MIU KAWASAKI / KADOKAWA SHOTEN

STOP!

This is the back of the book.
You wouldn't want to spoil a great ending!

This book is printed "manga-style," in the authentic Japanese right-to-left format. Since none of the artwork has been flipped or altered, readers get to experience the story just as the creator intended. You've been asking for it, so TOKYOPOP® delivered: authentic, hot-off-the-press, and far more fun!

DIRECTIONS

If this is your first time reading manga-style, here's a quick guide to help you understand how it works.

It's easy... just start in the top right panel and follow the numbers. Have fun, and look for more 100% authentic manga from TOKYOPOP®!